THE SENTENCE AND ITS PARTS

THE
SENTENCE
AND
ITS PARTS

A GRAMMAR OF CONTEMPORARY ENGLISH

RALPH B. LONG

THE UNIVERSITY OF CHICAGO PRESS
CHICAGO & LONDON

Library of Congress Catalog Card Number: 61-11895

The University of Chicago Press, Chicago and London
The University of Toronto Press, Toronto 5, Canada

© 1961 by The University of Chicago. All rights reserved
Published 1961. Third Impression 1965
Printed in the United States of America

CONTENTS

INTRODUCTION

The subject matter of this book is grammar in the broad sense of the term, including word formation, phonology, spelling, and punctuation. The central interest is in grammar in the narrow sense: syntax, of which inflection is here regarded as a division. The central interest in syntax gives shape to the whole book.

The book is organized around the patterns of grammatical form which English now employs, not around meanings. Meanings that are fundamentally identical can be expressed by different grammatical structures, as when we say now *we hope we'll get back by summer* and now *we hope to get back by summer*. On the other hand, a single grammatical structure can express very different meaning relationships, as when the subject is now responsible actor as in *Smith makes a great deal of trouble* and now simply "involved" as in *Smith has a great deal of trouble*.

But meanings are not ignored. When matters of grammatical patterning are noted, their usual contributions to meaning are taken into account. This is the reason that sentences as unlike in form as *what convincing excuses does Dora give?* and *who gives convincing excuses?* are classified together as interrogatives, while *what convincing excuses Dora gives!* and *not one convincing excuse does Dora give* are put together in another category. When such a phrasal verb form as *is smoking* is identified, its special contribution to meaning is similarly taken into account: sequences such as *George is smoking* are distinguished from sequences such as *George smokes* not only in form but in characteristic meanings. The primary function of language is to convey meaning: grammatical structures exist for this purpose. Often a word follows different patterns of syntactic behavior as it expresses different meanings.

1

Thus the *get* of *be sure to get your coat dry* has two complements and the *get* of *be sure to get your dry coat* has only one, and the difference in construction is obviously bound up with a difference in meaning. Contexts are of extreme importance in our understanding of language. When *they're ready to eat* is spoken in a situation in which it is clear that "they" is some children, *they* suggests the subject of *eat;* when the same sentence is spoken in a situation in which it is clear that "they" is some baked potatoes, *they* suggests not the subject but the complement of *eat. His sister is buying antiques* will always be understood to have *is buying* as predicator and *antiques* as complement; *his hobby is buying antiques* will always be understood to have *is* as predicator and *buying antiques* as complement. We know something about sisters and about hobbies; our analysis takes this into account.

This grammar begins with relatively large units—clauses and their nucleuses, and words—not with relatively small units such as phonemes. Attempts to base syntax in phonemics have not been successful. No single syntactic function and no single part of speech can be defined in terms of anything phonemic. No single category of clauses can be set up on the basis of anything phonemic. In particular uses *what convincing excuses does Dora give?* is without real question force: it is equivalent to such a declarative as *Dora gives no convincing excuses at all.* Intonation, manner, and situation are of decisive importance in matters such as these; but classification of clauses cannot be based on criterions of these types. *What convincing excuses does Dora give?* remains an interrogative, intent of the speaker notwithstanding, because it employs a grammatical pattern whose ordinary function is to elicit information. Similarly, *you'll give convincing excuses* can have the force of an order or of a question, but the sentence remains a declarative in syntactic patterning. Our sentences can be whispered, chanted, or sung without change in their grammar. They can be written and read by people who lack both hearing and speech.

English can be regarded as primarily an instrument used in the formulation and expression of thought. All languages can be regarded as collections of molds and patterns, extremely conventional in form, within which thought can be shaped. "Language and our thought-grooves are inextricably interrelated, are, in a sense, one and the same," wrote Sapir. We can listen and talk, unless we are deaf and dumb, and can read and write, unless we are illiterate; and we can work out problems in our minds in consciously verbal ways. The "thought" which we formulate is often no more than expression of emotion, or of desire to influence the actions of others. Feelings find expression in words, and we can speak these words to others or to ourselves or leave them unspoken. Words are more than combinations of sounds, as people are more than flesh and blood: words are more, even, than ghosts of sounds. However it is used, language is primarily an activity of the human brain, not of the human mouth and throat or of the human hand.

For a grammar which begins with clause structure, the concept of the morpheme is of little value. To describe *reactions* as a cluster composed of four morphemes is grammatically less significant than to say that it is the plural form of a complex noun whose components are the prefix *re*, the word *act*, and the suffix *ion*. Whether the complex was put together in English or not is of historical importance only. The relation of the *act* of *reaction* to the *ag* of *reagent* is of more than historical importance: we can most conveniently consider *ag* a stem which functions as a variant of *act*. When we start with clause structure, we are able to postpone the enormously intricate problems morphological analysis faces. It is a curious fact that those who insist that morphological analysis must precede syntactic cannot even agree on procedures for identifying morphemes. Phonemic identification results in such things as dividing *thermometer* into *ther* and *mometer*, since the clearest phonemic division parallels that in *the monitor*. Identification of morphemes on the basis of meaning runs into the fact that children learn words as units in the main, and division of as common a word as *thermometer* is inevitably somewhat sophisticated and is based in part on knowledge of spellings and history. Even for the linguistically sophisticated, when *thermometer* is divided into *thermo* and *meter* there remains the question of what view to take of the *o* of *thermo* and the *er* of *meter*. Syntactically derived morphemes are naturally of great interest to the grammarian, but when the *wh* of *who* (where no /w/ is pronounced) and of *which* is said to have the *that* of *a flower that had dropped* as a variant, followed by a zero variant of the *ich* of *which*, the analysis seems unrealistic. It is not the use of *wh* or /hw/ or /w/ that marks clauses of certain types, for *wh* occurs also in such words as *whack*, *wheel*, and *whip*. The clause markers of modern English are words and phrases, not fractions of words. And it seems simpler to say that the *'d* of *I'd be ready* and that of *I'd been ready* are reduced forms of two words which occur in their full forms in negated *I wouldn't be ready* and *I hadn't been ready*, than to say that they are the same morpheme following zero variants of *will* and *have*. Words are easier to deal with than morphemes, in spite of the obvious problems compounds, mergings, and fixed phrasings confront us with. Bloomfield called the word the smallest unit of speech "for the purposes of ordinary life." Grammar should begin as close as possible to the purposes of ordinary life—not with single words, many of which do not ordinarily occur alone, but with the most usual combinations in which words occur.

Assignment of decisive grammatical importance to inflection and "function words" seems unjustified for contemporary English. Uninflected words are to be found in all the part-of-speech categories: examples are *ought*, *machinery*, *extinct*, *now*, *each*, and *ouch*. Such a sentence as *people always spread bad news* is entirely clear in its structure, and yet *people* is a plural without characteristic plural inflection, *always* has an old inflectional ending not clearly felt in modern times, *spread* is the basic form of a verb that employs its basic form as both a present and a past, *bad* is an adjective whose comparative and superlative forms are strikingly unlike it and unlike most such forms, and *news* is an old plural form that is now felt as quantifiable—and the sentence contains no function words. Actually, the inflectional endings of contemporary English are not even recognizable except in combination with the words to which they are attached. In the sentence *forsaken oxen often sadden Helen* every word ends in *en* and yet is different in grammar from every other word. The spoken language does even less than the written to make inflectional endings genuinely distinctive. Thus the final inflectional /z/ of *trees* is identical with the final noninflectional /z/ of *breeze*, so that though in *the trees are very fine* the subject has plural force we cannot say that the /z/ of /triz/ carries this force apart from the rest of the word. Even the inflectional ending of *trees* is not unambiguous. *Trees* can be a third-person-singular verb form, as in *our dog trees too many cats*, as well as a plural noun. Attempts to distinguish "function" words and "content" words in modern English have been made by many grammarians, including Sweet at the end of the last century, and have never been successful. The truth is that almost all words have both grammatical and semantic value. Thus, *poetry* and *furniture* are learned as grammatically alike in that ordinarily they are both quantifiable (*much*) nouns, and *poetry* and *poem* are learned as semantically alike. Very few words are really semantically empty. *That* and *yourself* are semantically empty in *I knew that you'd enjoy yourself*, but if *hurt* is substituted for *enjoy* the reflexive *yourself*, now used much more characteristically, can no longer be called semantically empty. It is absurd to call prepositions semantically empty simply because sometimes the native speaker has difficulty defining them. The *to* of *what nature hasn't done to us will be done by our fellow man*, for example, is semantically of major importance to its sentence, so that if *for* is substituted there is a very considerable change in meaning. In this sentence it is true that *has, will,* and *be* are auxiliaries of tense and voice rather than full verbs, and so do express meanings that can be described as grammatical. It does not seem possible to accept a procedure which results in calling *that* a function word in *that concert* but a noun (or "Class I word") in *that small*, and in calling *had* a function word both in *the students had moved* and in *the students had to move* but a verb (or "Class II word") in *we had a perfectly wild time last night*. It would seem much better to say that *that* is a determinative pronoun used in two different ways in *that concert* and *that small* and in a third in *that's the new secretary*, and that *had* is the past form of *have* used as a full verb, with complements of different types, both in *we had a perfectly wild time last night* and in *the students had to move*, and as an auxiliary of tense in *the students had moved*.

Grammars of English have usually paid more attention to written English than to spoken. There are obvious reasons for this. The sentences of spoken English are often poorly constructed—and this is not a purist judgement—both when they are the products of rapid, spontaneous conversation and when they are the products of much more careful expression, as, for example, at a conference in which specialists in linguistic structure itself debate their problems while recording apparatus preserves what they say. What are generally regarded as satisfactory sentences appear much more regularly in the written language. Furthermore, once it is put in a book spoken English is written English. Methods of recording and reproducing actual spoken English are relatively new, and even yet bits of spoken English cannot be inserted in books in the midst of written English. Even worse, the spoken language cannot stand still. The written language does: the reader can take it at his own speed, skimming or pondering at will. Phonemicists and phoneticians find the usual written forms of English unsatisfactory for their purposes and employ their own written forms. Grammarians find the usual forms relatively satisfactory at most points. Though the ordinary written forms do not represent pitches and stresses accurately, they do give fairly adequate representation to the units with which syntax deals. Much of the time they provide extremely convenient representations, too, for phonemically variable formatives with which morphology must deal: for example, the *tele* of *telegraph* and *telegraphy*, the *hibit* of *exhibit* and *exhibition*, and the *gon* of *pentagon* and *trigonometry*.

There are strong arguments for employing the usual written forms in analysis wherever possible. They are established ways of using the language, precisely as the spoken forms are, and so require attention in themselves. In the schools of earlier generations, two of the "three R's" were concerned with written language and none with spoken. Recorders and television notwithstanding, it seems safe to predict that in the foreseeable future complex thought will still be communicated most satisfactorily by the written language. In everyday life also, the ordinary written forms are holding their own: indeed, they are put to more and more uses in supermarkets, for example, where the storekeeper of the past is no longer always at hand, and on superhighways, where increasingly complex directions must be given silently to all who drive by. The usual written forms are easily read; precise phonetic or phonemic transcriptions are much harder to read. The usual written forms do not call attention to matters of regional or personal pronunciation that are irrelevant to grammatical analysis: the ordinary written language is a broadly unifying instrument with a minimum of involvement in the local and individual. The usual written forms both represent and shape the native speaker's view of the structure of his language at many points. Thus the *used* of *I used to like him* is indistinguishable in speech from the *use* of *I didn't use to like him*, but the difference in spelling is jealously maintained for grammatical reasons.

It is obviously not possible for a short grammar to deal satisfactorily with very many varieties of a language. Here all that is attempted is a description of standard American English of the present time. Standard American English is the English most widely useful in the New World. Social considerations make it standard, not linguistic ones. Its patterns are complicated at some points by the existence of what can best be called styles. We will need to deal with three main categories of styles, which we can call informal, careful, and formal. Each kind of style has its appropriate sphere of usefulness. Informal styles are suitable in conversation and in a great deal of writing. There is a very considerable place for somewhat more carefully ordered prose that is neither notably informal nor notably formal. Formal styles, like formal clothing, are the least useful, though they sometimes seem the most beautiful. It is in "formal" styles that archaisms of various kinds, and echoes of the literature of the past, appear most often.

At some points the line between what is standard and what is nonstandard can be located only tentatively. Even where it seems fairly clear how the line should be drawn, those who use the language most effectively do not always confine themselves to standard locutions. Correctness is one of the less important of the linguistic virtues. Nonstandard phrasings sometimes have an aptness or a vigor that makes them very attractive, at least for the moment. Moreover, as has been said, rapid comfortable speech leaves many syntactic patterns unfinished, and carefully thought out speech commonly is felt to need revision and "correcting" when it is copied from an exact mechanical recording. Even in careful and formal written use, lapses occur: Homer was not alone in nodding occasionally. In the end, what we are calling standard American English is normalized English. A rigid dogmatism is obviously out of place under such circumstances.

This grammar is written primarily for teachers and prospective

teachers of English. There is an effort at every point to avoid
sharp breaks with the analysis of English that has been taught in
the schools. New terminology is avoided and terminology in general is kept to a minimum. But this grammar is written against a
background of widespread dissatisfaction with the school analysis
of the language. It is written, too, in the conviction that every
branch of human learning requires constant reformulation as the
generations go by and that nothing has ever been finished once
and for all. Samuel Butler remarked that it is a mercy of God
that every generation does its work badly enough to leave something for the next generation to do.

I have put twenty years of steady work into the making of this
grammar. I have collected examples both from my miscellaneous
reading and from what I have heard: only a fraction of these could
go into this volume. I have written and rewritten, and term after
term I have used preliminary versions of this grammar with considerable numbers of students who were themselves teachers of
English grammar, the great majority of them in the English-
speaking United States but many of them in very different linguistic situations. I have learned a great deal from my students. I
must acknowledge a heavy underlying indebtedness to the standard grammarians of Latin, Greek, and the older Germanic languages, and to the grammarians of modern foreign languages. They
were my first teachers, and I have not forgotten the lessons I
learned from them. I have a very great indebtedness to the Old
World grammarians of English, and especially to Palmer and
Poutsma. My indebtedness to such American students of language as Sapir, Bloomfield, Kenyon, Pike, Bolinger, Harris, and
Chomsky is considerable. In the last chapter the pronunciations
are based on material in *A Pronouncing Dictionary of American
English*, copyright 1953 by G. and C. Merriam Co., publishers of
the Merriam-Webster Dictionaries. The lines by Conrad Aiken on
page 414 are from his *Collected Poems* (Oxford University Press,
1953). For my title I am indebted to Rodolfo Lenz, whose *La
Oración y Sus Partes* is known by all serious students of Spanish
grammar. Finally, I am greatly indebted to Dwight L. Bolinger,
Tatsuyoshi Sakamoto, and Dorothy R. Long.

CHAPTER I

SYNTACTIC FUNCTIONS

Sentences are linguistic units of a certain magnitude. In written discourse they are ordinarily the most clearly marked units smaller than paragraphs and larger than words: capital letters begin them, periods or equivalent marks end them, and there is characteristic spacing before and after. Sometimes a single word can be a sentence, and even a paragraph; but the distinction in magnitudes is a real one nevertheless. Most sentences are dependent on the context of preceding sentences or of situation for some of their meaning. Thus such a sentence as *we got Phelps in* is syntactically complete, and yet neither *we* nor *Phelps* has adequate effective meaning apart from context, the time of *got* must be indicated by context, and some kind of completer for *in* must be implied by context. In unnormalized material, such as the unpunctuated twenty-five-thousand-word reverie at the end of *Ulysses*—and comparable stretches of spoken English—we cannot always be sure where the boundaries between sentences come. Analysis of sentence structure had better begin with sentences whose boundaries are not in doubt. It can best begin with sentences in which sequences of simple familiar words combine in familiar patterns to express readily understood meanings through a symbolism which, as Sapir said, "can be transferred from one sense to another, from technique to technique." An underlying assumption is that, in normal uses of language, words which follow each other without decisive breaks have syntactic relationships to each other or are parts of larger units that do.

We can begin the analysis of sentences by noting the syntactic functions found in them. These can be divided into three groups, which we can call major functions, contained functions, and secondary functions. We can draw our examples almost entirely from clausal sentences of a single type: the main declarative. The main declarative is the basic pattern for statements of fact and opinion. Examples of minimal main declaratives—declarative "nucleuses" to which nothing is added—can well begin with everyone's commonest name for himself, the pronoun *I*.

I am Ake.	I call him Butch.
I am sad.	I make him sad.
I am here.	I put work off.
I have time.	I snore.
I like soup.	I travel.

We will need to pay attention to nonclausal sentences also.

Ouch!	Thanks.
Yes.	Well!

We will, of course, need to look beyond minimal structures such as these very quickly, since not even all our major functions find illustration in them. And we will need to note part-of-speech distinctions.

Predicators.—The key to main declaratives and to clauses of every type is what we can call predicators: *am, have, like, call, make, put, snore,* and *travel* in the declaratives given above. We can define predicators as second major components in declarative nucleuses. From the point of view of part-of-speech classification, predicators are normally verbs, and the verbs are the most easily identifiable of the parts of speech, though phrasal verb forms such as *are traveling* and *has traveled* are not always clear. The subject matter of predicators is occurrences: actions, events, states of affairs. All predicators should be regarded as heads within their clauses. Even such an inconspicuous and variable form as the merged *am* of *I'm Ake*—which can be phonemically indistinguishable from *I make*—is what makes a clause of the sequence in which it is contained. Yet predicators are sometimes implied, or partially implied, rather than stated. Thus in reply to the question *where's James?* what is said may be only *here*, but *here* is then a main declarative and a sentence as truly as the full main declarative *James is here*. If the response to the main declarative *I've raised ducks* is *Harry has too*, the predicator *has* of the response is obviously a reduction of the full form *has raised,* and *ducks* is implied also.

Subjects.—All predicators have subjects, expressed or implied. We can define subjects as first major components in declarative nucleuses: *I* in *I am Ake, I am sad, I am here, I have time, I like soup, I call him Butch, I make him sad, I put work off, I snore,* and *I travel.* Meaning relationships are obviously varied. It will not do to say that subjects are "topics" in their clauses: what is topic and what comment in such a sentence as *I regret to inform you that your services are no longer needed,* where the syntactic main subject is *I?* Subjects can refer to something that is identified or classified or described or located, or to something that acts or is affected by action, or to something that is simply involved in an occurrence of some kind.

Sometimes it is possible to put into a subject the same content that can be put into a predicator.

> Our *conversation* continued till midnight.
> We *talked* till midnight.

One-word subjects are generally nouns or pronouns: the function of subject can be regarded as nounal, just as the function of predicator can be regarded as verbal. The person-and-number force of subjects is often reflected in the forms of their predicators, so that if the *I* of *I like soup* is changed to *he* then *like* is changed to *likes* also. Word order is of extreme importance and determines the subjects in such pairs as the following.

> *My worst day* is Monday.
> *Monday* is my worst day.
> *His eyes* are his chief problem.
> *His chief problem* is his eyes.
> *We*'ve been given a better schedule.
> *A better schedule* has been given us.

A somewhat artificial division of subjects occurs when *it* and *there* are employed in subject positions as representatives of words or longer units which embody the real content of the subjects but are postponed.

> *It*'s fortunate *that you came.*
> *It*'s hard *to understand Phelps.*

It's fifteen miles *to Parkersburg.*
There are *seats* now.
For your information *there* are inclosed *copies of all pertinent
    documents.*

Divided subjects not employing *it* and *there* are of less frequent
occurrence.

No one was present *that I'd ever seen before.*

Main declaratives with expressed predicators normally have expressed subjects also. *Thank you* is an exception. In informal styles
other exceptions are not hard to find.

Looks like rain.
He never does anything. Just talks.
Drove over to Akron yesterday, and did some shopping.

Complements.—We can define complements as third, fourth,
and (rarely) fifth major components in declarative nucleuses: *Ake,
sad, here, time, soup, him,* and *work* in *I am Ake, I am sad, I am here,
I have time, I like soup, I call him Butch, I make him sad,* and *I put
work off;* and *Butch, sad,* and *off* in *I call him Butch, I make him
sad,* and *I put work off.* In *I put work off* the two complements *work*
and *off* meet normal requirements of the predicator *put* just as the
subject *I* meets another normal requirement. Both *I put* and *I put
work* are less than minimal sequences; *I put work off* has the minimal adequacy nucleuses have. The function of complement, unlike
those of predicator and subject, cannot be related characteristically
to any single part of speech: it is sometimes nounal, sometimes
adjectival, and sometimes adverbial.

Though all verbs normally require expressed subjects when they
are used as predicators in declaratives, some verbs never take complements and many verbs do not take complements when they
express particular turns of meaning.

I snore.
I travel.
You're trembling.
Mr. Hayes is dying.
George is sleeping.
Sickness exists.

Sometimes a shift in meaning results in use with complements.

> George is sleeping the hours away.
> George is sleeping his headache off.
> The trailer sleeps six.

Some verbs sometimes have expressed complements and sometimes leave complements implied.

> We usually eat *lunch* at the cafeteria.
> We usually eat at the cafeteria.
> Sylvia married *an engineer*.
> Sonia never married.
> I don't care *whether you go or not*.
> I don't care.
> Yes, I'm *from Pennsylvania*.
> Yes, I am.
> They met *each other* in Mexico City.
> They met in Mexico City.
> He shaves *himself* on Sundays.
> He shaves on Sundays.

Some verbs take two complements. The one that comes first in the basic order can be called a first complement and the other a second complement. Second complements are italicized in the following sentences.

> I call him *Butch*.
> I make him *sad*.
> I put work *off*.
> The manager has turned us *down*.
> Harris locks his dog *in the car*.
> James puts up *with us*.

In each of these sentences the predicator has only its normal necessities, for the meaning expressed, attached to it. Second complements often become first, in effect, when more fundamentally first complements are implied rather than stated.

> He generally gets himself home.
> He generally gets home.
> I give the whole thing up.
> I give up.

Second complements sometimes precede first complements. Substitution of personal pronouns for nouns or nounal units generally reveals the basic order: the syntactically "second" complement then follows the first.

> Jack's lending *Mary* his car.
> Jack's lending it *to her*.
> The editorial takes *up* the subject of taxes.
> The editorial takes it *up*.

Three complements occur much more rarely than two.

> He has it in for us.

Meaning relationships between predicators and complements are extremely varied.

> They make electric fans.
> I hear an electric fan.
> George has an electric fan.
> I need an electric fan.

In *they make electric fans* we have an actor-action-product sequence, but the meaning relationships are different in the other three sentences. Some complements seem semantically empty.

> He lords *it* over us.
> We always enjoy *ourselves*.

Often, on the other hand, predicators are quite general in meaning and complements contain meanings that could be expressed by more exact predicators.

> He's taking part.
> He's participating.
> He's made his escape.
> He's escaped.
> He always lets out a whoop.
> He always whoops.
> I put work off.
> I postpone work.
> My wife gets it clean.
> My wife cleans it.

In combinations such as these the complements have a strict control over the writer or speaker's choice of predicator. Parts are taken, escapes are made, whoops are let out—or sometimes given. In complex sentence structure the use of general predicators often makes clearer modification possible.

> Most people enjoy watching television a great deal.
> Most people get a great deal of enjoyment out of watching television.

The President tipped the boys who carried his bags generously.
The President gave generous tips to the boys who carried his
bags.

If the first of these sentences is intended to mean what the second
one means, it is not very well constructed, since *a great deal* is
likely to seem to attach to the nearer *watching* rather than to the
more distant *enjoy*. Similarly, in the third sentence *generously* is
likely to seem to attach to *carried*.

 Adjuncts.—Subjects and complements are normal necessities
for their predicators, though (like predicators) they are sometimes
implied rather than stated. Predicators, subjects, and complements make up nucleuses. Predicators also take modifiers which
are not parts of nucleuses, and these can be called adjuncts.

> *Certainly* I'm Ake.
> I *certainly* am Ake.
> I'm sad *now*.
> I'm *always* unhappy.
> We wait for Marian *long enough*.
> We wait *hours*.
> He's kissed her *goodby*.
> *Tuesdays* George is very busy.
> *Fortunately* Harry's girl friends are *never* clever.
> Harrison turns me down *gracefully*.

The function of adjunct can be regarded as adverbial. But it must
be said at once that many kinds of words and multiword units
function as adjuncts. Such a unit as *this week*, for example, can
function as subject, complement, or adjunct.

> *This week* is Jack's last week here.
> We're wasting *this week*.
> *This week* everything is different.
> Everything is different *this week*.

In *letters and parcels come at ten* the unit *letters and parcels* is
pretty clearly the subject; in *Wednesday and Thursday come at ten*
the unit *Wednesday and Thursday* is pretty clearly not the subject
but an adjunct, and the clause is an imperative rather than a
declarative. In *the police stopped three cars* it is clear that *three cars*
is a complement and the predicator *stopped* means *brought to a
stop;* in *the police stopped three times* it is clear that *three times* is

only an adjunct and *stopped* means *came to a stop*. Words are used as representatives of meanings, and our knowledge of meaning relationships guides us in analysis of sentences such as these. In *fortunately Harry's girl friends are never clever* the predicator *are* and the complement *clever* are separated by the adjunct *never*, but there is no doubt that *clever*, not *never*, is the complement of *are*. Our knowledge of the functions particular words perform in sentences is operative in situations such as this, as are our feelings for meaning relationships. Part-of-speech classification makes us sure that *fortunately* is an adjunct. If closely related *fortunate* is substituted for *fortunately*, it will be taken as a part of the subject, within which it will modify *Harry*.

The adjuncts noted thus far are tight ones, smoothly incorporated into the flow of words in their clauses. From the point of view of meaning in particular situations, tight adjuncts are likely to be essential within their clauses. Thus the statement *Janet didn't marry her first husband because she loved him* becomes somewhat pointless if the adjuncts *not* and *because she loved him* are omitted. Some tenses of verbs often require adjuncts giving an idea of time. Thus *I studied French* is an unsatisfactory statement unless either an adjunct indicating (or at least suggesting) time is added or some idea of time is already implied. *I studied French in college* has an essential adjunct which *I'm studying French* and *I've been studying French* do not require. Present and present-perfect forms of verbs do not require adjuncts of time, expressed or implied; hence construction with these tenses shows the behavior of particular verbs, as opposed to particular tenses, most clearly. When adjuncts are essential, it is particular situations that make them essential. Subjects and complements are essential in a more general way.

Loose adjuncts must be recognized as well as tight ones. Loose adjuncts are felt as relatively nonessential, or incidental. The written language incloses them in commas or stronger marks, the spoken language generally sets them off with pauses.

Well, you're right.
John, it's your turn again.
Undoubtedly the old city still has charm, *though it cannot be called as comfortable as the new suburbs.*

Burned steak, canned peas, bad coffee, store cake—I felt my appetite deserting me rapidly.

One of my favorite teachers was Mr. Ries, *who taught me freshman Greek*.

Next weekend Barry goes to another convention, *in Chicago*.

Some loose adjuncts have secondary attachments within their clauses of types which will require notice later.

He hasn't read a new book, *good or bad*, in twenty years.

Inscrutable and sardonic, Veblen stood aloof from most of the currents of thought that swirled around him.

Loose-adjunct status can sometimes be assigned arbitrarily, but not always. Thus in *one of my favorite teachers was the man who taught me freshman Greek* the subordinate clause *who taught me freshman Greek* is necessarily a part of the complement in the main clause, not a loose adjunct. *Next weekend Barry goes to another convention in Chicago* will probably be understood to employ *another convention in Chicago* as a nounal unit comparable to *another Chicago convention*.

The commonest positions for adjuncts in declaratives are after complements—or after predicators, if there are no complements. Such positions are likely to be taken by adjuncts contributing meanings of manner, circumstance, respect, accompaniment, exception, means, condition, adverseness, result, place, time, duration, distance, degree, relatively exact frequency, cause, evidence, and reason for speaking.

He answered *politely*.

She isn't happy *with her husband acting like that*.

I'd put Puerto Rico at the top *for natural beauty*.

She shot him *dead*.

We waited *too long*.

We visited Cuba *several times*.

He must think he's important, *the way he talks*.

There's an article about Jamaica in this issue, *in case you're interested*.

Positions in front of subjects are likely to be taken by adjuncts contributing meanings of possibility, reservation, attitude, interjection, direct address, and order, and by adjuncts which refer to what has just been said.

> *Perhaps* you're right.
> *As politicians go,* he's a good speaker.
> *Fortunately* Harry's girl friends are very forgiving.
> *Well,* you may be right.
> *John,* it's your turn.
> *In the first place,* the town has no industry.
> *So* she married him.

Positions interrupting nucleuses (and even interrupting phrasal predicators) are likely to be taken by adjuncts contributing meanings of general frequency, assurance, and negation.

> They *often* get into difficulties.
> He's *certainly* doing good work.
> Phil *never* gets along with Jerry.
> He's *rarely* had a chance.
> She is*n't* being diplomatic.

Positions between predicators and complements are often not usable for adjuncts. Thus, if the adjunct *then* is added to *we knew the truth,* it can be put in any of three positions, but not between the predicator *knew* and its complement. But one-word forms of a few verbs are often separated from their complements by adjuncts which would precede one-word forms of most verbs.

> He's *always* here.
> He *always* comes here.

And adjuncts of types very much like second complements sometimes take positions between predicators and complements.

> Susan has made *Judy* a skirt.
> We've eaten *up* the cake.

In simple sentences interruptions of the nucleus are avoided for adjuncts of most types. The relationships of subject to predicator and of complement to predicator are indicated by juxtaposition as well as by part of speech and meaning. For this reason in *I always get there tired* the pressure of word order makes *there* a complement and *tired* an adjunct but in *I always get tired there* the same pressure makes *tired* a complement and *there* an adjunct.

A certain amount of varying of positions of adjuncts is quite possible if discretion is used—and is often desirable when clauses become complex in structure. Sometimes, however, changes in position involve changes in meaning relationships.

Naturally she speaks to us.
She speaks to us *naturally.*
She saw him on Tuesday, and he was happy *then.*
She saw him on Tuesday, and *then* he was happy.
These are easy days, but I'm *still* behind in my work.
These are easy days, but *still* I'm behind in my work.
She *just* won't say no.
She won't *just* say no.

Adjuncts modify more than predicators, of course: they modify nucleuses or combinations of nucleuses and other adjuncts. In *Janet didn't marry her first husband because she loved him* the adjunct *not,* in spite of being merged with the predicator, modifies all the rest of the sentence: *Janet did marry her first husband because she loved him.* The adjunct *because she loved him* modifies the nucleus *Janet did marry her first husband.* Adjuncts are added to nucleuses layer upon layer, and the precise order of the additions is not always clear. But the predicators are the ultimate heads, and it is convenient to speak of adjuncts simply as modifiers of predicators.

It remains true that it is not always easy to distinguish tight adjuncts from complements. The test is the normal requirements of present and present-perfect forms of the particular verbs used as predicators, when they have the turns of meaning in point. But it is not always easy to apply the test. Actually it is sometimes not easy to distinguish subjects from complements: for example, in *here's where I get off,* in *there isn't time, is there?* and in *who are the officers this year?*

Isolates.—The major syntactic functions found in clausal sentences are those of predicator, subject, complement, and adjunct. But alongside clausal sentences the language employs units which have no such structure even by implication and yet are given the same status clausal sentences are given. These can be called clause equivalents. They are of two types. First of all, there are what have the appearance of undeveloped clauses. Here there are words and multiword units such as clauses are made of, but no real clause structures are indicated clearly, so that it is not possible to speak of implied parts with certainty.

John!   Dear me!
Good night.   You and your big ideas!

Danger   Taliaferro Hall
No Smoking   Grape Juice

Signs and labels employ isolate construction very commonly. *John!*
sometimes amounts to a request for attention and sometimes is
simply an expression of emotion—pleasure, surprise, irritation.

The second type of clause equivalent makes use of words that
normally do not participate in clause structure at all but carry in
themselves the syntactic value of whole nucleuses.

Ouch!   Hello.
Whew!   Yes.

Isolates sometimes take adjunct modifiers, much as nucleuses do.
Adjuncts are italicized in the following sentences.

Thanks *very much*.   Good night, *Marian*.
Now for some music.   *Oh*, no!

In *like father, like son* two isolates are combined in a sentence of
exceptional type.

Major and contained syntactic functions.—From the point
of view of syntax everything that is put into English participates in
the performance of the major syntactic functions and is divisible
first into main clauses and main-clause equivalents and then,
within these, into predicators, subjects, complements, adjuncts,
and isolates.

The major syntactic functions can all be performed by single
words. They can also be performed by multiword units of various
kinds. Sometimes these units are clauses, with components of the
kinds that occur in main declaratives. Sometimes these units are
nonclausal, and within them must be recognized types of syntactic
functions which can be called contained functions.

Contained heads and contained modifiers.—Headed units
are made up of (1) contained heads and (2) contained modifiers
which attach to these heads.

Comfortable chairs are expensive now.
They have *three children*.
George is *diplomatic enough*.
She writes *very badly*.

The italicized headed units are used as subject, as complement,
and as adjunct. They are used in constructions characteristic of

their heads: *comfortable chairs* like *chairs, three children* like *children, diplomatic enough* like *diplomatic, very badly* like *badly.* The headed units given above can be classified as nounal, adjectival, and adverbial in type. Contained modifiers normally come next to their heads, as is the case here. Most one-word modifiers precede their heads, but the reverse order (as in *diplomatic enough*) is not rare. Headed units often function as contained modifiers within larger headed units.

> The island has *incredibly beautiful* vegetation.
> *Two-story* houses have disadvantages.

They perform other contained functions also.

In some headed units the heads are, for one reason or another, not freely usable alone in the ways the units are used.

> Our *apartment* can hardly be heated.
> The *poor* need health first of all.
> We came to Marietta six weeks *ago.*
> She irritates people too *much.*
> Our so-*called* expert is a fraud.

We are dealing with oddities of English construction here. Though *apartment* alone is hardly usable as subject without some modifier such as *our, this,* or *the,* the plural form *apartments* is usable. *The poor* is a nounal headed unit in which an adjective functions as plural head, and nounal use of adjectives is sharply restricted. *Ago* alone cannot be used as an adjunct, but *later* can—and *six weeks ago* must be analyzed, in modern English, as *six weeks later* is. Without such a modifier as *too, much* is now avoided in unnegated declaratives.

When two or more noncoordinate contained modifiers attach to the same head, they attach in layers. The precise order of the layers is not always apparent, but accumulation is a very different thing from coordination.

> Sarah has *two very satisfactory daughters.*
> *The excellent business opportunities there* interest him.

It is clear that in *two very satisfactory daughters* the most accurate analysis would say that the contained modifier *two* modifies the whole unit *very satisfactory daughters* and the contained modifier *very satisfactory*—itself a headed unit—modifies the single word *daughters.* But in *the excellent business opportunities there,* where three modifiers precede the head *opportunities* and one follows it, the order of layers is not quite so clear. It seems wise not to push the sorting out of layers very far but simply to say that in *two very satisfactory daughters* the head *daughters* has two modifiers and in *the excellent business opportunities there* the head *opportunities* has four.

Sometimes contained modifiers are separated from their heads.

Signs are not lacking *that the property will be divided.*
What business is it *of his?*
Let *someone* do it *that can.*
Of all these great volcanoes Popocatepetl is *the most famous.*

In *signs of division of the property are not lacking* the modifier of *signs,* here prepositional, follows it immediately.

Many contained modifiers are in fact complementary. Such a word as *fond,* for example, needs a completer, expressed or implied, as truly as such a verb as *like,* and such a word as *superior* may need one as truly as such a verb as *surpass.*

He isn't really *fond of her.*
The new tires are *superior to the old ones.*

It is noteworthy that the head words *fond* and *superior* determine the prepositions used in the modifiers. This is a common situation when modifiers are complementary. But the distinction between complementary and noncomplementary contained modifiers can generally be disregarded.

Phrasal verb forms are best regarded as headed units in which the auxiliaries are contained modifiers. Thus in *Mary is watching television with the children* the form *is watching* can be said to be made up of the head *watching* and the modifier *is.* *Watches* can replace *is watching* here without change in subject or complement; *is* hardly can. *Is watching,* like *watches,* is a form of *watch,* not of *be.*

The relationship of modifier and head is sometimes reversed. Thus *people of that kind,* with *people* the head and *of that kind* the modifier, is often made into *that kind of people,* with *kind* the head and *of people* a modifier. In *he's sort of nice* the relationship is similarly upside down: *he's rather nice* shows the syntactically more ordinary patterning. Upside-down construction would be hard to avoid for such a question as *what kind of person is he?* It is note-worthy that in such a phrasal verb form as *is watching* it is not the head word but the modifying auxiliary that is usable as a full predicator in main declaratives. Sometimes heads are implied. Thus the interrogative *is Mary watching television?* can be answered by *of course she is*, and the interrogative *is he diplomatic?* can be answered by *not very*.

Principals and appositives.—Apposed units are made up of (1) principals and (2) appositives set up alongside the principals and, in effect, duplicating their construction.

The year 1939 was the crucial one.
I like *the story "Dry September"* especially well.
You'll pay alimony yet, *you brute.*
You boys are welcome to go along.
We each had to make a choice.
You've met *my friends Lewis Williams and James McPherson.*
We're going *down to Mexico City* next week.
There aren't any seats *up front.*
Opportunities seem more numerous *out west.*
The girl *over there* is the new stenographer.

Apposed units obviously perform a variety of syntactic functions. Principals always precede their appositives and usually precede them immediately as in the sentences above. Phrases, as well as single words, are readily usable both as principals and as apposi-tives. Appositives are commonly more exact restatements of princi-pals; but this is not quite the case with respect to *you boys,* and in *we each had to make a choice* a representative singular is used in ap-position to a plural—a construction likely to be avoided in careful and formal styles. In informal *let's us go too* strongly stressed *us* is an appositive which actually repeats its principal, the *us* of *let's,* which rarely receives strong stress when *let's* means what it means here.

Though they perform a variety of syntactic functions, apposed units are of relatively few nounal and adverbial types. Headed units are preferred at many points where apposed units might seem usable: for example, in *the City of New York* and in *the month of August.* Adverbial apposed units such as *down to Mexico City, up front, out west,* and *over there* are in constant use, at least in informal styles. The principals here give expression to deep feelings for general relationships in space and the like: southernness, conspicuousness, remoteness from the historic spiritual centers of the nation, side-by-sideness. Occasionally two appositives follow a single principal.

> Phyllis went *back up north* last week.

Here *up* and *north* are semantically repetitive, but *up* (like *back*) is not usable without *north* or some more exact appositive stated or clearly understood from the context.

Postponing of appositives occurs when the principal is an *it* or a *there* whose function is to occupy the position the appositive would otherwise be expected to occupy.

> *It*'s fifty miles *from Youngstown to Akron.*
> He makes *it* hard *to work with him.*
> *There* isn't *time.*

Here the whole matter of the real content of the subject or the first complement is left in suspension until the appositive promised by the principal is arrived at.

Prepositions and objects.—Prepositional units are made up of (1) prepositions and (2) objects.

> He went *in debt* again.
> Jerry gives spectacular flowers *to his girl friends.*
> We bought the table *at a fire sale.*
> The man *with glasses* is a visitor.
> We drove up *to Quebec* last summer.
> It's an hour *till supper.*

In declaratives, prepositions almost always precede their objects and precede them immediately. But sometimes, as in *people want peace the world around,* a preposition follows its object; and sometimes, as in *we wanted him to give you more time,* a preposition (here *to*) occurs within its object (here *him give you more time*). In the following sentence an adjunct separates a preposition from its object.

> The study of contemporary English needs to develop some of
> the decorousness of, *for example,* Anglo-Saxon scholarship.

Objects of prepositions are sometimes single words and sometimes longer units of various types.

The relationship between prepositions and their objects has much in common with that between predicators and their complements. The following parallel constructions can illustrate.

> the room beside ours
> the room adjoining ours
> the room that adjoins ours
> students with eight-o'clock classes
> students having eight-o'clock classes
> students that have eight-o'clock classes

Prepositions are what gives syntactic character to prepositional units, and this character can be described as adverbial. The objects of prepositions are generally nounal, but a few prepositions (notably the *as* of *I regarded it as unimportant*) take adjectival objects in much the way such a verb as *be* takes adjectival complements.

Phrasal prepositions must be recognized. Often they embody a relational or directional meaning in a noun which is made the head word in the object of one one-word preposition and is followed and modified by a second.

Hatcher does everything *by means of* indirection.
We came *by way of* Miami.
The garage is *in back of* the house.
I keep an umbrella here *in case of* rain.
We went wrong *in spite of* everything.
There was considerable doubt *with respect to* Harrison's views.

They may contain a single preposition rather than two.

> We had a pleasant time *on board* both ships.
> The mountains *south of* San Juan are magnificent.

Another type of phrasal preposition embodies a preposition-like word followed and modified by an undoubted one-word preposition.

> He keeps *abreast of* the times.
> They entered the grounds *ahead of* us.
> Henry acquired three children *along with* his wife.
> He expressed himself frankly *apropos of* the change.
> Sensible people always run *away from* work.
> We postponed the meeting *because of* the weather.
> You need three wives *instead of* one.
> She buys them *regardless of* cost.
> The coat cost *upwards of* a month's pay.

Often phrasal prepositions can be paralleled by one-word prepositions which express their meanings less conspicuously, and perhaps
less explicitly, but more economically and sometimes more com-
fortably.

> I'm *in favor of* variety.
> I'm *for* variety.

Under some circumstances objects of phrasal prepositions are incorporated within them.

> They don't make errors *in the buyer's favor*.
> She gave up a great deal *for her family's sake*.

In such a unit as *since before Christmas* it seems preferable to
say not that *since before* is a phrasal preposition but that *since*
is a preposition with the prepositional unit *before Christmas* as its
object. *Before*, then, is another preposition with *Christmas* as its
object. For both *since* and *before* true prepositional use is normal.
In such a unit as *for George to call*, as in *it's time for George to call*,
it seems best to regard *for . . . to* as an apposed-unit preposition
in which *for* is principal and *to* is delayed appositive. The *for* is
obviously that of *it's time for his call*, and the *to* is obviously that
of *it's time to call*.

Coordinates.—Multiple units are made up of coordinates which
unite on a syntactically equal basis in performing either major
syntactic functions or contained ones.

> John *loves and leaves* them.
> *Harry and I* carried the trunk down.
> *Harry and I* drove our cars.
> Her new dress is *blue and white*.
> He works *slowly but accurately*.
> Marian is certainly worrying her poor *father and mother*.
> The startling *red and white* upholstery dominates the room.
> There's a *five-and-ten*-cent store in the block.
> We drove *up and down* the streets.
> The pen belongs to *George or Harry*.
> *More and more* people are bowling.

In *Harry and I carried the trunk down* there is joint action; in
Harry and I drove our cars there is something a little different, so
that *Harry drove his car, and I drove mine* means the same thing.
The multiple units given above all employ coordinators to mark

the relationship explicitly. Coordinators are best regarded as contained modifiers within coordinates which they begin. Thus in *loves and leaves* the coordinator *and* is best considered a modifier of *leaves*. Similarly, in multiple sentences, which have a great deal in common with multiple units within clauses, a coordinator joining two main divisions is best regarded as an adjunct within the second.

> Harry came out on the bus, *and* I did too.

Multiple units without coordinators are not at all rare.

> We took a bus *from Akron to Youngstown.*
> There were *thirty-two* seats.
> The *Sacco-Vanzetti* case attracted attention everywhere.
> He's *ignorant, opinionated, rude.*
> All we do is *work, work, work.*

Units of various types function as coordinates in multiple units.

> That's *the new man from Ohio and our friend McPherson.*

But though one coordinate is a headed unit and the other an apposed unit here, both are nounal. Especially in informal styles, there is often coordination of words and longer units which are not coordinate in sense.

> It made me *good and mad.*

Occasionally an adjunct separates coordinates.

> The pen belongs to George, who was here last, or to Harry.

In a series of three or more coordinates, commonly only the last has a coordinator, which then serves to mark it as terminal.

> Courses in English, Spanish, European history, calculus, and geology are listed.

Just as in some headed units the heads cannot be used alone as the units are used, the coordinates in some multiple units are not usable individually as the multiple units are used.

> *Slow and steady* wins the race.
> The program pleased *young and old.*
> It was *touch and go* for a while.
> The elephants are hunting *high and low* for Arthur and Celeste.
> He came at us *hammer and tongs.*

The baby cried *day and night.*
Job or no job, we have to have a holiday.
They're very conscientious people, *by and large.*
A *hit-and-run* driver almost killed her.
He's an *out-and-out* fraud.

Misleading parallelism in form sometimes suggests unintended coordination.

A conscious understanding of how grammatical patterns function is useful to *teachers and students* who are past childhood.

Here repetition of *to* before *students* would clarify the construction.

Items in unanalyzed strings.—Sometimes old relationships
are no longer felt, and analysis of syntactic units therefore
seems artificial. This is true, for example, of such a name as *James
Harvey Robinson,* where the divisions of the total name are quite
clear but their relation is not.

**Relation of major and contained syntactic functions to
secondary syntactic functions.**—The contained syntactic functions, then, are those of contained head, contained modifier, principal, appositive, preposition, object, coordinate, and item in an
unanalyzed string. Every word can be said to perform one of these
functions within a phrasal predicator, subject, complement, adjunct, or isolate, or to be a (one-word) predicator, subject, complement, adjunct, or isolate itself. Sometimes a word or multiword
unit can be said to perform two major or contained functions
simultaneously. Thus in *they separate the men with families from
those without* the word *without* can be considered both a modifier
of *those* and a preposition whose object is implied rather than
stated. Surely *without* has the semantic value of *without families*
here. In *he shouted, "Coming!"* the verb form *coming* is both the
complement in the main statement and the reduced predicator in
a quoted statement that has the force of unreduced *I'm coming
there.*

Secondary functions differ from major and contained functions
in that they can be regarded as always performed by words or
multiword units which also perform major or contained functions.

Half modifiers.—One kind of secondary function is that of half
modifier. Half modifiers appear in a variety of situations. Most

adjectival complements are half modifiers of subjects or preceding complements.

> The mountains are *very beautiful.*
> I finally got the shoes *clean.*

Here *very beautiful* and *clean* are first of all complements. Complements are needed where *very beautiful* and *clean* appear, and these items perform the necessary function. *I finally got the shoes clean* is structurally very much like *I finally got the shoes into good condition.* But a relationship which approaches contained modification is present also. The syntactic distance to *the very beautiful mountains* and *the clean shoes* is not great.

Many adjuncts have secondary functions as half modifiers.

> We ate the chicken *cold.*
> He married *young.*
> Sigrid was already composing *at the age of five.*
> Mary dropped the handkerchief *carelessly.*
> George slammed the door *furiously.*
> He speaks French *like a Frenchman.*
> The child was found three miles away, *hungry and cold.*
> *Familiar with the marvels of science and invention,* the American was reluctant to make commitments for future generations.
> Many clauses, *main and subordinate,* contain units for which the best name seems to be "complement."

In the last of these sentences *main and subordinate* is given half-modifier status for reasons that are largely rhetorical: in *many main and subordinate clauses* the same unit is a true modifier within the subject, and the meaning is not greatly different. In *we ate the chicken cold* the adjective *cold* is first of all an adjunct of circumstance, in the usual position of such adjuncts. *While it was cold* would be a similarly used adjunct if it replaced *cold.* In *he married young* the adjective *young* is primarily an adjunct of time or circumstance and secondarily a half modifier of *he,* which it cannot modify directly as it does *Payne* in *young Payne.* Secondary relationships as half modifiers may help to explain the construction illustrated in the following sentence.

> I saw a dress like that *in Hudson's window* yesterday.

Here the seeing has not taken place in the store window: the person who saw the dress was outside. The italicized unit is perhaps most conveniently regarded as an adjunct of place in the statement and, in addition, a half modifier of *a dress like that*. In *I never see him alone* it is similarly possible to regard *alone* as an adjunct of circumstance in the declarative and also a half modifier either of the subject *I* or of the complement *him*, depending on who is never alone.

Some half-modifier relationships are very strongly felt. Others are not clearly felt in modern English and can be ignored in all but the most careful analysis. But sometimes when even the least conspicuous relationships of this type are disregarded in practice, sentence structure is damaged.

> *At the age of five* Sigrid's teacher had her composing.
> The handkerchief dropped *carelessly* to the floor.
> *Good or bad*, he hasn't read a new book in twenty years.

In the first of these sentences *teacher* is syntactically more prominent than *Sigrid's*, and for this reason a false relationship is momentarily possible. In *the handkerchief dropped carelessly to the floor* there is no mention, and no real thought, of anything to which carelessness can be attributed. In the last sentence goodness or badness may seem to be related either to the adjacent subject, *he*, or to the whole state of affairs—rather than to *a new book*.

Half appositives.—Many loose adjuncts have secondary functions as half appositives.

> One factor, *prices*, was decisive.
> One old friend is especially missed: *Mozelle*.
> We hurried, *even ran*, to the door.
> He's a true Westerner—*natural, friendly, without pretensions*.
> Two cities—*Havana and Santiago*—dominate the opposite
>   ends of the island.
> That's what we do, isn't it?—*assume they won't come*.
> Some people consider hot weather, *especially tropical hot
>   weather*, unhealthy.
> Never before, *not even in the seventies*, had the outlook seemed
>   so bleak.
> Technology, *not art*, is what is needed.
> Anyone, *even the Little Woman*, can make good soup.
> I have no desk—*nothing but a table and two chairs*.
> These articles make sense, *most of them*.

In such a sentence as *one factor, prices, was decisive* the half appositive has no effect on the number form of the verb. The subject here is *one factor,* and *prices* is first of all a loose adjunct—even though from the point of view of meaning it is a more exact statement of the content of the subject. Some loose-adjunct half appositives approach clauses in force and in the type of modifiers they include.

> Wall Street and State Street, *so long the objects of popular execration,* could pose as saviors of the country.

Half-appositive relationships are present in certain kinds of loose adjuncts which precede their half principals.

> *As Maine goes,* so goes the nation.
> *The dictator of literary Boston,* Howells never forgot his frontier origins.
> *Child that he is,* he has always trusted her.
> *Windows, doors, beds, dressers*—everything in the room was burned to a crisp.
> *Money*—that was what he needed.
> And *John*—did he like it?

In the first of these sentences, *so* is a tight adjunct and *as Maine goes* can be considered in half apposition to it.

Tight adjuncts have half-appositive relationships much less frequently than loose adjuncts do.

> I'm occasionally right *myself.*
> We've *all* made that mistake.
> They don't *either one* eat enough.

In *I myself am occasionally right* it seems best to regard *I myself* as a true apposed unit used as subject, but when *myself* is delayed the situation is different: there is no suspension of the subject, since *I* alone is entirely adequate. Representative half appositives, such as *either one* in the third sentence above, occur chiefly in informal styles and put singular forms in half apposition with plural ones. Half-appositive construction may or may not be felt in sentences such as the following.

> The people of Hiroshima were the first to die *victims of the atomic bomb.*

Half coordinates.—Half coordinates which are primarily tight adjuncts occur. The *and the sound of voices* of *he could hear music somewhere and the sound of voices* can serve as an example. In a word-order language such as modern English, the postponement of *and the sound of voices* removes it from the status of a full coordinate with *music.* Half coordinates which are also loose adjuncts occur more often.

> He suffered with Latin and Greek, *and even with French.*
> Integrity was in the tower, *and decision.*
> We hurried, *or rather ran,* to the door.
> Avocados, *or alligator pears,* are a wonderful addition to our diet.
> The second part of the book, *and the best part in my opinion,* takes up the period of the Revolution.

Many half coordinates are semantically very much like half appositives, but are begun by *and* or *or.*

Coordinators.—Only four words function as basic coordinators: *and, but, or,* and *nor.* All four should be regarded as modifiers of the coordinates they begin: the function of coordinator is to be regarded as an additional, secondary one. Except that they are also coordinators, *and, but, or,* and *nor* function about as *also, nevertheless, else,* and (in some of its uses) *neither* function. The four basic coordinators, of course, always precede what they attach to. The multiple coordinator *and/or* is often useful.

> If you see Robert *and/or* Ruby, let me know.

The style here is informal, but *and/or* is most characteristically used in careful styles. It is likely to be avoided in formal styles.

It should be added that *and* and *but* do not always function as coordinators.

> Even the best stores—*and* they are very good stores—do not handle their vegetables well.
> All *but* two of the answers were wrong.

And is an adjunct beginning a loose adjunct of circumstance in the first of these sentences, and *but* is a preposition in the second. When they begin coordinates in multiple units, coordinators announce an equal sharing of a function. They announce something less than this, and yet much like it, when they begin half coordinates.

Precoordinators often accompany basic coordinators, normally beginning the first coordinate in a multiple unit and serving notice that it is a coordinate and will be followed by another. *Both, not, either,* and *neither* function as precoordinators before *and, but, or,* and *nor.*

> *Both* Mary and Jane liked the picture.
> *Not* a chemist but a physicist was needed.
> She's *not* only pretty but also fairly bright.
> He's *neither* for nor against it.

Like basic coordinators, precoordinators are modifiers within the coordinates they begin: their function as coordinators is a secondary one. In *he's neither for nor against it,* for example, there is a multiple preposition in which the first coordinate is *neither for* and the second is *nor against.* Each coordinate is a headed unit in which the contained modifier is also a coordinator. It is significant that the negative force of *neither* does not extend to the second coordinate as that of *not* does in *he isn't either for or against it.* The negative force of *not* is similarly confined in *not a chemist but a physicist was needed.*

Whether is often used as a precoordinator which comes somewhat before the first coordinate.

> I can't remember *whether* Jones came in 1953 or in 1954.

Here *whether* serves as a clause marker as well as a precoordinator. When other precoordinators move forward so that they are separated from what they attach to, the resulting construction meets with criticism. Thus *either Jones came in 1953 or in 1954* is less acceptable for careful or formal use than *Jones came either in 1953 or in 1954.*

Such pairs as *on the one hand* and *on the other hand* indicate coordinate relationships quite often. In such a sentence as *she is equally unhappy when Christianity is questioned and when it is practiced* the contained modifier *equally* functions rather similarly.

Clause markers.—Finally, whatever serves to distinguish clauses of other kinds from main declaratives can be said to function as a clause marker. The function of clause marker is best regarded as always a secondary one, performed by words and multiword units which also perform major or contained functions within the clauses they mark. Clause markers are italicized in the following sentences.

> *Has* Jack been waiting for us?
> Well, Robert, now *what*'s wrong?
> *Be* careful.
> I wonder *where* she's from.

Has is part of the predicator in the first sentence, *what* is the subject in the second, *be* is the predicator in the third, and *where* is the object in a prepositional unit used as complement in a subordinate clause in the fourth; but *has*, *what*, *be*, and *where* are also clause markers in these sentences. Clause markers tend to begin the clauses they mark, but they do not always do so. The use of clause markers in contemporary English is most conveniently described in connection with analysis of clause patterns.

CHAPTER II

PARTS OF SPEECH

Relation of syntactic functions to part-of-speech categories.—Words can be said to perform particular syntactic functions in particular sentences and at the same time to belong to part-of-speech categories. In modern English the part-of-speech classification of a word is primarily a matter of characteristic behavior in all the circumstances in which it is used with the particular meaning in point. In each of the two columns which follow, the italicized words must be classified alike with respect to function in these sentences but must be distinguished with respect to their grammatical behavior in general.

Coffee was enough. Summer is *fun* in Minnesota.
That was enough.   Summer is *delightful* in Minnesota.
Once was enough.   Summer is *over* in Minnesota.

Die and *death* mean essentially the same thing in *until I die* and *until my death*, but their grammatical behavior is different. The basic criterions for determining the part-of-speech classification of a word as used with a particular meaning are two, both of them syntactic: (1) the functions it characteristically performs, and (2) the kinds of modifiers it characteristically accepts. A third criterion is less generally useful, and does not help at all with large numbers of words such as *ought, fun, extinct, then, ouch,* and *each:* the ways in which the word inflects. A fourth criterion is sometimes useful but is hard to manipulate: the kind of meaning it expresses. A fifth possible criterion—the presence in some words of noninflectional formatives associated with particular part-of-speech classifications, such as the *ize* of *pasteurize* and the *less* of *careless*—is limited in usefulness and unreliable.

It seems best to recognize six parts of speech: verbs, nouns, adjectives, adverbs, absolutes, and pronouns.

Verbs.—The function characteristically performed by verbs is that of predicator, and the structures characteristically built around them are clauses. Their most characteristic modifiers are subjects. and these precede them in declaratives. Almost all verbs can be run through such series as *I want, you want, he wants,* though many of them need complements as well as subjects; and words of no other kind take the nominative and common-case forms of the personal pronouns as prepositive modifiers in this way. Almost all verbs make inflected forms by adding what the written language represents by *s* or *es* in the third person singular of the present and *ing* in the one-word gerundial; and every word which inflects in these ways is a verb. Verbs have other inflected forms too, but these two are sufficient for purposes of identification. Verbs express meanings of occurrence—action, event, or state of affairs.

A few defectives must be classified as verbs and yet do not fully meet the tests almost all verbs meet. Seven verbs have neither *s* forms nor gerundial forms: *can, may, must, ought, shall, should,* and *will.*

All verbs normally accept only subjects and other modifiers that are semantically compatible with them. This is the reason such a verb as *rain,* used as in *it rained last night,* takes only *it* as subject: only "it" can rain real rain. But people can rain blows on each other if they want to, and *rain* can hardly be called a defective verb. Compatibility of meanings sets bounds on the development of all syntactic relationships.

The patterning of particular verbs with respect to complements requires notice because of its importance to other parts of speech. Some verbs characteristically take nounal first complements and are called transitive.

> We *make* fudge.
> I*'ve dropped* a plate.
> I *remember* Tony well.
> Not even Californians *understand* Californians.
> She *has* no brothers or sisters.
> Columbus *is* the capital.

Some transitives also take second complements. These may be characteristically nounal.

> We*'ve elected* Haynes chairman.
> They *call* it efficiency.

Or they may be nounal ("indirect" complements) if they precede syntactically "first" complements. The verbs with which this is usual form a limited group: it is not usual, for example, to say *he's dedicated her another song.*

> They*'ve assigned* Wilson another class.
> She*'s handed* him his hat.
> Larry*'s sent* us some pictures.
> They *teach* the children a little French.
> We *owe* our friends a great deal.

Or they may be adjectival, with half-modifier relationships to the first complements.

> He *gets* his clothes wet.
> They*'ve made* their friends angry.

Or, more often, adverbial.

> We*'ve elected* Haynes to the chairmanship.
> They*'ve assigned* it to George.
> We *owe* a great deal to our friends.
> He *gets* his clothes into very bad condition.
> I*'ve put* the typewriter in its case.
> I*'ve put* the typewriter away.
> I*'ll take* you there.
> We*'ll look* the Littles up.
> He*'s turned* his key in.
> We*'ve* finally *rid* the place of roaches.
> You *deprive* me of my best excuses.

Some verbs characteristically take adjectival first complements with half-modifier relationships to the subjects and are called copulative.

> The older residents *are* now wealthy.
> He *gets* too emotional.
> She *looks* healthy enough.
> She *acts* silly.
> The dog *breaks* loose.
> Everything *went* black.

Some verbs characteristically take adverbial first complements (including prepositional units) and can be called oblique.

> He *looks* away.
> He *looks* at the ceiling.
> We *go* there.
> He *is* here.
> A new manager *has taken* over.
> Everyone *longs* for security.
> He *refrains* from criticism.
> Harris *participates* in the protests.
> They'*re infringing* on our rights.
> The car *belongs* to Jack.
> The purse *harmonizes* with her gloves.
> The dog *breaks* out.

Some oblique verbs also take second complements.

> He *doesn't fall* in with such suggestions.
> He'*s going* on with the novel.
> She'*s made* up with him.
> We'*ve done* away with the rugs.
> She *puts* up with a great deal.

Some verbs are used without complements and can be called terminant.

> He *snores.*

Meaning relationships are very complex, as has been said. Copulatives most often express ideas of being, becoming, remaining, and seeming (including impressing particular senses, as in *the milk smells sour*); but they are not confined to such meanings. Many verbs are used with varied turns of meaning with which varied complement patterns are normal. Thus, from the point of view of contemporary English grammar, *be* is transitive in *Columbus is the capital* (and even in careful or formal *it was he who had asked the White House to issue a denial*), copulative in *you're right*, oblique in *he's here*, and terminant in *there aren't enough seats*. *Get* is transitive in *he got another drink* and in *he got himself drunk*, copulative in *he got drunk*, and oblique in *he got back to his apartment*. *Look* is oblique in *she looked at him* but is transitive in *she looked daggers at him* and copulative in *she looked happy*. *Try* is transitive in *we try numerous recipes* but is oblique in *she tried for an* A. Truly exceptional complements, such as the adjective *long* with the transitive verb *spend* in *we didn't spend long there*, are another matter. Some verbs are used in patternings of extremely restricted types. Thus *bestir*, for example, is used only with reflexive first complements.

Nouns.—The functions which are characteristically performed by nouns and are most helpful in part-of-speech classification are four:

1. Subject, as in *paper isn't strong enough*.
2. Complement of a transitive verb, as in *we've used paper*.
3. Object of a preposition, as in *we wrapped it in paper*.
4. Head in a nounal headed unit, as in *this paper isn't strong*.

Other functions characteristically performed by nouns are those of principal and appositive within nounal apposed units (as in *Johnny my boy* and *my friend George*) and of coordinates within nounal multiple units (as in *Harvey and I*). The most characteristic modifiers of nouns in positions in front of the nouns are (1) determiners, such as *the* and possessives, and (2) adjectives. Their most characteristic inflections serve to mark plural number and possessive case. Meanings are of limited help in identifying nouns as such, since meanings of practically any kind can be expressed in nouns; it is true, however, that the names of people, places, and "things" are characteristically nouns.

But nouns are of three types with somewhat distinct patterns of behavior. The basic forms of pluralizer nouns are most often used as heads within nounal units, since they generally require determiners. Thus it is hard to use the basic forms of such nouns as *house* or *wife* alone as subjects without determiners such as *the*, *your*, or *Richardson's*. Proper nouns such as *Robert* and *Richardson* rarely take determiners and do not accept adjectives freely; when they are made plural or take determiners (as in *the Richardsons*) they generally cease to be proper nouns. Quantifiables such as *courage, fun, pneumonia, milk, spaghetti, machinery,* and *furniture* are not made plural, though it is true that some quantifiables have pluralizer status also. A word that has an *s* plural is clearly a noun or a pronoun, but only one of the three varieties of nouns forms plurals. Inflection for the possessive is fundamentally a nounal and pronounal variety of inflection, but it is often added to multiword units, as in *someone else's*, where *else* is an adverb. Actually, quantifiables and many pluralizers are rarely made possessive.

A number of functional defectives require classification as nouns. Examples are italicized in the following units.

on *behalf* of	in good *stead*
Mr. Jones	on the *verge* of
for your *sake*	for a short *while*
Dear *Sir:*	in no *wise*

These are words which now occur as nouns only in sharply limited situations. *Mr.* has the plural *Messrs.* and is clearly a noun honorific like *doctor, judge,* and *colonel.* In contemporary American use the *while* of subordinate clauses is best considered an adverb with the secondary function of clause marker, like *when.*

Nounal headed units fall into patterns of a complexity surpassed only by clause structure itself. Adjectival modifiers, descriptive or qualifying in force, normally precede their heads immediately.

quiet girls	*medieval* France	*better* clothes
motherly women	*poor* George	*older* countries

Determiner modifiers, pronominal in function, normally precede adjectival modifiers when both are used, and are concerned with identification, number, or quantity.

the tall boy	*two* bad starts
no good reason	*a great many* old friends
Fred's new house	*too much* water

But the presence of extremitive and near-extremitive elements sometimes forces the article *a* inside units it might be expected to begin.

> I didn't realize how high *a* price he had paid.
> It isn't as big *a* room as that.
> She's too good *a* cook to make such a pie.
> It isn't that big *a* city.

Predeterminer modifiers generally are adverbial in function, and mensurant, selectional, differential, conjunctive, or adjunct-like in force.

twice the time	*and* the young people
only the older children	*then* a struggling lawyer
considerably the best room	*scarcely* an hour

Postpositive modifiers are most characteristically adverbial or clausal.

> the price *alone* people *with children*
> the weather *here* people *who have children*

Postpositive position is normal even for adjectival units if they include prepositional or clausal modifiers of their own.

> Main statements *roughly equivalent to these subordinate clauses* would be as follows.
>
> *Roughly equivalent* main statements would be as follows.

When there is no determiner, a pluralizer or quantifiable noun or nounal unit usually has general force. Sometimes the force is truly generic.

> *Children* hate *irony*.
> *Water* is the best drink.
> *Statistics* require interpretation.
> *Man* still finds *germs* and *insects* dangerous.

Sometimes there is simply an unwillingness to get involved in ideas of identity, number, or quantity.

> We eat *baked potatoes* quite often.
> He writes *short stories*.
> He spent five years in *college*.
> Almost all our shoes are *machine* made now.
> We spend a third of our lives in *bed*.

Without determiners nouns sometimes approach adjectives in force.

> Mona is located in beautiful *mountain* country.
> Some *university* students were on the plane.
> *Faculty* social life tends to be dull.
> He isn't *man* enough.
> The other suit is *wool*.
> Summer is *fun* in Minnesota.
> The food is *tops*.
> He's *good company*.
> It's *biological nonsense* to call women the weaker sex.

This kind of thing is exceptional for nounal complements. Determiners are necessary with nounal complements in such sentences as the following.

He's *a lawyer.*
His wife is *a Canadian.*

But in the plural the inflectional endings show nounal construction and determinatives are not needed in the same situations.

Both men are *lawyers.*
Both the wives are *Canadians.*

In some special situations there is really specific force without the aid of determiners. This is notably true where there is a kind of pairing in more or less fixed phrasings.

I searched the room from *top* to *bottom.*
Mother and *child* are doing well.

It is true in upside-down construction where indefinite articles are commonly dropped, at least in careful and formal styles.

Some kind of *solution* is necessary.
A solution of some kind is necessary.

It is true in the light of context in such a sentence as the following.

I'm driving to *town* after supper today.

Proper nouns, of course, are basically specific in force without the aid of determiners. In *only John* the adverb *only* is essentially pre-determinative exactly as it is in *only the older children.*

Adjectives.—The functions which are characteristically performed by adjectives and are most helpful in part-of-speech classification are two:

1. Prepositive modifier of a noun head, as in *new houses are being built.*
2. Complement of a copulative verb, with a half-modifier relationship to the subject, as in *these houses are new.*

Adjectives are generally usable as *new* is used in these two sentences. Other functions characteristically performed by adjectives are that of head in an adjectival headed unit, as *new* is used in *these houses are very new,* and that of coordinate in an adjectival multiple unit, as *new* is used in *these houses are new and pleasant.* The most characteristic prepositive modifiers of adjectives are adverbs. Some adjectives employ the endings *er* and *est* to make comparatives and superlatives. As for meanings, generally adjectives express meanings that can be described broadly as qualitative or descriptive: they name "characteristics."

As modifiers of nouns, adjectives are normally preceded by determiners when determiners are used along with them: for example, in *the new house, some new houses,* and *Fred's new house. New house* and *new houses* are undetermined units, like *house* and *houses* alone; and *new house* is no more usable as a subject than *house* alone. Adjectives do not modify proper nouns such as *Lucy* and *Stephenson* freely, though emotional combinations such as *poor Lucy* occur. Some adjectives express meanings of identification, number, and quantity and are at the borderline with determiner use.

that *very* moment	forty-*odd* seats
innumerable occasions	*considerable* experience

In *forty-odd* there is even coordination of a determinative pronoun and an adjective.

A fairly large number of functional defectives must be included among the adjectives. Some are usable before nouns but not as complements of copulatives. This is true of the following.

utter
quondam
gala
very (meaning "exact" or "true")
live, lone, outdoor, faraway
foster (as in *foster parents*), vice (as in *vice president*)
main, chief
fore, hind, mid
mere, sole

A number of words that ordinarily require prepositional completers seem to require classification as adjectives and yet are not usable as prepositive modifiers of head nouns. Examples follow.

afraid	desirous
content ("satisfied")	irrespective
proof	tantamount
sorry ("regretful")	unable

All these words are freely usable, with completers expressed or in some cases implied, after copulative verbs. Such words as *ready* and *glad* have limited use before head nouns, as in *a ready wit* and *a glad smile*, but are much more freely usable after *be*.

For particular meanings, too, severe limits on use sometimes exist. Thus, in American English, *the baby feels bad* is not matched, with the same meaning, by *the bad baby* or even by *the baby is bad*, though *the baby is worse* is quite acceptable.

Adverbs.—The functions characteristically performed by adverbs which are most helpful in part-of-speech classification are (1) that of adjunct, (2) that of prepositive modifier of an adjective or another adverb, (3) that of postpositive modifier, and (4) that of preposition.

> The situation improved *then.*
> He was *very* frank.
> Someone *else* can do it.
> There's a good public library *in* Marietta.

The function of predeterminative modifier in nounal units (as in *twice the usual price*) is also fundamentally adverbial. Adverbs also function characteristically as heads in adverbial headed units (such as *very badly*), as principals and appositives in adverbial apposed units (such as *down there*), and as coordinates in adverbial multiple units (such as *now and then*). Many adverbs are highly specialized words that are quite limited in functioning.

A very few adverbs share with some adjectives (and with the pronoun *few*) the use of the inflectional endings *er* and *est* to make comparatives and superlatives. This is true of *often* and *soon*. Adverbs in *ly*, such as *faintly*, *quickly*, and *sadly*, reject *er* and *est* (preferring *more* and *most*), though various adjectives in *ly*, such as *deadly* and *friendly*, make use of these endings. As for meanings, adverbs used as adjuncts of predicators contribute ideas of time, place, manner, and so on, as adjuncts in general do. Adverbs used as prepositive contained modifiers express ideas of degree (as in *very arrogant*), attitude (as in *disturbingly ignorant*), reference (as in *rhetorically neater*), and so on. Adverbs used as prepositions generally express relational or directional meanings. But meanings are undependable guides once again.

The basic coordinators *and*, *but*, *or*, and *nor* are best regarded as a small but important subcategory among the adverbs, as are such clause markers as *if*, *than*, *when*, and *whether* and such linking adverbs as *consequently*, *nevertheless*, and *also*, which neither subordinate nor explicitly coordinate. All of the words which function as one-word prepositions are most conveniently classified as adverbs, though for such words as *worth* and *like* this classification is an arbitrary one.

Absolutes.—The one function characteristically performed by absolutes is that of isolate.

Some absolutes are substitute words. This is true of *yes* and *no*. Others have a more stable content of meaning. This is true of such absolutes as the following.

ah	hey	O. K.	pooh
bah	hi	ooh	scat
boo	hmm	ouch	tsk
gee	hurrah	ow	ugh
hello	oh	phooey	wow

Some absolutes take adjuncts of various kinds, as in *yes, indeed* and in *hello, John;* but it is noteworthy that absolutes tend to reject modifiers, so that, for example, *no* gives way to *not* in such sentences as *certainly not.* Absolutes do not inflect. Most of them are emotional, but this cannot be said of *yes, no,* or *hello.*

Some absolutes function as adjuncts on occasion.

> *Oh,* I guess not.
> *No* I didn't!

No I didn't! is a somewhat emotional declarative disagreeing with something that has just been said. *No, I didn't* is a very different matter: a semantically repetitive double sentence answering a question, with *no* used as an isolate in the main-declarative equivalent which constitutes the first division of the double sentence.

Such isolates as the following are not to be classified as absolutes.

> Danger   My!   Gracious!   Well!

Danger is a noun, *my* a pronoun, *gracious* an adjective, *well* an adverb.

Alone among the six parts of speech, absolutes will require no further attention at a later point.

Pronouns.—The pronouns make up a small part-of-speech category distinct from the others in that it is practically closed and the words that belong to it can be listed. The language adds new verbs, nouns, adjectives, adverbs, and absolutes, easily and constantly; but there is no easy entry for new pronouns.

The one characteristically pronounal syntactic function is that of determiner modifier of nounal heads, but not all pronouns perform this function. Pronouns do not take prepositive modifiers very freely. They express meanings (1) of identification and/or (2) of number or quantity. Some pronouns inflect in highly individualistic ways; others do not inflect. Pronouns are of two syntactically distinct kinds. Those which can be classified as determinative pronouns have the function of determiner as their basic use. They can be listed as follows.

I. Full determinatives of identification.
    1. Definiteness: *this* (and *these*), *that* (and *those*), *the*.
    2. Indefiniteness: *a* (and *an*), *some*.
    3. Indifference: *any, either*.
    4. Universality: *every, each*.
    5. Negation: *no* (and *none*), *neither*.
    6. Clause marking: *what, which, whatever, whichever*.
II. Partial determinatives of identification.
    7. Identity: *same*.
    8. Type: *such*.
    9. Difference: *other* (and *others*).
    10. Sequence: ordinal numerals, *last, next, former, latter*.
    11. Possession: *own*.
III. Determinatives of number and quantity.
    12. Cardinal numerals.
    13. Small number and quantity: *few* (and *fewer, fewest*), *little* (and *less, least*), *several*.
    14. Sufficiency: *enough*.
    15. Large number and quantity: *many* and *much* (and *more, most*).
    16. Totality: *all, both*.

The determinatives of identification are freely usable as determiner modifiers of singular forms of pluralizer nouns. Those which are called full determinatives of identification are usable thus without the presence of another (and superimposed) determiner in front of them.

        this house   some house
        the house   either house

each house	what house
no house	whichever house

Determined units such as these are usable in nounal functions as their pluralizer nounal heads ordinarily are not. Thus *this house* can be used as a subject though *house* normally cannot. Determinatives listed as partial determinatives of identification do not ordinarily begin similarly usable nounal units. Full determinatives and possessives can be superimposed on partial determinatives to make fully determined units. But where *such* is the partial determinative it precedes the indefinite article *a*, so that, in effect, the partial determinative is superimposed on the full one.

the same house	every second house
no such house	the latter house
such a house	your own house

Some of the pronouns listed as determinatives of identification, both full and partial, can modify plurals such as *houses* and quantifiables such as *furniture;* others cannot.

The pronouns listed above as determinatives of number and quantity are characteristically used to modify (1) plural forms of pluralizer nouns and/or (2) quantifiable nouns. Except for the cardinal numeral *one*, they modify singular forms of pluralizers only very exceptionally.

three houses	enough furniture
little furniture	many houses
enough houses	much furniture

The classification of the determinatives given here is somewhat arbitrary, especially from the point of view of meanings. There is a frequent mixing of interest in identification with interest in quantity and number. Moreover the patterning of the determinatives of number and quantity is often followed by *some, any,* and *no* as well, so that in effect these pronouns often take their places—syntactically as well as semantically—in a kind of number-and-quantity series along with *few, little, several, many, much, enough,* and *all. No* may even seem to deserve membership in the series of cardinal numerals: *no wife and no children, one wife and one child. two wives and two children,* etc.

The characteristic use of determinative pronouns is the use as determiners within nounal units. But most determinative pronouns are also usable rather freely in nounal functions. In nounal uses they are best considered forms which have assimilated the meanings and the functions of what would be their heads in unreduced construction. In general, determinative pronouns can represent larger nounal units only when it is clear exactly what they are representing. Often obvious parallelism is the key to the matter.

> Most tourists are interested in the life of the people, but *some* are interested only in nightclubs.

Clearly *some* represents *some tourists* here: the parallelism with *most tourists* makes this plain. Often determinative pronouns are followed by modifiers that are the key to what is not expressed.

> *Some* of Bill's old friends have turned against him.
> The *last* of the students has left.
> *Two* of the girls are from Haiti.
> *Many* of these apartments are furnished.

Unreduced expression—*some friends from among Bill's old friends,* etc.—would be objectionably repetitive here. Sometimes what suggests the unstated head for a determinative pronoun is simply something stated prominently in what immediately precedes.

> There are six apartments, *each* with a garage.

Sometimes it is something prominent in the situation at the moment, as when *that just isn't true* means *that story someone has told you just isn't true.* Sometimes no very precise unstated head is really thought of.

> She's on her *own* now.
> *This* is Fred Johnson.

If Fred Johnson uses *this* as an indirect equivalent of *I* in identifying himself on the telephone, some such noun as *speaker,* or some such nounal unit as *person who is calling,* may suggest itself as an omitted head for *this,* but it is not likely that it will suggest itself immediately and automatically. Nevertheless it remains true that the total pattern of behavior of the word must be kept in mind. Among the determinative pronouns only *the, a,* and *every* do not occur in nounal uses. *No* has a variant *none* which replaces the basic form in nounal uses, and *other* has an *s* plural for nounal use.

> This job takes patience, and I have *none*.
> Some old friends write oftener than *others*.

Here *none* obviously represents *no patience*, and *others* represents *other old friends*.

This and *that* have inflected plural forms, and such numerals as *dozen* and *hundred* have *s* plurals used in oddly restricted ways; but determinative pronouns in general lack number inflection. Possessive forms of determinative pronouns occur occasionally. *Few, little, many*, and *much* compare. *Many* and *much* share *more* and *most* as comparative and superlative.

As has been said, in general pronouns do not accept prepositive modifiers freely. Their most common prepositive modifiers are perhaps certain adverbs: for example, in *almost all of the houses*, in *very few houses*, and in *too much noise*. When they are used in nounal constructions, determinative pronouns often have modifiers that in unreduced constructions would belong to the nounal heads which are, with varying degrees of clarity, implied.

> her own   the latter
> some others   the third of the month

A few determinative pronouns take the indefinite article *a* as a modifier even when the units thus formed are used as determiner modifiers.

> *a few* occasions   *a great many* reasons
> *a little* fun

Nounal pronouns can be listed as follows.

1. The personals *I, you, he, she, it, we, they*, with their objectives, possessives, and *self* forms.
2. The reciprocal *each other*, with its possessive.
3. The expletive *there*.
4. General *one* ("a person"), with its possessive and its *self* form.
5. Substitute *one* (as in *a large house and a small one*), with its plural and possessive forms.
6. The compounds *someone, somebody, something, anyone, anybody, anything, everyone, everybody, everything, no one, nobody, nothing*, with their possessives.
7. The clause markers *that, who*, and *whoever*.

Naught and *nil* are little-used pronoun equivalents of *nothing*, and *aught* is a rare equivalent of *anything*. The personals are repeatable as nouns (and most other pronouns) are not, so that though it is not normal to say *George does George's work when George feels like it* it is quite normal to say *he does his work when he feels like it*. Expletive *there* is sharply limited in syntactic functioning, but so is such a noun as *behalf*.

Almost all of the nounal pronouns have the syntactic value of determiner modifiers and heads together. Thus *who's he?* is comparable syntactically to *who's that man?* rather than to the reduced *who's that?* The element of identification in terms of situation which is central in *that* is also prominent in *he*, though except in the possessive *he* is never used as a determiner modifier. It would be quite possible to regard the nounal pronouns as a subcategory of the nouns like the proper nouns in their behavior, but it seems wiser to group them with the determinatives.

Pronoun status should not be assigned on the basis of meaning alone. Meanings of identification, number, and quantity are often expressed by words of other kinds. The idea of number expressed by the pronoun *two*, for example, occurs also in the verb *double*, in the noun *pair*, in the adjectives *double* and *twofold*, and in the adverbs *doubly* and *twice*. The category of pronouns is primarily a syntactic one, not a semantic one.

Multiple part-of-speech classifications.—Many words must be classified sometimes as one part of speech and sometimes as another. When this is the case, it is normally because they accept two or more distinctive types of modifiers. Sometimes it is because they express distinct meanings in functions characteristic of different parts of speech. Patterns of inflection are significant too. Only verbs have *s* forms, *ing* forms, and *ed* forms. Only nouns and a few pronouns inflect for plural number—though verbs inflect for person and number at some points. Almost all the words that add *er* and *est* to form comparatives and superlatives must be granted adjective status: a few adverbs and pronouns are the only exceptions.

A considerable number of words must be classified as verbs and also as nouns. *Jump* can serve as an example: *jump* provides both verbal and nounal names for an action. As a verb it accepts such prepositive subject modifiers as the personal-pronoun forms *I, you,* and *he*. As a noun it accepts determiner and adjectival prepositive modifiers. As a verb *jump* follows the inflectional pattern of the regular verbs, as a noun the inflectional pattern of regular pluralizer nouns.

> He jumps up and down on the bed.
> He crosses the room in three big jumps.

Often where a single word is both a verb and a noun the meaning relationship is not so simple. Thus the verb *dust*, used as in *no one dusts the furniture now*, expresses the meaning expressed by the noun *dust* plus the additional meaning expressed by the verb *remove*. The following brief list of words which are both verbs and nouns can serve to suggest something of the complexity of the meaning relationships which develop.

air	desire	picnic	sandwich
amount	dress	play	ship
attack	drink	pocket	side
bite	elbow	powder	skin
book	face	profiteer	slum
bottle	farm	puncture	sponsor
button	hand	rain	station
cook	hit	run	summer
copy	iron	reason	walk
corner	must	referee	weather
cost	paint	sail	word

These matters are highly individual: each word has its own history and its own accumulation of uses.

A smaller number of words must be classified as verbs and also as adjectives. *Warm* can serve as an example. As a verb *warm* takes such prepositive subject modifiers as *I*, *you*, and *he*: as an adjective it takes such prepositive modifiers as the adverbs *too* and *very*. As a verb *warm* has an *s* form and an *ing* form, as well as a regular past form in *ed*; as an adjective it has an *er* form and an *est* form.

> It's warming up a little today.
> It's warmer today.

Warm is both verb and adjective, but *hot* is only an adjective. Again, these matters are highly individual: each word must be

known with respect to its grammar as well as its central meaning.
A few other words which are both verbs and adjectives are the
following.

busy	double	profane	steady
clean	empty	secure	tame
complete	forward	select	thin
cool	free	smooth	triple
correct	lower	sober	weary
corrupt	open	sour	wet

Verbs which are also adjectives are likely to express the meanings
of the adjectives plus such meanings as *become* or *cause to become*.
A few words are verbs, nouns, and adjectives.

better	faint	slack	trim
blind	limp	slight	void
calm	parallel	square	wrong
equal	quiet	total	yellow

A few words are verbs and are also pronouns, adverbs, or even
absolutes.

own	up	O. K.
second	down	hurrah

Second is of course a noun also. *Back, down,* and *while* seem to require classification as verbs, nouns, and adverbs.

A considerable number of words must be classified as nouns and
also as adjectives. *Conservative* will do as an example. As a noun it
accepts such prepositive modifiers as the determiner *a* and the
adjective *true* and it inflects for plural number, as in *he is a true
conservative* and *they are true conservatives.* As an adjective it ignores
considerations of number and accepts such prepositive modifiers
as the adverbs *very* and *too,* as in *they are very conservative.* The
word *French* can serve as a second example. As the name of the
language, *French* is a quantifiable noun and is hence modifiable by
such determiners as *much* (as in *he doesn't know much French*) as
well as by adjectives (as in *she speaks Canadian French*). But
French is also an adjective, usable as in *French customs, French
wines,* and *the French people.* Other examples of words which must
be classified as both nouns and adjectives follow.

characteristic	extreme	intellectual	plastic
criminal	general	material	secret
cold	inferior	native	solid
evil	innocent	opposite	uniform

A few words which require classification as pronouns require other part-of-speech classifications too. Thus *little* is best classified as a pronoun in *a little fun*, where it is quantitative and is modified by *a* (which cannot modify *fun*), but as an adjective in *a little boy*, where it is descriptive and is concerned with size rather than with quantity. In *a little fun* it functions (with *a*) as *some* functions; in *a little boy* as *small* functions. *There* is best regarded as a pronoun in *there isn't time*, where it is the principal in an apposed-unit subject and has no place meaning, but as an adverb in *there she is*, where it is complement and has a place meaning. *No* is best classified as a pronoun in *he has no friends*, where it is a determiner like *some*, but as an absolute when it answers questions as *yes* does. *Thirty* is a pronoun in *he's thirty years old* and in *he's thirty*, but it is best considered a noun in *he's in his thirties*. *Fourth* is a pronoun in *the fourth day* and in *there were five meetings, but she came only to the fourth;* but it is best classified as a noun in its use as the denominator in fractions, as in *one fourth* and *three fourths*.

When problems of part-of-speech classification touch the category of the adverbs, meanings furnish important criterions more often than at any other point. Adjectives and adverbs cannot be distinguished on the basis of differences in the kinds of prepositive modifiers they characteristically accept. In general, no word should be granted both adjective and adverb status unless either (1) sharply distinct meanings occur in the functions characteristic of the two parts of speech or (2) prepositional and nonprepositional uses seem to require this double status. *Right* is best regarded as an adjective in *he gave the right answer* but (for contemporary English) an adverb with quite different meaning in *he went right ahead*. *Round* is an adjective in *a round table* but an adverb with different meaning in *he went round the corner*, where the more distinctive form *around* is now preferred. *Still* is an adjective in *a still night* and in *the still figure*, but an adverb in *he still remembers a little Latin*, in *still, he remembers a little Latin*, and in *his Greek is still worse*. *Right, round,* and *still* are verbs and nouns also. *Pretty, real,* and *very* are to be classified as adverbs with meanings of degree in *pretty late,* informal *real new,* and *very high,* but as adjectives in *pretty girls, real mahogany,* and *the very man, the very same, my very own,* and *the very best* (where the old meanings of attractiveness, truth, and exactness have not faded away). The double part-of-speech status indicated for such words as these is made necessary by the correspondence between distinctions in syntactic functions and distinctions in meaning. Prepositional use seems to make double status necessary for a few words. Thus the *due* of *all due consideration* and of *our success was largely due to your help* is best regarded as an adjective, but the *due* of *twenty dollars is still due him* is most conveniently regarded as an adverb used prepositionally.

Uncharacteristic functioning.—A word that in a particular meaning or cluster of meanings clearly has unquestioned membership in one part-of-speech category should not be granted membership in another merely on the basis of performance of functions characteristic of this second part of speech. Thus the italicized words which follow are best classified as nouns in all the uses illustrated.

an *hour* went by	Eastern *universities*
hours later	*university* students
a *graduate* of Swarthmore	he teaches *English*
a *graduate* student	an *English* teacher from Ohio
a bright *future* is ahead	these songs are my *favorites*
his *future* employer	my *favorite* songs
Marietta is her *home*	on my *right*
she isn't a *home* girl	we turned *right*
she went *home* early	raise your *right* hand
the frozen *north*	the *back* of the chair
the *north* wind	the *back* road
he went back *north*	in *back* of the house
silk is too expensive	is made of *iron*
a *silk* dress	an *iron* will
the dress is *silk*	

The italicized words which follow are best classified as adjectives in all the uses illustrated.

a *fast* car	*fast* colors
he drives *fast*	he held *fast*

bodily injury	*hard* work
toss him out *bodily*	he works *hard*
the *right* answer	a *weekly* paper
he answered *right*	it's delivered *weekly*
a *defensive* psychology	an *early* hour
on the *defensive*	we left *early*
loud voices	a *rough* game
they talk too *loud*	they play *rough*
a *forward* look	an *extra* shirt
we went *forward*	*extra* large
an *easy* job	*poor* people
easy does it	the *poor* suffer most
take it *easy*	he died *poor*
deep feelings of guilt	a *long* time
deep in his heart	hasn't been here *long*
hasn't dug *deep* enough	not for *long*

Those which follow are best classified as adverbs in all the situations illustrated.

went *off* sadly	offices *up* on the third floor
an *off* day	the *up* button
she sings *well*	we *only* borrowed it
would be *well* to consult	he's *only* a child
let *well* enough alone	he's an *only* child
she isn't *well*	

Yes is best classified as an absolute in all the uses illustrated.

Yes, I saw him.
George says *yes*.
He's no *yes* man.

The words that follow are best classified as pronouns in all the situations illustrated.

she never helps	*the* city
that *she* devil	so much *the* better
neither of us went	his *first* wife
neither loved nor hated	let's go home *first*
not *much* time	we need *more* money
doesn't work *much*	money is *more* important
brought *no* ice	*all* children
feels *no* better	*all* right

For assignment of more than a single part-of-speech classification, acceptance of characteristic modifiers, clear distinctions in meaning, and inflection are all more significant than simple performance of syntactic functions of varied types. Thus though in *my favorite songs* the word *favorite* is performing a function more characteristically performed by adjectives, the fact that it will not accept adverbs as prepositive modifiers as adjectives do, together with the fact that in such sentences as *these songs are favorites among our students* it is not possible to replace *favorites*, which is clearly a plural noun, by *favorite*, should make it seem unwise to classify *favorite* as an adjective. *Favorite* is a noun used, in *my favorite songs*, like an adjective; but it is not an adjective. The *poor* of *the poor suffer most* is not as clear a case. Here *poor* does take one modifier characteristically taken by nouns rather than by adjectives: the determiner *the*. But *poor* rejects inflection for plural number, is not usable nounally in the singular (*a poor suffers in times like these* is not possible), and generally accepts only *the* and occasionally a possessive (as in *Mexico does not forget her poor*) among the modifiers characteristically accepted by nouns; consequently it seems best to regard *poor* not as a noun but as an adjective used, in *the poor suffer most*, like a noun—as a head in a nounal headed unit.

To the extent that meanings permit, words which hold membership in two or more part-of-speech categories must always be assigned, in particular uses, to the category most characteristically usable in the construction. Thus in *a cold day* the word *cold* is to be classified as an adjective whereas in *the bitter cold penetrates to the bone* the same word is to be classified as a noun. In *a French teacher* meaning cannot be ignored. If the unit is equivalent to *a teacher of French*, the word *French* is a noun. If the unit is equivalent to *a teacher from France* or something of the kind, the word *French* is an adjective.

Situation and common sense often play a major part in our assignment of part-of-speech classifications. Thus the sign *open Sundays* on a store will not often be misunderstood. It is clear that *open* is an adjective used as complement, not a verb used as predicator in an imperative clause. It is clear too that what is open is the store, not the Sundays—though under other circumstances *open* might well modify *Sundays*. In one situation *fire!* will be understood as a verb meaning "shoot," in another as a noun mean-

ing "conflagration." The reader or hearer solves jigsaw puzzles
such as these rapidly and accurately, even though the pieces which
he must put together have considerable flexibility. The words are
known, both with respect to their central meanings and with respect to the ways they can combine with other words; and the
patternings of clauses and clause equivalents are known.

Classification of inflected forms.—It is one of the complexities of syntax that inflected forms do not always behave syntactically as the corresponding basic forms behave. In general, it is
desirable to give inflected forms the same part-of-speech classifications their basic forms are given. But exceptions must be made at
some points.

A few comparatives and superlatives seem to require different
classifications from their basic forms. *Inner, outer,* and *upper* seem
to require classification as adjectives (since they are freely usable as
prepositive modifiers within nounal headed units), though *in, out,*
and *up* are best classified as adverbs. *Better, best, worse,* and *worst*
are conveniently classified as adjectives when they function as
inflected forms for *well* and *badly* as well as when they function
thus for *good* and *bad.*

> The cookies were *good,* but the cake was *better.*
> Dora cooks *well,* but Mary cooks *better.*

A great many words which in some uses clearly are gerundial or
participial forms of verbs require classification as nouns or adjectives in others and are doubtful in still others. When such words
are employed as head words in nounal headed units, it is generally
most convenient to classify them as nouns.

> Loud *singing* makes George nervous.
> Miles was involved in the *taking* of bribes.
> Not much *building* is going on now.
> Window *washing* is exciting this far up.

When they are employed as head words in adjectival headed units,
it is most convenient to classify them as adjectives.

> Our Spanish-*speaking* students expect long holidays.
> It's a God-*forsaken* desert.

Verbal force is strong in the examples given: this can be recognized
by describing the italicized words as gerundial nouns and adjec-

tives and participial adjectives. In units such as *the wounded* and *the dying* the heads are best described as adjectives, like *poor* in *the poor*, not nouns.

Where words of gerundial or participial type are unmodified but clauses would not be used, classification as nouns or adjectives seems best. Thus gerundial and participial forms used as prepositive modifiers in nounal units are best described as gerundial and participial nouns and adjectives.

her *chewing* gum	a *born* salesman
good *farming* country	his *given* name
rising prices	a *hated* professor
winding roads	a *satisfied* customer
the *winning* team	*spoken* English

Here *chewing* and *farming* are gerundial nouns (*gum for chewing*, not *gum which chews*) and the other italicized words are adjectives. As postpositive modifiers within nounal units the same forms are best described as verb forms, predicators in one-word clauses.

the students *answering*	the name *given*
the team *winning*	the English *spoken*

When such forms are used as complements of copulatives, they are best classified as gerundial and participial nouns and adjectives.

Patton's only recreation is *bowling*.
The principal occupation of the area is still *farming*.
Peanuts are *fattening*.
Joe is always *irritating*.
A spoon is *missing*.
The procedure is *complicated*.
I'm *depressed* today.
The doors have been *closed* for an hour.
The door won't stay *put*.
We finally got *rid* of our pets.

Here *bowling* and *farming* are gerundial nouns used as *chess* and *agriculture* might be used, and the other italicized words are adjectives. When modification by *very* and *too* (meaning "excessively") is possible, classification as adjectives is doubly warranted: *very* and *too* simply do not modify true verbs. But *very* and *too* will not modify the *missing* of *a spoon is missing* or the *closed* of *the doors have been closed for an hour*. In careful and formal styles participial adjectives, much more than gerundial, are quite slow to accept *very* even where it seems semantically compatible. Phrasings such as *greatly amused, thoroughly bored, deeply concerned, extremely disgusted, quite encouraged, decidedly interested, genuinely pleased*, and *quite surprised* result from avoidance of *very*. Even the most informal American English would probably reject *very* as a modifier of the participial adjective *hated* in *a hated professor*.

Often gerundial and participial nouns and adjectives are quite unlike the corresponding verbs in the matter of normal completers. Thus the verb *disturb* requires a nounal complement: *it disturbs everyone*. But the participial adjective *disturbing* gets along quite well without a completer, as in *it's disturbing*, or takes a prepositional one, as in *it's disturbing to everyone*. In *it's disturbing everyone* the predicator is *is disturbing* and the complement is *everyone: is disturbing* is like *disturbs* in function. Similarly in *the doors have been closed by the watchman* the predicator is *have been closed* and the complement is *by the watchman:* the sentence is a reversal of *the watchman has closed the doors*.

Meanings are untrustworthy guides, but they are helpful nonetheless. When *building* (as in *a tall building*) no longer names an action, but rather names the product of an action, the word is no longer a verb form. When *irritating* comes to be a qualitative, descriptive word—as in *her manner is always irritating*—then *irritating* is no longer a verb form. Inflection is occasionally decisive. When *coming* forms an *s* plural, as in *I can't keep up with her comings and goings*, the word requires noun classification.

Nonce uses.—Nonce uses cut across normal part-of-speech lines. In *he uses too many "if's"* the word *if* is a nonce noun and has taken on both a determiner modifier (*too many*) and a plural ending. In *don't "if" me* the same word has become a nonce verb and has taken on an auxiliary modifier (*do*). Italics, underlining, or quotation marks commonly mark nonce uses in the written language.

CHAPTER III

MAIN-CLAUSE PATTERNS AND THEIR SUBORDINATE-CLAUSE DERIVATIVES

A variety of well-defined clause patterns is available in contemporary English. These fall into two general categories: main-clause patterns and subordinate-clause patterns. Main clauses have characteristics that make them freely usable as sentences. Subordinate clauses, on the other hand, are normally incorporated within other clauses, and many of them have characteristics which ordinarily make them seem unacceptable as sentences, at least in careful and formal styles. Four main-clause patterns can be distinguished in contemporary English: the patterns of the main declarative, the main interrogative, the main imperative, and the main assertive. Four subordinate-clause patterns clearly derive from these main-clause patterns.

Main declaratives.—As has been said, the main declarative is the ordinary main-clause pattern for statements of fact and opinion. The order subject-predicator-complement is employed in the nucleus, and there are no special clause markers such as are found in clauses of other types. The predicator is a common-mode or hypothetical-subjunctive verb form.

> You'*ll like* San Francisco.
> You'*d like* San Francisco.

Main declaratives sometimes have question force. Intonation and/or manner, and context, can make this intention clear in the spoken language.

> You're coming along?
> Segall was chairman?
> Perhaps you think I'm unsympathetic?
> I don't remember your name.

All of these sentences remain declaratives in syntax. In some situations main declaratives have the force of orders.

You're coming along.

The situation is much the same when clause equivalents such as *yes?* and *well, George?* have question force without the syntactic marks of interrogatives, and when clause equivalents such as *sh!* and, in an elevator, *third* have imperative force without the syntactic marks of imperatives.

Sometimes main declaratives are incorporated within other clauses, as are the italicized main declaratives in the sentences which follow.

They really were going, with a flutter of *"We did have the best time!"*
I thought to myself, *this is it!*
The fact is, *I never liked him.*
They know only one thing about him: *he's honest.*
I don't need any help, *thank you.*
I don't care what you say, it's too expensive.
If the situation of the past two years is typical—*and I believe it is*—we must resign ourselves to decreasing sales for some time.
It's time to start, *I suppose.*
I hated to say much, *he was so nice.*
The state of jitters seemed almost normal, *it had prevailed so long.*

In the last three sentences the construction is upside down: such forms as *I suppose it's time to start* show the more ordinary pattern. In *it's time to start, I suppose* the adjunct *I suppose* lacks a complement because its complement has become the main nucleus for the whole sentence. Incorporation of main clauses subordinately within other clauses is of course exceptional. In general, it is also less smooth than incorporation of subordinate clauses, and so requires punctuation more commonly in the written language.

The main declarative can conveniently be regarded as the basic clause pattern. Other clause patterns can be regarded as transforms of the main-declarative pattern and can be described in terms of matters of structure which distinguish them from it.

Subordinate declaratives.—Subordinate-declarative clauses are in form little more than smoothly incorporated main declara-

tives. When subordinate declaratives are marked, it is normally
by the addition of an unstressed pronoun *that* which functions as
a semantically empty adjunct and clause marker.

I knew that I was right.

This *that* is required in some situations, optional in most, and
unusable in a few. Informal styles employ it less than careful and
formal ones. When *that* is not used, subordinate declaratives are
distinguished by their declarative form and their tight incorporation within larger clauses.

Subordinate-declarative clauses have some use in the nounal
functions of subjects, complements of transitive verbs, appositives in nounal apposed units, and objects of prepositions.

> *That the committee was fortunate in its choice* is amply demon-
> strated by the twenty-nine years of service Miss Holmes
> rendered.
> They say *they'll send us copies.*
> The fact *that he grew up in Mexico* helps.
> She makes it clear *that she isn't pleased.*
> We can't help it *that things went badly.*
> He kept on in spite of the fact *that he was very unhappy.*
> Life was hard the year after *her husband died.*
> Few dogs prowl among the rubble, for *refugees catch and eat
> the dogs.*
> It looks like *it's going to rain.*
> I can't say but *that I agree with you.*
> The budget is unrealistic in *that it disregards increased costs.*

There are sharp limits on the use of declaratives in all the nounal
functions. They are often quite unsatisfactory as subjects: such
a question as *is that he's coming true?* is especially unacceptable,
and the reduction of the declarative to delayed-appositive status
in *is it true that he's coming?* is a welcome way out. Only a few
prepositions accept declarative clauses as objects. *After, before, for,
since, till* and *until, in* when it expresses respect, informal *but*
within negated larger clauses, and informal *like* accept them; but
only *in* and *but* among these will tolerate a marker *that* in a declarative which serves as object for them. Some phrasal prepositions
such as *because of, for fear of,* and *in case of* accept declarative
objects but are shortened when they do so.

> We went because *we wanted to.*
> Here's the paper, in case *you're interested.*

Subordinate declaratives are often used where nouns would not be usable.

> We were hoping *we'd finish in time.*
> He convinced us *that we were unwise.*
> What has he done *that he should deserve this?*
> There is some indication *that others are involved.*
> We're glad *you came.*
> He bought another car so *his wife would have one.*
> We arrived early, so *that we got good seats.*
> The situation is such *that agreement is unlikely.*
> He's such a good speaker *he doesn't need subject matter.*

Prepositions can be said to have fallen out in many such uses of declaratives, and the declaratives alone function as complements, adjuncts, and contained modifiers where prepositional units would be syntactically more ordinary.

> We were hoping *for* a quick job.
> He convinced us *of* our mistake.
> What has he done *to* deserve this?
> There is some indication *of* the involvement of others.

When a declarative modifies a *so* or *such*, immediately preceding or earlier in the larger clauses, it is harder to think in terms of lost prepositions.

In informal styles *what* sometimes replaces *that* as clause marker in declaratives used as objects of the preposition *but* within larger negated clauses.

> I'm not sure but what I agree with you.
> I never talked to him but what he told me his troubles.

Exceptional reduction is illustrated in the following declaratives.

> That's the house Mary said *was for sale.*
> I hope *not.*

In somewhat archaic styles subordinate declaratives, generally with the adjunct *oh* preceding the marker *that,* are occasionally given sentence status as expressions of desires.

> Oh that she knew the truth!

Main interrogatives.—The main interrogative is the ordinary main-clause pattern for asking for facts and opinions. Like the declaratives, it normally has a common-mode or hypothetical-subjunctive predicator.

> *Do* you *like* Jamaica?
> *Would* you *like* Jamaica?

Main interrogatives are marked by the use of predicators or parts of predicators in front of subjects.

> *Was* Jack at the University?
> *Did* he take you around the island?

Or by the use of marker pronouns or adverbs as subjects or parts of subjects.

> Well, Bill, *who*'s coming?
> *Which house* was built first?
> *How old a child* drew that?

Or by the use of both predicators or parts of predicators in front of subjects, and marker pronouns or adverbs (or units including them) in front of the verb-form markers.

> *When are* the Richardsons coming back?
> *Exactly how much would* we be paid?
> *Why in the world did* you skip Haiti?

Main interrogatives which do not employ marker pronouns or adverbs can be called yes-or-no interrogatives. The pronouns and adverbs which can mark main interrogatives are very few in number: *who, which, what; when, where, why, how.* The verb forms which can mark main interrogatives form a limited group also: *are, am, is, were, was; can, could, may, might, must, ought, shall, should, will, would;* in their auxiliary uses *have, has, had, do, does, did;* infrequently *need.* In combination with *better, had* functions as a main-interrogative marker even when it is not an auxiliary: for example, in *hadn't we better telephone?* Exceptional main interrogatives such as *how goes it?* occasionally occur. In *who's a linguist?* the subject is *who;* the interrogative is a transform of *A is a linguist.* In *what's a linguist?* the subject is *a linguist;* the interrogative is a transform of *a linguist is X.* In such an interrogative as *who's the chairman this year?* two analyses are possible.

The markers used in interrogatives are not superimposed on clause structures to which they add nothing but the marks of the interrogative. They perform major syntactic functions, or participate in the performance of major syntactic functions, which are also performed in the corresponding main declaratives.

> You *would* like Jamaica.
> Jack *was* at the University.
> He *took* you around the island.
> Well, Bill, *she*'s coming.
> *A nine-year-old child* drew that.
> The Richardsons *are* coming back *tomorrow*.
> You *skipped* Haiti *for some ridiculous reason*.

The marker pronouns and adverbs are not themselves usable in declaratives ordinarily, but the marker verb forms are, though expanded verb forms with *do*, such as *did take*, have somewhat special emotional force in declaratives not negated by *not*.

When a marker pronoun or adverb is used as the object of a preposition, or as part of the object of a preposition, in informal styles the preposition generally takes the position it would have in the corresponding declarative.

> What are you looking for?
> Which office are they putting Olga in?
> Where are you from?
> What has Wilson been up to?
> What does the new library look like?
> Who is the package for?

In formal styles the preposition sometimes moves forward with its object. Sometimes, however, it simply cannot go forward.

Sometimes the structure of the main interrogative is mixed with that of another clause type. *Why be so particular?* is thus a main interrogative with verbid-clause characteristics: the predicator is an infinitive, and there is no expressed subject. *He said what?* is a declarative with something of the syntax of an interrogative: *what* has interrogative-marker force but is not in the interrogative-marker position.

Though they operate subtly and do not themselves establish the interrogative pattern, the presence of interrogative reinforcers in many interrogatives deserves notice. *Any* and *ever* are perhaps the most-used interrogative reinforcers.

> Have there been *any* hurricanes since you came?
> Do flowers *ever* stop blooming in Puerto Rico?

The corresponding unnegated declaratives would certainly not employ *any* and *ever*. Nor would the corresponding unnegated declaratives employ the words and longer units italicized in the following sentences.

> Why did you go into teaching *at all?*
> Will George be away *long?*
> Does Jack have *much* time for it?

Highly reduced main interrogatives have constant use in informal styles.

> Anyone at home?
> Why?

Even in careful and formal styles parts of main interrogatives are often implied rather than stated.

> What virtues did the nineteenth-century American extol, what vices condemn, what heroes exalt, what villains execrate?

When *what* is used as the reply to a call or to ask for a repetition of something not understood, it is best described as an isolate. In *why so much noise?* the unit *so much noise* is best described similarly, and *why* is best called an adjunct. *What about George?* is best described as a main interrogative composed of two isolates, the second of them a prepositional unit.

Main interrogatives are sometimes incorporated subordinately within other clauses, as are the italicized main interrogatives in the sentences which follow.

> The first question is, *how much can we spend?*
> St. Thomas, *may I add*, is fully as interesting.
> Rebellion was inevitable, for *what other course was open?*

St. Thomas, may I add, is fully as interesting has upside-down construction, and what in more ordinary patterning would be the complement of *add* (in *may I add that St. Thomas is fully as inter-*

esting?) has become the main nucleus to which *may I add* attaches as an adjunct.

The main-interrogative pattern has some use where no real question is intended.

Was it hot!
What was my surprise to learn that Andrews had left.
Will you please send the information requested.
Will you be quiet!

The first two sentences have extremitive force (*it was extremely hot!*), and the last two have the force of requests; but the sentences are main interrogatives in syntax nevertheless.

Subordinate interrogatives.—Subordinate-interrogative clauses employ markers of the same types employed by main-interrogative clauses. Some subordinate interrogatives have clear question force, others do not. The category is a category of syntactic form as it is here described.

Marker verb forms preceding subjects are employed very much less than in main interrogatives. They occur chiefly in subordinate interrogatives used as adjuncts of condition, without other markers. Usually the marker verb form is *had, should,* or *were.*

Were prices to rise further, the government would have to take action.

Subordinate interrogatives marked by verb forms sometimes perform nounal functions in doubtfully standard informal use.

Then he said he didn't know any other girls in New York *and would I play around with him this week.*

The marker pronouns and adverbs used in main interrogatives are all employed in subordinate interrogatives, without other markers. Subordinate interrogatives marked by *who, which, what, when, where, why,* and *how* are all usable in nounal functions.

What you need is a change of scene.
What clothes she has are unsuitable.
We didn't know *who he was.*
That's *how I learned German.*
I remember *when the family was very poor.*
I was thinking about *what you said.*
It isn't clear *where he got it.*

Like subordinate declaratives, subordinate interrogatives marked by these words are also used in nonnounal functions where prepositions can be considered to have dropped out.

> I don't care *how you finish it.*
> Look *what I did!*
> I have no idea *why he said that.*
> Make up your mind *what you want.*
> I'm not sure *when they'll get here.*
> *What is more important,* he knows his subject.

Subordinate interrogatives marked by *when* and *where* are used as adjuncts quite freely.

> The city was much smaller *when we lived there.*
> *Where I come from,* people are polite.

Adjunct-like modification can be extended to nounal heads.

> I'll never forget his surprise *when we told him.*

Subordinate interrogatives marked by *who* and *which,* and to a lesser extent by *when, where,* and *why,* have considerable use as contained modifiers following heads which are also referred to by the marking pronouns and adverbs.

> People *who talk like that* are dangerous.
> The man *whose car was wrecked* is our neighbor.
> He ended with the argument *with which he had begun.*
> The day *when we arrived* was a holiday.
> Now *when we want to start,* Larry isn't here.
> The reason *why he can't come* is clear.
> There's no industry in the area *where he grew up.*

They function also as loose adjuncts following words or longer units to which the markers refer.

> We went with Larry, *who knew everyone.*
> Then we went on to Cleveland, *where my sister lives.*

Chiefly in informal styles, subordinate interrogatives marked by *which* are used as loose adjuncts following nucleuses to which *which* refers.

> Jerry argued that emotional loyalties are dangerous, *with which contention Henry disagreed.*
> He answers when he wants to, *which isn't often.*

Many clauses which are best classified as subordinate interrogatives have as clause markers pronouns that are rarely or never used in this way in main interrogatives. Clauses marked by the compounds *whoever*, *whichever*, and *whatever* occur in nounal functions.

> *Whoever said that* was very shrewd.
> He'll do well in *whatever course he takes.*

They also occur as adjuncts.

> *Whatever he said,* we need his help.

The unstressed pronoun *that* marks many subordinate-interrogative clauses used as contained modifiers of preceding heads to which *that* refers.

> I didn't see anything *that I liked.*
> I've never seen children *that made less trouble.*
> The day *that we arrived in Mexico City* was a holiday.
> I see Julia everywhere *that I go.*
> Harriman was one of the original New Dealers *that was able to survive the Truman Administration.*
> This is one of the best books *that have come out lately.*

Subordinate interrogatives marked by *that* are sometimes not distinguishable in terms of their own internal form from subordinate declaratives.

> Now *that you're here* we'll open the box.
> We're glad *that you're here.*

The *that* of interrogatives is syntactically in competition with *who* and *which;* the *that* of declaratives is not. The *that* of *now that you're here* is used in the clause it begins as *at which* is used in essentially equivalent *at this time at which you're here:* it is an adjunct of time and refers to the *now* which precedes it. The *that* of *we're glad that you're here* is the superimposed *that* of declaratives: *who* and *which* are not used in this way. Interrogatives marked by *that* are sometimes used as adjuncts (characteristically tight ones), with *that* referring to whole preceding nucleuses, often with other adjuncts.

> He didn't even apologize *that I know of.*

Sometimes they are used as delayed appositives within apposed-unit subjects, and *that* refers to what precedes them immediately.

> It's your own dead *that matter.*
> It was in Miami *that he met his future wife.*
> It was then *that I became convinced.*

Many clauses that we can most conveniently classify as subordinate interrogatives have as clause markers adverbs which are not used similarly in main interrogatives. *Whether* marks subordinate interrogatives used where nouns are usable and also where prepositions can be considered to have dropped out.

> No one knows *whether he's coming.*
> There's some question *whether he likes it.*
> *Whether it's expensive or not,* Mary wants it.

Subordinate interrogatives begun by *whether* have much of the force of main-clause yes-or-no interrogatives marked only by verb forms.

> Is he coming?
> Does he like it?
> Is it expensive or not?

Or not is felt as necessary after *whether* in subordinate interrogatives used as adjuncts within larger clauses. *Whenever, wherever,* and *however* mark interrogatives characteristically used as adjuncts.

> He tells that story *whenever anyone will listen.*
> *Wherever he grew up,* his English is colorless enough now.
> You won't be able to please him *however hard you try.*

Such compounds as *whereby* and *whereupon* mark subordinate interrogatives used as contained modifiers and loose adjuncts, chiefly in somewhat formal styles. *Where* is equivalent to *which* in these compounds and refers to something (often a whole nucleus) preceding it.

> He has an arrangement *whereby a car is available.*
> In New Mexico the Mossers tried to escape, *whereupon Cook threatened to kill them.*

Although and *though, as, if, once, only, unless,* and *while* mark subordinate interrogatives characteristically used as adjuncts within larger clauses.

Though he wouldn't admit it, he was very tired.
The story seemed plausible *as he told it.*
We'll come *if we can.*
You'll like the place *once you get settled.*
The food is good, *only they serve too much pie.*
The hospital was very full *while I was there.*
George won't contribute *unless he has to.*

Besides serving as markers, these words function in their clauses as adjuncts semantically much like nonmarker *nevertheless, thus, perhaps, soon,* and *then.* Clauses marked by *as* have a considerable range of use even apart from their use in comparisons.

Chicken pie *as Harriet makes it* is a work of art.
That's *as it should be.*

If competes with *whether* as a marker for subordinate interrogatives in nounal constructions, especially in informal styles.

We asked the watchman *if we might look around.*

Grammatical complexity of subordinate interrogative clauses.—The prepositional adverbs *but* and *like* sometimes enter into subordinate clauses (then best regarded as interrogative in type) instead of preceding them and functioning as prepositions with declarative-clause objects.

There is not a university in the area *but follows public opinion in fear and trembling.*
He looks *like he did twenty years ago.*

Here *but* is a subject, equivalent to *it* plus negator *not* in the corresponding statement *it does not follow public opinion in fear and trembling,* and *like* is a complement, equivalent to *like that* in the corresponding statement *he looked like that twenty years ago.* *But* is used in this way chiefly in somewhat formal styles, and *like* chiefly in informal styles.

The use of *than* and *as* in clauses of comparison is syntactically remarkable. *Than* functions as a marker in subordinate interrogative clauses used as contained modifiers of comparatives (including *rather*), *other* and *else,* and sometimes *differently* or even *different.* Though best considered an adverb in part-of-speech classification, this *than* (like *but* and *like*) performs major and contained syntactic functions of a remarkable variety of types.

The cost was greater *than seemed reasonable.*
More people drink milk *than used to.*
We got more tomatoes *than we had bargained for.*
I'd rather take the course in English *than in Spanish.*
Rice is prepared differently *than it is in the States.*
You may often say something with a different intonation *than we indicate here.*

Besides functioning as a marker in clauses used much like those marked by *although* and *if*, the adverb *as* also marks subordinate interrogatives used as contained modifiers of another *as* (which cannot precede marker *as* immediately) or (somewhat formally) of a *so* in a negated containing clause or of the pronouns *such* or *same*. Like *than*, this *as* performs a remarkable variety of functions in addition to marking the clauses it begins.

Not nearly as many students take Latin here now *as did twenty years ago.*
He isn't as energetic *as he once was.*
We have as many points of view *as we have members.*
We went to Saba as well *as to Nevis.*
Houses such *as yours* aren't built now.
Harriet has alienated such friends *as she has.*
My feelings are the same *as yours.*

Occasionally the first *as* is omitted.

He's strong *as an ox.*
Late *as we were*, Mary was later.

In subordinate interrogatives as in main interrogatives, when a marker pronoun or adverb is used as object of a preposition in its clause it is likely to be separated from its preposition, coming at the front of the clause it marks while the preposition remains where the whole prepositional unit would be in a declarative.

I wonder *who he's looking for.*
Machinery is *what he knows most about.*
No one knows *what the box is for.*
This is the goal *that we are striving toward.*
There are some things *which people cannot do without.*
I wonder *where she's from.*
We got more tomatoes *than we had bargained for.*
That's about as much teasing *as Jack will put up with.*

Clause-marker adverbs such as *where, than,* and *as* cannot follow prepositions for which they serve as objects, and neither can the clause-marker pronoun *that*. Clause-marking *what* is apparently limited in much the same way in subordinate interrogative clauses. *Who* and *which* often follow prepositions, at least in somewhat formal styles—though hardly in subordinate interrogatives used in nounal constructions.

Is there a candidate *in whom we can have confidence?*
Dr. Jordan has three sons, *two of whom are also physicians.*
This is the goal *toward which we are striving.*
There is a residence requirement *the effect of which is not quite clear.*
People are impressed by the assurance *with which he speaks.*

Subordinate interrogatives function as impinging clauses sometimes.

He's never *what you'd call deceived her.*
She's attractive, industrious, and *what passes for intelligent.*
They lost little, *if any*, of their investment.

So do clauses of mixed construction in which declarative word order is combined with the use of subordinate-interrogative clause markers.

We'll get there *heaven knows when.*

Sometimes subordinate interrogatives are parts of predicators and predicator-and-complement sequences in upside-down construction.

He as much *as said so.*
He has more *than satisfied us.*

Sometimes they are given sentence status.

Labor felt that prices and profits had risen more rapidly than wages. Which was to a considerable extent true.
Franklin finally married, in fact. While his mother was visiting an ailing relative.
If only she knew her own mind!
If it isn't our old friend Hubert!
As if we didn't know what she was up to!

Noteworthy reduction of varied types occurs in subordinate-interrogative clauses. Where it does not function as subject of the interrogative it marks, *that* is often implied rather than stated.

> I didn't see anything *I liked.*
> He ended with the argument *he had begun with.*
> The leaders are disturbed at the situation *the party is in.*
> The reason *he can't come* is clear.
> I see that girl everywhere *I go.*
> That's the house *Mary said was for sale.*

In the last sentence if a clause-marker *that* is added, as in *that's the house that Mary said was for sale,* it functions as the subject not of the subordinate interrogative it marks but of the subordinate declarative which is contained, as complement, within the interrogative—as *it* functions in *Mary said it was for sale. That* can be said to be the only dispensable clause-marker of interrogative clauses. A common pattern of reduction drops the subject and the predicator (*be*) but keeps the marker.

> I didn't know *where to look for you.*
> There is no set point *at which to begin.*
> He has a new car *in which to see Puerto Rico.*

Such main interrogatives as *where was I to look for you?* show the construction. Reduction is especially notable in clauses of comparison, where a great deal is commonly left to be inferred from what has just preceded.

> It's pleasanter here in the winter *than in the summer.*
> He spoke better *than usual.*
> More *than fifty* students enrolled.
> He's doing more *than being polite.*
> It's easier said *than done.*
> A house should be convenient as well *as beautiful.*
> I read as far *as the fifth chapter.*

Oddly different reductions lie behind the following sentences.

> Joan is more impatient *than her sister.*
> Joan is more impatient *than that.*
> Joan is more impatient *than bad-tempered.*

There is often a kind of telescoping of subordinate interrogatives.

> Haynes acts *as if he were a millionaire.*
> The town looks *as though it's very old.*
> She welcomed us with excessive cordiality *as though to compensate for her earlier neglect.*
> *Hard as we worked,* we didn't finish.

Syntactically complete equivalents here would seem unnatural.

Haynes acts *as he would act if he were a millionaire.*
The town looks *as a town looks if it's very old.*
She welcomed us with excessive cordiality *as she would welcome us if she did so to compensate for her earlier neglect.*
Though we worked as hard as we did, we didn't finish.

In *hard though we worked, we didn't finish* a line has been crossed, and it seems necessary to say that *hard* is an adjunct in the clause marked by *though,* preceding the clause marker quite exceptionally. Reduction of still other types is common.

Tell me *when!*
I'll tell you *what.*
Whatever the reason, he refused.
Their religious and political differences, *though great,* never produced a clash.
He seemed excessively timid, *if not unfriendly.*
They lost little, *if any,* of their investment.
In the nineteenth century, *as in the seventeenth,* great social changes took place.
As taught here, economics is very stimulating.

Isolates occur in subordinate interrogative clauses. The italicized interrogative in the following sentence is best regarded as composed of two isolates.

Young people can't be expected to read, *what with automobiles, sports, and television.*

The fact that the following main subject may seem momentarily to suggest a wrong subject for the subjectless interrogative lays the reduction in the following sentence open to criticism.

Although seriously damaged by the earthquake of 1917, restoration work has almost brought the cathedral back to its original beauty.

Sometimes the structure of the subordinate interrogative is mixed with that of another clause type. In the following interrogatives there is assimilation of the form (1) of the main interrogative, (2) of the main imperative, and (3) of the verbid.

1. We'd pick San Francisco, *as who wouldn't?*
2. I'll tell you *what let's do.*

The cost is $2.65, *which please remit to Ralph D. Fall, Ithaca, New York.*

It is certain that the President's action will be severely criticized, *as witness the account in this morning's paper.*

3. The American did not so much disparage other peoples and countries *as ignore them.*

Rather *than live near Ruth,* Andy went to sea.

Many of those who wrote on language were retired clergymen who, *though possessing some skill in the classics,* had no conception of the history of English.

Occasionally a subordinate interrogative has word order that is characteristic of assertives.

The road into Gyangtse was lined on each side with small stones, *as was the entire route.*

In careless nonstandard use, what begins as a subordinate interrogative modifying a preceding nounal head to which the clause marker in the interrogative seems to refer, sometimes shifts to subordinate-declarative construction as it proceeds.

Now she has a husband *that she never has any idea where he is.*

Present-subjunctive verb forms sometimes occur as predicators in subordinate interrogatives used, in formal styles, as adjuncts of condition or circumstance. Here they have none of the force they have in imperatives.

A liberal education is of value to anyone, whether he *be* a teacher, a businessman, or a farmer.

In interrogatives in which *lest* serves as marker, present-subjunctive verb forms do have something of the force they have in imperatives.

The visitors sat in silence lest they *be* guilty of offense.

Main imperatives.—Main imperatives give main-clause expression to requests and desires. The predicators are always present-subjunctive verb forms, usable without expressed subjects much more freely than the common-mode verb forms with which they are often identical except in syntax. Since present-subjunctive verb forms are never employed as the predicators of main clauses of other kinds, they serve as clause markers as well as predicators in main imperatives and are indeed the only clause markers used in them. Main imperatives most often express direct requests of one kind or another, varying in force from supplication through invitation, hope, and warning to command and challenge.

Just give me one more chance.
Come in.
Have a good time.
Be careful.
Pick those toys up this instant!
Just say one more word if you're looking for trouble.
Try to tell them that human nature has changed, and they respond that it cannot possibly change.

When a direct request does not have an expressed subject, its implied subject is of course *you,* singular or plural. Sometimes main imperatives used to express direct requests do have expressed subjects.

You be careful coming down that mountain.
You boys drive carefully.

You boys drive carefully can be either a declarative or an imperative: context, manner, and/or intonation provide the key.

Main imperatives with third-person subjects are used less frequently.

Heaven help us!
The devil take the hindmost.
Somebody do something!

Somebody do something! has the force of a direct request. In such imperatives as *bless your heart!* and *confound it!* the third-person subject *God* is implied rather than stated.

Main imperatives without expressed predicators occur.

Down, Rover!
Good luck to you!
Shame on you!

Main imperatives are sometimes incorporated within other clauses.

Please don't say that.
He hardly seems middle-aged, *let alone old.*
She gave him a *come-hither* look.

It's a *dog-eat-dog* situation.
Say what you will, we got the job done.
We never get away *except in the summers.*
All *except one* were air-conditioned.
It's the best restaurant here, *bar none.*
You can depend on Mary, *bless her heart.*
Win or lose, he'll do it his way.
We were ready in time, *thanks to you.*
There is something irresistible about a method of classification
  that starts with two poles, exemplified, *say,* by Chinese and
  Latin.
Explain ourselves as we might, we couldn't placate him.

In the last of these sentences the implied subject of *explain* is
first-person *we.* Modifying units beginning with *except* and *bar*
are often regarded as prepositional, not clausal.

Some main imperatives have the basic subject-predicator-complement word order altered as it is in assertive clauses to be
described at a later point.

Far be it from me to tell Logan the truth.
May the best man win.
Suffice it to say that the point was never pressed.
Be that as it may, the gesture was a wise one.
Come Easter, Barbara will buy another outfit.

Sometimes main imperatives have the force of questions: for
example, *suppose John calls?* The imperatives of direct request
tend to be avoided where delicacy is thought desirable—as when
would you mind closing the window? replaces *please close the window.*
Main imperatives of other kinds are confined chiefly to formal, or
even archaic, styles and to fixed phrasings.

Subordinate imperatives.—Subordinate-imperative clauses
are like main-imperative clauses in having present-subjunctive
(and occasionally present-perfect-subjunctive) verb forms as predicators, and they are like main-imperative clauses in force. They
are like subordinate declaratives in using an unstressed *that* as an
adjunct and clause marker. Subordinate imperatives are unlike
main imperatives in requiring expressed subjects, which are of
all persons; they are unlike subordinate declaratives in the mode
of their verb forms and in their constant use of the marker *that.*
Subordinate imperatives occur as subordinate clauses affected

by desire (or by influencing normally rooted in desire) expressed in larger containing clauses by such verbs as *advise, ask, beg, demand, desire, forbid, insist, intend, order, prefer, propose, recommend, request, require, suggest,* and *urge,* and by nouns and adjectives with related meanings.

> The students ask only that they not *be bored.*
> The situation demanded that our efforts *be concentrated* at home.
> In case of my death I desire that this insurance *be paid* to my wife.
> The Press prefers that footnotes *be grouped* at the end of the manuscript.
> Various members of the faculty have urged that the library *be kept* open.
> It is important that the child *recognize* good informal English and *be* able to use it.
> We were anxious that there *be* no misunderstanding.
> The Dean approved Fenton's proposal on condition that he *get* the consent of the departments involved.
> The insistence that each student *pay* an activities fee had put another burden on those whose families were poor.
> We had already received Miss Lay's request that she *be transferred* to another department.

In the examples given above the subjunctive forms are clearly distinct from common-mode forms. In great numbers of subordinate imperatives this is not the case, so that in internal form the clauses are not distinguishable from declaratives.

> It is important that children *recognize* good informal English.
> The police demanded that we *move* our car.
> There is no good reason for the requirement that all students *have completed* a course in phonemics before enrolling for the course in grammar.

Subordinate imperatives occur characteristically in rather formal styles. Verbid clauses tend to replace them.

> The students only ask *not* to *be bored.*
> The Press prefers to *have footnotes grouped at the end of the manuscript.*
> It is important for *the child* to *recognize good informal English and be able to use it.*

Main assertives.—Like main declaratives, main assertives are main-clause expressions of opinion or of fact. Like declaratives (and interrogatives) they have common-mode or hypothetical-subjunctive verb forms as predicators. They characteristically differ from declaratives in that their subjects are preceded by complements (or parts of complements) and/or by predicators (or parts of predicators); in some assertives, however, the parts of the nucleus occur in the order in which they occur in declaratives, just as they do in such an interrogative as *who broke the cup?* Four types of main assertives occur.

One type uses *what* or *how*, or a unit including one of these words, in or before the subject.

> *What strange people* come here!
> *What a beautiful city* San Francisco is!
> *How* I suffered with that dentist!

The clause markers are italicized here. In the first and third sentences the parts of the nucleus are in declarative order. *What* and *how* have extremitive force in assertives: *how I suffered* is much like *I suffered extremely* in meaning. Expression of opinion or fact felt as extraordinary is accompanied by construction that is extraordinary. Reduced *what* and *how* main assertives are common.

> What a day!
> How sweet!

What and *how* main assertives are generally regarded as exclamatory, and so punctuated. But exclamatory sentences employ all main-clause patterns and (as in *if only we agreed on restaurants!*) even some subordinate-clause patterns. In expressions of enthusiasm *what* and *how* main assertives are commoner in feminine use than in masculine. *What* is used more widely than *how*.

A second type of main assertive uses before the subject (1) *so, such, especially, still more*, or similar locutions, or units containing them, or (2) negatives or near negatives. In this position these words and multiword units function as clause markers, besides functioning as adjuncts or as complements. In addition, in this position these markers make necessary the use of still other clause markers before the subjects: marker verb forms. There are thus two markers in all clauses of this type. Clause markers are italicized in the following main assertives.

1. *So ridiculous were* his charges that it seemed pointless to try to answer them.

   To such an extreme did they go that all moderate solutions became impossible.

   Especially did we enjoy the life of the plaza.

   Still more were we pleased with the beaches.

   Well do I remember the day we arrived.

2. *Nowhere is* there a lovelier island.

   Not since Wilson nosed out Hughes had the country seen such an upset.

   Not only in summer is the climate of these states unpleasant, but in winter also.

   Not one word did he say.

   Rarely does the temperature go above ninety in San Juan.

   Only when he is addressed directly does Jasper look up.

The marker verb forms are those that are used in main interrogatives: *are, am, is, were, was; can, could, may, might, must, ought, shall, should, will, would;* in their auxiliary uses *have, has, had, do, does, did;* infrequently *need.* Main assertives of this second type have something of extremitive force, though less of it than those employing *what* and *how.*

Reduced main assertives of this second type occur.

They won't finish by June, *much less* by April.

Main declaratives closely paralleling main assertives of this second type are generally possible.

His charges were so ridiculous that it seemed pointless to answer them.

There is no lovelier island anywhere.

The declarative pattern is more generally satisfactory. At one point, however, this second assertive pattern holds its own in competition with the declarative pattern: *so* and *neither*, accompanied by marker verb forms, are constantly used before the subjects in reduced assertive clauses that are parallel in their content to previous declaratives.

We enjoyed the trip, and so did Harry.

Harry hasn't paid his bill yet. But neither have I.

Here the assertives are not felt as different in force from the corresponding declaratives *and Harry did too* and *and I haven't either.*

A third type of main assertive is essentially extremitive also but includes nothing as distinctive as the *what* and *how* of the first type or the marker verb forms of the second. Assertives of this third type—simple main assertives—merely have their subjects preceded by complements or parts of complements and/or by predicators or parts of predicators.

> *There* it is
> *Off* he went.
> *In* you go!
> *Right* you are.
> *One thing* I'm sure of.
> *Oversights* we can pardon.
> *His habits of waste* the American transmitted to a generation that could no longer afford them.
> *Of all these great volcanoes* Popocatepetl is the most esteemed.
> *A lot of good* it did me!
> *Here's* your pen.
> *In came* three of the neighbors' children.
> *Sixty miles to the north is* the city of Cleveland.
> *Many's* the time he's done it.
> *Coming up the street was* the Congregational minister.
> *Inclosed is* my check for the amount due.
> *Enjoy it* we did.

The clause markers in these sentences are of course the italicized complement and predicator units which precede the subjects in their nucleuses. All of these assertives could be made into declaratives simply by changing the word order. But English is a word-order language, and departures from the normal subject-predicator-complement order of declaratives are significant. Simple assertives are something special: sometimes emphatic, sometimes excited, sometimes rhetorically useful for varied reasons, sometimes just feebly literary. Ordinarily the basic declarative pattern is preferable. Much of the time, as a matter of fact, it would be difficult to avoid it in expression of fact or opinion. Exceptional assertive sentences such as *here's your pen* can readily employ complement-predicator-subject order simply because *here* does not readily function as subject. *Dogs like children* will always be taken as in subject-predicator-complement order.

Reduction occurs occasionally in simple main assertives.

Not for him the easy paths, the glib answers, the simple solutions of a material civilization.
Here goes!

Simple main assertives are sometimes incorporated subordinately within larger clauses.

Roosevelt's dead, *more's the pity*.

The fourth type of main assertive is proportionative rather than extremitive. This type is marked by the use of *the* and a comparative, or a unit containing *the* and a comparative, in or (much more often) before the subject. Assertives of this kind occur in pairs, combined in multiple sentences; the occurrence of the first constitutes a promise that a second is ahead.

The more he spends on that car, *the worse* it runs.
The sooner you decide, *the better* it will be.
The fewer visitors come, *the more* we'll accomplish.

Reduced assertives of the proportionative type are common.

The smaller the town, *the friendlier* the people.

In pairs of proportionative assertives the meaning relationship makes it reasonable to regard the first as an adjunct included, in front position, within the second.

In proportion as the town is small, the people are friendly.

But the parallelism in form makes it seem best to regard pairs of proportionatives as coordinate main clauses in closely unified multiple sentences in which the main parts are interdependent. Sometimes a single proportionative clause is used as an adjunct within a larger clause of another type.

The situation got worse and worse *the more he said*.

Subordinate assertives.—Subordinate assertives differ from main assertives as subordinate declaratives differ from main declaratives: in their smooth incorporation within larger clauses and/or in their use of an unstressed pronoun *that* as semantically empty adjunct and clause marker.

Subordinate *what*-and-*how* assertives cannot employ *that* as a clause marker.

> I didn't realize *what strange people came here.*
> You have no idea *how I suffered with that dentist.*
> It's amazing *how good Jack's steaks are.*

In internal syntactic form, subordinate *what*-and-*how* assertives are commonly indistinguishable from subordinate interrogatives, though manner and intonation serve to distinguish the two types in the spoken language. Doubtful instances are most conveniently classifiable as interrogatives. But the use of an indefinite article between *what* and a singular pluralizer head does distinguish subordinate assertives from subordinate interrogatives syntactically.

> I had forgotten *what a department Mills worked in.*
> I had forgotten *what department Mills worked in.*

Subordinate assertives corresponding to the other types of main assertives occur infrequently.

> I tried to explain *that not one word had we said.*
> It was at precisely this point *that in came three of the neighbors'*
> *children.*
> We knew *that the more we offered Hartford, the more he would*
> *want.*

CHAPTER IV

OTHER MATTERS OF CLAUSE PATTERNING

The four patterns of structure, or clusters of patterns of structure, characteristically found in main clauses—those of the main declarative, the main interrogative, the main imperative, and the main assertive—are matched by clearly derived patterns of structure characteristically found in subordinate clauses. It remains to describe a pattern of clause structure—or a cluster of two patterns—characteristically employed in subordinate clauses and not so clearly derived from any main-clause pattern, and to say something about the effects of negation on clause structure, about clause splitting, and about the coordination of clauses.

Infinitival verbid clauses.—What can conveniently be called verbid clauses are like main imperatives in that the predicators are verb forms usable without expressed subjects much more freely than the common-mode verb forms with which some of them are identical except in syntax. The verb forms used as predicators in verbid clauses are sometimes infinitival in mode and sometimes gerundial, and they serve as the only clause markers, unless special case forms of subjects are also regarded as clause markers when they occur. Infinitival verbid clauses are sometimes identical in internal form with main imperatives. This is true of *be careful,* for example, in *it's wise to be careful.*

The commonest use of infinitival verbid clauses without expressed subjects is the use as object of the preposition *to.*

Circumstances forced us to *postpone the trip.*
We came to *feel very happy in New York.*
We were too late to *see our friends.*
We decided to *take Edward along.*
He lived to *be ninety.*
To *tell the truth,* we all want comfort.

He left home in 1945, *never to return.*
We're to *bring our own food.*
He has a family to *think of.*
She wants a new bag to *match her shoes.*
To *have admitted the truth* would have been to *endanger the whole venture.*
It takes a low bush to *stand in a strong wind.*
We wanted to *go with you.*
People like to *be liked.*
We asked nothing except to *be let alone.*

Units made up of *to* and infinitival completers of *to* sometimes occur as exceptional complements in sentences in which there has been a shifting of subjects.

He is said to *have been indicted before.*
Everyone is supposed to *bring a small present.*
She seems to *have accepted the situation.*
He's likely to *get into trouble again.*

Like the shifted constructions of such passives as *we weren't given enough time,* the shifted constructions above commonly serve to give earlier notice, and greater syntactic prominence, to the involvement of human beings.

It is said that *he* has been indicted before.
He is said to have been indicted before.
Not enough time was given *us.*
We were not given enough time.

Units made up of *to* and infinitival completers are sometimes given sentence status even in careful and formal styles.

To return to what was happening in Mexico City.
To think that all that money has been wasted!

When infinitival clauses used as objects of *to* are negated by *not* or *never,* the negator is usually advanced to a position in front of *to,* at least in careful and formal styles.

It's a shame *not* to *be there.*
I try *never* to *offend her.*

The word *so* moves forward similarly in the formula *so to speak. Simply, only, merely,* and *just* seem to move forward without difficulty.

I hope that it will be possible *simply* to *drop my name.*
You have *only* to *read the introduction.*

Other adjuncts of infinitives generally do not take the position in front of *to* very gracefully.

It was not the General's function *openly* to *attack his superior.*

Openly could follow *his superior* to advantage here. There is a prejudice against putting adjuncts of infinitives between *to* and the infinitives, and the name "split infinitives" has been attached to the constructions which result when adjuncts are put there. But sometimes no other position is really very satisfactory.

She's too young to *really* understand what age means.
It's a terrible thing to *almost* kill your best friend.
To *actually* steal a contract seemed a great sin.
People seem to *deliberately* avoid talking to newcomers.
On his deathbed he asked his children to *at least* give him a
funeral at which his old friends would feel comfortable.

Especially in informal styles, there is frequent use of the preposition *to* alone to represent a prepositional unit in which the expressed object of *to* would be an infinitival clause.

She speaks English, but she doesn't like *to.*
She speaks English only when she has *to.*
More people drink milk than used *to.*

The reduction here is basically the same as that which occurs when *come in* is used in place of *come into the house.* Another noteworthy type of reduction is common after *want.*

The cat wants *in.*

The construction is similar to that in *did you let the cat in?* except that after *let* an expressed infinitive (*get* or *come*) would not be preceded by *to.* A third type of notable reduction is found in such sentences as *he has a family to think of,* where the infinitival clause *think of* lacks an object for the preposition *of* just as the interrogative clause does in *he has a family he thinks of.*

Two phrasal prepositions often occur where *to* alone might be expected.

We stopped *in order to* look at the old forts.
Will you be so kind *as to* explain what happened?

In order to is simply an expansion of *to* often used in adjuncts of purpose. *As to* is a combination of a head word, *as*, here made necessary by the preceding *so*, and a modifying *to* which prepares for the following infinitival clause in the common fashion.

Subjectless infinitival clauses are by no means confined to use as objects of the preposition *to*. A few verbs take them as first complements: the defectives *can, may, must, shall, should*, and *will*, but not the defective *ought; had*, when it is used with present force along with *better, rather*, etc.; *need*, when it is used with a negator or near negator and (formally) when it is used in interrogatives; *dare*, when it is used (formally) with a negator and in questions.

> John can *help you.*
> You may *be right.*
> Shall we *call a taxi?*
> To this day Mary won't *say a word to John.*
> We'd better *tell her the truth.*
> Dare we *trust our own representatives?*

Among these verbs, *will* functions as an auxiliary of tense, as well as a full predicator expressing volition and related meanings; and *shall* functions similarly where it competes with *will* as a true tense auxiliary, as in formal *we shall be glad to send further information if you wish.* Occasionally an infinitival clause without *to* completes *be*.

What the author does is *attribute to Charlie every kind of trouble a student ever has.*

In informal styles such clauses sometimes complete *go* and *come*.

> Let's go *tell him.*
> Come *see us.*

Subjectless infinitival clauses are used (1) as second complements after a few very important verbs of influencing, assisting, and permitting, and (2) as tight postcomplementary adjuncts (and in some cases as second complements) after a number of verbs of experiencing.

> 1. She had the store *deliver the dresses.*
> She makes her husband *take her to operas.*
> John helped me *pack my books.*
> They let us *leave when we finished.*

2. I saw Mary *drop the box.*
I watched him *pick it up.*
Look at the boy *run!*
Jane heard us *come in.*
I felt the atmosphere *change.*
I've had people *ask me whether I'm Scotch.*

Where the infinitival verb form is passive, auxiliary *be* is omitted.

I had my watch *cleaned a year ago.*
I saw George *put out of the restaurant for brawling.*

More extreme reduction is common after *let* and *help.*

Let me *in.*
I'll help you *up.*

Most verbs of influencing, assisting, permitting, and forbidding take *to* and infinitival clauses, not infinitival clauses alone, as second complements.

Circumstances forced us *to* delay the trip.
Hugh got us *to* ask for a postponement.
His wife's income enables Herbert *to* send his children to the very best schools.
They allowed us *to* leave when we finished.
He forbade his daughter *to* see George again.

Help takes both types of second complements: *John helped me to pack my books* is used alongside *John helped me pack my books.* In the passive *make* and *help* always have *to* in the complementary construction.

We've been made *to* wait much too long.

A few verbs of experiencing take *to* and infinitival completers after first complements.

I've always found him *to* be reasonably diplomatic.
I've known him *to* be candid.

After a passive verb of experiencing *to* makes its appearance regularly.

A stranger was seen *to* pick up the purse.

What are at bottom infinitival second complements occur without expressed first complements in a few fixed phrasings.

He didn't let *go.*
Live and let *live.*
Children like to make *believe they're adults.*

Sometimes infinitival second complements are implied rather than expressed.

She went because her mother made her.

Infinitival clauses without expressed subjects of their own appear occasionally under other circumstances.

He won't even thank you, let alone *pay you.*
That's what I'll do: *marry a fortune.*
He's never done anything besides *tell funny stories.*

A feeling for parallelism has a great deal to do with the use of infinitival clauses in the first two of these sentences: such clauses as *he won't pay you* and *I'll marry a fortune* are vaguely in mind. In the last sentence an infinitival clause serves as a neutral substitute for a less manageable structure. In informal conversational use infinitival clauses without *to* sometimes function as contained modifiers of nounal heads.

There have been lots of people *try it.*

The subjects of infinitival clauses.—When infinitival clauses lack expressed subjects, subjects are always implied. Often the subject of the larger clause within which an infinitival clause is contained suggests the subject for the infinitival clause.

We came to *feel* very happy in New York.
He has no home to *go* to.
He is said to *have been* in trouble before.
You may *be* right.
He's never done anything besides *tell* funny stories.
He has a family to *take* care of.
The *children* are ready to *eat.*

Sometimes a complement in the larger clause suggests the subject of a following infinitival clause.

Circumstances have forced *us* to postpone the exhibition.
She wants *a new bag* to match her shoes.
They let *us* leave when we finished.
I watched *him* pick it up.
He has *a family* to take care of him.

Sometimes even a possessive within the larger clause suggests it.

His desire has been to be frank without giving offense.

Sometimes situation or context suggests the subject.

To return to what was happening in Mexico City.
The invitation to visit the laboratory came at an awkward moment.
It was very disturbing to see John so upset.
The potatoes are ready to eat.

Sometimes the unexpressed subject is general—"a person."

Taking courses is a silly way to get an education.
Guadalajara is a delightful city to live in.
To tell the truth, we all want comfort.
It's easy to underestimate quiet people.
The fruit is just to look at.

Infinitival clauses with expressed subjects of their own tend to be used as objects of the apposed-unit preposition *for . . . to*, much as those without expressed subjects tend to be used as objects of the simple preposition *to*. This *for . . . to* occurs, like the *to*, both where a preposition is syntactically normal and where a preposition would hardly occur except before an infinitival clause. The *to* is put inside the infinitival clause, before its predicator.

We waited for *the clock* to *strike*.
There's no need for *you* to *be indirect*.
There were children for *Susan* to *play with*.
For *religion* to *divide the country so bitterly* is tragic indeed.
It is important for *the discussion* to *be frank*.
One way of finding Jones would be for *you* to *inquire at all the bars*.
She hates for *anyone* to *ignore her*.
We intended for *you* to *be there*.

Infinitival clauses made objects of *for . . . to* are identical in appearance with combinations (from which they originally developed) in which *for* is a preposition completed by the noun or nounal unit which follows it, while *to* is another preposition completed separately by an infinitival clause with no stated subject of its own within it.

It's hard for me to explain my feelings.

Here *for me* is an adjunct of the main predicator *is* and *to explain my feelings* is in apposition with *it*.

Infinitival clauses with their own expressed subjects are also used as objects of the simple preposition *to*. This *to*, like the *to* of *for . . . to*, comes inside the infinitival clause, before its predicator. Units made up of *to* and infinitival clauses with expressed subjects are used as complements (1) after certain verbs of wanting and liking, and (2) after certain verbs of knowing, thinking, declaring, and the like.

1. Mildred wants *her friends* to *visit her constantly.*
   I like *people* to *tell the truth.*
2. Hamilton knew *the facts* to *be otherwise.*
   We expected *rents* to *be high here.*
   He conceives *it* to *be his duty to correct his colleagues.*

After *like* units with *for . . . to* compete.

I like for people to tell me the truth.

Verbless infinitival clauses without *to* or *for . . . to* are common.

Everyone wants *lemonade very cold.*
Small-town people consider *us bad-mannered.*
Those who did not know him thought *him rude.*

Sometimes only an auxiliary *be* and *to* are omitted.

We don't want *anything said about this.*

The corresponding infinitival clause with common-voice predicator is *anyone (to) say anything about this.* Occasionally infinitival clauses with their own expressed subjects and with *to* develop after verbs of influencing and permitting.

The company requires *bills* to *be paid by the tenth.*
The court ordered *the property* to *be sold.*

The infinitive is passive, and the construction is only doubtfully standard. But when auxiliary *be* and *to* are omitted, the construction sometimes becomes more acceptable.

The manager ordered *the floor cleared at once.*

This kind of reduced infinitival clause also develops after such verbs as *hear* and *have.*

> I've had *three pens taken from my desk.*
> I've heard *him criticized unmercifully.*

Infinitival clauses with expressed subjects and without *to* occasionally have sentence status with the force of somewhat emotional questions.

> Him teach English?
> Me be careful?

Gerundial verbids.—Gerundial verbid clauses have gerundial-mode verb forms as predicators. Gerundial clauses without expressed subjects of their own are used as subjects in larger containing clauses.

> *Seeing Montreal* occupied Monday.
> *Washing windows this far up* is very exciting.

They are used as complements of verbs of various types, notably verbs of stopping, finishing, postponing, avoiding, resenting, and tolerating, and a few verbs of approximately opposite meanings such as *begin*, *keep* ("continue"), *enjoy*, *appreciate*, and *recommend*, and such verbs as *imagine*, *consider*, and even *be*.

> John mentioned *having seen Fred in Rochester.*
> We enjoyed *being with you.*
> She hasn't finished *mending her stockings.*
> We put off *buying a car* as long as we could.
> I recommend *trying diplomacy.*
> We're considering *buying a new car.*
> It would be *playing with fire* to invite Walter.
> George went on *eating his breakfast.*
> They kept us *wondering what the trouble was.*
> We kept *wondering what the trouble was.*

They are used as adjuncts, both tight and loose, chiefly with relationships of circumstance, manner, cause, or similar meanings.

> We kept busy *seeing Montreal.*
> The neighbors heard us *coming in last night.*
> The police caught him *robbing a gas station.*
> *Coming into town,* we had a hard time finding a garage.
> *Beginning in June,* prices will be five percent higher.
> *Having had good debate training,* Thomas can make a case for
> either side.

To the end of his life Veblen was alone and imperturbable, *seeking truth along the byways rather than in the cultivated fields of scholarship.*
Scientific knowledge can be good or bad, *depending on the use to which it is put.*
Considering everything, it was a good deal.

They are used as contained modifiers of nounal heads.

In came a small girl *carrying a puppy.*
Students *desiring additional training in spoken Spanish* should register for Spanish 202.
Religion is God *moving among men.*

They are used as postponed appositives, though in American practice infinitival clauses with *to* are generally preferred in this construction.

It's no use *reasoning with Jack.*
It's very pleasant *sitting here in the sun.*

They are used as objects of prepositions. Here they are the most widely usable of all subordinate clauses.

Jester won't get cooperation by *threatening people.*
I'm in favor of *making some money.*
He was arrested for *knocking a policeman down.*
Her color comes from *getting out in the sun.*
There's no use in *reasoning with Jack.*
She talked him into *giving her a job.*
Smith isn't past *being taken in by pretty girls.*
The newspapers have devoted a great deal of space to *telling the public about advances in this field.*
I have no objection to *writing the letter.*
I'm used to *getting my own breakfast.*
The sales are worth *waiting for.*
Countries are often thought of as *having feminine qualities.*

At some points gerundial clauses and infinitival clauses with *to* are usable with about the same meanings.

He began questioning us.
He began to question us.

At other points there are clear differences in meaning.

Do you remember closing the door?
Do you remember to close the door?

> I tried being polite to her.
> I tried to be polite to her.

At some points gerundials with normal prepositions compete with infinitives with the generalized preposition *to*.

> There's no time for singing silly songs.
> There's no time to sing silly songs.
> She was delighted at being included.
> She was delighted to be included.

When gerundial clauses lack expressed subjects, subjects are of course always implied. They are suggested as in infinitival clauses. When there is a possibility that a wrong subject may suggest itself, however ludicrously, subjectless gerundial clauses (or infinitival clauses, or interrogative clauses) are best avoided, at least in written English. Thus such a sentence as *walking around the campus, the Tower dominates everything* had better be rephrased.

Gerundial clauses without expressed subjects are sometimes begun by determinative pronouns which modify what follows much as they would modify nouns.

> There's *no* telling what he thinks.
> There isn't *any* getting along with him.
> *This* treating us all like children is a little offensive.

The pronoun modifiers can be regarded as adjuncts of an exceptional type within the gerundial clauses. The situation is not wholly different in such a sentence as *he's behaving exactly as he's always behaved*, where *exactly* can be regarded as an adjunct within the adverbial clause even though it precedes the clause marker *as*.

Gerundial clauses with expressed subjects are sometimes used as subjects within larger clauses.

> *John's staying away* complicates the problem.
> *The children's taking music lessons* added to the expense.

Sometimes as complements.

> Pardon *my being so frank*.
> We resented *Foster's treating us so arrogantly*.
> We appreciate *your inviting us*.

Sometimes as adjuncts.

> We prefer a lower altitude, *all things being equal*.

There being no objection, the meeting adjourned.
I have often seen him marching magnificently up the street, *wife and children following respectfully a few steps behind*.

Sometimes as objects of prepositions.

Rosemary's usefulness is increased by *her having lived in Mexico*.
They insisted on *our being there*.
You're right about *there being no time*.
There's no use in *everyone's getting upset*.
I'm in favor of *people like him making some money*.
Instead of *the passing months assuaging his grief*, they only increased it.
I have often seen him marching magnificently up the street with *his wife and children following respectfully a few steps behind*.
How can we get anything done with *him acting like a prima donna?*
Harriet can't do anything without *her husband criticizing her unmercifully*.

Expressed subjects in gerundial clauses are likely—but not certain—to be marked by possessive inflection if the gerundial clauses are used as subjects, complements, or objects of prepositions other than *with* and sometimes *without*. But where possessive inflection cannot be added very satisfactorily, even careful and formal styles get along without it. And apostrophes are not very likely to be added to plural subjects, as in *instead of the passing months assuaging his grief*. Possessive inflection is not usable for subjects in gerundial clauses used as adjuncts or as objects of the preposition *with* within adjuncts of circumstance.

Verbless gerundial clauses with expressed nonpossessive subjects have considerable use. They function as loose adjuncts of circumstance.

We left Cairo on the seventh with still more passengers, *most of them beautiful women*.
There were dozens of poems, *some of them good and some bad*.
While they were talking—*the family about their small ambitions and he about leadership*—a huge stone rolled down the mountain.

Verbless gerundial clauses are fairly common as objects of the preposition *with*. The implied predicator in such clauses is *being*.

We can't buy much with *prices always so high.*
We went into it with *our eyes open.*
It's lonely with *the children away.*
An airliner with *forty people aboard* crashed west of Denver
   last night.

Where there is more or less fixed phrasing, as in such locutions as
*day after day, word for word, step by step, arm in arm, eye to eye,
year in and year out, hat in hand, sight unseen, inside out,* and *head
first,* verbless gerundial clauses are much more widely usable. They
occur, for example, as tight adjuncts, as subjects, as modifiers
within nounal units, and as complements.

> They slept *three in a bed.*
> *Car after car* went by without stopping.
> A *head-on* collision was the result.
> The table was *upside down.*
> We were *face to face* with the thief.

Gerundial clauses with both expressed subjects and expressed
predicators seem somewhat stiff and uncomfortable much of the
time. Competing constructions tend to replace them.

John's staying away complicates the problem.
It complicates the problem for John to stay away.
We resented Foster's treating us so arrogantly.
We resented having Foster treat us so arrogantly.
We resented it that Foster treated us so arrogantly.
No one can prevent John's seeing the manager.
No one can prevent John from seeing the manager.
Of course she minds her husband's acting like that.
Of course she minds it when her husband acts like that.
Weather permitting, the meeting will be held in the stadium.
If the weather permits, the meeting will be held in the stadium.

When full gerundial clauses would have passive predicators, the
passive auxiliary *be* is commonly omitted. Such clauses without
subjects of their own are used as adjuncts, chiefly with relationships of circumstance, manner, cause, or similar meanings.

Williamson taught at the University for thirty years, disliking
   his colleagues *and disliked by them.*
Seen from a distance, Our Most Holy Lady of the Miracles of
   Tlaltenango looks like a pretty doll.
Long neglected by literature, the city now achieved a notoriety
   as unlovely as that of the frowzy country town.

Such clauses are also used as contained modifiers of nounal heads.

Hidalgo appealed to resentments *built up by centuries of oppression.*
You won't like the accommodations *furnished by the college.*
A friend in power is a friend *lost.*

When there are no expressed subjects, subjects are of course implied. Sometimes there are expressed subjects.

All things considered, you did very wisely.
There are also advanced courses in history, philosophy, and sociology, *some of them taught in English.*
It's hard to go ahead with *so many people offended by our plans.*

If the passive auxiliary were stated in gerundial clauses such as these, sometimes the form used would be *being* and sometimes *having been.* Often it would seem unnatural to express the auxiliary.

Some gerundial clauses have the normal subject-predicator-complement word order altered as it is in many assertives. When this is the case, generally *being,* as full verb or as auxiliary in a passive, is implied but not stated.

Babbitt had various profitable contacts, *among them the officials of the traction company.*
No matter what he says, we're going ahead.
Some solution is possible, *provided no further errors are made.*
Given a reasonable amount of good will, the conflict of interests can be resolved.
Granted that universities need business managers, it still does not follow that these men should run the universities.

Negation.—Fundamentally negation is the language of dissent. Its favored word is *not,* and the central meaning of *not* is one of otherness. Thus negated *George doesn't drive very prudently* dissents from unnegated *George drives very prudently.* Here, in terms of layers, *not* is best regarded as the outermost modifier of the predicator *does drive,* though the focus of dissent obviously lies in the words *very prudently* and *George drives rather imprudently* is probably a roughly equivalent statement. *Half his students don't understand him* does not seem to dissent from unnegated *half his students understand him,* but this is because the two sentences speak of different groups of students—one of one half, the other of the other half. Sometimes negation is semantically specialized to convey meanings of "lessness," as in *I don't have a dime*, and (though usually not with *not*) zero, as in *no coffee is raised on the island now*.

When *not* negates a declarative, it normally must follow one of the same verb forms that are used to mark main interrogatives and some main assertives: *are, am, is, were, was; can, could, may, might, must, ought, shall, should, will, would*; in their auxiliary uses *have, has, had, do, does, did; need*.

> Fred was not there.
> We can't leave before Thursday.
> There won't be time next week.
> The economic problem has not been solved.
> You needn't return the jars.

In interrogatives also *not* must follow one of these same verb forms. The subject commonly intervenes in careful and formal styles but not in informal ones.

> Has the economic problem not been solved?
> Wasn't Fred there?

In main imperatives *not* follows *do* even when the predicator is *be*.

> Don't tell him.
> Don't be reckless.

When main imperatives have expressed subjects, negation with *not* produces a word order like that of main interrogatives.

> Don't you tell him!
> Don't anyone move!

Not is used without *do* in subordinate imperatives.

> It is important that exceptions *not* be made.

In some assertives of the second type *not* is attached to a complement or adjunct on which the negation is focused and, as has been said, this negated unit then moves in front of the subject and must be followed by a marker verb form which is also in front of the subject.

> *Not since Wilson nosed out Hughes* had the country seen such an upset.
> *Not one word* did he say.

In verbid clauses *not* is used without the preceding verb forms required in main declaratives. As has been said, when *not* negates infinitival verbid clauses used with *to*, it moves forward before *to*.

> I tried *not* to offend him.
> He resents *not* being invited.

Not is by no means the only adjunct with negator force.

> It was *no longer* possible to have confidence in Jackson.
> Marian *never* acts hastily.
> It is *by no means* the only adjunct with negator force.
> *Never* mind what I said yesterday.

Marker verb forms are not required with negator adjuncts other than *not*. Equivalents employing *not* and a marker verb form compete with the constructions illustrated by the sentences given above, and are often preferred in informal styles.

> It *wasn't* possible to have confidence in Jackson any longer.
> Marian *doesn't* ever act hastily.
> It *isn't* the only adjunct with negator force by any means.

Negative subjects and negative complements can serve as negators.

> Nothing was done.
> Not everyone would agree with you.
> No home could be pleasanter.
> It's none of his business.
> He's no mathematician.
> I had no way of knowing his attitude.
> We got nowhere.
> They did nothing.

It is noteworthy that the negative subject of such a declarative as *nothing was done* disappears in the corresponding main interrogative, at least in informal styles.

> Wasn't anything done?

When negators turn up as late as the complement area, they are likely to produce special effects either of emphasis or of formality. But the use of negative complements often results in neater sentences than alternative patternings produce, and so is favored in careful and formal styles.

> They did nothing.
> They did not do anything.

The desire for early expression of negators sometimes leads to attaching them to main predicators when attachment to later subordinate predicators might seem more orderly and exact.

> I don't think we've finished.
> I didn't use to like him.

It is not really illogical to put the negators early here. As the sentences stand, what is negated is the main nucleuses *I think we've finished* and *I used to like him.* If the negators are moved to the subordinate predicators, the effect is likely to seem too direct.

> I think we haven't finished.
> I used not to like him.

Negation is the language of dissent, and dissent can seem a little graceless when it is precise. Occasionally in informal styles a negator is moved forward to a main predicator when it would seem that meanings should prevent.

> When we parted, I never expected to see her again.

Negative words tend to push forward under other circumstances also. In the following sentences negative modifiers which from the point of view of the most careful structure should be contained modifiers later in their clauses have moved forward to the normal position of adjuncts functioning as clause negators.

> The *Observer* does *not* appeal to emotion but to reason.
> One is *never* engaged in farming in general, but in farming a
>   particular tract of land under specific conditions.

Neither full declarative is really negated here: certainly there is no negation of what begins with *but.* Sentences such as these are frequent even in careful and formal styles: it is not possible to regard them as nonstandard. But from the point of view of clause structure, revisions are preferable to the two sentences as they stand.

Not often moves forward after *whether,* with which it is coordinated.

> Whether or not he said it, it isn't true.

Whether he said it or not is a split clause of syntactically ordinary type.

Like interrogative reinforcers, negative reinforcers are of minor importance syntactically but deserve notice. Negation and interrogation are related in idea, and the same reinforcers are used in both situations.

> Shelton doesn't have *any* real convictions.
> He hasn't *ever* expressed himself on the basic issues.
> He doesn't vote *any more*.
> He doesn't think about them *at all*.
> He doesn't like candor *a bit*.

The italicized negative reinforcers would not be used in the corresponding unnegated declaratives. *Much*, too, is often a negative reinforcer, and for this reason the following questions involve different implications.

> Doesn't Harris know a great deal of Spanish?
> Doesn't Harris know much Spanish?

The use of *a great deal* here suggests that a positive answer (*yes, he does*) is expected. The use of *much* suggests that a negative answer is expected. As has been said, the influence of reinforcers is subtle, but is real. They are quite likely to be present in negated clauses: there is an obvious preference for multiple indication of negation when it affects nucleuses. Yet though standard English prefers multiple indication of negation when it affects nucleuses—by marker verb forms, by *not*, much of the time by reinforcers also—it is now reluctant to combine, attached to a single predicator, two or more of the invariably negative words beginning with *n*. *I don't know nothing*, for example, is nonstandard if it means what is meant by *I don't know anything* or *I know nothing*. *Why don't we just not go!* is standard, however—with two negators attaching to the nucleus independently, as different layers.

At the semantic borderline between positive and negative are concepts expressed by such words as *only, just, hardly, scarcely, seldom,* and *rarely* on the one hand and *nearly* and *almost* on the other. The first six words, though semantically positive in their relations to what they modify, often affect clause patterns as negators do. Marker verb forms accompany them when they precede the subjects of their clauses, and the clauses are assertives rather than declaratives.

Rarely *does* the thermometer go above ninety.
Only when he is addressed directly *does* he look up.

Only, just, hardly, and *scarcely* tend to push forward to clause-negator positions, just as *not* does, even when later positions seem more appropriate.

We *only* kept one of the puppies.
He *just* shaves on Saturdays.
The law should *only* be invoked, we believe, when all other
    means of influencing the parents have been exhausted.
At present we *hardly* have a hundred names and addresses.

The desire that negative or near-negative coloring begin early is very strong, and sentences such as these cannot be called nonstandard, though they would be revised in the most careful writing. Negative reinforcers combine with the near negatives also.

I've hardly ever seen Jack angry at all.

And there is objection to combining near negatives with *n* negatives, as in nonstandard *I don't hardly think so. Nearly* and *almost,* on the other hand, have no negative syntactic force, though from the point of view of meaning they are negatives.

We nearly missed the train.
He almost hit the window, didn't he?

In informal styles combinations of *n* negatives and near-negative *but* are fairly common, and they occur also in other styles.

There's no doubt but what he means it.
I can't help but wonder about Barnes.
We never saw but one tarantula while we were there.
There can be no question but that onomatopoetic forms exist.

Hardly and *scarcely* can be negative in real meaning as well as in syntax: for example, in *I hardly think so. Little* is really negative in *little did we realize that we would never see Maurice again.* There is negative meaning, though not negative syntactic force, in *it was anything but satisfactory* and in *she was far from well.* A variety of adjuncts take on negative meaning in informal styles: for example, *like fun* in *like fun you can!* Irony gives negative force to ordinary positive patterns at times.

> A lot of good it did me.
> I'll teach him to talk like that.

Comparison occurs in negation where higher degrees of dissent are indicated.

> What he says is not true of the older generation, and *still less* is it true of the young people.

Layers of modification are sometimes of great importance where negation is concerned.

> Harriet isn't from a wealthy home like most of our students. Unlike most of our students, Harriet isn't from a wealthy home.

The two sentences mean much the same thing; yet in the second the loose adjunct preceding the subject requires a negative prefix *un* which is not usable in the tight adjunct following the complement in the first sentence. The loose adjunct in the second sentence is the outermost modifier of the main predicator *is* and is not affected by the fact that the nucleus is negated. Layers of meaning are involved somewhat differently in sentences such as the following.

> Nobody who can stay at home wants to be out every night.

Here *nobody* is a zero word, but the *who* which refers back to it is not a zero word. *Nobody can stay at home* is no main-declarative equivalent of *who can stay at home: who* refers to the unnegated core of *nobody*, and actually *no* modifies *body who can stay at home*. The presence of a negator in the main predication seems to be responsible for the illogical loss of one in the subordinate predication in the following sentence.

> He didn't stay any longer than he could help.

Positive and negative forms often take on special implications in interrogatives. *Is it a pretty baby?* can be an open question, without any suggestion of the type of response expected. Spoken enthusiastically, the sentence can lose question force and become equivalent to *it's an extremely pretty baby*. An exclamation point generally replaces the question mark in the written language when this sense is intended. Spoken skeptically, the sentence can indicate expectation of a negative answer. The corresponding negative interrogative can hardly be an open one. *Isn't it a pretty baby?* in one situation and with one manner suggests expectation of a positive response; under other circumstances and with another manner, the sentence suggests expectation of a negative response. Confirmational questions invite specific answers. In *it's a pretty baby, isn't it?* the negative question invites a positive answer confirming the positive statement which has been made somewhat tentatively. In *it isn't a pretty baby, is it?* the positive question invites a negative answer confirming the tentative negative statement. This is the basic pattern for confirmational interrogatives. Where the positive-or-negative force of a statement is not entirely clear, it is difficult to add a satisfactory confirmational interrogative.

There is a good deal of negation that does not affect clause structure. The negative affixes do not disturb it, for example. *Uncertainty has paralyzed us* is as positive in force as it would be if the subject were *certainty*. *The paper was illegible* is as positive a statement as *the paper was messy*, though *the paper wasn't legible* is a negated statement. Even the words that commonly negate clauses do not always do so. The negatives in the following sentences do not negate their clauses: their force is contained.

You're no doubt right.
He wastes no end of time.
He'll repair it for nothing.
Not infrequently the native upper classes did more harm than the foreigners did.
In 1861 the Southerners justified secession not on the basis of the right of revolution but on constitutional grounds.
The *Observer* appeals not to emotion but to reason.
We had a pleasant week in Costa Rica not long ago.

Split clauses.—Sometimes what begins as a single clause divides as it proceeds. The division can occur at various points. In the following sentences the split comes at the end of the italics.

On Thursdays John keeps the baby and his wife plays bridge.
Clark loves God dearly, hates the devil enthusiastically, and tolerates his fellow man.
Harris has always liked women but never understood them.

It was good to see you but sad not to have more time.
Are you going to town or not?

Here *on Thursdays* is followed by two complete nucleuses, tied together in Siamese-twin fashion by joint possession of the introductory adjunct—the second nucleus also modified by the adjunct *and*. *Clark* is the subject of three predicators, all of them with complements and adjuncts of their own. *Harris has* is the subject and part of the predicator of two joined nucleuses, the first with its own adjunct *always*, the second with the two adjuncts *but* and *never*. *It was* is part of the subject and all of the predicator for two joined nucleuses, the remainder of the subject in the first nucleus being *to see you* and the remainder in the second being *not to have more time*. *Are you* is the subject and part of the predicator for two joined nucleuses, the second given highly reduced expression.

Sometimes split clauses terminate in single words or sequences.

Adjuncts most often follow but sometimes precede and occasionally interrupt the nucleuses they attach to.

Here three predicators, each with an adjunct or two of its own, share both a single subject and a single complement.

Impinging modifiers produce a variant type of split clauses terminating in single words or sequences.

They took us heaven knows where.
Philips is an honest, if not a diplomatic, Administration man.

In the first of these sentences *heaven knows where* is an impinging declarative whose complement *where* has the syntax of a complement of the main predicator *took* also—as, for example, in *they took us somewhere*. This sentence has something of the quality of upside-down construction: it is not unlike a twisted variant of *heaven knows where they took us*. In the second sentence *Administration man* is a part of the complement in the impinging reduced subordinate clause *if not a diplomatic Administration man* and a part of the complement in the main nucleus *Philips is an honest Administration man*. When split clauses terminate in a single word or sequence, the result is likely to have a labored, conscious quality that is hardly desirable even in careful and formal styles, whatever the ingenuity and efficiency of construction. Other patterns are generally preferable.

A great deal of dubious sentence structure is produced by careless or insensitive use of split clauses. The basic principles of careful structure here are very simple: everything which precedes a point at which splitting begins must fit both or all of the branches which begin there, and everything that follows a point at which splitting ends must fit both or all of the branches which unite there. Such sentences as the following violate these principles.

In 1930 Mrs. Allen came to the University and taught there twenty years.
This car is as good or better than the last one we had.
He is one of the worst if not the worst teacher I've known.
This is an upsurge of opinion that officials cannot ignore and stay in office.
Language is something that people should sit back and enjoy.
I'm going downtown and buy a hat.

Sentences like these occur inevitably in rapid, natural speech, and should be regarded as acceptable in informal styles.

Split clauses whose structure is less than ideal also occur when the splitting makes single words, or larger units, perform two or more structural functions of different types.

She is beautiful and admired by everyone.
He is polite to, but does not respect, those under whom he does his work.

In the first of these sentences *is* functions both as a main predicator and as an auxiliary within the predicator *is admired*. In the second sentence *those under whom he does his work* functions both as object of the preposition *to* and as complement of the predicator *does respect*. The first sentence can hardly be called standard. The second must be described as standard but a little painful. Yet when a completing unit precedes what it completes, little or no pain is felt if it completes two constructions of dissimilar types.

Is this the haven *that* he searched for and found?
What we had bought and paid for was enough.

Coordination of clauses.—Quite often two or more main clauses are united as coordinates within multiple sentences. Analysis of such sentences must begin by separating the coordinates.

We met your friend, *and* he impressed us.
Are you coming along, *or* aren't you?
Don't be too dishonest, *but* don't be too truthful either.

Here the coordinates are united by coordinators functioning as adjuncts within the coordinates they begin. The first sentence is made up of two declaratives, the second of two interrogatives, the third of two imperatives. Precoordinators are used in the following multiple sentences.

Either he thinks she's wonderful, or he finds her father's money very attractive.
Not only is their patriotism commonly mixed with feelings of humiliation and shame, but it is probably stronger because of the admixture.

The precoordinators are adjuncts in the first clauses, just as the basic coordinators are adjuncts in the clauses they begin. Many multiple sentences, of course, employ no coordinators at all.

His manner became less abrupt: he was almost polite.
He sat still for a few more minutes; then he walked over to the table.

The interdependent relationship between the two main clauses in proportionative assertives is indicated by the parallel constructions with which they begin.

The more he said, *the less convincing* he was.

Exceptional reduction is often present in coordinates after the first.

The European had his wheat *and the Indian his corn.*
You won't like the course, *but you will the teacher.*

To a considerable extent, multiple sentences are made up of main clauses of the same type. Various types of assertives, however, are frequently coordinated with declaratives.

She didn't understand the teacher, much less the text.
Wages are high, but so are prices.
We urged him to go, and go he did.

Imperatives are often coordinated with following declaratives to which they have the meaning relationship that clauses of condition would have.

Give in to her once, and you'll never have your way again.
Let an honest man enter politics of this kind, and all the
established groups will be at his throat.

Nonstandard coordination of an interrogative and a declarative
occurs in the following sentence.

Would you like to lose fat but you just can't control your appetite?

Confirmational interrogatives (always reduced) unite with the
declaratives for which they ask confirmation, in multiple sentences
for which no coordinator is usable.

The food's very good, isn't it?
I'm doing well enough, don't you think?

Emotional and meditative interrogatives unite with declaratives
similarly.

She persuaded you, did she?
He doesn't like the food, doesn't he?

Semantically repetitive interrogatives unite with imperatives in
much the same way.

Bring your friend along, won't you?
Let me in, will you?
Let's go again, shall we?

A kind of half coordination sometimes unites clauses of different
types where true coordination might seem a little uncomfortable.
A dash often indicates this in the written language.

Bring your friend along—and won't you try to come a little
early?

Multiple sentences sometimes combine a main clause and an
isolate with or without adjuncts.

The American tolerated in others minor infractions of law and
custom and expected to be similarly indulged in his own
transgressions: hence his vast patience with noise, litter, the
invasion of privacy, and sharp practice.
Every effort was made, but to no avail.
It's a hard life, and no mistake.
One more story like that, and out he goes.
Yes, I saw it.
No, I don't.

Sometimes they combine two isolates with or without adjuncts.

> Well, well!
> Another day, another dollar!
> Tsk, tsk!
> Oh, oh!
> Easy come, easy go.
> First come, first served.
> So far, so good.

Multiple sentences can themselves be made up of multiple units composed of main clauses.

> His wife wanted to make the trip, and he did too; but the children were a problem, and the expense was great.

At the other extreme, coordinators often begin new sentences, where they are best regarded as no more than adjuncts of order or sequence.

> Centerville is a few miles south. And Fillmore is even closer to the north.

What must be considered a lapse in sentence structure occurs when what ought to be the second of two subordinate clauses is allowed to take the form of a main clause, or to appear to take it.

> Horace was a wild young fellow whose father was cruel to him *and his mother was drunk much of the time.*
> Cokeson believed Falder had committed a crime, *so he should be punished.*

Multiple units within larger clauses often have clauses as coordinates. In general, the clauses are alike in type.

> Cokeson believed that Falder had committed a crime and that therefore he should be punished.

Quite exceptionally, both interrogatives and gerundials are sometimes combined even with nonclausal coordinates.

> She has *beauty and what passes for intelligence.*
> I saw him *at nine and when he left.*
> *Dazzled by the concept of infinity, prodigal of the resources of nature, greedy and reckless,* the American did more damage in a century than nature could repair in a thousand years.

Nonclausal transforms of the basic clause pattern.—Units that are best regarded as nonclausal are often strikingly similar to clauses in meaning and structure and can be regarded as nonclausal transforms of the basic clause pattern. Units such as are italicized in the following sentences are best considered nounal and adjectival headed units, not clauses.

stopped *the taking of bribes*   *labor-saving* machinery
necessitates *constant window*   *church-going* families
    washing   *home-cooked* meals

Taking and *washing* are best described as gerundial nouns used as heads in nounal headed units here, and *saving*, *going*, and *cooked* as gerundial and participial adjectives used as heads in adjectival headed units—somewhat as *crazy* is used in *boy crazy*.

CHAPTER V

VOICE AND ASPECT

Complexity of the grammar of English verbs.—The syntactic function characteristically performed by verbs is that of predicator. Within phrasal predicators (such as *is playing*) individual verb forms function as modifiers and heads. Verbs often function as clause markers, notably in imperatives, verbids, and many interrogatives. Verbs can of course be used as coordinates within multiple predicators.

> We washed and dried the dishes.
> I tried and tried to warn him.

They can constitute one-word subordinate clauses and so perform another syntactic function along with that of predicator.

> We have work to *do*.
> I can't look at Jim without *laughing*.
> The time *given* was insufficient.

Here *do* and *laughing* are predicators and objects of prepositions as well, and *given* is a contained modifier within the main subject as well as the predicator in a one-word gerundial clause. Truly exceptional uses of verb forms are of very few types. Especially in informal styles, upside-down construction sometimes puts verb forms in objects of prepositions within headed-unit predicators.

> It all but *ruined* him.
> I kind of *like* it.

Occasionally what seem to require classification as verb forms are used in purely nounal and adjectival functions.

> They're in the *know*.
> As a *would-be* scholar he's pathetic.

As the heart of the predications in which they occur, verbs indicate by their forms a variety of circumstances affecting these predications. Verbs have far more forms than words of other parts of speech have. They are inflected in various ways, as pairs such as the following indicate.

play, plays	go, went
sing, sang	play, will play
think, thought	play, is playing

Inflectional endings are added, parts of basic forms are replaced, forms that originally belonged to other verbs are (for *be* and *go*) brought into the paradigms, and auxiliaries are employed. In regular verbs such as *play* inflection is by the addition of the endings *s*, *ing*, and *ed* and the auxiliaries *do*, *will* (and in formal styles *shall*), *have*, and *be*. In such a form of *play* as *would have been playing* several devices of inflection have been employed together.

We will need, then, to note the inflectional patterns that are followed and their relation to meaning. Inflection is for voice, aspect, mode, tense, expansion (with *do*), and person and number.

The two voices.—For almost all verbs two sets of voice forms exist side by side: a common-voice set, often called active, and a passive-voice set. Passive-voice forms are phrasal. They have at least two components: (1) a form of the verb *be*, used as auxiliary; and (2) the participle of the verb whose passive is formed, used as head. The participial head is invariable: all indications of aspect, mode, tense, expansion, and person and number are carried by the auxiliary (as in *is played*) or auxiliaries (as in *would have been played*). The use of a passive form indicates that the verb's normal direction of predication is reversed: that is, that the subject is what in the basic common-voice pattern would be a complement or the object of a preposition in a prepositional unit used as a complement or (exceptionally) as an adjunct.

Common-voice verb forms with reversed direction of predication.—The common-voice forms of some verbs are themselves usable with opposite directions of predication. This is notably true of verbs whose common-voice forms can take both active responsible subjects and neutral subjects, the latter usable also as complements when the same verbs have active responsible subjects.

They *ring* the bells at six.
The bells *ring* at six.
Something *has changed* Mary greatly.
Mary *has changed* greatly.
I'*m wearing* my shoes out.
My shoes *are wearing* out.
A sailor *opened* the door and came in.
The door *opened* and a sailor came in.
George *waked* us up when he left.
We *waked* up when George left.
John dropped the candy dish and *broke* it.
John dropped the candy dish and it *broke*.
We *didn't digest* the supper very well.
The supper *didn't digest* very well.
We *smelled* the flowers.
The flowers *smelled* good.

In the second sentence in each of these pairs what is predicated is seen as an event or a state of affairs rather than as an action, and the matter of responsibility is ignored. In *the bells ring at six* there is no thought of people or mechanisms responsible for the ringing: all that is said is that a ringing of bells takes place. In *the door opened and a sailor came in* the opening of the door is told of (in the first main clause) without reference to the sailor who is opening it but is not seen at first. In *John dropped the candy dish and it broke* there is no fixing of responsibility for the breaking, though responsibility for the dropping is assigned. The subjects in sentences such as these are comparable to the subjects in such sentences as *my grades have gone down* and *his wife died last year*. Events are predicated, not actions: subjects are thought of not as responsible but as merely involved.

In some pairs with opposite directions of predication, both subjects seem to be active and responsible.

> The Democrats ran Roosevelt again in 1944.
> Roosevelt ran again in 1944.

In modern English when reflexive complements are expressed or can readily be expressed, the subject is normally an active responsible one.

She tires herself out talking on the telephone.
Mr. Dobie's books sell themselves.

We kept poking George in the side, and finally he turned over.
Jack shaves twice a day.

But in *we enjoyed ourselves* apparently an event rather than an action is spoken of, as in *we had a good time*.

The ability of common-voice forms to take either active responsible subjects or neutral subjects, with reversed direction of predication, belongs to a limited (though considerable) number of verbs. Thus *see* and *hear* are not reversible but *smell* is, so that *the baby sees, hears, smells* becomes regrettably ambiguous when *smell* is reached. Though it is usual to say *the water is boiling* as well as *Judy is boiling the water*, it is not usual to say, for example, *the floor is sweeping* or *a house is building*. It would perhaps be difficult to visualize the sweeping of floors and the building of houses without some notice of sweepers and builders also. There are limitations also on the extent to which some verbs that take either active responsible subjects or neutral subjects can take the latter. Though it is possible to say *the water for our tea is boiling*, it is not possible, with the same freedom, to say *water for tea boils every afternoon*. Here visualization of the total process of boiling, as opposed to a mere central segment of the process, is likely to require notice of a responsible person.

The common-voice forms of *be* are reversible when *be* is a true equational verb.

> The worst thing is the lights.
> The lights are the worst thing.

Pairs of etymologically related verbs exist in which an essential distinction lies in opposite directions of predication. This is true for *lay* and *lie*, *raise* and *rise*, *set* (and *seat*) and *sit*, and *fell* and *fall*. Such pairs give trouble: *lay* and *lie*, in particular, are constantly confused, with *lay* tending to take over the functions of *lie*. Where opposite directions of predication are expressed by etymologically unrelated verbs, the situation is better.

> Flattery pleases us all.
> We all like flattery.

Implications in use of passive forms.—The use of passive-voice forms ordinarily indicates an awareness that the basic direction of predication has been reversed, and a feeling that responsibility for what is predicated is assignable to someone or something distinct from the subject. The subject is marked unmistakably as a passive subject. A comparison of the following sentences is instructive.

> The chairman *began* the meeting promptly.
> The meeting *began* promptly.
> The meeting *was begun* promptly.

In the second sentence there is no hint of an awareness of an active agent, apart from the meeting itself, responsible for the meeting's beginning. In the third sentence there is such an awareness. In the third sentence it is quite possible to add a direct notice of the responsible agent: *by someone I didn't recognize*, for example. There is in fact a kind of syntactic reduction in the third sentence as long as no notice of the responsible agent is included, and such units as *by someone I didn't recognize* are best regarded as complements.

Passive-voice predicators do occur sometimes, though quite exceptionally, without any hint of responsible agents apart from the subjects.

> One boy fell out of a canoe and *was drowned.*
> Lincoln *was born* in Kentucky.

For most verbs reversal of the basic direction of predication normally necessitates use of passive-voice forms.

> The neighbors disturb us every night.
> We're disturbed every night.
> They rob us whenever we buy there.
> We're robbed whenever we buy there.

Yet, though it is hardly possible to make *we disturb every night* approach *we are disturbed every night* in meaning, it is quite possible to make *we disturb easily* roughly equivalent to *we are disturbed easily.*

The subjects of passive verb forms.—The subjects of passive verb forms are most often what would be nounal first complements if the basic direction of predication of the verbs were not reversed.

> The bells *are rung* every morning at six.
> The door *was opened* by a sailor.

The candy dish *has been broken.*
Mr. Dobie's books *are sold* everywhere.
He'*ll* always *be dominated* by his wife.
We *were called* idlers.
Such things *aren't* ever *lived* down.
He *was heard* to object.
We *were forced* to economize.
You'*ll be picked* up at seven.
He *is regarded* as undiplomatic.

Quite often the subjects are what would be objects of prepositions in adverbial first complements if the basic direction of predication of the verbs were not reversed.

You'*re being imposed* on.
The objectives *have* never *been agreed* on.
She likes to *be looked* at.
The house *has been lived* in.
The box *has been broken* into.
The funds *were accounted* for carefully.
You'*ll be called* on for help.
A doctor *had been sent* for.
The box *had been run* over by a car.

Sometimes the subjects of passive verb forms are what would be second complements if the basic direction of predication of the verbs were not reversed.

We *weren't given* enough time.
She *was promised* improved facilities.
Students who request them *will be mailed* permits.

The construction is exceptional, and when it occurs it is usually where the second complement of the common-voice sentence could precede the first complement, without a preposition. Occasionally what would have to be objects of prepositions in adverbial second complements if the basic direction of predication of the verbs were not reversed become subjects of passive verb forms.

Every detail *will be taken* care of.
He'*s been made* fun of too much.
The pictures *have been done* away with.
He *is looked* up to by everyone.

Again the construction is exceptional; usually it is not possible.
Occasionally what would be objects of prepositions in adjuncts if

the basic direction of predication of the verbs were not reversed become subjects of passive verb forms.

> The bed *has been slept* in.
> The baby *is* always *being cooed* over by aunts and grand-mothers.
> On the way home we *were rained* on.

Here again the construction is very exceptional and is ordinarily not usable. The use of passive verb forms with subjects that have been shifted to them from subordinate clauses to which they more logically belong has been mentioned elsewhere.

> The preparations *were thought* adequate.
> It *was thought* that the preparations were adequate.
> Several congressmen *are said* to be involved.
> It *is said* that several congressmen are involved.

Analysis must accept what it finds, and what it finds as subjects of passive verbs can be very strange from the point of view of Indo-European grammar of more conservative types. Generally nothing is thrown away in the passive, except that the active subject is likely to be implied rather than stated. Thus in *the pictures have been done away with* the passive verb form has both *away* and *with* as complements, though the object of *with* in the unreversed equivalent *they've done away with the pictures* has become the subject. Nothing is really added in the passive either. For this reason *it is danced here* is not possible as a reversal of *people dance here*, though it is quite possible as a reversal of *people dance it here*, where *it* represents the name of some particular dance.

Usefulness of the passive.—Passive-voice forms are bulkier than common-voice forms, and where there is no real reason to prefer passives common-voice forms are generally preferable. But passive forms are often quite effective. Sometimes what would be the subject of a common-voice form seems unimportant or is only vaguely identifiable.

> The old house *has been torn* down.
> We've *been locked* out again.
> The figure *is said* to represent the rain god.

Sometimes what would be the subject of a common-voice form is important, and is included in the clause, but for valid rhetorical reasons seems better as complement of agency than as subject.

> The college *was founded* by two frontier preachers.
> He*'ll* always *be dominated* by his wife.

When the passive is an infinitive or a gerundial, sometimes its use eliminates awkward subject constructions.

> > Everyone likes to *be liked*.
> > We resented *being treated* like that.
> > We got out without *being seen*.

In impersonal written styles the passive often serves as a way of keeping the writer out of sight.

> The use of shifted subjects *has been mentioned* elsewhere.

Some verbs, however, have no passive forms. *Be* and *seem* have none, nor do the defectives *can, may, must, ought, shall, should,* and *will. Happen* and *occur* have none: it is hardly possible to say, for example, *I've been happened to by some very inconvenient things lately. Cost* has no passive: *a lot of money is cost by his wife's clothes* is hardly allowable. *Belong* seems to have no passive. The list could be extended. Other verbs are not reversed in particular turns of meaning. Thus *have* has no passive when it is statal, as in *she has red hair. Let* cannot be reversed in *they let us continue,* though *we were allowed to continue* is entirely acceptable, and *we were let in,* without an infinitive after *let,* is also acceptable. On the other hand, though *she's been taken sick* occurs *something has taken her sick* does not.

Direction of predication in infinitives, gerundials, and participles.—In the infinitival mode, common-voice forms without expressed subjects frequently occur where passives might be expected. The direction of predication the common-voice verb would have in other modes is maintained, and the unstated subject is likely to be either very general (*people* or *someone*) or something that the situation suggests.

> > There isn't much to *say*.
> > There are larvae to *feed* and eggs to *tend*.
> > The bread is too hot to *eat*.
> > The reason is not far to *seek*.

> This is to *chop* with.
> Of course he's to *blame.*

There is no need to regard the italicized verb forms as passive in force. *There isn't much to say* is equivalent to *there isn't much that I* (or *a person*) *can say. Of course he's to blame* is equivalent to *of course he faces people's blaming him: is to* is here semantically close to *faces*, as *is toward* would be.

In the gerundial mode, common-voice forms without expressed subjects sometimes occur under similar conditions.

> The situation needs *looking* into.
> The suggestion is worth *thinking* about.

The situation needs looking into is comparable to *the situation requires that someone look into it.* When gerundials become nouns and adjectives, however, they very often do show reversal of the basic directions of predication of the verbs to which they are related. Thus *earnings* and *savings* have a kind of passive force, and so does *clipping* in *a newspaper clipping. Lacking* and *missing* seem to have passive force in sentences like *my best tie is missing.*

Participles are a special case. They are most conveniently listed among common-voice past forms, since for regular verbs and many irregular verbs they are identical with the common-mode and subjunctive-mode common-voice past. Used with auxiliary *be*, or with auxiliary *be* implied, participles have passive force.

> The cameras that are now *made* in Japan are among the world's best.
> *Seen* from the plane, the islands are very beautiful.

English participles are ordinarily not used as *returned* and *climbed* are used in *returned to his country, Froebel started kindergartens* and *this is a picture of my little brother climbed up a tree.* But there is nothing passive about participles in modern English when they are used with auxiliary *have.*

> He has *finished* the job.
> He would have *become* more irritable if we had kept on.

And participial adjectives are often clearly not passive.

> an *escaped* prisoner   he's a well-*read* man
> a *grown* person   he's *given* to boasting

a *decayed* tooth   we're *paid* up now
a *dissipated* fellow   she feels *run* down

Constructions that resemble passives.—Combinations of *be*
and participial-adjective complements are identical with passives
in form.

John's copy *is bound* in leather.
The old Mormon houses *are* very solidly *built*.
Apparently the lock *is broken*.
Are you *married?*

But in true phrasal passives the auxiliaries set the time for actions
whose semantic centers are the head-word participles. The auxiliaries in the four sentences given are all present, but there is no
present action: rather there is a present state of affairs consequent
upon earlier actions. *John's copy is bound in leather* is not a reversal of *the publisher binds John's copy in leather*. In *John's copy
is bound in leather* the predicator is *is*, not *is bound*, and the complement is *bound in leather*. *Apparently the lock has been broken* is
a reversal of *apparently someone has broken the lock:* the predicator
is the passive verb form *has been broken*. The situation is not the
same in *apparently the lock is broken*, where the participial adjective
broken is a complement, not a part of the predicator, just as such
a nonparticipial adjective as *defective* would be.

The verb *get* is used in many combinations which resemble
passives to a greater or less extent. Often the resemblance is very
superficial indeed.

Jack *got* married last month.
Olds *got* elected without difficulty.
We *got* rid of him finally.
He finally *got* dressed and went out.
We *got* started at noon.

There is no reversal of common-voice nucleuses in these sentences.
Jack got married last month is not a reversal of *someone married
Jack last month;* rather, *married* is the complement of copulative
got just as *sick* or *rich* might be. *We got started at noon* is structurally
parallel to *we got ready at noon*. *Get* seems closer to the true passive
auxiliary *be* in sentences such as the following.

Jack *got* arrested for speeding yesterday.
My trousers *got* torn.
I *get* blamed for everything.
We *got* soaked on the way home.
She *gets* upset easily.
Caroline *gets* teased by the other children.

Even in sentences like these, however, *get* is best regarded as a full predicator expressing arrival or attainment, whether purposed or not, much as it does in *Jack got in trouble, my trousers got dirty*, and similar sentences. In *Caroline gets teased by the other children*, then, the complement is the headed unit *teased by the other children*, in which *teased* is the head. Phrasings employing *get* as the predicator are often used in preference to passives because true passives would not be clearly distinguishable from combinations of full-predicator *be* and participial-adjective complements. Thus *he was married a year ago* can mean either (1) someone authorized to perform the ceremony did so a year ago, or (2) he was in possession of a wife a year ago, having gone through the ceremony before that time. *He got married a year ago* is unambiguous: it can mean only that he arrived at the married state a year ago.

The two aspects.—For almost all verbs except the defectives *can, may, must, ought, shall, should*, and *will*, two sets of aspectual forms exist side by side: a common-aspect set and a progressive set. Progressive-aspect forms are always phrasal. They always have at least two components: (1) a form of the verb *be*, used as auxiliary; and (2) a one-word gerundial following this auxiliary. When a progressive is also passive, the one-word gerundial is *being*, which serves as the auxiliary for the passive and is followed by the participle of the verb whose progressive passive is being formed, as in *was being cheated*. Unless the phrasal progressive form is passive, the gerundial is head for the whole progressive form, and indicates the verb whose progressive is being formed, as in *has been cheating*. Mode, tense, and person and number are indicated by what precedes the gerundial in the phrasal form.

The use of common-aspect forms.—For most verbs the use of a common-aspect form suggests that the predication is viewed with perspective. The point of view is not always external, but it often is. Common-aspect forms are normal in narrative, in which sequences of actions or events are seen from outside, not while they are in process.

> Every morning George *takes* the children to school, *parks* his car about six blocks from his office, *walks* to a restaurant near his office, *drinks* two cups of coffee and *reads* his newspaper, and then finally *gets* to work.
>
> In the third act the robots *destroy* their masters and *assume* control.
>
> In February my parents *will come* down by plane. They*'ll stay* a month or so, and we*'ll take* them around the island. Then they*'ll take* the boat to New Orleans.
>
> When the Spaniards *came* to the islands, they *found* a considerable Indian population; but new diseases and bad treatment *eliminated* the Indians, and Negro slaves *were brought* in.

Common-aspect forms are similarly normal wherever actions or events are spoken of as wholes, not as in process either at the time of speaking or writing or at any other time taken as a temporary center.

> Mary *learns* new tunes with no effort at all.
> Our dog *has bitten* the mailman twice since September.
> He*'s picked* up some French somewhere.
> Martin *has had* a great deal of trouble with his teeth.
> What *have* you *told* her?
> People *have been shot* for less.
> Rosemary *will fly* back to Puerto Rico after Christmas.
> Phelps *got* back yesterday.
> Roosevelt *made* the Democratic Party what it is.

In uses of both these types, except in the present tense, the verb forms are not affected by considerations either of duration or of repetition or the lack of repetition.

Common-aspect forms are sometimes used for special effects in telling of actions or events in process at the time of writing or speaking, where progressives would seem normal. This occurs in various situations where the external point of view of spectators at a play is approached. Assertive-clause word order sometimes helps to give the effect of something special.

> Here they *come!*

In you *go!*
He doesn't answer.

Sometimes a flavor of objectivity and detachment is gained through the use of common-aspect forms in requests, warnings, promises, and other delicate communications actually in process of formulation and directed at the reader or hearer. Here the verbs are often "performatives" whose use in itself sometimes is a performance of the action they name.

We *ask* that you return these forms promptly.
I *warn* you that diplomacy is needed.
We *raise* this question reluctantly.
I *promise* that this will not happen again.
I *congratulate* you on your promotion.
I *give* up.
I *pass.*
I *inclose* a check for the amount due.

Progressive forms are of course usable also in these examples. But it is noteworthy that main imperatives rarely employ progressive forms.

Common-aspect forms are ordinarily used when verbs express what can best be thought of as reflexes—more or less automatic responses, whether sensory, emotional, or intellectual. An explicitly internal view is normally not taken when such predicators are used.

I *hear* you.
She *sees* you.
I *don't believe* that.
I *remember* that face.
I *forget* your address.
I *think* so.
She's dreaming and *doesn't know* what's happening.
I *wonder* what time it is.
It *occurs* to me that I may have misunderstood you.
It *surprises* me that you should say that.
That *suits* me.

Common-aspect forms are used in predications which are not thought of as confined within relatively narrow time limits. Verbs expressing actions and events then have repetitive force; verbs expressing states of affairs simply imply relatively great continuance.

1. The bells *ring* at six.
   Mary *talks* too fast.
   William *walks* to school.
   We *don't eat* much meat.
   Jack *smokes* too much.
2. Mary's parents *live* across the river in West Virginia.
   A church *stands* at the corner.
   Judy *looks* like her mother.
   Williamson *is* very inconsiderate.
   My father chose a spot that *overlooked* the river.

Ownership and "possession" of varied types are usually stated in nonprogressive forms even when explicitly temporary.

> The car *belongs* to me this week.
> Sarah *has* a headache this afternoon.

Sarah is having a headache this afternoon might suggest that Sarah was making a point of the headache.

The use of progressive-aspect forms.—Progressive-aspect forms are normal where predications tell of actions, events, or states of affairs that are in process at the time of writing or speaking and are thought of as begun but not ended, with beginnings and/or ends felt as relatively close to the time of writing or speaking.

Mary's *talking* too fast.
William had an early breakfast and *is* now *walking* to school.
Mary's parents *are living* across the river in West Virginia.
A policeman *is standing* at the corner.
Judy's *looking* well, for a person just out of the hospital.
Williamson *is being* very inconsiderate.
I'm *listening* to you.
She's *watching* you.
She's *seeing* the sights.
I'm *thinking* about what you said.
Jack *is having* a wonderful time in England.
Johnny's *dropping* his plate.
Are your parents *living?*

Sometimes what is in process is a series of actions or events, so that the progressive forms have repetitive force.

William *is walking* to school this semester.
We *aren't eating* much meat nowadays.
Jack *is smoking* too much.
Is the paper *coming?*

Spoken while Mary was talking, *Mary's talking too fast* would imply nothing about Mary's habit. *Mary's parents are living across the river in West Virginia* implies that their residence there is regarded as temporary, or began recently. *Williamson is being very inconsiderate* views Williamson's lack of considerateness as a relatively brief phenomenon; *Williamson is very inconsiderate* views his lack of considerateness as a rather permanent quality. *I'm thinking about what you said* differs from *I think so* in that there is an element of deliberateness about the thinking where progressive forms are used: thought is here a kind of work, with fairly well-defined beginning and end, not merely a quick darting of opinion rising instantaneously to the surface when something calls it into play. *I'm listening to you* differs similarly from *I hear you:* listening is conscious and deliberate, but hearing, in this sense, is a reflex. In *Johnny's dropping his plate* what is going on is apparently preliminary to the actual fall of the plate, and the plate may never fall. In *are your parents living?* the progressive form is a reminder of the shortness of life. *Do your parents live?* is not likely, though *do your parents live here?* is quite common because in this sentence "living" is simply a matter of residence and for residence feelings of relative permanence are easily achieved. In *William is walking to school this semester* what is felt as in process at the time of speaking is not a particular walk to school but the semester-long series of walks. No single walk need be in process. The reason for the choice of the progressive here is the feeling that the series of walks is of relatively short duration, not a long-time, relatively permanent habit.

Progressive-aspect forms are normal where predications tell of actions, events, or states of affairs in process, begun but not ended, at the time of other occurrences which at the moment are more prominent in the speaker or writer's attention. Here the progressive marks a kind of overlapping simultaneousness, at the same time indicating an awareness of relatively near beginning and/or end.

Henry *is leaving* for work when Louise gets home.

The wife of the dead man hides near the house, and the mother runs for the neighbors, who *are working* in their garden.

If I *were being waited* on, I wouldn't be so unhappy.

Jack always knows what he'*s doing.*

When you arrive, I'*ll be taking* examinations.

John went to the drugstore at ten. Two of his best friends *were having* coffee, and naturally he joined them.

Sometimes what has been begun is never ended.

Sarah *was drowning* when the boys got to her, but they saved her.

Sometimes what is in process is a series of actions or events, so that the progressive forms again have repetitive force.

When I first came to know Robertson, he *was spending* his summers in Mexico City.

Usually *Henry leaves for work when Louise gets home* views the departure and the arrival as alike members of a narrative sequence: first Louise gets home, then (very soon) Henry leaves. When *is leaving* is used instead of *leaves*, sequence is replaced by overlapping simultaneousness: the departure has begun, at least in the marginal phase of preparation, before the arrival takes place; but the departure has not been completed. A kind of linguistic economy sometimes results in the use of the simpler common-aspect forms in clauses subordinated by *while* and *as*, where progressives might seem reasonable.

While you *enjoy* the boat trip, I'll take my examinations.

The crowd grew restless as the moment *approached.*

Sometimes progressives are concerned simply with occurrences in progress—begun but not ended—at some time in the past.

George was taking a Greek course in October.

Progressive-aspect forms in present-perfect and present-future tenses sometimes emphasize closeness to the moment of writing or speaking, and in past-perfect and past-future tenses closeness to a past time that is central in the attention at the moment. The point of view is internal, as with all progressives.

Martin*'s been having* a great deal of trouble with his teeth.
Mary*'s been crying.*
Mrs. Harris *has been dying* for days and cannot possibly live
  much longer.
He*'s been learning* some French somewhere.
I*'ve been writing* a letter home.
I*'ll be seeing* you.
I*'ll be retiring* in June.
The children *had been pestering* me outrageously.
I knew I*'d be seeing* him.

Martin's had a great deal of trouble with his teeth leaves the trouble
undated: it may have been at any time in Martin's life. *I've written
a letter home,* on the other hand, almost certainly speaks of a recent
action—a whole action, resulting in a finished letter. *I've been
writing a letter home* stresses recentness a little more and does not
imply that the letter has been finished. Perhaps the letter has been
finished, perhaps it has not: all that is said is that the speaker or
writer has very recently been engaged in writing it.

Progressive-aspect forms sometimes merely suggest greater emotional realization than simple-aspect forms. The hearer or reader
is asked to stop for a moment at a point between the beginning and
the end of the action, event, or state of affairs predicated, or within
a series of actions, events, or states of affairs.

She asked whether he was hurt, and he replied that he was.
  A moment later he *was dying.*
He*'s* constantly *seeing* things that aren't there.
*H*aven't you *been buying* yourself another car?
I suppose I*'ll* still *be worrying* about grammar when I'm super-
  annuated.
Sally got the job in June, and by August she *was lunching* with
  the boss pretty regularly.
He *was* always *wanting* to be consulted.
In 1932 Hitler came to power. From 1932 to 1939 Germany
  was preparing for war. In 1939 she struck.
I *had been waiting* half an hour when she arrived.

They haven't been seeing each other this fall suggests a responsible
subject, and a broken relationship, much more clearly than *they
haven't seen each other this fall* would.

Aspectual force of gerundials.—In phrasal progressive forms
such as *is playing, will be ending, are being made,* and *has been work-*

ing the gerundial forms—head words except in progressive passives—obviously contribute heavily to the progressive force. Sometimes, however, gerundials are not progressive in force at all.

My father chose a spot *overlooking* the river.
Having come prepared to deal with savages, Cortez sent Moctezuma a cap and some toys and necklaces.
After *taking* the test, Mary decided there was hope for her.

Constructions that resemble progressives.—As has been said, the progressive involves an awareness of beginnings and/or ends. But verbs which express beginning, continuance, or end explicitly are another matter, and should not be regarded as auxiliaries of aspect. This is true of such verbs as *begin, start, come (to)*, *get (to), take (to), keep, go (on), used (to), stop,* and *quit.*

Susan *began* writing letters at six.
Mattie *came* to play the role Zeena had played.
Ben *has taken* to wearing ties only an artist can wear.
I *kept* saying I was sorry.
I *went* on eating my lunch.
We *used* to walk long distances.
Most men *have quit* carrying pocket watches.

The italicized verb forms should be regarded as the main predicators in these sentences. Some of them have gerundial-clause complements, others have prepositional complements in which *to* is the preposition and what follows is the infinitival-clause object of *to.*

CHAPTER VI

MODE

The five modes.—Mode has to do in part with distinctions between the actual and the hypothetical (and sometimes the merely doubtful) and in part simply with distinctions between clause patterns. It seems necessary to recognize five modes: the common (or indicative), the subjunctive, the infinitival, the gerundial, and the participial. It seems best not to recognize any modal auxiliaries at all. The modes of modern English are distinguished primarily by different practices with respect to (1) the use of tense forms and (2) the relative dispensability of expressed subjects. Differences in verb forms are relatively slight. The basic verb form *listen* requires three classifications with respect to mode in the following sentences.

> Usually you *listen* to the music.
> *Listen* to the music!
> You like to *listen* to the music, don't you?

And the past form *listened* requires three classifications with respect to mode in the following sentences.

You *listened* to the music yesterday.
Rosemary would like the music if she *listened* to it.
Music *listened* to in times of weariness and frustration has
    something of the therapeutic value of religion or of love.

Whatever may be true of more highly inflected languages, in modern English modal distinctions, like part-of-speech distinctions, are primarily matters of syntax, not of differences in inflection.

The common mode.—The common mode is the normal main-clause mode for predications formulated as actualities. Except where predications are formulated hypothetically, it is the mode normally used in main-clause expressions of fact or opinion and in questions. It dominates most subordinate-clause patterns as well, but it is of course not usable in verbid clauses.

The common mode is the mode of actuality, but it is used for fiction as well as for what is spoken of as fact. Moreover actuality has its margins in which colorings of uncertainty and doubt appear and yet do not cause the kind of rejection implicit in hypothetical predication. Noncommittal conditional sentences almost always employ common-mode verb forms, whether (1) from the present set of tenses or (2) from the past set.

1. If he *isn't* in his office, he*'s* on his way there.
   The poor boy *deserves* sympathy if he*'s* in love with Janet.
   If I*'ve* ever *met* him, I*'ve forgotten* about it.
   Nothing *will happen* unless we *get* busy.
   If I said the wrong thing, we*'ll hear* about it.
2. If Joe *was* angry, he *concealed* his feelings.
   If I*'d* ever *met* him, I*'d forgotten* about it.
   If I *said* the wrong thing, we'll hear about it.

Other nonfactual uses of common-mode forms are italicized in the following sentences.

1. I doubt that he *has* enough experience.
   We're hoping you*'ll be* there.
   Suppose we*'re* late.
   We're looking for a stenographer who *has* a thorough mastery of English, Spanish, and Portuguese.
   Anyone who *learns* to control hurricanes will deserve an island or two as a reward.
   Who's silly enough to say things *will be* better next year?
2. I doubted that Jack *knew* the facts.
   I had heard an absurd rumor that Hugh *was remarrying*.
   Arsat's brother had asked him to wait until the woman *was* dead, but she did not die.
   There wasn't anyone in the little town that *had seen* more of the world.

Doubt finds expression, in sentences such as have been given, in such words as *if* and *doubt*, or simply in context—not in modal verb forms.

Hypothetical subjunctives.—In modern English the subjunctive is employed, first of all, to mark predications as formulated not in the stream of actual occurrences but in a stream of imagined occurrences which can be thought of as flowing phantom-like along-side it. When the time is past or narrowly present, hypothesis rejects all idea of actualization: what is spoken of is regarded as unreal. When the time idea is future, hypothesis generally involves provisional rejection rather than complete, since in human affairs complete accuracy about the future is usually out of the question. Present time and future time are often not clearly separated in the stream of the hypothetical.

The verb forms used as hypothetical subjunctives are forms belonging to the four past tenses—past, past perfect, past future, and past future perfect—never forms belonging to the four corresponding present tenses. "Past" forms are thus used not for what has already been passed, and lies behind, in the stream of the actual, but for what is passed over to one side (as a building on the other side of the street is passed) in the parallel stream of the hypothetical. At most points hypothetical-subjunctive forms are identical with common-mode forms; but they are sharply distinguished from common-mode forms by their use of the four past tenses with altered time values. The following pairs show the distinction.

Virginia *knows* the Dunhams well. I wish you *knew* them.
Virginia *knew* the Feders when they were students. I wish you
    had known them then.

In the first pair the subjunctive past *knew* has the time value of the common-mode present *know*. In the second pair the subjunctive past perfect *had known* has the time value of the common-mode past *knew*.

Main-clause uses of hypothetical-subjunctive predicators are illustrated in the following sentences.

Mary *would be* a good teacher.
It *would be* hard to find a worse husband than Hugh.
Would Jack *mind* moving?
Phyllis *had* better see a psychiatrist.
Hugh *would*n't *have enjoyed* the party.
Olga *would have known* about that.

Mary is not a teacher, and is not planning to be one. No one is trying to find a worse husband than Hugh, or has any intention of trying: if *is* or *will be* were substituted for *would be*, the search would be brought into the stream of actuality; but here it is wholly imaginary. In *would Jack mind moving?* Jack is not moving, and so is not in a situation to mind moving or not mind it. In *Hugh wouldn't have enjoyed the party* and in *Olga would have known about that* the time is past. Hugh did not attend the party; Olga's knowledge was nonexistent for all practical purposes, since it did not come into play.

Hypothetical subjunctives are of course not confined to main clauses. Subordinate clauses which are parts of larger hypothetical frameworks employ them.

What would Jane be doing if she *were* here now?
Not many stores would keep a salesman who *was* as irritable as that.
Hugh would be healthy enough if he *ate* sensibly.
If Napoleon *had unified* Europe, the history of the last century would have been very different.

In the second sentence both predications are formulated hypothetically, but it is entirely possible that an actual salesman who is "as irritable as that" is being kept in mind. The time is present in the first two sentences, vaguely present or future in the third, and past in the fourth. *Hugh will be healthy enough if he eats sensibly* is a noncommittal conditional sentence, formulated in the stream of actuality though obviously colored by doubt. *Hugh would be healthy enough if he ate sensibly* is a rejected conditional sentence, formulated in the stream of hypothesis though the rejection is provisional and leaves room for a possibility of reformation on Hugh's part.

Sometimes hypothetical predications or even sets of predications occur within larger clauses formulated in the stream of actuality rather than in that of hypothesis.

She acts as if she *were* his wife.
The room he has now is better than anything he *would find* if he *looked* for another.
San Francisco is a city you *would enjoy* living in.

Conversely, clauses which are predicated hypothetically sometimes have within them smaller clauses which are predicated as actualities.

It would be hard for Fred to accept the climate of Maine, now
that he *has lived* in the tropics so long.

A new house would probably not be as well constructed as this
one *is*.

My grandmother wouldn't have liked the way people *spend*
Sundays now.

I'd say Julia *is* a genius.

Sometimes it is even possible to make mixed noncommittal-rejected conditional sentences, though ordinarily such mixtures are
not acceptable.

If you *can* tell me what books are needed, I'*d appreciate* your
doing so.

If I *buy* the gas, *would* you *furnish* the food?

If you *would like* to meet him, we'*ll invite* him to the house.

Hypothetical subjunctives are normal in subordinate-declarative clauses used as complements of the verb *wish*.

We wish we *were* back in the islands.

I wish Hugh *had apologized*.

For a long time we've wished we *had* two cars.

Declarative clauses completing *wish* express what is felt as unreal
or impossible. *We wish we were back in the islands* is very close to
we regret that we're not living in the islands in meaning. In *I wish
Hugh had apologized* it is implied that he has not; in *I hope
Hugh has apologized* there is no such implication. Hypothetical
subjunctives are normal in declarative clauses after *it's time*.

It's time I *did* some work.

It's time he *was getting* married.

Here the hypothetical subjunctives of the subordinate clauses can
express not only what is felt as highly improbable but also what
is an actuality but a surprising actuality, pulled out of the jaws
of the unreality to which it has seemed to belong. Subordinate
clauses used as sentences to express wishes which amount to expressions of regret employ hypothetical subjunctive forms also.

Oh, that we *had known* what was coming!

If only he *knew* the truth!

Hypothetical subjunctives are often used as softened equivalents

of common-mode forms. In this use the rejection of actualization
is not genuine.

> I'*d think* so.
> That *would seem* reasonable.
> When *would* the Dean *be* likely to come in?
> *Would* you *happen* to have a map of the city?
> *Would* you please close the window?
> *Could* you tell me the time?
> Mary *might* like the picture.
> I'*d* rather you told the Dean yourself.
> We'*d* just as soon he *did*n't *know*.

What the hypothetical-subjunctive forms contribute here is an
effect of indirection and delicacy. By a kind of syntactic metaphor,
they transfer predications from the stream of the actual to which
they really belong to the remoter stream of the hypothetical.
Thus *Mary might like the picture* states the existence of the possibility hypothetically and so implies that there is less chance than
Mary may like the picture would imply. Common-mode forms often
seem too direct where opinions, requests, and similar sensitive
matters are in point. *I prefer that you tell the Dean yourself,* for
example, may seem too forthright in many situations. In informal
styles the indirectness which hypothetical-subjunctive forms can
contribute is sometimes used for emotional effects bordering on
sarcasm.

I *would*n't *know* about minor poets of the eighteenth century.

Coactual subjunctives.—The subjunctive is used not only in
predications formulated within the stream of the hypothetical or
unreal but also in predications formulated in marginal reaches of
the stream of the actual where there are colorings of uncertainty.
Subjunctives of this second type can be called coactual. The verb
forms employed are present forms or (rarely) present-perfect forms,
identical with common-mode forms for the same tenses except
that (1) they have no *s* ending in the third person singular and (2)
in the case of *be,* as full predicator or as auxiliary, the basic form is
employed throughout the present rather than the *are, am,* and
is of the common-mode present.

By far the commonest use of coactual subjunctives is the use as the predicators of imperative main clauses. Imperative main clauses are implicitly objects of desire or of twisted counterfeits of desire such as lie behind challenge; there is present a basic uncertainty with respect to actualization, though there is nothing approaching even provisional rejection of the possibility of actualization.

Be sure to bring the children.
Stay single till you're thirty, and you'll inevitably be a social lion.
Just *say* one more word and out you go!
Someone *say* something!
May the best man win!

The use of *may* as a subjunctive in indirect imperatives such as the last sentence is confined to archaic styles and more or less fixed phrasings.

The predicators of subordinate imperative clauses are also coactual subjunctives.

The Administration asks that no exceptions *be made*.
It is important that every member *come* prepared to discuss this problem.

In somewhat formal styles coactual subjunctives like those of subordinate imperative clauses in force occur in interrogative clauses subordinated by *lest*.

The visitors sat in silence lest they *be* guilty of offense.

In more or less formal styles coactual subjunctives occasionally occur in adjunct clauses of condition (and concession) of noncommittal type, where common-mode forms are usual. The predications made in these adjunct clauses are not in any sense objects of desire.

If the major subject *be* psychology, the student must select a first minor from the following list of subjects.
A liberal education is of value to anyone, whether he *be* a businessman, a farmer, or a teacher.
It is hard to compose out of many separate impressions, *aided* though they *be* by sketches and color notes, a new complete conception.

Infinitival, gerundial, and participial modes.—The infinitival and gerundial modes have required extended notice in connection with clause structure and for this reason require only very brief notice here. They provide varied patterns for subordinate-clause use and compete now with the common mode and now with the subjunctive.

1. I'm sorry to *have disturbed* you.
   I'm sorry I *disturbed* you.
   We urged her to *make* other arrangements.
   We urged that she *make* other arrangements.
2. After *climbing* the pyramid, we were ready for a little rest.
   After we *climbed* the pyramid, we were ready for a little rest.
   She always insists on Jack's *going* along.
   She always insists that Jack *go* along.

The infinitives of modern English have no genuinely distinctive forms: they are to be classified as infinitives for syntactic reasons only. Most verbs have six infinitives.

play	be playing	be played
have played	have been playing	have been played

Gerundials have the ending *ing* as their characteristic mark. Most verbs have five gerundial forms.

playing		being played
having played	having been playing	having been played

In each phrasal gerundial form the first word carries the ending *ing*. Infinitives and gerundials inflect for tense, aspect, and voice. Participles make no such distinctions. Most verbs have a single past form used in common, subjunctive, and participial modes. This is true, for example, of regular *play*, and of irregular *sell*, *send*, *cut* (which uses its basic form unchanged as a past), and *stick*. A few irregular verbs have participles distinct from common-mode and subjunctive pasts: *sink*, *steal*, *eat*, and *be* are examples.

Participles, basic-form infinitives, and one-word gerundials are all used as heads in phrasal verb forms: for example, in *is played*, *will play*, and *has been playing*. Other verb forms are not used in this way. Unlike infinitives and gerundials, participles do not function as predicators alone: that is, without an auxiliary expressed or implied. The defectives *can, may, must, ought, shall, should,* and *will* have no forms usable as infinitives, gerundials, or participles in standard American English.

One-word infinitival and gerundial forms often pass over to the part-of-speech category of the nouns, and one-word gerundial and participial forms to that of the adjectives. Phrasal infinitival and gerundial forms do not.

The problem of modal auxiliaries.—A category of modal auxiliaries is often set up for modern English, to include various verbs expressing ideas of possibility, constraint, and desire. The verbs most often regarded as modal auxiliaries are those which are normally followed by infinitives: *can, may, must,* and *should;* perhaps *shall* and *will,* in uses in which they are not regarded as simply auxiliaries of tense. *Ought* is sometimes added to the list in spite of the *to* which precedes following infinitives, as in *the work ought to be done by Thursday.* Sometimes such combinations as *had better* and *let's,* as in *the work had better be done by Thursday* and *let's give it all up,* are also regarded as modal auxiliaries, though obviously not on the basis of form. But we will have a neater analysis of contemporary English, as has been said, if we recognize no modal auxiliaries at all. We will then have to say of such a verb as *can* that it is a transitive whose complement must be infinitival, somewhat as we have to say of such a verb as *pride* that it is a transitive whose first complement must be reflexive. We will still need to give special notice to verbs expressing meanings of possibility, constraint, and volition.

Expression of possibility.—Among verbs expressing possibility of various types *can, may,* and *let* are most deserving of attention. *Can* is sometimes concerned with ability, of whatever type, thought of as belonging to the subject.

> Julia *can* translate that, I'm sure.
> I *can* stand that fellow only for a limited time.
> She was a woman who *could* weep becomingly.
> The trunk is so heavy I *can* hardly budge it.

Perhaps the most frequently expressed meaning of *can,* however, is really feasibility, or the absence of anything to prevent.

> I *can* go home next weekend.

You *can* spend the night with us.
I *can* only report that she labors heavily to add a little fun to a
   dreary comedy.
I *could* see Ixtaccihuatl from the plane.
Can I be of any help?
Florence interrupted before Julia *could* finish.
Snow *can* cover the ground for months here.
The building *can* be entered at either end.
Faulkner's stories *can* be compared with Poe's.

In negated clauses and in interrogatives *can* appears where *may*
would be likely, or almost certain, in the corresponding unnegated
declaratives.

> English *can't* be as hard as you think.
> He *can't* have left.
> These figures *can't* be right.
> Who *can* that be?
> *Can* we be mistaken?

In *he can't have left* the idea of possibility is present in time
(*it isn't possible*) and the idea of leaving is past (*that he has left*).
A negator used with *can* almost always negates *can*, not the following complement alone. *Can* is of course defective, with two tense
forms only and with the present form used only in the common
mode and the past form not used as a participle. Other modes of
expression often have to replace *can*.

You'*ll be able to* drive after a few more lessons.
I'*d had an opportunity to* spend some time in New York the
   preceding summer.

Ideas of ability and feasibility creep into various constructions
where they find no explicit expression. Thus *he speaks three languages* is equivalent in force to *he can speak three languages* and
there's no knowing what he'll do is equivalent to *what he'll do can't
be known*. Moreover the preposition *to* often comes to express
possibility such as *can* also expresses.

> He has a good home *to* go to.
> Shoes of this type are *to* be seen everywhere.

May, like *can*, is a full predicator expressing possibility of various
types. Most often it expresses a kind of possibility that involves

uncertainty on the part of the speaker or writer, much as the adverb *perhaps* does.

I *may* go home next weekend.
We *may* have been wrong about George.
You *might* not want to come back with me.
If the rain had been harder, it *might* have washed away the
    hurdles course.

In interrogative clauses after *any* and after *such*, the *may* of uncertainty expresses a shade of meaning also expressed by *happen to* and by *by chance*. The style is careful or formal.

We shall be glad to answer any questions that you *may* wish
    to ask.
The local representative in each city had to bear the responsibility for any serious errors that *might* occur.
The student was expected to see his advisor at such hours as
    might be posted.

The *may* of uncertainty is sometimes used in making admissions where there is really no uncertainty at all.

I *may* be a woman, but I have some rights.
Bad as the situation *may* be, there are reasons for restrained
    optimism.

Sometimes *may* expresses feasibility. It is used in this way chiefly (1) in more or less fixed phrasings and (2) in slightly archaic formal styles and in usage that is perhaps justly described as genteel.

1. I *may* as well give up.
   He decided he *might* as well clear out and have a stroll
       before catching the train home.
   I *might* have known you'd be dissatisfied.
   I've been calling since noon, I *might* add.
   Cost what it *may*, she'll have to have it.
   May the best man win!
2. The prescriptions of the reformers were gathered into
       textbooks and *may* still be found in the books we are
       now using.
   Inclosed is a postcard that you *may* use.
   The arm of the chair *may* be detached.
   We shall be careful to inform you of all developments, in
       order that there *may* be no misunderstandings.

After somewhat formal *in order that* it is usual to employ *may* or *shall*. *May* is sometimes used also in clauses that have the force of quite indirect request.

>Thursday you *might* read the next chapter.

Sometimes *may* expresses a kind of possibility that involves permission and direct recognition of authority.

>*May* I borrow your pen for a moment?
>*Might* we have a little air?
>I'll go along with you if I *may*.
>We asked the watchman whether we *might* take a walk through the premises.
>Husband and wife *may* file a joint return even though one of them had no income.

The *may* that recognizes authority has honorific force where authority is imputed to the person or people addressed. It is consequently a graceful form in such sentences as *I'll go along with you if I may*, where *if I may* is equivalent to *if you permit*. It cannot be described as graceful where it suggests open arrogation of authority (however rightly) by the speaker or writer, as in *you may have my copy until tomorrow*. *Can* is preferable in granting or denying permission, since it states the case simply in terms of feasibility, ignoring the superior status of the speaker or writer. Institutional granting of permission, in regulations and the like, is another matter: authoritative *may* is more satisfactory here, though *can* is satisfactory also. Sometimes *may* suggests vaguely located authority, as *it is permissible* would.

>We are concerned with what I *may* call the mechanics of flowers.

Can is usable in asking permission, though here *can* lacks the polite deference that *may* has.

>*Can* I open a window?
>*Could* I borrow your dictionary for a few minutes?

The hypothetical subjunctive *could* has the politeness of indirection here—a more delicate kind of politeness, perhaps, than that of the directly honorific *may*. Like all polite forms, the *may* of deference to authority can be used ironically.

May I ask whether you have any idea of paying me?

Permission is of course expressed in other ways also.

> Is it all right if I open a window?
> We're allowed to use dictionaries if we want to.

In interrogatives *may* is pretty well confined to permissive use. The question corresponding to *he may go home* will employ some such phrasing as *is there a possibility of his going home? Hadn't we might as well leave?* illustrates the nonstandard use of *had* with *might* in interrogatives. The *may* which recognizes uncertainty is not negated: in *you may not like it,* for example, there is no negating of *may.* Permissive *may* can be negated, as in *students may not keep cars at the College;* but *must* and *can* are both preferred where permission is denied. Where defective *may* cannot be used other locutions occur: *there is a chance, it is possible, it is permitted, we're allowed to,* etc.

Like *may* and *can, let* is best regarded always as a full predicator, never as an auxiliary. As the predicator in main-imperative clauses it has a remarkable range of uses. Where *let us* becomes a suggestion that the hearer or hearers unite in some action with the speaker (or the reader or readers with the writer), the use of *let* is honorific in origin. *Us* is the first complement, and an infinitival clause is the second.

> *Let* us pray.
> *Let* us assume that what we call human nature is a conglomeration of processes.

Though quite informal, the merged form *let's* always has this once-honorific force.

> *Let's* go to a movie.

The implication once was that control of the situation lies with the person or people addressed. *Let* is also used as the predicator of main-imperative clauses when the person or people addressed cannot be thought of as in any way able to influence the situations in point. Here too *let* is a full predicator with two complements.

> Our reasons for granting loans should be reasons of humanity. If instead they are reasons of power, *let* them at least be on the side of the popular movements all over the world.

If Henry doesn't like the school, *let* him go elsewhere.
Just *let* him try to get out of this!
Let the study of Latin be dropped from our schools, and the English of the next generation will reach a level unknown heretofore.
He doesn't look middle-aged, *let* alone old.

Expression of constraint.—A number of verbs expressing constraint of various types require attention. *Must*, like *can*, *may*, and *let*, is never a true auxiliary. *Must* expresses a degree of constraint that is felt as too strong to permit escape: necessity, in other words.

> I *must* do some studying tonight.
> We *must* be going.
> You *must*n't let things worry you.
> We *must* not forget the part religion has played.

Sometimes *must* expresses the compelling force of evidence which is felt as almost conclusive: this is the *must* of conviction, or probability—semantically not far from the *may* of uncertainty.

> That *must* be the new manager's wife.
> It *must* be almost twelve.
> George *must* not have been consulted.

Must is never negated: when *not* follows *must*, and even when it is merged with *must* in *mustn't*, what is negated is the complement of *must*, not *must* itself. *George must not have been consulted* is equivalent to *it seems clear that George wasn't consulted: not* goes with *have been consulted*, not with *must*. *Must* has only a single form. It is not liked in main interrogatives, so that, for example, the confirmational question for *you must be an engineer* is often *aren't you?*

Constraint felt as inescapable is also expressed by *have* with *to* and an infinitival completer of *to*. *Have* has the advantage of not being defective.

> We've *had* to put up with that for weeks.
> You'll *have* to be diplomatic with Harrison.
> Everything *had* to have his approval.
> You *don't have* to return the book.

Where there is negation of necessity—or near negation, or even questioning or doubt—*need* is often used, though *have* is usable also.

You *need*n't return the book.
He *need*n't have been so frank.
There *need* be only a few of these.
Need I add that nothing more was said?

Elsewhere *need* usually expresses not constraint, which is felt as pressure from outside, but simple lack or deficiency, as in *we need more information* and in *we need to get a little more information*. In informal styles the strongest way of expressing constraint is *have got* followed by *to* and an infinitival completer of *to*.

I'*ve got* to do some studying tonight.
We'*ve got* to get started.

But *have got to* expresses compulsion only in a single tense, and it is commonly avoided in main interrogatives and with negators. Constraint felt as inescapable can also be expressed by such locutions as *have no alternative but, cannot help*, and *be necessary*. Conviction is expressed by *be bound to* as well as by *must*.

That'*s bound to* be the new manager's wife.

Be bound to can express conviction about the future course of events, as in *he's bound to be here tomorrow; must* cannot. *Have to* occasionally expresses conviction also, at least in informal styles. Both *have to* and *need* occasionally display remarkable mutations in meaning.

She just *has to* have a new dress for each party.
He *need*n't think he can get away with that.

In the first of these two sentences strong desire is treated as a compelling force. *There's no use in his thinking he can get away with that* phrases the meaning of the second sentence more exactly.

Shall is a special case among the verbs expressing constraint felt as inescapable. *Shall* is used in main interrogatives which assign the hearer or reader authority to make decisions for the speaker or writer or even for others.

Shall we have some coffee?
When *shall* I come by for you?
Let's go again, *shall* we?
Shall John get your mail too?

The use is honorific, like the *may* of *may I bring you some coffee?*

and (originally) the *let* of *let's get some coffee*. Sometimes the authority of the person or persons addressed—the readers of a book or article, for example—is obviously fictitious.

Who *shall* say that landscaping is not one of the fine arts?

Like *may*, *shall* has a certain amount of use in regulations, where the authority is clearly collective or institutional.

Passengers *shall* not converse with the driver while the bus is in motion.

There may even be a control vested in physical things.

The velum determines which way the air *shall* escape.

In formal styles authoritative *shall* occasionally occurs even where authority clearly resides in the speaker or writer.

The visitor was the president of a university that *shall* be nameless here.

But in general *shall* is avoided where authority resides in the speaker or writer. Both *you shall have an answer by Thursday* and *my son shall do as I say* now seem a little graceless.

Especially in more or less formal styles, *shall* occurs in subordinate clauses affected by desire (or by influencing normally rooted in desire) expressed in the larger containing clauses, and in subordinate clauses subordinated by *lest*.

Her only desire is that her daughter *shall* never see want.
We are anxious that there *shall* be no misunderstanding.
One senses in the older man a constant solicitude lest the younger man *shall* burn himself out.
He was determined that the truth *should* be known.
Her only desire was that her daughter *should* never see want.
The visitors sat in silence lest they *should* be guilty of offense.

Shall is very close to *may* in uses such as these. In a variety of other situations styles that can be described as careful or formal to a variety of degrees employ *shall* to express uncertainty, much as *may* is employed.

Williams was expected to act as dean only until someone better qualified *should* become available.
If the exchange *should* become more unfavorable, most of our Mexican students would have to leave.

Any person who *shall* make any false statement in an attempt
to defraud this retirement system shall be subject to pros-
ecution under the law.

In the first of these sentences *should*, here the common-mode past
of *shall*, has a good deal of the semantic value of *if anyone did.*
In the second sentence *should* has the semantic value of *by any
chance:* the condition is a rejected one, formulated in the stream
of the hypothetical (so that *should* is a subjunctive past), but the
effect of *should* is really to soften the rejection and make it equiv-
ocal as compared with the simpler *if the exchange became more
unfavorable.* The *shall* of the legalistic third sentence is semantically
very close to the *may* of *someone may make a false statement.*

Finally, *shall* is used in formal styles as an auxiliary of tense
alongside *will.*

As separate common-mode-present defective verbs (no longer
to be thought of as inflected forms of *shall* and *owe*), *should* and
ought are now used to express a degree of constraint that is felt as
escapable: desirability of some kind, whether based in duty, propriety, civility, prudence, or simply probable benefit or pleasure.
Examples of this use of *should* follow.

> Children *should* obey their parents.
> How *should* I know what they want?
> Peas *should* not be eaten with a spoon.
> *Should* we tell him the truth?
> I *should* study tonight.
> I *should* have told you what to expect.
> You *should* see our garden now.

Ironic uses occur, at least in informal styles.

> I *should* worry what she thinks.

Should is also used to express what can be called reasonable
probability.

> You *should*n't have much trouble finding him.
> The situation *should* improve by fall.
> A coat like that *should* cost about fifty dollars.

I have to study tonight implies that no escape from the task is in
sight. Escape may later be found, but this is another matter.
I had to study last night implies that no escape was found. *I should*

study tonight implies that escape from the task is quite possible, and *I should have studied last night* implies that escape was actually found. *A coat like that must cost about fifty dollars* expresses conviction. *A coat like that should cost about fifty dollars* expresses reasonable expectation—something weaker than conviction.

Like *shall, should* sometimes expresses uncertainty. It has considerable use of this kind, even in informal styles, in the subordinate clauses of noncommittal conditional sentences and in other subordinate clauses of similar types.

> If anyone *should* call, please say that I'll be back at five.
> If the Consul *should* be in town tomorrow, we'll make our arrangements then.
> He always prepares his argument carefully, in case there *should* be opposition.

Here *should* is semantically close to *happen to*. It gives a shading that is often felt as desirable. Possibility of actualization is not rejected, even provisionally; but it is discounted somewhat—sometimes, as in the first of the three sentences given, because a kind of modest underestimating of the possibility seems called for. Noncommittal conditions become less than completely noncommittal.

Should sometimes has essentially the semantic value of *actually* or *the very idea*. This occurs in subordinate-declarative clauses following ideas of appraisal, emotional or nonemotional, expressed in the larger containing clauses.

> It amazes her that informal English *should* be considered standard.
> It is strange that there *should* be so few complaints.
> It's a shame that you *should* have so much trouble.
> It seemed entirely natural that during the Civil War privates *should* elect their officers.
> It was appropriate that the American's favorite philosopher *should* have founded a newspaper.

It also occurs in main clauses which employ the main-interrogative clause pattern but are really not questions at all.

> When I looked out, what *should* I see but three cars full of teenagers.

Ought has a much narrower range of use than *should*. It is used only to express desirability (duty, propriety, etc.) and reasonable expectation.

> I *ought* to study tonight.
> They *ought* to have told you that.
> Mary *ought* to be getting back now.

Though *ought* belongs to the small group of verb forms performing clause-marker functions, it is a relatively uncomfortable member of the group and is likely to give way to *should* where a marker is needed. Nonstandard *had ought* sometimes occurs where a clause marker is needed.

> *Had*n't we *ought* to tell George?

Other methods of expressing desirability are of course available, and some of them are especially attractive where defective *should* and *ought* are unsatisfactory. *Be desirable, be wise,* and similar phrasings are often used. *Behoove* has become somewhat archaic.

> It *behooved* every ambitious politician to get himself born in a
>   log cabin.

Had better is used, like *should* and *ought*, with common-mode-present force, but *had* is a past-subjunctive form of *have* in this combination, and it can hardly be dissociated from *have* as *should* and *ought* can be dissociated from *shall* and *owe*.

> We'*d better* hire anyone that wants the job.
> You'*d better* see a doctor about that.

Colorings of warning, sometimes even of threat, appear with *had better* rather more often than with *should* and *ought*. Ideas of reasonable probability can of course be expressed in many ways—simply by the adverb *probably*, for example, and by *is likely to*.

Be to expresses a kind of constraint that grows out of arrangements, stipulations, and expectations of various kinds. It occurs only in two tenses, the present and the past.

> Charles *is to* get us at eight.
> You *were to* phone me this afternoon.
> How *was* I *to* know they were married?
> Your father says you'*re to* get the car back by ten.

Arrangements and schedulings represent a relatively inoffensive kind of constraining influence, and *be to* is often, in effect, a polite substitute for more direct *have to*, as in the last of the four sentences just given. With passive infinitives *be to* often represents stronger constraint, becoming equivalent to *must*.

Difficulties *are to* be expected.

Sometimes, on the other hand, *be to* expresses destiny, and is equivalent to *be destined to*.

In 1860 she met the man who *was to* be her husband.
We were quite prosperous when my father remarried. Within a year we *were to* lose everything.

In subordinate clauses in sentences of rejected condition *be to* comes to be roughly equivalent to *should* and *happen to*.

Even if the Administration *were to* undergo a last-minute conversion and decide that the wisest course was to reverse its present policy, it could not easily do so.

Arrangements and expectations find frequent expression in *be supposed to*, *be expected to*, and similar locutions.

I*'m supposed to* get back tomorrow.

Expression of volition.—As a full predicator *will* expresses various types of volition, ranging from reluctant consent to determined insistence. Consent is expressed most often.

Will you do me a favor?
Come here, *will* you?
Won't you stay awhile?
Would you be so kind as to explain yourself?
Phil can help if he *will*.
If you*'ll* excuse me, I'll phone the store.
He'd study music if his family *would* let him.
Wilson *would*n't commit himself when we talked to him.
I *would*n't have a car like that.
I*'d* just as soon finish now.

Preference is expressed by *would rather*.

I*'d rather* you didn't tell him.

Desire of a variety not nearly as strong as insistence is expressed in such sentences as the following.

Say what you *will*, you won't convince him.
Will you have sugar for your coffee?

The desire is pessimistic when the past subjunctive *would* is used (archaically) with a declarative-clause complement but usually without an expressed subject.

Would that it were true!
Would to God that we could believe him!

With dominant stress *will* can express insistence.

She *will* tell the awful truth.
Why *will* he do such things?
They *would* invite him, in spite of everything.

A kind of animism often extends volition to weather, machinery, and inanimates of various other types, especially when they are regarded as obstinately negative.

If only it *would* rain!
The motor *won*'t start.
His stomach *won*'t let him sleep.
I do wish the phone *would* ring.

Adaptability is just a step from this and is hard to distinguish from it.

The auditorium *would*n't hold the crowd.
The new car *will* go a hundred miles an hour.
I tried the suit on, but it *would*n't do.

Habit is just a step from volition too.

He'*ll* talk for an hour or so, and then he'*ll* become apologetic about wasting time.
When we were children, Mother *would* read to us in the evenings from a big book of Bible stories.

Will is best regarded as a full predicator in all these uses. It is also used as an auxiliary of tense, of course. Often it is extremely difficult, without very clear context, to tell whether *will* is a full predicator expressing volition, adaptability, or habit, or simply a future auxiliary. Sometimes such ambiguity exists even with context. *Will* is of course defective, and so gives way to other methods of expressing volitio n, etc., at many points. *Be willing to* is much used for consent. There is no possibility of ambiguity, and it is usable where defective *will* is not.

> I'm not sure I can translate that paragraph, but I'*m willing to* try.

Apparently *want* is now the commonest verb for expressing desire directly, as in *she wants to see you*. *Wish* involves rejection of possibility when declarative clauses follow, as in *I wish I were a good mechanic*, and is largely confined to formal styles when it has complements of other types, as in *whom did you wish to see?* The hypothetical subjunctive *would like* is much used for expressing desire somewhat indirectly, as in *what would you like to see?* In interrogatives, negated clauses, and adjuncts of condition *care* is used as a delicate way of expressing desire, as in *we'd enjoy having you if you care to come along*. *Feel like* and *feel inclined to* have somewhat similar uses.

> Take off your coat if you feel like doing so.

Determination is most likely to be expressed by locutions such as *be determined to*, *insist on*, and *be bent on*.

CHAPTER VII

TENSE

The eight tenses.—The tenses are the recognition that verbs give to the passage of time. The common mode makes more distinctions than any other. In the common mode four tenses have the time of speaking or writing as their center: the present, the present perfect, the present future, and the present future perfect, the last with some future time as a more immediate center. These are the tenses of proximity, or the present tenses. In the common mode four other tenses normally have some specific time in the past as their center: the past, the past perfect, the past future, and the past future perfect. These are the tenses of severance, or the past tenses.

Tense forms are marked in two ways. Futures and perfects employ auxiliaries: *will* (and in limited first-person uses in formal styles, *shall*) in all future tenses, *have* in all perfect tenses. Almost all one-word past forms are distinguished from basic forms (1) by the addition of endings to the basic forms, as when *played* and participial *eaten* are formed from *play* and *eat;* or (2) by changes in the vocalic and/or consonantal composition of the basic forms, with or without the addition of endings, as when *dug, sent, felt, stood, sold,* and participial *broken* are formed from *dig, send, feel, stand, sell,* and *break;* or (3) by replacement with originally un-related forms, as when *were* and *went* replace *be* and *go.* A few basic forms are used as pasts without change: for example, *put, spread,* and (as a participle) *come.* Except for such one-word pasts as *put, spread,* and participial *come,* all the forms of the four past tenses are marked by past inflection. In phrasal past forms past inflection occurs in the first word. Ignoring variations for person and number, the forms of the four past tenses of the regular verb *play* in the common mode can be listed as follows:

played *and* did play, had played, would play, would have played
were playing, had been playing, would be playing, would have been playing
were played, had been played, would be played, would have been played
were being played

Corresponding forms in the four present tenses lack the past inflection which marks past forms:

play *and* do play, have played, will play, will have played
are playing, have been playing, will be playing, will have been playing
are played, have been played, will be played, will have been played
are being played

In phrasal forms employing more than one auxiliary, *will* (or *shall*) always comes first and *have* can be preceded only by *will* or *shall*.

It is not surprising that the time of speaking or writing should serve as a center for one group of tenses. This is the time that we live in, and it is all that we have. In the narrowest sense the present time is a point so minute that it is already a part of the past before we can finish the sentence. But the present with which verbs are concerned is not this uncomfortable pin-point present: an infinite variety of durations is covered in verbal presents. As for the past, it is dead, but we are products of it, and everything that we have comes out of it. The past stirs us deeply. We cannot know the future as we think we know parts of the past, and it has not affected us as clearly. Bit by bit new presents emerge from the future, and we try to shape the present with the future in mind. We make predictions with varying degrees of certainty. Yet the language has long had only two main centers in its tense system. There are no one-word futures to match the one-word presents and pasts, and the language gives no such attention to future time as it gives to present and past time. The future is always ahead and is always looked forward to from some point in the present or the past. Sustained narrative has difficulty using future tenses on and on: a

novel about the future, for example, runs into much less difficulty
with its verbs if it makes a past out of its future by looking at it
from a still later point in time.

Each tense has its characteristic time range, though every tense
meets competition from other tenses within its characteristic range.
The time spans actually covered in particular predications are
another matter. Thus in *George has knocked that silly friend of yours
down* the felling of the friend is placed by the tense form within a
time range that terminates at the moment of speaking or writing.
The time span actually covered by the felling of the friend is
probably a very brief one, and unlike the time range within which
it is set, it pretty clearly has not terminated just at the moment of
speaking or writing. Nothing is implied about the situation before
the time actually spanned by the predication. Nor is anything
implied about the situation at the moment of speaking or writing:
probably the silly friend has got up and gone about his business.
Similarly in *Mary was sick yesterday* nothing is implied about what
preceded yesterday or about what is following it. Some actions,
events, and states of affairs leave lasting effects; but this is not a
matter tense forms are concerned with. Often the time spanned by
a predication is not really filled: there is simply recurrence of an
action or event through the span. Thus in *I'm eating lunch downtown this week* the time spanned is the week within which the
sentence is framed, but the lunches eaten take up only a fraction
of the time contained in the week, and no lunch need be in process
when the sentence is framed. The time ranges assigned to tense
forms vary notably from mode to mode. Thus in *we drove very carefully coming through town* the gerundial present form *coming* is
used for the same time as the common-mode past *came* in *we drove
very carefully as we came through town.*

The present in the common mode.—In the common mode
the time range of the present tense is fixed only by the normal
requirement that it include the moment of speaking or writing.
Whatever their length, the time spans covered by common-mode
presents are normally thought of as extending both before and after
the moment of speaking or writing. These time spans can be long
enough to include millions of years, or they can be a few brief

moments, or they can be segments of time somewhere between these extremes.

> Water *is* basic to life on this planet.
> Johnny *is dropping* his plate.
> The Johnsons *live* in New Jersey now.
> We*'re eating* supper out this week.

It is quite natural that the common-mode present should be used in speaking of what is said and done in stories, novels, plays, and the like, which continue to express themselves to those who read or see them.

> The book *begins* with an account of the building of the first
>   Mormon temple at Kirtland.
> Shakespeare's Cleopatra *says* that women should be haughty.

For many verbs the common-mode present is also quite natural in telling about what is scheduled, at the time of speaking or writing, to take place in the future.

> We *leave* for Mexico City at seven tomorrow morning.
> The mayor *is speaking* over television tonight.
> Classes *begin* next Wednesday.

Here what extends through the moment of speaking or writing is a marginal phase of the actions or events predicated: planning, arranging, or scheduling. Similarly, in *Johnny's dropping his plate* what is already happening is almost certainly marginal, and there is a possibility that the actual fall of the plate can even be headed off. It is noteworthy that where presents have to do with schedules or arrangements, ideas of constraint are sometimes involved.

> Where *do* we *pay?*
> Where *does* this piece *go?*
> You*'re seeing* the Dean at three this afternoon.

Under certain conditions common-mode presents are used for time spans which lie entirely before the moment of speaking or writing. In a very few situations common-mode presents are used for very recent past time which is felt as practically present.

> I *hear* that Eugene is in town.
> Why *do* you *say* that?
> It*'s* four months since we left Mexico City.

Sometimes the present is used in narrative for what lies farther back in the past, in an effort to make the past seem alive again.

> The bus *reaches* the top and *begins* to descend. Soon we *see* a small whitish town deep in the valley below.
> At some time before the thirteenth century Teotihuacan *is abandoned* and Ananuac *becomes* the prey of Nahua invaders from the north.

Finally, a few present forms that were originally pasts, and *need* when it expresses constraint, are used like pasts in limited circumstances where the past time is clear from the context.

> I knew I *must* be wrong.
> We supposed that we *ought* to make some apology.
> It seemed entirely natural that during the Civil War privates *should* elect their officers.

Ought, should, and *need* are used with perfect-infinitive complements where past forms of these three verbs with present-infinitive complements would seem more reasonable.

> I should have told you what to expect.
> You needn't have done that.

The equivalent phrasings *it was desirable that I tell you what to expect* and *you didn't have to do that* show combinations of tenses that are not so exceptional.

In subordinate clauses common-mode presents have considerable use for time spans which lie entirely after the moment of writing or speaking. Usually the predicators of the larger clauses within which these subordinate clauses occur set the time clearly enough, but sometimes the time is indicated in other ways.

> We'll welcome anyone who *comes.*
> I'll talk to him as soon as he *arrives.*
> They'll continue to have trouble until they *solve* the economic problem.
> If you*'re* in New York next summer, hunt us up.
> Do you mind if I *skip* the meeting tomorrow?

Future-tense forms are used economically. For the verbs, future time is a kind of horizon for present time, entitled to its own tense forms but only within limits.

The present in other modes.—In the subjunctive mode the present tense is very commonly used for time spans which lie entirely after the moment of writing or speaking.

> *Come* in!
> *Don't* *miss* next week's issue.
> I suggest that we *try* the steak.

Present subjunctives also occur in subordinate clauses incorporated in larger clauses with predicators whose time is past, and in such contexts they commonly are used for time spans which are future in relation to the time of the main predicators, not in relation to the moment of speaking or writing.

> I suggested that we *try* the steak.

In the infinitival and gerundial modes, present forms are normally concerned not with the time of speaking or writing but with the time of the predicators of the larger clauses within which the infinitival and gerundial clauses are incorporated, or with time that is future in relation to this time. In the following sentences the time of the infinitives is the same as that of the main predicators.

> She likes to *be flattered.*
> She always liked to *be flattered.*
> There's no one to *be seen.*
> He's never done anything but *tell* silly jokes.
> You'll see him *leave* at six tomorrow morning.
> Besides *being* ignorant, Beecham was very arrogant.
> We always got lost *coming* through town.
> Weather *permitting,* the meetings were held in the stadium.
> The Indians went forward on their knees, *carrying* candles and *intoning* prayers.

The time is future in relation to that of the predicators of the larger containing clauses in the following sentences.

> The hero is gone from serious modern literature never to *return.*
> George was planning to *leave* the next day.
> Jack had recommended *trying* again.
> We're afraid of *offending* him.
> They've always insisted on our *being* there.

In the gerundial mode, present forms in clauses used in nounal constructions are sometimes concerned with time earlier than the time of the larger clauses within which the gerundial clauses are incorporated. Perfect gerundials might be expected, but sometimes they would seem a little heavy.

> John mentioned *seeing* Mary in Washington.
> George was arrested for *knocking* a policeman down.
> I can't understand Perry's *doing* that.
> We appreciate your *inviting* us.

In gerundial clauses used as adjuncts present forms are concerned with earlier time only when there is no real interval.

> *Taking* off his coat, he sat down at the counter and went to work.

In exceptional circumstances present infinitives and gerundials are sometimes concerned with the time of writing or speaking rather than the time of the larger clauses in which they are incorporated.

> To *tell* the truth, I never felt that I understood him.
> That man *sitting* next to the hostess was a teacher here ten years ago.

The present perfect in the common mode.—In the common mode the time range of the present perfect is ordinarily fixed only by the requirement that it terminate at the moment of speaking or writing. The time spans covered by common-mode present perfects are of widely varying lengths, and they vary also in their placing within the characteristic time range. Sometimes they terminate at the moment of speaking or writing or just before it. This is commonly true when adjuncts of duration are attached to them.

> Jack's *been* in town for a week.
> Mary's *had* a headache all morning.
> How long *has* Bill *lived* in New York?
> Since its beginnings the industry *has developed* steadily.
> She's *been deceiving* him for months.

Sometimes there is simply an implication of recentness, without explicit recognition of intervals of time that have actually elapsed, and without explicit dating of the predications.

The mail *has come.*
We*'ve sold* our house.
They*'ve caught* the robber.
It's the first time Bill *has tried* to marry anyone.
She*'s been crying.*

Sometimes the time spans lie farther back in the past. Here again there is no explicit recognition of the intervals of time—sometimes very considerable—that have elapsed, and no explicit dating of the predications. Experiences lying at unspecified points in the past are thought of as not severed from the present.

I*'ve seen* that face before somewhere.
I*'ve heard* my grandmother sing that song.
The city *has been destroyed* by invaders repeatedly.

When the time spans covered by present perfects terminate at the moment of speaking or writing, what is predicated often continues, in reality, through this moment. *Jack's been in town for a week,* for example, can be spoken or written just as Jack leaves town or when he intends to stay longer. In either case what the present-perfect verb form is concerned with is the week that has just come to an end, not the situation at the moment of speaking or writing. *Jack's in town for a week* places the moment of speaking or writing within the week, not at the end of it. *Mary's had a headache all morning* is usable either at the end of the morning or at any point well along in the morning. The sentence is concerned with the period of headache preceding the moment of speaking, whether it is really a whole morning or simply the considerable part of the morning which has elapsed; whether or not the headache has ended is outside the scope of the predicator. Wherever adjuncts of duration name periods of time terminated (exactly or inexactly) just before the moment of speaking or writing, present-perfect tense forms are normal for the predicators. This is felt to be true when the adjuncts are made up of the preposition *since* and an object indicating a point at which the time span of the predication begins.

We*'ve lived* here since 1952.
The city *has changed* since we came here.

But exceptional presents occur occasionally in informal styles where *since* and an object make up an adjunct of duration.

> It's dull here since George left.
> Since when *is* he an authority?

Something comparable occurs occasionally in careful and formal styles with such adjuncts as *to this day*.

> They *regret* the decision to this day.

When the time spans covered by common-mode present perfects do not extend to the moment of speaking or writing, it is normally impossible nevertheless to include in the clauses any mention of the intervals of time that have elapsed. Thus *the mail has come* cannot keep its present-perfect verb form if *half an hour ago* is added—or, for that matter, if *five seconds ago* is added. Nor can there be any dating of predications employing common-mode present-perfect verb forms. Thus *I've seen him at ten o'clock this morning* is unnatural; the perfect must give way to the past here. Even so vague a dater as *once*, as used to refer to unspecified times in the past, requires the use of past verb forms rather than present perfects. *I've once discussed the problem with Perry* is unnatural: the past is needed again. Dating as within units of time uncompleted or barely completed at the moment of speaking or writing is another matter: the present perfect permits this readily. Thus *I've been to town this morning* is quite natural if the morning is not yet completed or is barely completed.

Though it deals with past time and has exactly the same time range as the past tense, the present perfect is one of the four present tenses in force as well as in form, and when it is used what it deals with is seen as still not cut off from the present. In *I've heard my grandmother sing that song* the grandmother may be dead at the time of speaking or writing but the active subject is not, and is not willing at the moment to use a verb form that would cut his experience off from the present. *My grandmother has sung that song* is normal, however, only when the grandmother is still living. Death makes us all parts of the past, and at the moment of the grandmother's death verb forms belonging to the four past tenses would become inescapable in most sentences in which the grandmother was the subject.

When the fact is clearly indicated, the common-mode present perfect sometimes deals with segments of time that extend to more than one point in a longer present which includes the moment of speaking or writing, rather than to the precise time of speaking or writing.

> Every time I see him, he *has* just *made* some startling discovery.
> I always know when she *has had* a letter from her son.

Sometimes it deals with segments of time that extend to points in the future (in relation to the time of speaking or writing) rather than to the time of speaking or writing itself.

> When I*'ve had* lunch, I'll call you.
> George won't give up till he*'s used* every argument.

With *after* present-perfect forms are sometimes used where they are really redundant.

> After he*'s given* up, he always despises himself.

In informal styles the present perfect is used exceptionally in sentences such as the following.

> It's nine hours since I*'ve eaten* anything.

It's been nine hours since I ate anything employs tense forms more normally.

In informal styles common-mode present-perfect forms of *get* are often equivalent in force to the present forms of *have* where meanings of possession and necessity are expressed.

> He*'s got* two automobiles and a boat.
> I*'ve got* to go downtown.

This is an exceptional use of the present perfect. Ordinarily the present perfect implies nothing about the moment of speaking or writing, and certainly implies no continuance after it. This is the reason *your son's been having trouble with his arithmetic* is likely to seem a little politer than *your son's having trouble with his arithmetic*. The present perfect places the trouble in a very recent past whose effects are still felt, but suggests that there need be no more of it. The present places the trouble in the present—and not a pin-point present—and inevitably suggests a certain amount of continuance beyond the moment of speaking or writing.

The present perfect in other modes.—In the subjunctive mode present-perfect tense forms occur only rarely.

> It is important that the candidate *have completed* all the required courses.

The time is earlier than the time of the predications of the larger clauses or than some other time indicated by the situation.

In the infinitival and gerundial modes (where there are no past forms), present-perfect forms normally deal with time earlier than the time of the predicators of the larger containing clauses, whatever this time is:

1. I'm glad to *have met* you.
   You seem to *have been* in the rain.
   Moore was known to *have falsified* his returns.
   I must *have said* the wrong thing.
2. Paul bitterly regretted not *having gone* into music.
   Having read three detective novels that week, I wasn't interested in a fourth.

Sometimes present-perfect infinitives and gerundials deal with time earlier than a time indicated by an adjunct within their clauses.

> I hope to *have finished* by June.
> I was supposed to *have finished* by last June.

With *after* present-perfect gerundials involve redundancy, but they occur.

> After *having visited* Trinidad, we were eager to see Martinique also.

Sometimes present-perfect infinitives indicate unreality. This occurs characteristically after *were* (or *was*) *to*, *could*, *might*, *ought to*, and *should*.

> A second conference was to *have been held* the following summer.
> Mary could *have warned* us.
> They might *have died*.
> George should *have waited* longer.

The first of these sentences means that a second conference was scheduled but was not actually held. The second means that Mary was able to give a warning but did not. The third means that there was a possibility of death but death did not actually occur. The fourth means that it was desirable for George to wait longer but he did not. In the absence of past infinitives, present-perfect infinitives have taken on the function of predication in the stream of the hypothetical and the unreal.

The present future.—Present-future forms occur only in the common mode. The time range of the present-future tense extends from the moment of speaking or writing to indefinitely remote points in what presumably lies ahead. The moment of speaking or writing is not included. The time spans covered by present-future forms are of infinitely varied lengths.

> It *won't take* five minutes for me to pick George up.
> We'*ll be* happier next year.
> The poor *will* not *accept* poverty forever.

The time spans covered are usually pegged at definite points in the future, explicitly or by implication; but sometimes they can be left unpegged.

The present future is used chiefly to make predictions. These can be hedged about with conditions, reservations, and qualifications of many other types. Subordinated predications underlying the predictions made by present-future forms are generally assumed rather than predicted directly, and present forms are used for them even though their time spans do not include the time of speaking or writing. Thus in *your friends will miss you while you're gone* the main-clause predicator *will miss* is a present-future form and makes a prediction, but the subordinate-clause predicator *are* is a present form used of future time. Present futures occur quite normally in subordinate clauses whose predications follow those of the larger clauses in some sequence of cause and effect or of time, instead of preceding them.

> John will come Thursday, so that it *will be* possible for you to
> see him on Friday.
> He won't be able to find a house that *will suit* his wife.
> Please send a telegram telling when you *will arrive.*

Present futures occur in other subordinate clauses used as loose adjuncts in larger clauses.

> We'll meet the ten-o'clock plane, which *will* naturally *be* late.
> He'll come, though he *won't do* so very cheerfully.
> Hughes will have a relatively easy job, since he*'ll be* an outsider not involved in local quarrels.

Present futures occur in subordinate clauses used as adjuncts of comparison.

> They'll miss us more than they*'ll miss* you.

They occur in subordinate clauses within larger containing clauses whose predicators are of other tenses.

> It isn't likely that Perry *will agree.*
> He has a wife that *will make* life interesting.
> If the building *won't be finished* till August, we have a problem.

Where what is predicted is likely to benefit the hearer or reader and the speaker or writer seems able to bring about what he predicts, present futures are likely to be taken as equivalent to promises.

> I*'ll be* in my office at four.
> You*'ll be* satisfied with our work.

Where what is predicted is likely to seem troublesome to the hearer or reader and the speaker or writer possesses, or seems to possess, authority that enables him to compel actualization of what he predicts, common-mode present futures develop notions of constraint.

> Students intending to take this examination *will sign* the list in the office of the secretary.
> You*'ll do* as I tell you.
> That *will be* all.

This latter use of present-future forms has a quality of assurance that often seems highhanded. Present futures have occasional use in expressing assumptions about the present. Here there is a kind of prediction that the assumptions will be verified.

> A car's coming in. That *will be* Hugh, I guess.
> They*'ll be* in the balcony. Let's go on up.

Present futures are sometimes used where the present seems a little too direct.

> That *will be* twenty dollars, please.·

The present future perfect.—The present future perfect normally has a time range whose distinguishing characteristic is that it terminates at some point in the future and is thought of primarily with respect to this terminal point. Time spans actually covered vary in length and sometimes extend to the terminal points of their time ranges and sometimes do not.

> We'*ll have lived* here three years in August.
> Surely the world *will have solved* the problem of war by the time the children grow up.

Occasionally the present future perfect is used to express assumptions where the present perfect would otherwise seem normal.

> He'*ll have finished* the examination by now.

Present future perfects are relatively heavy forms. The construction out of which they originally developed is generally preferred, where it is usable.

> Surely the world will have the problem of war solved by the time the children grow up.

But present future perfects cannot always be avoided, and they do occur even in informal styles.

The past tense in the common mode.—The point from which the passage of time is noted is of course the moment of speaking or writing. But all our presents become pasts, and in part the past is very real to us. Parts of the past can be viewed as attached to the present: present-perfect tense forms are then usable. But much of the past cannot be looked at very easily in this way. The past had its own validity, quite apart from the tiny present; and the past has its own tenses, quite distinct from the four present tenses. The past tense is the most important of these. The past tense is not a satellite on the present tense; the past tense is indeed a center for satellite tenses exactly paralleling the three satellite tenses surrounding the present tense. The time range of the past tense is identical with that of the present perfect, and extends to the moment of speaking or writing: but the past tense belongs to the enormous dead past, not to the brief present. The time spans with which the past tense deals are of enormously varied length and can occur at any point in the past.

Since the past tense belongs to the enormous past, it usually requires some kind of time modifier to date it, unless what has been said previously makes dating clear.

I didn't sleep a wink last night.
Students worked harder when I was in college.
After the Spaniards hunted for the fountain of youth in the
    sixteenth century, mankind gave up the dream.

Sometimes dating is unnecessary because it is assumed that the hearer or reader possesses an adequate notion of chronology.

The Mayans developed a magnificent architecture.
Lincoln was born not far from here.
Barry grew up in Mexico.

Sometimes dating seems unnecessary for other reasons.

Who invented the safety pin?
My father gave me this watch.
Did you know the new manager has arrived?

Where *used to* is used, no dating is necessary.

He used to sell automobiles.

Where dating seems necessary with past-tense forms, such vague words as *once* are sufficient.

I once heard Paxton say he saw no point in restricting people
    to one marriage at a time.

The past tense is quite usable for the very recent past, always with the implication of separation from the precise present moment.

I just *saw* George talking to Millard.
What *did* you *say?*
Did you *hear* that?

It is usable with time modifiers naming units of time not yet completed at the moment of speaking or writing.

He just this minute *left*.
Where *did* you *have* lunch today?

The common-aspect, common-mode past is the normal narrative tense used for series of occurrences thought of as forming sequences of one kind or another in the past. It occurs even in subordinate clauses attaching to predicators of other modes and tenses where a probable sequence is looked at from the point of view of some point in the past.

> They considered it necessary that they *fight* until one of them *killed* the other.
> Three years ago we decided to *build* a house as soon as costs *went* down a little, but they are still as high as ever.

Where main predicators are past-tense forms, common-mode predicators in subordinate clauses, and even in other main clauses which follow immediately, are likely to be past-tense too if a choice between past forms and presents is possible. Unnecessary wrenches in point of view are avoided.

> Columbus believed that the world *was* round.
> We stopped in a small village where the inhabitants *spoke* Nahuatl.
> I thought you *were* an Englishman.
> What did you say your name *was?*
> We found this book in the living room, and we were sure it *was* yours.

The past tense generally leaves the whole matter of the present open, and does not imply that it differs from the past. But the pull to present forms is sometimes strong, and certainly should not be resisted when it is felt.

> George said yesterday that his brother still *wants* to run the family's affairs.
> We lived near Chapultepec, which *is* one of the world's great parks.

In these sentences the use of past verb forms might very well suggest that the situation has changed. But sometimes even present perfects used as main predicators pull subordinate predicators to the past tense, since present perfects deal with the past also.

> I've always known you *were* a good speaker.

Common-mode past-tense forms are sometimes used as softened equivalents of presents which might seem a little too direct.

Did you *wish* to look at our higher-priced suits?
We *were wondering* whether you *were going* to be at home next
    Sunday.
I *thought* you said we'd have a day off this week.

Common-mode past-tense forms are often substituted for present perfects where the time relationship of the present perfect has
been established and repetition of the tense seems undesirable.
Series of past-tense forms are entirely acceptable; series of present
perfects sometimes seem less so.

He's one man who *has studied* French and remembers what he
    was taught.
These are just a few of the things he*'s done* when he *had* a little
    spare time.

Past-tense forms are sometimes used with *ever* and *never* where
present perfects would seem more normal.

This is the best gumbo I ever *tasted.*
This is the first time he ever *admitted* his guilt.
Did you ever *find* out who broke the window?
George never *did know* how to pick a tie.

They can be used for time earlier than a central future time.

If you buy an old house, you will live to regret that you *did.*
I'll mail you a card when I reach New York, and let you know
    I *arrived.*

Progressive past-tense forms can involve ideas of planning or
arranging for later actions or events, especially when the verb
is *go.*

I stayed at the University that Christmas because I *was
    going* home the next summer.

The past tense in other modes.—In the hypothetical subjunctive the past tense is used for the time of speaking or writing
and for time that is future in relation to the time of speaking or
writing. This use of the past tense occurs chiefly in clauses incorporated in larger clauses similarly formulated in the stream of
the hypothetical.

You would think Jerry *was* incapable of guile if you *saw* him
    under such circumstances.

He'd pay you if he *could*.
George would help anyone who *was* in trouble, no matter what the trouble *was*.
I'd rather you *stayed* here.
If I *left* now, my family wouldn't have any idea where I *was*.

The occurrence of past-tense forms in subordinate hypothetical clauses parallels the occurrence of presents in subordinate clauses whose time is future.

If I *leave* now, my family won't have any idea where I *am*.

Past-tense forms occur in declarative clauses used as complements of *wish*, whatever the mode and tense of *wish*, when the time of the declarative-clause predication is the same as the time of the main predication.

I wish Bill *had* a little patience.
I wish I *shared* your optimism.

The past subjunctives of the defectives *can*, *may*, and *will* are used not only in subordinate clauses where the past subjunctives of other verbs are used, but also in the situations where the past future subjunctives of other verbs are used.

Hugh *could* take us all if he wanted to.
You *might* like the music if you listened to it for a while.
I *might* add that I never got my money.
George *would* rather we didn't say much.

This use of *could*, *might*, and *would* has made it hard to use them as common-mode pasts in some situations. Thus in *on the way home we were able to visit Yucatan* it is not possible to use *could* rather than *were able to*. The past subjunctive of *have* is used when *better* follows and is followed by clausal complements (always infinitival after *had better*) or has such complements understood.

You*'d* better talk to Perry about it.

When hypothetical subjunctives occur in clauses incorporated in larger clauses with past time ideas, the hypothetical forms sometimes have their time values in relation to the time of the larger clauses, not to the moment of speaking or writing.

I knew I*'d* better explain.
She spoke of God as if she *managed* the world for him.

Infinitives and gerundials do not have past-tense forms: instead their present-perfect forms function much as both present perfects and pasts function in the common mode. Participles, on the other hand, occur only in the past tense.

The past perfect in the common mode.—In the common mode the time range of the past perfect is fixed with relation to some past time, which is taken as the terminal point. The past perfect deals with time farther in the past than another past time on which attention is centered. The time which fixes the terminal point for the range of the past perfect may find expression in any of the past tenses.

> Spanish *was* easy for Mary because she *had studied* Latin.
> We*'d been waiting* an hour when she *got* there.
> That *was* the first time we*'d* ever *eaten* Arabic food.
> He did not know that years later he would return and *would wonder* that he *had been* so bitter.
> I*'d* never *seen* a man before that *had been beaten.*

Or even in a present perfect.

> I*'ve* rarely *had* students that *had had* much Latin.

Or in context.

> If a stranger came, they waited until he *had left.*
> I *had*n't *thought* of that.

In the first of these last two sentences *until he had left* is equivalent to *until after he left.* In the second something like *until you mentioned it a moment ago* is implied.

Sometimes the past perfect is used as a softened present perfect.

> We *had hoped* you would agree with us.

We have been hoping would often be a more accurate beginning in such a sentence.

The past perfect is likely to be avoided in telling of relatively quick sequences of actions and events occurring pretty much in series.

> John *jumped* to his feet the moment the bell *rang.*
> When he *finished* his coffee he *went* back to work.

At the other extreme the past perfect is ordinarily not used in telling of earlier occurrences which are not thought of as genuinely related to what is told of in the past tense.

> We *visited* Gettysburg last summer and *saw* the battlefield where the Confederacy *sustained* one of its most important defeats.
> The student from France *argued* that Napoleon's defeat *was* a catastrophe for Europe.
> My grandfather once *told* me that when he *was* a boy the village *was* very much larger.

Where the time is the same, the past perfect is not used in predications incorporated in larger clauses employing past-perfect tense forms.

> When Paul *was* a young man, he *had wanted* to travel.
> They *had*n't *found* us when they *called*.

The past perfect is usually not maintained in series of predications dealing with essentially the same time. It is likely to be used only at the beginning and the end of such series, being one of the relatively heavy tenses in effect and so being used sparingly.

> They *had seen* him once in the morning. As usual he *was walking* the deck for his daily exercise. He *passed* them several times and *looked* at them with interest, but without speaking. Margaret *said* she thought he wanted to speak but was too timid. Then he *had disappeared*.

The past perfect in the subjunctive.—In hypothetical-subjunctive uses the past perfect very commonly deals with the time range which in the common mode is divided between the present perfect and the past tense.

> If George *had been listening*, he would have understood.
> Jack would have better teeth if he'*d eaten* sensibly as a child.
> I wish we *had known* the truth.

Sometimes, however, the terminal point for the time range is not the moment of speaking or writing but some point in the stream of the hypothetical—probably vaguely future—at which a larger containing clause is pegged.

> What would you do if you waked up some day and discovered that you *had killed* someone in your sleep?
> I wouldn't buy a car that *had been* in a wreck.

The past future in the common mode.

—In the common mode the time range of the past future is fixed with relation to some past time and extends into the future from that time. The time which fixes the beginning point for the range of the past future may find expression in any of the past tenses, or in the present perfect.

She *told* him he *would find* her waiting when he returned.

If the magazines of the new day lacked distinction, they doubtless *served* the same purpose that the movies and the radio *would* shortly *serve*—that of killing time pleasantly.

Pierre *had thought* children *would bring* him happiness.

He was always afraid he *would marry* someone who *would tire* of him within a short time.

Smith *has* always *turned* his check over to his wife so that the money *would last* longer.

The common-mode past future is used chiefly in subordinate clauses incorporated in larger clauses whose time is past. Occasionally, however, it occurs in main clauses.

He watched the mists come creeping up the beach below the house. In a few minutes fog *would surround* the house too.

The past future in the subjunctive mode.

—In main-clause hypothetical-subjunctive uses the past future is concerned with the time of speaking or writing and with time that is future in relation to the time of speaking or writing. Predications employing the past future in this way are formulated in the stream of the hypothetical, in which the distinction between present and future is somewhat obscured. *Would* (and in formal first-person uses *should*) can be said to express a kind of lateral prediction, directed not at what lies ahead but at what belongs to a stream of occurrences distinct from that of actuality but more or less parallel to it.

You *wouldn't recognize* him now.

Most people *would say* she is too aggressive.

If you did your thesis next spring, you *would get* your degree in June.

In clauses incorporated within larger clauses whose predicators are hypothetical-subjunctive past-future verb forms, past subjunctives are usual—assuming that the subordinate predications are also formulated in the stream of the hypothetical. But past-future subjunctives are used when they deal with what follows in some sequence of cause and effect or of time.

> If foreign students got to know native students quickly, they *would learn* the customs of the country in a way that *would help* them greatly.
>
> If we moved out there, we'*d be* so far from my work that a car *would be* necessary.

Past-future subjunctives are also used in clauses that function as loose adjuncts within larger clauses with past-future subjunctive predicators. Here they deal with essentially the same time as that of the larger clauses.

> It *would be* fun to have them all to dinner, though it *would* also *be* hard to manage.

Past-future subjunctives also occur sometimes in subordinate clauses used as or in subjects, complements, and tight adjuncts within larger clauses which also employ past-future subjunctives and which are concerned with essentially the same time.

> A small house on a quiet street *would be* what we *would like* most.
>
> You *would*n't *think* they *would have* a cruise for schoolteachers, but they do.

In clauses incorporated within larger clauses whose predicators are hypothetical subjunctives of other tenses, past-future subjunctive forms often deal with time future in relation to the time of the larger clauses.

> I wish we *had known* you *would be* in town the next day.
>
> I *would*n't *have thought* anyone *would object.*
>
> If he *had* a job that *would keep* him on the payroll till next summer, he'd be all right.

In declarative clauses used as complements of *wish* (whatever its tense and mode), past-future subjunctives are sometimes used for time that is future in relation to the time expressed by *wish.*

> Judy wishes we'*d see* someone we know while we're in Acapulco next month.
>
> I wish that plane *would get* here.

But *hope* and a future are more satisfactory in expressing desires not felt as unrealizable. In complementary clauses after *wish, would* commonly is a full predicator expressing volition, as in *I wish Mr. Crawford would give fewer quizzes.*

When clauses whose predicators are past-future subjunctives are incorporated within larger clauses whose time is past, they are concerned with time that is present or future in relation to the time of the larger clauses within which they are incorporated.

We knew that if we moved out there we'*d need* a car.
The Marquis said that it *would be* hard to find the ideal wife he wanted.

A distinction that is useful in the present cannot be made here.

The Marquis says that it *will be* hard to find the ideal wife he wants.
The Marquis says that it *would be* hard to find the ideal wife he wants.

Past-future subjunctives have some use (like futures in the common mode) to express probability in present time.

Let's see. He *would be* in New York by now. We probably can reach him by telephone.

The same forms often serve as softened equivalents of common-mode presents.

It *would seem* that we aren't exactly popular here.
I *should think* you'd welcome a change.

The past future perfect.—The past future perfect has very little common-mode use. When it is used in this mode, its time range is fixed at the terminal point, which is future in relation to a past time taken, at least momentarily, as a kind of center.

We were afraid that by the following summer our jobs *would have come* to an end.

In hypothetical-subjunctive uses in main clauses, the time range of the past future perfect is that which the perfect and the past tense divide when predications are formulated in the stream of the actual.

Miss Hill *would have been* a wonderful mother and grandmother; instead she has been a rather dull teacher all these years.

We *would have appreciated* some cooperation last week, but we certainly didn't get any.

In subordinate clauses the time is sometimes past in relation to another past which is the time of the larger incorporating clause.

He often wondered what he *would have done* if he had not met Hana.

Sometimes the time range is that of the present or future, with the implication that all possibility has ended.

I'm doing as well as I can, but Hadley *would have done* the job better.

It *would have been* nice to spend next summer in Mexico, but it just doesn't seem possible now.

Constructions resembling futures.—Combinations composed of *be going to* and following infinitives are sometimes very close to futures semantically. Nevertheless it seems best to regard *be going* as a full predicator in all such uses, with *to* and its infinitival completer as the complement of *be going*. Often *be going to* expresses intention, and is really closer to *be intending to* than to the future auxiliary *will* in meaning.

We're *going to* sell the car.
Mr. Harris *isn't going to* give an examination.
You *were going to* tell us what happened.

Sometimes *be going to* expresses preparation without intention in the strict sense, or tendency or direction.

It's *going to* rain tonight.
The baby's *going to* fall out of his chair.
You're *going to* be disappointed, I'm afraid.
What's this *going to* cost me?

Be going to characteristically does more than simply place a predication within a time range, as the auxiliary *will* does. In *she's going to have a baby* the processes leading to birth have begun. *We're going to show you the town while you're here* suggests that plans, and even preparations, are in process. *You're going to regret this* is more ominous than *you'll regret this:* it is an assertion that the person addressed is already on the way to regret. *We're going to move next month* is semantically very close to *we're moving next month. We're moving* treats planning and the like, already begun, as a part of the action of moving; *we're going to move* gives separate status to such preparations, as is made clear by the naturalness of such a sentence as *we were going to move next month*, with *were going* in the past.

Be about to is one of a number of common ways of expressing imminent action. *I was about to say so* is like *I was approximately at the point of saying so* in construction except that the phrasal preposition *at the point of* takes a gerundial clause as its object, not an infinitival clause. When it is used of past time, *be about to*, like *be going to*, is likely to carry the implication that what was then imminent did not really occur. *They're about to get a new car* is semantically and syntactically quite distinct from *they'll get a new car.*

CHAPTER VIII

EXPANSION, PERSON AND NUMBER, PARADIGMS, IRREGULAR VERBS

Expanded presents and pasts.—With the exception of the defectives *can, may, must, ought, shall, should,* and *will* all verbs have expanded forms in which the basic-form infinitive serves as the head and *do* serves as the auxiliary. The chief use of expansion of this kind is to provide verb forms which can function as clause markers and in negation, in addition to serving as parts of predicators.

> *Did* you *try* the roast beef?
> Not only *did* Butch *serve* excellent soups and meats, but his desserts were the best in Cuernavaca too.
> People *do* not *eat* much mutton in this region.

Expanded forms also serve as vehicles for expression of exceptional emotion of varied types, with *do* semantically much like such adverbs as *really, certainly,* and *actually.*

> They *do know* how to cook steaks.
> *Do come* to see us.
> I *do wish* the children weren't so noisy.
> If I *do tell* Dora, she'll repeat it.
> What difference would it make if we *did get* there late?

Occasionally, needed parallelism is made possible by the use of expanded forms.

> They *can* and *do escape* such duties.

If we refuse auxiliary status to *can,* we will have to say that we have an oddly split clause here.

Expanded forms occur alongside one-word unexpanded forms in the present and the past tenses. They are normally confined to

177

use in (1) the common mode, (2) the coactual subjunctive in main-imperative clauses, and (3) the hypothetical subjunctive.

He *doesn't waste* much time.	(He *wastes* some time.)
Don't waste so much time.	(*Waste* less time.)
I wouldn't get much done even if I *did use* all my time well.	(Even if I *used* all my time well.)

Expanded forms of *be* are clearly standard in main-imperative clauses and dubiously standard in some other uses.

> *Don't be* so concerned.
> *Do be* careful.
> Why *don't* you *be* diplomatic?

Expanded forms of infinitives occur after *let's* in doubtfully standard informal styles.

> Let's *don't say* anything.
> Let's *do go* to see him.

The *do* of expanded presents and pasts is closely related to the *do* which serves as a substitute verb replacing present-tense and past-tense common-mode and subjunctive forms of all verbs except *be, can, may, must, ought, shall, should, will,* and perfect-auxiliary *have,* in contexts in which they have just had prominent expression and repetition is not desired.

> She *speaks* Portuguese better than she *does* Spanish.

Substitute *do* often represents more than a verb.

> You *speak Spanish,* don't you?
> She *wants more money, does* she?
> No one expects Ferris to *write another textbook now.* In fact, if he *did* no one would read it.
> Martin *gets angry easily,* and Williams *does* too.

With *so* or *it* as complement, substitute *do* is usable in other tenses and in other modes.

> Someone else would have told George if we *had*n't *done so.*
> Collins asked Jennings to make the motion because he was afraid to *do it* himself.

The verbs which substitute *do* cannot replace can represent larger units which are suggested by what immediately precedes.

He isn't a student, *is* he?
You can persuade him better than I *can*.
He'll eat up the rest of the pie, *will* he?
He'll take suggestions better than he *will* orders.
You haven't known him as long as we *have*.
The noise has annoyed my wife as much as it *has* me.

With some of these forms a second form, *have*, must often be kept as a time indicator.

We stayed longer than we *should have*.

Sometimes *be* cannot be left unexpressed after them as other verbs can.

I was as diplomatic as I *could be*.

In somewhat formal styles both substitute *do* and representative forms of *be, can, may, must, ought, shall, should, will*, and perfect auxiliary *have* are sometimes dispensed with in adjunct clauses of comparison where informal styles, and perhaps careful styles, would employ them.

She speaks Portuguese better *than Spanish*.
You can persuade him better *than I*.
He takes suggestions better *than orders*.
The bank has waited as long *as we*.
The delay has inconvenienced you as much *as us*.

Where *as well as* means *as truly as* or *besides*—as in *parents are invited as well as children*—this verbless reduction is the only possibility. In such a sentence as *Linda understood Willy better than anyone else*, the verbless reduction may be ambiguous: it can be equivalent to *than anyone else did* or to *than she did anyone else*.

Person-and-number forms.—With all verbs except the defectives *can, may, must, ought, shall, should*, and *will* there is sometimes inflection for person and number. Three "persons" are recognized by the language. The first is that of the speaker or writer, or of a group with two or more members including the speaker or writer, or of two or more writers (or, rarely, speakers) expressing themselves jointly. The second person is that of a person or people directly addressed, or of a group with two or more members including a person or people directly addressed but not including the speaker or writer or speakers or writers. Sometimes what is directly addressed is not really human: everyone talks to dogs, for example, and children talk to dolls. The third person is that of everyone and everything else. Two numbers are recognized: singular and plural. When verbs are affected by considerations of person and number, ordinarily what influences them is something primarily a characteristic of their subjects, not of the verbs themselves. Thus in *Mrs. White goes to town twice a day* the inflectional *s* of *goes* makes it clear that the form is third person singular; but what is third person singular at bottom is Mrs. White, not the repeated trips to town.

At many points the verbs of contemporary English are quite indifferent to person and number. Thus the past form *played* is usable with subjects of any person and either number. The defectives *can, may, must, ought, shall, should*, and *will* do not inflect for person and number at all.

Person-and-number distinctions are carried farther in the verb *be* than in any other verb. In the common-mode present the verb *be* has *am* in the first person singular, *is* in the third person singular, and *are* as common-person-and-number form used in the second person singular and throughout the plural. In the common-mode present perfect *be* has *has been* in the third person singular alongside the common-person-and-number form *have been*. In the common-mode present future and present future perfect *be* has the formal first-person forms *shall be* and *shall have been* alongside the indifferent-person-and-number forms *will be* and *will have been*. In the common-mode past *be* has the first-and-third-singular form *was* alongside the common-person-and-number form *were;* in the subjunctive-mode past it has *was* as a first-and-third singular form alongside a *were* which in some situations is a common-person-and-number form and in others is indifferent to person and number. In the subjunctive past future and past future perfect it has the formal first-person forms *should be* and *should have been* alongside the indifferent person-and-number forms *would be* and *would have been*. The complexities of *be* affect all progressives and passives, since *be* is used as auxiliary in these. And among the common-aspect, common-voice forms of other verbs, the defectives excepted, there are such forms as *plays, does play, has played, shall play, shall have played, should play*, and *should have played* alongside common-person-and-number forms or even indifferent-person-and-number forms.

The use of *shall* as an auxiliary in present-future and present-future-perfect forms is confined to formal and careful styles, and is general only in formal styles.

Formal: We *shall* not *be* able to furnish additional copies.
Careful: We *will* not *be* (or *shall* not *be*) able to furnish additional copies.
Informal: We *won't be* able to send any more copies.

The reductions *ll* (as in *we'll*) and *wo* (as in *won't*) are clearly reductions of *will*, not *shall*. The *shall* which appears in formal styles as an auxiliary of tense in the first person is normally not used, in contemporary American English, in main interrogatives.

Will we *be* living in peace a decade from now?
Will I *be* able to find the place?
Will we *have* a holiday at Easter?
Will I *need* a sweater?

In American English if *shall* is used in such interrogatives as these the effect is disturbing: the semantic center of gravity of *shall* makes itself felt, and a decision from someone supposedly able to determine the course of events seems to be asked for, rather than a prediction. The full-predicator *shall* of *shall I take a sweater?* is quite distinct from the tense-auxiliary *shall* of formal *I shall be in New York all next week*. The use of *shall* in such a sentence as the following can be described as genteel nonstandard.

A new road is being cut around the island, and the foundations of the old house *shall be uncovered*.

The use of *should*, the past of *shall*, as an auxiliary in past-future and past-future-perfect forms is similarly characteristic of careful styles and (more especially) of formal ones, and is similarly avoided in questions. In these two past tenses *would* is almost universally preferred, in American use, in the common mode.

We were paid what we had thought we *would be paid*.
In September we were confident that we *would have completed* the work by May.

Here *should* would suggest the meaning *ought* also expresses. In the hypothetical subjunctive *should* is used in formal styles much as *shall* is used in the common-mode present future and present future perfect.

> If you pressed us we *should admit* that some students are liberally educated with thirty hours of credit.
> We *should have preferred* an earlier date.

Even in informal styles *should* occurs as an auxiliary of tense in the hypothetical-subjunctive past future with *think* and in a few fixed phrasings.

> I *should think* George would like it.
> I *should say* not!

But *would* is preferred in the past future and the past future perfect almost everywhere in all but the most formal styles.

In the past subjunctive, *were* is sometimes used as an indifferent-person-and-number form of *be* and sometimes as a common-person-and-number form, with *was* used alongside it in the first and third persons singular. *Were* can function as an indifferent-person-and-number form only in adjunct clauses of rejected condition and in declarative clauses used as complements of *wish*.

> If the expense *were* justifiable, the situation would be different.
> Everyone wishes war *were* a thing of the past.
> I shouldn't avoid him if I *were* you.

But even in these situations *was* is used in the first and third persons singular in informal styles and to some extent even in careful styles, just as it is used in the common-mode past.

> Everyone wishes war *was* a thing of the past.
> If he *was* my friend, I'd warn him.

In subordinate clauses of other types *were* is not similarly usable in the first and third persons singular of the past subjunctive.

> If I had to write a thesis, I would pick a subject that *was* not very involved.
> I wish I thought war *was* a thing of the past.
> I wondered whether the expense *was* justified.

When *were* is employed with first- and third-person singular subjects in clauses such as these, its use can be described as genteel nonstandard. The tendency is obviously toward making the past subjunctive identical with the common-mode past, for *be* just as it is for other verbs.

> She wouldn't read a novel that *bored* her.
> She wouldn't read a novel that *was* dull to her.
> She wouldn't read a novel if it *bored* her.
> She wouldn't read a novel if it *was* dull to her.

But in the adjunct clause of rejected condition in the last of these four sentences, *were* can still be said to be preferred in formal styles and to some extent even in careful ones.

Person-and-number force reflected in verbs.—As has been said, when verbs are affected by considerations of person and number, ordinarily they simply reflect something primarily characteristic of their subjects, not of the verbs themselves. Only a few pronoun subjects—*I*, *we*, *you*, and very infrequently the subordinators *who* and *that* when they refer to *I*, *we*, or *you*—actually exert first- and second-person force with visible effects on their verbs. With other subjects first- and second-person verb forms are not used even where they might seem most logical.

> I'm the person that always *has* to pay the bill.
> Neither of us *is* very tactful.
> Poor little me always *gets* the blame.
> One of you *is* responsible.
> Who*'s calling?*

Who are you? with subject *you* is a possible, but very direct, way of asking a person who is making a phone call to identify himself; but *who are calling?* would not occur. Similarly when a person refers to himself as *this* in identifying himself on the telephone, he cannot employ *am* as he would if he referred to himself as *I*.

> This *is* Fred Andrews.
> I'*m* Fred Andrews.

In quoted uses, even *I* and *you* have third-person-singular force.

> Just who *is* "I" in this story?

Very infrequently *I* and *you* are used as final coordinates in multiple-unit subjects in which the first coordinate is either a rejected one or an alternative, and first- or second-person force is assigned the total subject.

> *Not you but I* am to blame.
> *Either Jack or I* am to blame.

The construction is usually avoided, since there is no very satisfactory solution to the problem it poses.

Where there is third-person force, the distinction between singular and plural is more complex than the terms traditionally employed suggest. The "singular" forms are really nonplural rather than singular in the strict sense. Indifferent-number subjects and quantifiable subjects normally influence verb forms exactly as true third-person-singular subjects do.

> Home is always in the men's thoughts.
> Money is of inescapable importance.

Here *home is* is semantically equivalent to *their homes are. Home* is not truly singular here, as it is in *he has never had a real home.* And *money* is not a pluralizer ordinarily; it is a quantifiable, like *fun* and *lettuce,* to which concepts of number are not directly applicable.

When words or multiword units usable with either singular or plural verb forms function as subjects, it is obviously necessary to look beyond them for the key to the number force they can be thought of as transmitting.

> *The goldfish* is dead.
> *The goldfish* are dead.
> *Some* were damaged.
> *Some* was damaged.

Clearly the key to the number of the verb used with *the goldfish* is the number of goldfish the speaker or writer has in mind. The key to the number of the verb used with *some* is what *some* represents in particular contexts: *some chairs were damaged,* but *some furniture was damaged.*

When clauses are used as subjects, they are ordinarily assigned singular force.

> *Buying cars on the instalment plan* is an expensive avocation
>   for a teacher.
> *Case after case* has been cured.

But interrogative clauses in which *what* is clause marker can have plural force.

> *What people I met* were very friendly.

Here *what people I met* has the same number force as *the people I met*. But if clauses of this type contain nothing in themselves to suggest plural force, and what immediately precedes has not suggested it, singular force is normal for them even before *be* and plural complements of *be*.

> *What we all want* is health and security.

Prepositional units used as subjects are assigned singular force.

> *Over the fence* is out.
> *To admit the truth* would be to endanger the whole enterprise.

So are double units in which prepositional units function as coordinates.

> *From here to Cleveland* is seventy miles.

When subjects are apposed units having *it* as principal and clauses as postponed appositives, they are regularly assigned singular force.

> *It*'s true *that we always have difficulties.*
> *It*'s the wives *who make the problem.*

But when *there* is principal the number force of the subject is determined, at least in careful and formal styles, by the appositive.

> *There* isn't *time.*
> *There* are still *a few seats.*

When headed units determine number forms for verbs (or for pronouns), their force is generally indicated by their heads. Thus *a man of exceptional talents* has singular force, and this force is indicated by the head word *man*. Sometimes, however, it is necessary to look beyond the contained head to a modifier. This is true especially when the head is a noun or pronoun capable of expressing meanings either of quantity or of number.

> Half of our time was wasted.
> Half of the cups were broken.
> Some of our time was wasted.
> Some of the cups were broken.

It is true also in such units as *Mr. and Mrs. Smith* in *Mr. and Mrs. Smith are coming,* as opposed to *the Smiths.* Sometimes a unit whose head is plural is used nevertheless as the name of what is felt as singular.

> Fifteen minutes is too long to wait.
> Ten dollars is too much to pay.
> Three fourths of the distance was behind us.

Here there is no interest in separate minutes or dollars or fourths. Headed units representing arithmetical processes (addition, subtraction, multiplication, division) commonly have singular force whatever the head words.

> Two plus two is four.
> Nine divided by three is three.

Upside-down units generally have the number force they would have if they were not upside down.

> That kind of people annoy me.
> People of that kind annoy me.

More than one has singular force.

> More than one of our customers has complained.

When multiple units determine number forms for verbs (or for pronouns), problems sometimes come up. If pluralizer coordinates are added, the unit resulting normally has plural force.

> *A mother and her child* were waiting for the bus.

The multiple head in *a husband and wife were sitting across from me* gives the headed-unit subject plural force; the multiple head in a *colleague and friend was sitting across from me* does not because the coordinates here are simply two designations for a single person. Multiple units representing the arithmetical process of addition commonly have singular force.

> *Two and two* is four.

Representative singulars are sometimes added without producing plural force.

> *Every tone of voice and every facial expression* was painful.
> *Everything he did and everything he said* was too dramatic.
> *One thing and another* has gone wrong all year.

Quantity is often added to quantity to produce simply a bigger quantity, not anything felt as plural.

> *All of his own money and most of his wife's* has been wasted.
> *Your assistance and that of your friends* is greatly appreciated.
> *Very little building and not much repairing* is being done.

Sometimes clauses are added without developing plural force.

> *Lecturing for an hour and then batting questions about* is hard work.

When representative singulars are added to plurals, and when quantifiables and pluralizers are added, somewhat awkward situations result. The combinations generally are felt to have plural force.

> *Every city and many smaller places* have adequate facilities now.
> *The tables and other furniture* are for sale.

When a multiple subject follows its predicator, the first coordinate in the subject is likely to determine the number form of the verb.

> On the table was a runner of gold-threaded Chinese fabric, four magazines, a silver box containing cigarettes, and three "gift books."

Multiple units in which the first coordinate is rejected but the second is accepted have the number force of the accepted member.

> *Not the boy himself but his parents* are responsible.

This is true even where the rejection of the first coordinate actually centers in its employment of some such word as *only* or *merely*.

> *Not only the parents but also the boy himself* is in trouble.

But multiple units of this type are likely to be kept out of situations in which their number force becomes significant.

Multiple units in which the coordinates are alternatives, whether open or rejected alternatives, in general have the number force of the coordinate nearer the point at which number force operates.

> *Either the climate or the houses* are wrong.
> Is *the climate or the houses* wrong?

Similarly the multiple modifier *one or more* gives the subject plural force in *one or more pages are missing*. But where number force is important it is generally wise to avoid using multiple units in which the coordinates are alternatives that differ in number.

Split clauses sometimes have two or more subjects and a single predicator. The two subjects function quite differently from multiple-unit single subjects.

> First the necessity of helping support his younger brothers and then the period of service in the war was responsible for his failure to get the formal training in music he always wanted.

Here *was* functions as predicator for the two subjects separately, as for the two adjuncts *first* and *then*.

Paradigms.—It remains to list the forms of the verbs. Verbs do not have many one-word forms. Regular verbs have only four. *Play, plays, playing, played* can illustrate; the four forms here are the basic form, the *s* form, the gerundial form, and the past form. A number of irregular verbs have five one-word forms, two of them past forms: *write, writes, writing, wrote, written* can illustrate. *Be* has eight one-word forms; at the other extreme such verbs as *put* and *spread*, which use their basic forms as pasts also, have only three distinct one-word forms and yet are not syntactically defective. The syntactic defectives *can, may, must, ought, shall, should,* and *will* have only a form or two. For all verbs except the defectives phrasal forms are made with the aid of auxiliaries: *be* followed by a participle in passives, *be* followed by a gerundial in progressives, *have* followed by a participle in perfects, *will* (and sometimes *shall*) followed by an infinitive in futures, *do* followed by an infinitive in expanded forms. From the point of view of syntax the use of auxiliaries is not greatly different from the use of other inflectional devices. Thus the separable *will* of *George will probably start tomorrow* is syntactically quite like the attached *ed* of *I started yesterday*.

Paradigms illustrating the inflectional pattern of regular verbs follow. The paradigms are simplified in that they give no indication of the variability of auxiliaries. *Will*, for example, becomes *ll* in *he'll start tomorrow* and *wo* in *he won't start today*.

COMMON ASPECT, COMMON VOICE

Tense	Form	Mode	Person and Number
A. 1.	play	common	common
		subjunctive	indifferent
		infinitival	indifferent
	plays	common	third singular
	playing	gerundial	indifferent
	do play	common	common
		subjunctive	indifferent
	does play	common	third singular
2.	have played	common	common
		subjunctive	indifferent
		infinitival	indifferent
	has played	common	third singular
	having played	gerundial	indifferent
3.	will play	common	indifferent
	shall play	common	first person
4.	will have played	common	indifferent
	shall have played	common	first person
B. 1.	played	common	indifferent
		subjunctive	indifferent
		participial	indifferent
	did play	common	indifferent
		subjunctive	indifferent
2.	had played	common	indifferent
		subjunctive	indifferent
3.	would play	common	indifferent
		subjunctive	indifferent
	should play	subjunctive	first person
4.	would have played	common	indifferent
		subjunctive	indifferent
	should have played	subjunctive	first person

PROGRESSIVE ASPECT, COMMON VOICE

Tense	Form	Mode	Person and Number
A. 1.	be playing	subjunctive	indifferent
		infinitival	indifferent
	are playing	common	common
	am playing	common	first singular
	is playing	common	third singular
2.	have been playing	common	common
		subjunctive	indifferent
		infinitival	indifferent
	has been playing	common	third singular
	having been playing	gerundial	indifferent
3.	will be playing	common	indifferent
	shall be playing	common	first person
4.	will have been playing	common	indifferent
	shall have been playing	common	first person
B. 1.	were playing	common	common
		subjunctive	common or indifferent
	was playing	common	first and third singular
		subjunctive	first and third singular
2.	had been playing	common	indifferent
		subjunctive	indifferent
3.	would be playing	common	indifferent
		subjunctive	indifferent
	should be playing	subjunctive	first person
4.	would have been playing	common	indifferent
		subjunctive	indifferent
	should have been playing	subjunctive	first person

COMMON ASPECT, PASSIVE VOICE

Tense	Form	Mode	Person and Number
A. 1.	be played	subjunctive	indifferent
		infinitival	indifferent
	are played	common	common
	am played	common	first singular
	is played	common	third singular
	being played	gerundial	indifferent
2.	have been played	common	common
		subjunctive	indifferent
		infinitival	indifferent
	has been played	common	third singular
	having been played	gerundial	indifferent
3.	will be played	common	indifferent
	shall be played	common	first person
4.	will have been played	common	indifferent
	shall have been played	common	first person
B. 1.	were played	common	common
		subjunctive	common or indifferent
	was played	common	first and third singular
		subjunctive	first and third singular
2.	had been played	common	indifferent
		subjunctive	indifferent
3.	would be played	common	indifferent
		subjunctive	indifferent
	should be played	subjunctive	first person
4.	would have been played	common	indifferent
		subjunctive	indifferent
	should have been played	subjunctive	first person

PROGRESSIVE ASPECT, PASSIVE VOICE

Tense	Form	Mode	Person and Number
A. 1.	are being played	common	common
	am being played	common	first singular
	is being played	common	third singular
B. 1.	were being played	common	common
		subjunctive	common or indifferent
	was being played	common	first and third singular
		subjunctive	first and third singular

In the paradigms given above, the tenses are indicated by letters and numbers as follows:

> A. 1. Present
> 2. Present perfect
> 3. Present future
> 4. Present future perfect
>
> B. 1. Past
> 2. Past perfect
> 3. Past future
> 4. Past future perfect

Other progressive passive forms are possibilities rather than normal actualities. Combinations of the forms *be* and *being* and of the forms *been* and *being* are generally avoided. *The last game of the series is being played now* is quite acceptable; *the last game of the series will be being played then* is much less so.

The form *would have been played* will serve to illustrate the structure of complex phrasal verb forms. The head is *played*. *Would* is the past form of *will*: the total form is therefore a past future. *Have* marks the total form as a perfect, *been* marks it as a passive. *Would have been played*, then, is a past-future-perfect passive form of the verb *play*. It can be used in either the common mode or the subjunctive, and in American English it is generally indifferent to person-and-number force in its subject. In aspect *would have been played* is common, since it lacks the sequence of *be* and a gerundial which marks the progressive.

The category of regular verbs to which *play* belongs includes the overwhelming majority of English verbs. Verbs of non-Germanic origin—including the many acquired from French, Latin, and Greek—are characteristically regular, and most verbs of Germanic origin are regular also.

The inflected one-word forms of regular verbs.—Regular verbs have *s* forms made by adding to their basic forms an ending which in the written language is represented by *s* alone where its addition does not increase the number of syllables in the spoken forms.

aim s	crie s	play s	froth s
allow s	die s	ski s	knife s
bar s	huddle s	stir s	pick s
bathe s	live s	tag s	seat s
bow s	marrie s	vetoe s	wipe s

Where the addition of the ending does increase the number of syllables in the spoken forms, *es* is added rather than *s* alone.

amaz es	catch es	judg es	rag es
box es	danc es	lunch es	reach es
buzz es	gass es	pass es	roug es
cash es	hatch es	quizz es	whizz es

Involvement in more or less regular complexities of the spelling system when inflectional endings are added does not constitute grounds for calling a verb irregular.

Regular verbs have gerundial forms made by adding to basic forms an ending which in the written language is represented by *ing*. Here again complexities of spelling appear.

agree ing	danc ing	liv ing	study ing
bend ing	dy ing	occurr ing	ty ing
better ing	dye ing	picnick ing	travel ing
blam ing	hoe ing	quizz ing	utter ing
bow ing	fill ing	rubb ing	veto ing
cry ing	fix ing	ski ing	worry ing

Regular verbs have past forms made by adding to their basic forms an ending which the written language represents by *ed* even where its addition does not increase the number of syllables in the spoken form.

amus ed	dragg ed	quarrel ed	bas ed
buzz ed	flow ed	quizz ed	diminish ed
carri ed	fre ed	referr ed	froth ed
chuckl ed	lean ed	seem ed	photograph ed
crochet ed	long ed	sinn ed	reach ed
cri ed	play ed	stirr ed	trapp ed
deaden ed	purr ed	ti ed	trick ed

Where the addition of the ending does increase the number of syllables, *ed* is added exactly as where it does not.

avoid ed	educat ed	permitt ed	start ed
correct ed	mold ed	provid ed	want ed
disgust ed	padd ed	rott ed	wound ed

Once again complexities of spelling appear.

Irregularities affecting one-word present forms.—Irregular verbs differ from regular verbs almost entirely in that their one-word inflected forms are not made, in the written language, simply by adding *s*, *ing*, and *ed* to their basic forms. A very few of them differ also in the uses to which their one-word forms are put. Except that the defectives *can, may, must, ought, shall, should,* and *will* do not take auxiliaries at all, irregular verbs do not differ from regular verbs in the use they make of auxiliaries.

Only a few verbs have irregularities affecting the uses to which their basic forms are put. The most notable is *be*, whose basic form serves only as a subjunctive and an infinitive.

> The Chairman suggests that speeches *be* brief.
> We want to *be* fair.

The common-mode present of *be* substitutes forms quite unlike the basic form: *are* in the second singular and throughout the plural, *am* in the first person singular. The defectives *can, may, must, ought, shall, should,* and *will* are notable also: their basic forms are used only as common-mode presents, not as infinitives and (except for *may* as used in *may the best man win*) not as subjunctives; but on the other hand their basic forms serve as indifferent-person-and-number forms in the common-mode present and thus take over the function performed in the third person singular by the *s* forms of regular verbs. The basic form *need* sometimes functions as an indifferent-person-and-number form in the common-mode present also, generally in negated clauses in which *need* is completed by infinitival clauses without *to*.

> The tourist need not provide himself with a passport.
> No tourist need worry about hotel accommodations.

In doubtfully standard informal styles a somewhat similar extension sometimes carries *do* into the third person singular in the merged form *don't*.

> He don't like the food very well.

Irregularities affecting one-word *s* forms are very few. *Be* has an *s* form quite unlike its basic form: *is*. *Have* has the *s* form *has*, with *ve* lost. *Say* and *do* have *s* forms that are regular in the written language but irregular in the spoken. The seven defectives have no *s* forms.

There are no real irregularities affecting gerundial forms. The seven defectives, again, do not have such forms.

Irregular verbs with single one-word past forms.—Almost all irregularities in the formation and use of English verb forms involve one-word past forms. Since the verbs that are irregular in other respects are also irregular here, it is convenient to make past forms the basis for classification of all irregular verbs. On this basis the irregular verbs of contemporary American English fall into eight categories, most of which can be divided into obvious subcategories. The verbs included in the first four of the eight categories have single one-word past forms which function in common, subjunctive, and participial modes.

One category of irregular verbs is made up of verbs which employ the spoken inflectional ending /d/ or its variant /t/ in forming single one-word past forms, but which accompany the addition of /d/ and /t/ by changes in the forms to which they are added. These verbs do not use the written *ed* of regular verbs. They fall into six subcategories.

1.	lay: laid	feel: felt
	pay: paid	kneel: knelt
	O. K.: O. K. 'd	mean: meant
2.	flee: fled	buy: bought
	hear: heard	4. bereave: bereft
	say: said	leave: left
	sell: sold	lose: lost
	tell: told	5. have: had
	shoe: shod	make: made
3.	creep: crept	6. seek: sought
	keep: kept	teach: taught
	sleep: slept	bring: brought
	sweep: swept	think: thought
	weep: wept	catch: caught
	deal: dealt	

In *laid*, *paid*, and *O. K. 'd* there is of course irregularity only in spelling. *Kneel* sometimes has the regular past *kneeled*. *Dream, leap, burn, dwell, spell*, and *spill* are usually regular in contemporary American use. Where death is involved, *bereave* is usually regular. *Beseech* has *besought* as a past form, or it can be a regular verb. *Work* has *wrought*, but is more commonly a regular verb.

A second category of irregular verbs is made up of verbs whose basic forms end in /d/ and whose single one-word past forms differ from the basic forms only in that /t/ is substituted for /d/. The category is a small one, but the verbs within it fall into two subcategories.

1. bend: bent   send: sent
   lend: lent   spend: spent
   rend: rent   2. build: built

Gird has *girt* as its past sometimes, but probably is a regular verb more often.

A third category of irregular verbs is made up of verbs whose basic forms also function as pasts in common, subjunctive, and participial modes. The category is small, and the verbs within it have basic forms ending in /t/ or /d/.

1. bet: bet   set: set
   burst: burst   shut: shut
   cast: cast   slit: slit
   cost: cost   spit: spit
   cut: cut   split: split
   hit: hit   thrust: thrust
   hurt: hurt   2. bid ("offer"): bid
   let: let   shed: shed
   put: put   spread: spread
   quit: quit

Spit uses both *spit* and *spat* as pasts. *Fit, knit, sweat, wet, rid,* and *shred* all use both regular pasts and their basic forms. *Acquit* is a regular verb, unlike *quit.*

A fourth category of irregular verbs is made up of verbs whose single one-word past forms differ from their basic forms only in their vowel sounds. The verbs within this category can conveniently be grouped according to their vowel sounds.

1. bleed: bled   string: strung
   breed: bred   swing: swung
   feed: fed   wring: wrung
   lead: led   slink: slunk
   read: read   dig: dug
   meet: met   stick: stuck
2. sit: sat   spin: spun
3. cling: clung   win: won
   fling: flung   4. get: got
   sling: slung   tread: trod
   sting: stung   5. hang: hung

6. light: lit   8. fight: fought
   slide: slid   9. shine: shone
7. bind: bound   10. strike: struck
   find: found   11. hold: held
   grind: ground   12. shoot: shot
   wind: wound

In spite of its non-Germanic origin *plead* sometimes has a past *pled* as well as the regular and better established *pleaded*. *Speed, heave, stave,* and *abide* are usually regular now; but the past forms *sped, hove, stove,* and *abode* occur. *Get* has a participial form *gotten* which occurs in some uses of *get,* so that for some users of American English in *he's got a new car now* the verb *get* expresses possession only and is different in sense from *get* in *he's gotten a new car now,* where acquisition is expressed. *Gotten* is generally avoided in careful and formal styles. *Trodden* occurs occasionally as a participial past of *tread. Hang* is sometimes kept regular where executions are spoken of. The verb *light* is sometimes regular, and the compound *alight* is always regular. *Shine* is regular with nounal complements, as in *he shined his own shoes in those days. Strike* has *stricken* as a participle used with the general meaning "afflicted."

Irregular verbs with two one-word past forms.—Three more categories of irregular verbs are made up almost entirely of verbs that have two one-word past forms, one used as a past in common and subjunctive modes and the other used as a participle. The first of these categories, the fifth category of irregular verbs, is made up of verbs whose common-mode and subjunctive past differs from the basic form only in its vowel sound, and whose participle is distinct from the other past only in its vowel sound. The category is a small one, made up of verbs whose vowel sound is followed by a nasal consonant sound; but it divides into two subcategories.

1. come: came, come   spring: sprang, sprung
   run: ran, run   drink: drank, drunk
2. swim: swam, swum   shrink: shrank, shrunk
   begin: began, begun   sink: sank, sunk
   ring: rang, rung   stink: stank, stunk
   sing: sang, sung

The verb *swim* is likely to be avoided where the participial form is called for. *Sprung* and *shrunk* sometimes drive out *sprang* and *shrank*. Uncertainty about past forms is common, in fact, in all the verbs of the subcategory to which *swim*, *spring*, and *shrink* belong.

A sixth category of irregular verbs is made up of verbs that have two past forms of which one, used in common and subjunctive modes, differs from the basic form only in vowel sounds and the other, the participle, is marked by the use of an infectional ending which in the written language is represented by *en* and (after vowel letters, and *r* and *w*) *n*. The verbs of this category fall into three subcategories, and these can conveniently be subdivided further.

1. a. freeze: froze, frozen
      speak: spoke, spoken
      steal: stole, stolen
      weave: wove, woven
   b. break: broke, broken
   c. beget: begot, begotten
      forget: forgot, forgotten
   d. bear: bore, borne
      swear: swore, sworn
      tear: tore, torn
      wear: wore, worn
   e. bite: bit, bitten
      hide: hid, hidden
   f. lie ("recline," "extend"): lay, lain
   g. choose: chose, chosen
2. a. eat: ate, eaten
   b. see: saw, seen
   c. give: gave, given
   d. bid ("order," "express"): bade, bidden
   e. forsake: forsook, forsaken
      shake: shook, shaken
      take: took, taken
   f. slay: slew, slain
   g. fall: fell, fallen
   h. draw: drew, drawn
   i. blow: blew, blown
      grow: grew, grown
      know: knew, known
      throw: threw, thrown
3. a. drive: drove, driven

ride: rode, ridden
rise: rose, risen
smite: smote, smitten
stride: strode, stridden
strive: strove, striven
write: wrote, written
    b. fly: flew, flown

Bear also has a participle *born*, used only in passives where birth
is spoken of. For many speakers of American English the *borne*
of *she had already borne six children* and the *born* of *her seventh was
born that Christmas day* are distinct only in the written language.
The participles *lain* and *stridden* are rarely heard: these verbs are
simply avoided where a participle would be called for. *Strive* is
sometimes regular.

A seventh category of irregular verbs includes a few highly individualistic verbs that combine inflectional patterns normally
characteristic of different types of verbs or that behave in some
other highly unusual fashion.

stand: stood   go: went, gone
do: did, done   be: were, was, been
beat: beat, beaten

Stand has only one one-word past form. In vigorous, slightly
slangy informal styles the basic form *beat* is used as a participle
also, as in *they've beat us again*. *Show, sow, strew,* and *swell* are
commonly regular verbs, but they also have as participles the
forms *shown, sown, strewn,* and *swollen*. *Wake* is commonly a regular verb, but the irregular common-mode and subjunctive past
form *woke* is also widely used. *Dive* is normally a regular verb, but
the past form *dove* also occurs; *thrive* is usually regular, but the
past form *throve* occurs. *Prove* has a participle *proven*, in spite of
its non-Germanic origin.

The defectives.—The remaining category of irregular verbs is
made up of the seven defectives. Four of these have one-word
past forms which function as common-mode and subjunctive pasts,
but not as participles. All these pasts are irregular formations.

1. can: could   will: would
   shall: should   2. may: might

Three defectives have no inflected forms at all.

must   should
ought

Should was originally a past form of *shall* and is still best regarded as the past of *shall* in various situations where it has past-tense force. When *should* is equivalent to *ought* in meaning, and in certain other uses where it has present-tense force, it is best regarded as a distinct verb in spite of its origin.

In particular turns of meaning some verbs are in effect functionally defective. *Use,* used as in *he used to be very strong,* as in *I didn't use to like him,* and as in *I'm used to him,* occurs only in past forms. But *use* occurs in much more varied situations with other turns of meaning: it is not defective basically. There is more reason to call such a verb as *be,* which never occurs in passive forms, defective; but it seems wisest to keep the word for verbs which fail to fill out even the common-aspect, common-voice pattern.

Irregularities in participial adjectives and in compound verbs.—Participial adjectives are sometimes oddly distinct from the true participles of the living language. A few examples follow.

on *bended* knees   *molten* metal
his *bounden* duty   *roast* beef
I'm *broke*   a *rotten* apple
a *drunken* beast   a *sunken* garden

In addition, participial adjectives in *ed* sometimes make a syllable of *ed* where the true participles would not: for example, in *her aged parents, his beloved sister, not a blessed one, that cursed fool,* and *he seemed very learned. Gotten* occurs in *his ill-gotten gains* even in the usage of those who generally reject the form. *Lit, swelled,* and *ridded* are not usable in *a lighted room, a swollen finger,* and *we finally got rid of him. Pent, sodden,* and *staid* now seem hardly related to *pen, seethe,* and *stay.*

Compound and complex verbs normally follow the related simpler verbs in their inflectional behavior. *Awake* inflects like *wake, become* like *come, foresee* like *see, outrun* like *run, uphold* like *hold, withstand* like *stand,* and so on. *Beget* and *forget* are exceptions to this rule. Irregularities in verb inflections characteristically appear in monosyllabic forms. *Forsake,* however, has no corresponding verb *sake* among living English verbs. *Beware* and *daresay* are really merged forms. *Beware* is usable in constructions where the basic verb form *be* is usable; *daresay* is ordinarily used only with *I* as subject.

CHAPTER IX

PLURALIZERS AND QUANTIFIABLES

Pluralizer nouns have plural forms whose use often correlates with the use of particular person-and-number forms of verbs and with the use of particular pronoun forms.

> *This* island *has* a quality of *its* own.
> *These* islands *have* a quality of *their* own.
> *That* sheep *has* a quality of *its* own.
> *Those* sheep *have* a quality of *their* own.
> *Those* trousers *have* a quality of *their* own.

The plural forms of pluralizers are also syntactically distinct from the singulars in that they are freely usable as subjects, for example, without determiner modifiers.

> *Islands* have a quality of their own.
> *Every island* has a quality of its own.

Regular inflection for plural number.—Most pluralizers have two common-case forms: a basic form, which is ordinarily singular in force; and a common-case plural form. The plurals of regular pluralizers are made by adding to the basic forms an ending which in the written language is represented by *s* alone where its addition does not increase the number of syllables in the spoken forms.

auditorium s	egg s	son s	bandit s
countrie s	piano s	stove s	cap s
crie s	rattle s	taxi s	cape s
day s	shoe s	tomatoe s	wreck s

Where the addition of the ending does increase the number of syllables in the spoken forms, *es* is added rather than *s* alone.

box es	church es	guess es	quizz es
buss es	dish es	hostess es	sandwich es
chanc es	fezz es	judg es	stag es
chorus es	fuzz es	mirag es	summons es

Involvement in more or less regular complexities of the spelling system when inflectional endings are added does not constitute grounds for calling a pluralizer noun irregular.

Irregular plurals using the s ending.—One group of irregular pluralizers employs the *s* ending of regular pluralizers but in the spoken language changes a final voiceless consonant sound to the corresponding voiced sound. Sometimes the change is from /f/ to /v/.

beeve s	knive s	scarve s	thieve s
calve s	leave s	selve s	wharve s
elve s	live s	sheave s	wive s
halve s	loave s	shelve s	wolve s

Sometimes the change is from the first sound of *thin* to the first sound of *then* and is not indicated by the spelling.

| bath s | moth s | oath s | truth s |
| booth s | mouth s | path s | |

In the word *houses* the change is from the /s/ of *sue* to the /z/ of *zoo*. *Beef, scarf, wharf, moth,* and *truth* have regularly formed plurals as well as the irregular ones noted here.

The irregularities noted in the formation of such plurals as *beeves, baths,* and *houses* occur only in small groups of words. They are not present in the following plurals.

belief s	cliff s	fourth s	kiss es
berth s	death s	growth s	proof s
birth s	depth s	gulf s	roof s
breath s	dos es	hearth s	safe s
chief s	dwarf s	hoof s	staff s

Hooves and *staves,* the latter with a change in vowel sound, occur.

Letters, numerals, words mentioned as words, and abbreviations form *s* plurals which commonly use apostrophes in the written language but are regular in the spoken.

three *A*'s and two *B*'s   in the *1950*'s
no *if*'s or *but*'s   too many *Ph.D.*'s

Irregular plurals inflecting in other ways.—A few native nouns have plurals which differ from their basic forms in their vowels and/or in their employment of the inflectional ending *en*.

geese	lice	women
teeth	mice	oxen
feet	men	children

Women is extraordinary in having changed the vowel of the first syllable in the spoken language but not in the written and having changed the vowel of the second syllable in the written language. *Brother* has a regular plural ordinarily, but *brethren* occurs also, chiefly in religious use.

A considerable number of nouns of foreign origin make plurals in English following foreign patterns. The best-established foreign pattern is that followed by the following plurals, in which weakly stressed final *es* has been substituted for unstressed final *is* of the basic forms.

analyses	diagnoses	neuroses	psychoses
axes	hypotheses	oases	synopses
crises	metamorphoses	parentheses	theses

A second foreign pattern substitutes weakly stressed final *i* for unstressed final *us*.

alumni   bacilli

A third foreign pattern substitutes weakly stressed final *ae* for unstressed final *a*.

algae   alumnae   larvae   minutiae

A fourth pattern substitutes unstressed *a* for unstressed *um* or *on*.

addenda   bacteria   desiderata   phenomena

Mr. and *Mrs.* have highly anomalous *Messrs.* and *Mesdames* as plurals, but these are commonly avoided except in very formal styles and at the beginning of lengthy lists. A good many words sometimes have plurals following foreign patterns and sometimes have regular *s* plurals. Examples include *cactus, focus, fungus, gladiolus, nucleus, radius, stimulus, syllabus, terminus; antenna, formula; compendium, curriculum, encomium, medium, memorandum, spectrum, stratum, automaton, criterion;* and *appendix, beau, genus, seraph, stigma,* the last five words sometimes following foreign patterns not noted above.

In general, when words from other languages have been added to the English word stock they have been made to follow the established inflectional pattern of English (when they inflect at all), just as their pronunciation has in general been made to fit into the English sound system. Only a basic form has been taken into English. Thus the verb *move* inflects in English as a regular English verb: the French and Latin inflections of the source verb are completely disregarded by the English verb. Sometimes the English basic form is itself an inflected form in the language from which the word comes. Thus Latin inflected forms of various kinds have become English nouns in *affidavit, deficit, fiat, ignoramus, imprimatur, quorum, recipe, requiem, tenet, veto,* and *vim.* But from the point of view of contemporary English grammar embedded inflections such as occur in words like these are irrelevant. The foreign plurals found among English nouns are not irrelevant. They are of course commonest in learned special vocabularies. They are troublesome: *mass media,* for example, is sometimes taken to be singular rather than plural. Very common words, such as native *foot,* can follow exceptional inflectional patterns; less common words can hardly afford to try, if they are to flourish in the non-esoteric general vocabulary. The substitution of foreign plurals for the regular English plurals of such words as the following would seem quite affected in most contexts.

| area | bandit | cello | isthmus |
| auditorium | bureau | gymnasium | stadium |

Sometimes regular plurals replace even firmly established native irregular plurals: for example, in *she does still lifes* and in *those boys are dumb oxes.*

Other plural forms.—A small number of nouns use their basic forms both as singulars and (unchanged) as plurals. These include (1) a few words used of animals and fish, (2) a few nouns applied to people as members of national and tribal groups, and (3) a few other nouns of miscellaneous types.

deer	goldfish	salmon	swine
fish	moose	sheep	trout
fowl	perch	shrimp	vermin

Chinese	Japanese	Siamese	Swiss
Iroquois	Portuguese	Sioux	
aircraft	grapefruit	means	series
counsel	head	offspring	species
craft	horsepower	pick	

Counsel is used in this way when it is applied to lawyers, *craft* when it is applied to boats, *head* when it is used of cattle and the like in counting, *means* when it is close to *method* in sense, *pick* when it is close to *the best* in sense. In the spoken language *Iroquois* and *Sioux* sometimes add /z/ in the plural.

A few nouns use their English basic forms as unchanged plurals less consistently. In informal styles a few nouns naming measurements use their basic forms occasionally as unchanged plurals when numeral pronouns modify them, as in *six foot one* and *five gallon of gas*. Sometimes family names ending in *s*, and even some family names ending in *x* and *z*, are made plural without change of form. Thus *the Bridges* occurs alongside *the Bridgeses, the Hendrix* alongside *the Hendrixes, the Stephens* alongside *the Stephenses, the Andrews* alongside *the Andrewses, the Hughes* alongside *the Hugheses*, and *the Schwartz* alongside *the Schwartzes*. The regular plurals, made by adding *es*, are commonly regarded as preferable; but the basic forms of names like these have something of the feeling of inflected forms in which inflectional *s* has already been employed. It may seem preferable to avoid making plurals for family names such as have been mentioned, just as it is preferable to avoid making a plural of *Socrates*, or of *commons* (as used of college eating places), or of *lazybones*, or of *upstairs* or *whereabouts*. Such locutions as *the Bridges family* and *Mr. and Mrs. Bridges*, the latter with number shown only in the multiple modifier, get around the difficulty.

A few nouns of French origin use basic forms ending in *s* as unchanged plurals in the written language but in the spoken language have nothing corresponding to the final *s* for the singular and add /z/ for the plural.

chamois	faux pas	precis
corps	patois	rendezvous

An essentially opposite situation exists in compounds terminating in unstressed *man*, which is changed to *men* in the written language but remains unchanged in the spoken.

> Englishmen   Irishmen   policemen   workmen

The noun *person* generally employs an etymologically unrelated plural, *people*.

> Several *people* have tried to reach you.

Persons occurs too, chiefly in formal styles. *People* is still a singular also, in its application to groupings of human beings such as nations.

Plurals without corresponding singulars.—In general, plurals represent more instances of what is represented singly by their basic forms. Thus *boys* is used of young male people, just as *boy* is ordinarily used of a single young male person; and *fathers* is used of male parents, just as *father* is ordinarily used of a single male parent. A few plurals are more general in application than the corresponding singulars. Thus *alumni* can include female graduates, though *alumnus* is ordinarily applicable only to a single male graduate. *Our hosts* can be equivalent to *our host and hostess*, and *the George Hendersons* can be applied to a group made up of a single George Henderson and his wife and children, or to George Henderson and his wife. *Dishes* can include cups and plates, though *dish* is not likely to be used of a cup or a plate. But this kind of thing is limited in occurrence; ordinarily plurals are not more general in application than corresponding singulars.

Uncountable plurals for which equivalent singulars are not employed are much less limited in occurrence. The italicized words in the following sentences are plurals both in form and in the force they exert on verbs and pronouns.

> Her present *surroundings* are very satisfactory.
> Her *travels* have taken her everywhere.
> The *dues* are not very high.
> He gives me the *creeps*.
> His *statistics* are more impressive than accurate.
> The *proceeds* from the sale were considerable.
> George's new *trousers* are rather startling.
> These *scissors* need sharpening.

There is no clear feeling here for such individual units as normally compose pluralities. In the concept of *surroundings*, for example, though there is some feeling that more than one element is involved, there is a certain vagueness about the identity of the elements, and it is not possible to speak either of *a surrounding* or of *three surroundings*. *Travels* has a clear feeling of plurality in it, but the components of the plurality, again, are not thought of clearly enough to be definitely countable. If they were so thought of, *trips* would replace *travels; trips* is a true countable pluralizer. If all feeling of plurality were gone, *travel* would be used; and *travel* is a quantifiable, in syntax not the singular form of the pluralizer *travels*. *Dues* reflects in its plural form and force an awareness of repeated payments; yet the number of payments is of minor importance. *Creeps* shows an old feeling that emotional states are multiple in character and yet cannot be broken down into clearly defined divisions. For *statistics*, a corresponding singular does occur, especially where there is expression of contempt.

You have corrupted every statistic you have used.

A list of plurals without semantically corresponding singulars would include such words as the following.

ashes	doldrums	oats	teens
backwoods	dregs	outskirts	thanks
belongings	earnings	police	throes
blues	environs	premises	tropics
bygones	fidgets	proceeds	valuables
cattle	fireworks	quits	wilds
clothes	groceries	remains	winnings
confines	headquarters	riches	wits
contents	lodgings	savings	woods
credentials	morals	statistics	works

Cattle and *police* are without inflectional *s*, but are plurals nevertheless. Number words can be used only in a limited way with words such as are listed here. Words which express number concepts exactly—the numeral pronouns—are not usable. Even as accurate a word as *several* is hardly usable. *Many* and *few* and *a few* are usable with some plurals of the kind.

She has entirely too many clothes.
I have to pick up a few groceries on the way home.

But it is not usual, for example, to speak of *few morals* or *few savings*. Words that express both number and quantity concepts—

such as *all, enough, some, any*, and *no*—are usable with most of the plural nouns that have no singulars. In these words the number concepts are largely lost in less troublesome concepts of totality, sufficiency, and the like. But some plural nouns reject even modifiers such as these. *Police*, for example, normally gives way to *policeman* under such circumstances.

A rather distinct subcategory among the plural nouns without freely used corresponding singular forms is made up of nouns used as the names of single articles whose structure, at least in part, is double.

breeches	pajamas	scissors	suspenders
drawers	pants	shears	tights
glasses	pincers	shorts	tongs
jeans	pliers	slacks	trousers
overalls	scales	spectacles	tweezers

The old singular *forceps* seems to have become a plural of this kind now. *Hose* (meaning "stockings") is a plural of the same kind in spite of the fact that the members of a pair are not joined. Usually words naming members of pairs that are not physically attached to each other are ordinary countable pluralizers, as is true of *glove, stocking, sock,* and *shoe*. When a plural form is used for a single double unit, plural forms in themselves indicate nothing about the number of double units. *My new trousers* can refer to one garment or more than one. When the number of double units is of consequence, and is not clear from the situation, the word *pair* can be applied to the double units. Number words can then be used with *pair*.

> Did you see a pair of glasses on my desk?
> We keep several pairs of pliers in the car.

But such words as *enough, some, any,* and *no*, again, can be used without the insertion of *pair*.

> Surely we have enough scissors already.

It should be added that refusal to accept determinatives of number occurs also with a few exceptional pluralizers whose basic forms are used with both singular and plural force. Thus *counsel* (used of lawyers) and *pick* (meaning "the best") can hardly be given such modifiers.

Collectives.—Nouns applied to various types of groups, organizations, and the like sometimes raise number problems when their basic forms are used. Ordinarily the basic forms of collectives have singular force. The pronoun forms that modify other singulars can modify the basic forms of collectives, as in *this audience, a committee, each family, another government.* In their relations with marker pronouns referring back to them, the basic forms of collectives normally show singular force and require a *which* or *that* with singular force. In their relations with verbs for which they function as subjects, the basic forms of collectives, again, usually show singular force.

> The Army was not much interested at first.
> The audience was very quiet.
> A committee is investigating the matter.
> The family has its black sheep.
> The government has been following a dangerous course.

Exceptions to these generalizations occur. It is possible to find combinations such as *fewer faculty,* as in *it is suggested that fewer faculty be assigned to each institute* where *fewer faculty members* would be more in accord with normal patterning. When a collective names a group of people in which the individual members stand out with considerable prominence in the speaker's mind, and when the verb names an action or state of affairs that is felt as more individual than collective, the basic forms of collectives sometimes are employed with plural verb forms and transmit plural force to marker pronouns also.

> Tom's family aren't impressed by his new wife.
> The young couple who are moving next door are from Utah.

The basic forms of collectives are most likely to exhibit plural force when personal pronouns are made to refer to them in new main clauses or in later parts of split clauses.

> The Army wasn't much interested in him. They took one look
>   at him and turned him down.
> The audience was in a bad mood. They had expected a more
>   familiar kind of music.
> The class does good work on phonetics. They like it better
>   than they do syntax.

A committee is studying the situation. They want a statement
from everyone involved.

The crowd was stirred, and their responses showed it.

A delegation from the union was waiting. They had come a
long way to present their case.

The faculty was behind the President. They had shown this
repeatedly, and now they showed it again.

We brought the baby home from the hospital yesterday. We
had hoped they would keep him longer.

The Institute will support us. They almost have to.

The Republican machine was fighting hard. They had money,
and they were winning.

I wrote the Cleveland office twice, but they never answered.

Our Production Department is having trouble and will need
more time than they had thought.

The neuter, nonhuman character of *it* operates in favor of *they*
in situations of this type. In careful and formal styles, however,
desire for consistency usually leads to elimination of avoidable
shifts in number. The sentences above are likely to be rephrased in
such styles. *It* will replace *they*, or the sentences will be changed
still more radically. Sentences such as the following will result.

The Army wasn't much interested in him. It took one look at
him and turned him down.

The audience was in a bad mood. Everyone had expected a
more familiar kind of music.

The students do good work on phonetics. They like it better
than they do syntax.

A committee is studying the situation. Its members want a
statement from everyone involved.

A list of more or less typical collective nouns follows:

association	club	herd	press
band	crew	intelligentsia	public
bureau	flock	management	set
choir	gang	mob	staff
clergy	generation	orchestra	swarm
clique	group	population	team

Most collectives name human groupings, but some, such as *flock*,
herd, and *swarm*, name animal groupings, and a few, such as *set*,
usually name inanimate groupings.

Most collectives have plural forms with normal plural force. Collectives are simply pluralizers whose basic (normally singular) forms sometimes have plural force in varying degrees.

Nouns of number and quantity.—Nouns of number are much like collectives in their behavior, and they also resemble pronouns. The number force of whatever they count makes itself felt through them; much more often than the collectives they resemble, they combine singular forms with plural force.

> An *average* of ten students are absent each day.
> When the papers reached me, a *couple* were missing.
> No *end* of errors were found.
> One *fourth* of the students were Spanish majors.
> *Half* of the students were English majors.
> A *lot* of people feel that way.
> A *number* of possibilities were mentioned.
> The greater *part* of our people were favorable.
> *Plenty* of rooms were available.
> A *quarter* of the games were lost.
> Some papers were excellent, but the *rest* were poor.
> A *wealth* of examples are given.

Nouns of number often retain a degree of singular force, as is shown by their acceptance of such modifiers as *a* and *one*. Nevertheless the verbs which follow them are rightly plural in such sentences as those above. Most nouns of number are usable in other ways also. *Number* itself, for example, is an ordinary singular pluralizer in such a sentence as *the number of possibilities has increased*. *Half* has an extraordinary range of uses, and even supplants *second* in fractions much as *quarter* sometimes replaces *fourth*.

Nouns (or nounal units) of quantity are sometimes like nouns of number in exerting number force that is not suggested by their forms.

> *Ten minutes* is too long.
> *Three glasses* of lemonade seems like a great deal.
> *Two dollars* is a high price.
> *Ninety horsepower* seems enough.

Names of quantities such as these have pluralizer force. Sometimes, as in *he gave us a bad ten minutes*, determiners involving number ideas are superimposed on them; in informal styles occasionally they are even made plural, as in *there was a long line of people paying their eighty centses.* Some nouns of number are also used as nouns of quantity. This is true of the denominators in fractions (*half, third,* etc.) and of such words as *lot, part, plenty, remainder,* and *rest.* As nouns of number such words are used with plural force; as nouns of quantity, with singular. In this respect they are strikingly like various pronouns of number and quantity, such as *all* and *some.*

> *Some* of the chairs were in good condition, but the *rest* were not.
> *Some* of the furniture was in good condition, but the *rest* was not.

Sometimes singular forms and plural forms compete to express practically identical meanings of number and quantity. Thus *a great number of voters* means about the same thing as *great numbers of voters,* and *a lot of time* as *lots of time.*

Indifferent-number force in basic forms of pluralizers.— Ordinarily the basic forms of pluralizer nouns have clearly singular force in all respects. Thus *chair* in *her chair didn't seem very strong* can be applied only to a single specimen, just as *chairs* in the same sentence could be applied only to two or more specimens. If *be* replaced *seem,* the sentence would read *her chair wasn't* (not *weren't*) *strong;* if a personal pronoun were made to refer back to *chair,* the form used would be *it;* and if a demonstrative pronoun were substituted for *her,* the form used would be *this* or *that,* not *these* or *those.* Collectives like *family* and nouns of number like *part* sometimes exhibit plural force, as has been noted.

There is, however, a limited and yet rather considerable use of undetermined basic forms of pluralizers as indifferent-number forms. The construction is normal when pluralizer nouns are used as common-case modifiers of other nouns.

animal crackers	*cigar* boxes	*student* activities
automobile salesmen	*fool* boys	*taxi* drivers
baby girls	*girl* babies	*telephone* books
baby sitters	*insect* powder	*tourist* business
baby talk	*letter* writing	*window* washing
card playing	*oyster* stew	*woman* haters
cherry pie	*street* signs	*word* order

Some pluralizers that are ordinarily not used except as *s* plurals are without *s* in this use.

> an *ash* tray   an *oat* field   *pajama* trousers

Even the *s* of such compounds as *outdoors* sometimes falls off in prepositive uses, as in *outdoor sports*, though *an upstairs apartment* illustrates the opposite practice.

In prepositive-modifier common-case use plural forms would tend to be confused with possessives. Thus *girls babies* would be indistinguishable from *girl's babies* and *girls' babies* in the spoken language, and even in the written language the distinction would be a weak one. Nevertheless some plural forms do occur in this use.

> *clothes* closet   *United States* government   *savings* bank
> *glasses* case   *sales* technique   *women* lawyers

A glass case could hardly mean *a case for glasses*. *Men friends* and *women lawyers* employ common-case plurals as prepositive modifiers of other plurals without any possibility that the modifying plurals will be confused with possessives. *Women lawyers* is oddly distinct from *woman haters*. In *women lawyers* the modifying noun is semantically equivalent to the adjective *female*. In *woman haters* the noun *woman* is semantically equivalent to postpositive *of women*.

Undetermined basic forms of pluralizers are normal, without reference to number, as prepositive modifiers of adjectives, including gerundial and participial adjectives.

> *ash* gray   *cigar*-smoking politicians   *machine* made
> *boy* crazy   *horse* drawn   *motor* driven

In paired constructions of various types undetermined basic forms of pluralizers are used without reference to number.

> We worked *day* and *night* till we finished.
> *Man, woman,* and *child*—the bomb destroyed them all.
> They fought *tooth* and *nail* for their freedom.
> The relationship between *husband* and *wife* has changed.
> The food isn't fit for *man* or *beast*.
> We get tired of *boy*-meets-*girl* movies.
> They built dozens of such houses *side* by *side*.
> He's read all Trollope's novels from *beginning* to *end*.

Undetermined basic forms of pluralizers are used with indifferent-number force as objects of prepositions in a considerable number of more or less fixed phrasings.

Most college students spend their summers *at home*.
You can see Mexico *by bus* cheaply and pleasantly.
Fine shoes are still made *by hand* in these countries.
The Captain knew practically all of us *by name*.
Such things can generally be worked out *by telephone*.
We were hunting *for squirrel*.
We spend a third of our lives *in bed*.
Millions of young people are *in college* now.
The best people were *in jail* at the time.
We had to stand *in line* for everything in those years.
Millions of men were *in uniform* at the time.
Few of us achieve real peace *of mind*.
Love *of country* was weaker than love *of family*.
We stacked the boxes *on end*.
The poor travel *on foot* as in the past.
The men have been *on strike* three times since then.
George is never *on time*.
The books are all *out of place*.
He's always speaking *out of turn*.
Country people go *to town* frequently all over the island.

People can see Mexico *by bus*, or *by car*, or *by plane*, or *by train;* but ordinarily not *by comfortable bus*, and not *in bus*. *To town* can be matched by *in town*, *out of town*, and *through town;* but in *islands without towns are pleasant places* it is hardly possible to employ *without town*. Such locutions as *in hospital* and *in university* would be useful but apparently are not established.

Undetermined basic forms of pluralizers have indifferent-number force in such phrasal adjectives as *black-eyed*.

She's a pretty little black-eyed girl.
She's a pretty little girl with black eyes.

Black-eyesed simply does not occur, however reasonable it may seem.

Undetermined basic forms of pluralizers are used with indifferent-number force as complements in fixed phrasings of various **types**.

The Jacksons had never set *foot* in Mexico before.
We all got *home* by midnight.
Many women keep *house* and work too.
The winners took *office* at a difficult time.
The children haven't learned to keep *step*.
A few of those who were captured turned *traitor*.

In all the constructions noted thus far, the indifferent-number force of basic-form pluralizers is unlikely to affect other parts of the sentences in which they occur, or of following sentences. When indifferent-number force is found in basic-form pluralizers used as generic subjects of expressed predicators, the situation is different.

Man, too, is stimulated by hunger.
Life is too short for hair-splitting like that.
Birth does not always involve pain.
Monday is always a hard day.
When *noon* comes, the stores close for two hours.
Breakfast always includes eggs.
Marriage is rarely a prison.
Home is always in the men's minds.

In such sentences number force is indifferent from the point of view of meaning, but choice between singular and plural is necessary for the predicators. Pronouns can refer to nouns used in this way too, or modify them; and again choice between singular and plural is sometimes necessary.

Man has had to fight *his* way step by step.
Birth should not involve pain, but *it* often does.
This life is too short for such hairsplitting.

The more usual patterning calls for the use of undetermined plurals, not undetermined singulars, where generic force is desired for pluralizers.

People, too, are stimulated by hunger.
Mondays are always hard.
Marriages should not be prisons.
Uniforms impress Sarah.

Basic forms of quantifiables function generically quite normally. The usual contrast is clear in the following sentence.

Thought is hostile to *fluency*, so that *politicians* are more fluent than *scientists*.

But such words as *man, life* (as applied to the period of time
separating birth from death), *birth,* and *Monday* can hardly be
classified as quantifiables, as *thought* and *fluency* can.

Extension of indifferent-number use to determined pluralizers
occurs in common-case nounal units employed as prepositive modifiers within larger nounal units.

a sixty-*dollar* suit	a three-hundred-*mile* trip
a six-*foot* man	a ten-*minute* nap

In *a dry-goods store* and *a two-thirds majority* plural forms are used
in similar situations. In units such as *three-year-old,* whether used
as phrasal nouns (as in *the three-year-old next door*) or as prepositive modifiers (as in *any three-year-old child*), the construction is
different but obviously related.

***Distributive singulars, representative singulars, singulars
by understatement and metaphor.***—Determined distributive
singulars compete with plurals.

When we go to the movies, we rarely stay till the *end.*
Both drivers had a good *sense* of humor.
The tender *part* of the horses' hoofs was sore.
The tests are given in the *form* of objective quizzes, discus-
     sion tests, and oral examinations.
All New Yorkers seem to be in a *hurry.*
Mothers give up too much for the *sake* of children.
Bring a *pencil* to class next time, please.

There are shifts in point of view here. In the first sentence, for
example, *movies* is plural, and each movie has an end; but *end* is
singular. In the last sentence each student is expected to bring a
pencil, but a group of students is spoken to jointly. A strong feeling against needless shifts in point of view holds the use of distributive singulars down in careful and formal styles, and to some
extent even in informal styles. Distributive singulars are avoided,
for example, in such sentences as the following.

The men brought their *wives* along.
They turned their *faces* to the camera.
Many of them have their own *homes.*
Do you all have your *badges?*

Here the complements are plural for much the same reason as the complement is plural in *his relatives are farmers*.

Representative singulars, determined by such pronouns as (1) *any, each, every,* and *a,* and (2) *the,* compete with plurals also.

(1) *Any student* of history knows that.
Does *each delegate* have a badge?
All her life *every woman* waits for the right man to come along, but meanwhile most women marry.
In order to get maximum enjoyment out of life, *a man* should have an Egyptian wife, a French mistress, a Chinese cook, and a home in the West Indies.
Here and there *an old Victorian mansion* is still kept up.
Many *a man* has tried and failed.
(2) He buys ties by *the dozen.*
It's a noisy district in *the evening.*
One trouble with higher education in the United States is that in *the fall* there is football and in *the spring* there is spring.
The Ph.D. should always be awarded posthumously.
The family has always perpetuated inequalities.
The Indian had no defense against the new weapons.

The chief disadvantage of the plural is illustrated in the following sentence.

In order to get maximum enjoyment out of life, men should have Egyptian wives, French mistresses, Chinese cooks, and homes in the West Indies.

Here there is no clear indication that what is suggested is an allotment of a single wife, for example, to a single man. The chief disadvantage of representative singulars turns up in sentences like *everyone paid his own way,* where *his* is less than completely satisfactory if *everyone* represents a group that includes members of both sexes but the *their* of informal styles leaves something to be desired also.

Some singulars are simply products of understatement or metaphor.

In *a word,* the new policy is doomed to failure.
Keep *an eye* on George, will you?

Distinctions between pluralizers and quantifiables.—
Quantifiable nouns characteristically reject both determinatives of

number (the cardinal numerals, *few, several, many, both*) and determinatives of identification which modify only true singulars (*a, either, every, each, neither*), but they accept determinatives of quantity (*little, much*). Similarly, quantifiable nouns are used harmoniously with such words as *amount*, as in *a certain amount of poetry*, and not with such words as *number*, as in *a certain number of poems*. Quantifiables are not made plural, though it must be added at once that many nouns must be classified as quantifiables in some uses and as pluralizers in others. When quantifiables determine number forms of demonstrative pronouns, personal pronouns, or verbs, these forms are singular, not plural.

Quantifiables used of what lacks obvious physical substance.—Nounal names of qualities, emotions, activities, and forces are often quantifiables. Some nouns of these kinds are rarely or never used as pluralizers.

applause	foolishness	lightning	stamina
behavior	fun	luck	thunder
blame	humanity	permission	transportation
courage	ignorance	progress	wisdom
flattery	laughter	sadness	work

Thus such locutions as *several applauses, an odd behavior*, and *another fun* seem quite strange; locutions such as *several bursts of applause, an odd piece of behavior*, and *another good time* generally replace them. *Laugh* is a pluralizer alongside quantifiable *laughter*, *job* is a pluralizer alongside quantifiable *work*. The situation is simpler when nouns naming qualities, emotions, activities, and forces are freely usable both as quantifiables and as pluralizers applied to particular instances.

ability	color	entertainment	service
accident	conscience	examination	shape
action	crime	fire	sin
amusement	death	life	sleep
business	depth	noise	sport
chance	difficulty	poison	thought
change	doubt	risk	war

Thus *I didn't have much chance* can be matched by *I didn't have a very good chance*, and *my hat doesn't have much shape* by *my hat doesn't have a very good shape*. The situation is different with such nouns as *heart, school,* and *sun. Heart* is a quantifiable in the sense of "enthusiasm," as in *I didn't have much heart for it;* it is a pluralizer as the name of the physical organ, as in *Maurice had a bad heart. School* is a quantifiable as the name of an activity, as in *school starts at nine* and in *we didn't have much school today;* it is a pluralizer as the name of an institution, as in *Susan was in four schools that year. Sun* is a quantifiable as the name of the emanation, as in *a little sun would do us good;* it is a pluralizer as the name of a star.

Gerundial nouns are likely to be quantifiable. Quite often alongside quantifiable gerundial nouns there are pluralizers whose basic forms are identical with the basic forms of the corresponding verbs. Thus *so much crying* is paralleled by *a good cry, that much guessing* by *several guesses, too much stopping* by *three stops,* and *a little whispering* by *a stage whisper.* But this patterning is followed only within limits. Thus *hearing* and *suffering* are pluralizers as well as quantifiables, and *sin* and *taste* are quantifiables as well as pluralizers.

Names of bodies of knowledge and of languages tend to be quantifiables. This is true of such words as *architecture, chemistry, English, French, grammar, law,* and *zoology.* It is also true of nouns in *ics* such as *economics, phonetics,* and *physics.* The words *language* and *science* are quantifiables in their broader, less differentiated senses, but pluralizers when applied to individual instances.

I never learned much science.
The sciences are more and more important.

Nouns applied to less extensive kinds of information (and misinformation) also tend to be quantifiables. This is true of such words as *advice, information, knowledge, nonsense, propaganda,* and *word* (meaning "news"). It is also true of the old plural form *news.* Such words as *piece* and *bit* are commonly applied to what are felt as countable units, as in *two or three pieces of news.* Names of games are generally quantifiables. This is true of such words as *basketball, bridge, football,* and *poker,* and even of such old plurals as *checkers* and *dominoes* when used as names of games and not as names of objects used in the games.

I don't play much checkers nowadays.

Names of ailments tend to be quantifiable. This is true, for example, of *anemia, appendicitis, arthritis, asthma, dysentery,* and *pneumonia.* It is true also of such old plurals as *measles, mumps,* and *rickets.*

There has been very little influenza this winter.
We've had entirely too much mumps in the neighborhood.

Disease is both a quantifiable and a pluralizer. *Fever* (unspecified), "ache" names (such as *backache, headache,* and *toothache*), and *cancer* are both quantifiables and, when applied to individual instances, pluralizers. But phrasal *scarlet fever* and *typhoid fever* are always quantifiables.

There's very little typhoid fever there now.

Indigestion is always quantifiable. Odd preferences appear in particular locutions. Thus the native would never say *I have headache,* but always *I have a headache;* yet he would say either *I don't have much headache* or *I don't have a very bad headache.* The word *case* is often used when particular instances of ailments without pluralizer names are to be discussed.

There were two cases of typhoid fever last year.

Time, applied to duration, is a quantifiable in its general application and either a quantifiable or a pluralizer in applications to specific periods.

I don't know how *much* time I wasted.
I waited *a* long time.

The names of the seasons are similarly sometimes quantifiables and sometimes pluralizers.

Minnesota has too *much* winter.
Florida usually has mild *winters.*

Vacation behaves like the names of the seasons. *Weather* is a quantifiable, *climate* is a pluralizer.

We have very *little* hot weather.
We have *a* very mild climate.

Space, place, and *room* are both quantifiables and pluralizers. As a pluralizer *room*, of course, has a very specific application to the divisions of buildings.

Names of colors are normally quantifiables.

> *A little* yellow would help the total effect.

But such nouns are used as pluralizers when particular shadings are referred to, as in *the hat was a pale blue*. And some color nouns have specialized uses as pluralizers, as when *the whites* means *the white people*.

Names of substances.—Nouns naming what are felt as uncountable substances are normally quantifiables, not pluralizers. This is true of names of solids, of liquids, and of gases. It is also true of names of grains and leaves and of other masses of particles whose natural units are commonly too numerous for counting to be a real possibility; but it is not true of beans and peas, berries, or nuts. Nouns such as the following are normally quantifiable when they name substances.

air	cloth	foliage	molasses
aspirin	coal	glass	oak
bacon	coffee	grass	oxygen
bread	corn	hair	sand
brick	cotton	iron	skin
butter	dust	lamb	soup
cabbage	fish	lettuce	water
chicken	flour	milk	wheat

With most names of substances measurement becomes possible with the aid of words such as *piece, grain, helping, gallon, pound*, etc., which are countable pluralizers. The quantifiable noun has to be subordinated in construction, as the object of a preposition—as, for example, in *a head of lettuce* and in *a quart of milk*. Some names of substances are used as pluralizers also, applied to particular varieties of the substances named.

> The bakery makes *a* very fine rye *bread*.
> American *soups* are uninspiring.
> Marble is *an* expensive *stone*.

Such uses are exceptional. It is commoner for nouns which are quantifiables as names of substances to have uses of other kinds as pluralizers.

She took two *aspirins* and went to bed.
He raises *chickens*.
The dog had *a cloth* wrapped around its leg.
We toasted marshmallows over the hot *coals*.
We need *a* new electric *iron*.
He buys *skins* from the trappers.

Names of miscellanies.—Names of aggregates whose components are of different kinds tend to be quantifiables. This is true of such nouns as the following.

baggage	equipment	lace	music
candy	food	livestock	poetry
cash	fruit	machinery	poultry
clothing	furniture	mail	scenery
country	hardware	medicine	shrubbery
cutlery	jewelry	money	slang

Such words as *piece* and *article* are generally applied to what are felt as countable units. Pluralizers are commonly used for distinct components within miscellanies. Thus quantifiable *baggage* is matched by pluralizer *suitcase*, quantifiable *country* by pluralizer *farm*, quantifiable *furniture* by pluralizer *chair*, quantifiable *machinery* by (hardly more specific) pluralizer *machine*, quantifiable *mail* by pluralizer *letter*, quantifiable *money* by pluralizer *dollar*, quantifiable *poetry* by pluralizer *poem* and (more specific) *sonnet*, quantifiable *scenery* by pluralizer *scene* or *view*. A few nouns of miscellany are also used as pluralizers when varieties are referred to.

The avocado is *a* valuable *food*.
The mango is *a* tropical *fruit*.

This kind of thing is commoner in quasi-technical use than in general use. *Country* is a pluralizer as well as a quantifiable, but with a sharp distinction in meaning.

There's *too much country* around us.
This is *a* big *country*.

Quantifiables applied to people are quite exceptional in contemporary English. The Shakespearean *much tall youth* and the biblical *much people* have given place to *many tall young men* and *many people*. *Company*, however, in the sense of "visitor or visitors," is a quantifiable which is applied to people.

We like to have *a little company* now and then.

But the neuter personal pronoun *it* can never refer to *company: it* would be felt as too devoid of personality. *Posterity* and *personnel* are basically quantifiables, like *company;* but the tendency is to avoid them, substituting *relatives, descendants*, and *employees* where their quantifiable force would be noticeable. Sometimes *personnel* is treated as a plural. *Population* is a highly impersonal quantifiable in some of its uses. Even for domestic animals a quantitative view is exceptional, though it persists in *livestock* and *poultry*.

Mixtures of quantifiable and pluralizer characteristics.— As has been noted, English has nouns that are plural in form but quantifiable in force. This is true of names of a number of diseases, though here, it must be said, there is a tendency to assign uncountable-plural status and *mumps are dangerous to adults* is heard alongside the preferred *mumps is dangerous to adults*. The names of such games as *checkers* and *dominoes* are plural in form but quantifiable in force. So are the names of bodies of knowledge ending in *ics—genetics, mathematics, physics*, etc. *Politics* is often treated as a quantifiable even when it names activities rather than any body of knowledge.

There's too much *politics* in what he's doing.

Statistics is an uncountable pluralizer when applied to particular figures, and such nouns as *acoustics, athletics, hysterics*, and *tactics* are uncountable pluralizers when they are applied to properties and activities.

The statistics he quotes are misleading.
His tactics are a little crude.

News is now quantifiable in force invariably.

The plural forms seen in *mumps, checkers, genetics*, and *news* are native ones employing the regular ending *s*. It is remarkable that they have developed quantifiable force. It is much less strange that a few foreign plurals should have crossed the same line, as *paraphernalia, regalia, stamina, confetti, macaroni*, and *spaghetti* have done. *Data* is moving in the same direction, and the old singular *datum* is rarely seen; but *data* has not become securely established as a quantifiable and is often avoided in constructions where it would determine a choice between singular and plural forms of verbs or pronouns. It is of course not surprising that *data* should move toward classification with such quantifiables as *information* and *advice*.

Quantifiable status is sometimes given, especially in informal styles, to such uncountable pluralizers as *ashes, brains, fireworks, morals, oats,* and *suds*.

> We have *too much ashes* in the fireplace.
> He just doesn't have *much brains*.

The situation is very similar in sentences such as *Johnny's eaten too much mashed potatoes*. *Many* is obviously not usable here: individual, countable potatoes are not present in mashed potatoes.

In somewhat literary styles, nouns which are ordinarily quantifiables are sometimes preceded by the indefinite article *a* when they are also modified by adjectives or, more often, clauses.

> an admiration which he did not try to conceal
> a thorough knowledge of the subject
> a prose that has rarely been equaled for force

In archaic usage a few ordinarily quantifiable nouns occasionally take plural forms as an indication of great quantity.

> the sands of the desert   the waters of the deep

Waters occurs also in such phrases as *American waters*. Sometimes nouns that are normally pluralizers are used as quantifiables with an effect somewhat like that of metaphor.

> He has *too much family*.
> I just didn't have *much morning* today.
> He isn't *man enough*.

Slightly less direct combinations of determinative pronouns of quantity and pluralizer nouns are commoner.

> Only a little of the contents of the bottle remains.
> I'd seen enough of the picture.
> Not much of the morning was left.

Quantifiables remain unchanged when pluralizers with which they are coupled change number.

The little girl's *hair* is very pretty.
The little girls' *hair* is very pretty.
He tries to guard his *health*.
They try to guard their *health*.
He got his *education* in the public schools.
They got their *education* in the public schools.

It is noteworthy that expression of abstract concepts is commonly better achieved by quantifiable nouns than by pluralizers. Thus *machinery* gets to the essence of the matter better than *machines*, which even as an undetermined generic plural does not get as completely away from the particular, and better than the representative singular *the machine* also.

Machinery has changed human life completely.
Machines have changed human life completely.
The machine has changed human life completely.

But when undetermined basic forms of pluralizers are usable with indifferent-number force, they are able to get at essences about as well as quantifiables can.

Marriage is an institution it is hard to be happy with and hard to be happy without.
Travel by *plane* makes the transitions between cultures disappear.

At the opposite extreme from abstraction, accurate measurement always requires the use of numerals, even when these cannot be attached directly to the nouns that name what is measured, as in *three quarts of milk*.

In most constructions basic forms of nouns used without determiners and without particular applications are best taken to be quantifiables if the nouns in point are clearly established as quantifiables in other constructions. Basic forms of pluralizers have only very exceptional use without determinative modifiers, as has been noted. Thus in *a great change took place* the noun *place* is best considered a quantifiable, as in *there isn't much place for it*, rather than a pluralizer, as in *there's a place for such things*. The use of basic forms without determiners is ordinary for quantifiables (and for proper nouns) and is exceptional for pluralizers.

CHAPTER X

PROPER NAMES, POSSESSIVES, SYNTACTICALLY EXCEPTIONAL USES OF NOUNS

Proper nouns.—Proper nouns differ from both pluralizers and quantifiables in having particular applications without the use of determiner modifiers.

George	Mars	Mexico	Christmas
Jack	Paris	Europe	February
Thompson	Ohio	Fujiyama	"Hamlet"
Moses	Martinique	Tuesday	*Erewhon*

Proper nouns are most characteristically used (1) as names of living beings, real or imaginary, that are thought of as individual personalities; (2) as names of geographical and political units and topographical features of various kinds; (3) as names of days and months; and (4) as titles of literary, musical, and artistic works, and of periodicals. Children use proper nouns as names of dolls and toy animals. Large rural estates sometimes have proper nouns as names. Hurricanes are given such names. Such names as *George* are likely to be assigned on an unsystematic basis (except that sex is taken into account), simply because they happen to appeal to those who (at birth or purchase) are doing the naming. Such names as *Jack* are likely to be nicknames. Such names as *Thompson* are usually given systematically, on the basis of membership in a family. Such names as *Tuesday* are assigned on the basis of position in a sequence. *Tuesday* is a pluralizer in *the last three Tuesdays*, but so is *George* in *another George* and *Paris* in *the Paris of Napoleon's day*. *Tuesday* is a proper noun both in *I'll see you Tuesday* and in *I saw George Tuesday*, but it is a pluralizer in *I'll see you next Tuesday* and in *I saw George last Tuesday*, where determiners are employed. Weeks do not have proper nouns as names, and neither do years or centuries. The written language assigns honorific initial capital letters to most proper nouns.

Such words as *George, Thompson,* and *Paris* have their most characteristic uses as proper nouns. Such words as *faith, mother, god,* and *tombstone* all have other uses as more basically characteristic; yet they function as proper nouns too.

> Where did *Faith* leave her umbrella?
> What does *Mother* think?
> George Fox thought that *God* was uninterested in theology.
> We visited *Tombstone* while we were in Arizona.

Here *Mother* is equivalent in meaning to *my mother,* in which the same noun is a pluralizer with a determiner; and *God* is equivalent to *my god* or *his god.* When such words as *faith* and *tombstone* become proper nouns, there is an obvious interest in the meanings they convey as words of another kind; but once they are attached to particular people and places, these meanings become, in varying degrees, irrelevant. Girls named *Faith* must not be assumed to be devout, just as men named *Johnson* must not be assumed to be sons of men named *John.* Family names such as *Young* and *Short* are of course proper nouns, though the same words are also adjectives.

Proper nouns are not confined to single applications. There are innumerable Georges, some of them people, some of them dogs, some of them dolls. The commonly used proper nouns can be unambiguous in their applications only when context or situation is favorable. *George phoned while you were out* is a satisfactory sentence only if in the thinking of both the speaker or writer and the hearer or reader a single person named George is prominent at the time. The effective meaning of such a name as *George,* in characteristic proper-noun uses, is quite individual—accumulated in years of acquaintanceship perhaps, and not to be found in dictionaries. *We'll be in Paris next week* is satisfactory only when a single Paris—whether in Kentucky or in France or elsewhere—is already more prominent in the minds of those concerned with the sentence than all other Parises.

Combination and modification of proper nouns.—Proper
nouns sometimes unite with other proper nouns to form phrasal
units whose application is clearer than that of one-word proper
nouns. Thus *George Carter* will often be clear where *George* alone is
not. A second given name can follow *George*, as in *George Harvey
Carter*. In actual practice, letters often replace given names. *T. S.
Eliot*, for example, is a much better known sequence than *Thomas
Stearns Eliot*. The relationships between the names which make up
phrasal units such as *George Harvey Carter* are highly ambiguous:
in modern English such units are best regarded as unanalyzed
strings. Combinations such as *Paris, Kentucky*, are a little like
combinations such as *George Carter;* but in the written language
the name of the larger geographical unit is treated as a loose adjunct and inclosed in commas.

Modification of proper nouns includes, notably, the use of honorific modifiers with names of people. These are usually nouns used
as prepositive modifiers of family names or of combinations of
family names and given names.

Mr. George H. Carter	President Eisenhower
Captain James J. Nichol	Bishop Manning
Judge McLendon	Senator Morse
Dr. Elder	Grandfather Clark

A few honorifics are attached to given names.

Uncle Leslie	Saint Paul
Aunt Mary	Queen Elizabeth

Two adjectives are used as honorific modifiers: *reverend* and, less
commonly, *honorable*. There is a feeling that these should be preceded by the article *the* and followed by given names and family
names together, as in *the Reverend George Brewster;* but there is also
a marked tendency to treat *reverend* exactly as the noun honorifics
are treated, as in *Reverend Brewster will preach at the eleven-o'clock
service*. The general tendency has long been toward simplification
and standardization in the matter of honorific modifiers of people's
names. The names of the famous and of the dead are commonly
used without honorifics: *Abraham Lincoln*, or just *Lincoln*, is generally preferred to *President Lincoln*, for example. At the other
extreme, also, when relationships become informal it is usual for

honorifics to disappear and for given names to replace family
names, though such things as differences in age may interfere.
Mrs. is often used with names which without it would belong only
to the husbands. Most honorific modifiers of people's names are
usable without the names where they can also be used in combination with the names. Without the names they usually take
articles, except in direct address.

> Tell me the truth, *Doctor.*
> Has the *Judge* come in?

But *Mr.*, *Mrs.*, and *Miss* are not standard without names, and
neither are *Reverend* and *Honorable.*

At least in journalistic styles, common-case nounal modifiers
naming professions or otherwise contributing toward identification
are sometimes attached to names of people and capitalized like
honorifics.

> Polio Fighter Salk   World Champion Tenley Albright

Other types of modifiers of proper nouns applied to people and
places can be illustrated as follows.

> *poor* Mary   *all* Germany
> *colonial* Virginia   Chicago *proper*
> *southern* France   my dear Mr. Fulton

Here the modifiers are not given initial capital letters. In *poor
Mary* the modifier is an emotional word, like the *dear* of *dear me.*
Some prepositive modifiers of proper nouns are of ordinary predeterminative types: *all Germany,* for example, is much like *all
that week.* Proper nouns do not take modifiers freely, as has been
said. But half modifiers relate to them with comparative freedom.

> Mary went home *sick.*

**Phrasal proper names including words other than proper
nouns.**—The proper nouns, alone and in combinations, form the
hard core in a much larger category of proper names. The remainder of the category is made up of phrasal units which combine
fixed wording with individual application. The wording of phrasal
proper names is often official in origin, but this is not always the
case. The written language uses honorific capital letters to mark

phrasal proper names. Words of all kinds are included in such names. In *the Republican Party*, for example, *the* is a determinative pronoun, *republican* is an adjective, and *party* is a pluralizer noun. No single word is a proper noun in this proper name, but the whole unit has a fixed quality, and the application is individual. In *Ohio State University* all three words are nouns. *Ohio* is a proper noun; *state* and *university* are pluralizers. *Ohio State University* normally has no determiner pronoun; *the Republican Party* requires one, the article *the*.

Sometimes official titles are used with reasonably fixed particular applications so that in some ways they compete with the more permanent given-and-family names of the holders.

> the President of Mexico
> the Governor of Michigan
> the Dean of the College of Education

The honorific capitals given *President*, *Governor*, and *Dean* here would not be normal in *the last three presidents*, *a meeting of governors*, and *another dean*. It is noteworthy that the honorific *Mr.* (and the less common honorific modifier *Madam*) can modify short forms of some titles such as these when they are used in direct address.

> Mr. President   Madam Chairman

Some old or exotic phrasal proper names applied to people and superhuman personages are not titles but approach titles in force.

> the Wife of Bath
> Our Most Holy Lady of the Miracles of Tlaltenango
> the Holy Ghost

Pseudoproper names are used ironically.

> Has the Great Man expressed himself yet?
> Even the Little Woman could learn to make good soup.

Names of geographical and political units and of topographical features are very frequently phrasal.

> North America   the Atlantic Ocean
> the United States of America   the Gulf of Mexico
> Puerto Rico   Hudson Bay

New York
the Far East
the Ukraine
Mexico City
Fort Wayne

Lake Erie
the Panama Canal
Mount Everest
Lookout Mountain
the Tropic of Capricorn

Roads, streets, buildings, addresses, and the like commonly have phrasal proper names.

the Pan-American Highway
Main Street
the Holland Tunnel
Schuyler Park
the Statue of Liberty

the White House
Carnegie Hall
the Stambaugh Building
5531 Maryland Avenue
Room 315

Ships, trains, and planes do too.

the Spirit of Saint Louis   the Capitol Limited

Institutions, organizations, commercial establishments, and the like have them.

Columbia University
the University of Illinois
McKinley School
the Republican Party

the Methodist Church
the United States Senate
the Ford Motor Company
the Viking Press

Historically important events, alliances, groupings, treaties, etc., may receive such treatment.

the Renaissance
the French Revolution
World War II

the Supreme Court
the New Deal
the Monroe Doctrine

Phrasal proper names are given to days.

January 7   New Year's Day

Courses of study commonly have phrasal proper names.

History 22   the Poetry of Milton

Literary, musical, and artistic works, and periodicals, very commonly have names of this kind.

"Dry September"
Passage to India
"I Got Rhythm"
the Cleveland *Plain Dealer*

the Bible
the Acts of the Apostles
the Iliad
the Canterbury Tales

Divisions of such works have them too.

Volume III   Appendix B

West Virginia is a proper name; *southern Ohio* is not, since the combination lacks the fixed status *West Virginia* has. *The White House* is a proper name as used of the President's residence in Washington; used of another building that simply happens to be white, the same series of words has no such status. *History 22* is a proper name; *history* is merely a quantifiable noun. *Volume III* is a proper name; *the third volume* is not. *January 7* is a proper name; *the seventh of January* is not.

What are felt as short forms of phrasal proper names occur frequently and retain the capitals of the full forms.

the United States	5531 Maryland
the States	the University
the Atlantic	the Senate
the Gulf	General Electric

But short forms of proper names are not similarly recognized in such locutions as *the mountain, the ocean, the lake, the street* (though *the Street* is possible for *Wall Street*), *the hotel*, and *the school*. *The Church*, with an honorific capital *c*, refers to a national church, or to the body of believers in general, not to a single local organization or building.

Phrasal proper names with both plural form and plural force occur. They are commonest as names of mountain ranges, groups of lakes, and groups of islands.

the Appalachian Mountains	the West Indies
the Rocky Mountains	the Philippine Islands
the Great Lakes	the British Isles

The Appalachians, the Rockies, and *the Philippines* are short-form phrasal proper names. *The Middle Ages* is a plural phrasal proper name of more exceptional type. Phrasal proper names with plural form but singular force occur also.

the United States	*Gulliver's Travels*
Niagara Falls	

Corresponding singulars do not occur for plural-form proper names. Sometimes sequences that in form are not nounal at all are used as phrasal proper names. Thus race horses are sometimes assigned names such as *In Dutch* and *Call the Cops*. Combinations of letters often replace complex phrasal proper names in common use. Thus the series of letters *U. C. L. A.* is a generally recognized reduction of *the University of California at Los Angeles*.

Uncapitalized and doubtful proper names.—The proper names thus far noted are marked in the written language by honorific capital letters. But some nouns that seem to require classification as proper nouns are not so marked. Among place names *heaven, hell, paradise*, and *earth* often require classification as proper nouns and yet are not begun with capitals. *World* is never a proper noun; like *sun*, it always requires the definite article if the application is to be specific. *Earth* is generally a pluralizer in its syntax, like *world* and *sun*; it is usually after prepositions (as in *no city on earth is more beloved than Paris*) that *earth* seems to require proper-noun classification. When it means "soil" or "dirt," *earth* is of course a quantifiable. The names of the seasons are sometimes proper nouns (as in *we'll be in Puerto Rico by winter*), sometimes pluralizers, and sometimes quantifiables. *Today, tomorrow,* and *yesterday* usually have the syntax of proper nouns and yet are left uncapitalized. Like *Tuesday*, these names are assigned on a fixed periodic basis; but every day is *today* once, somewhat as every human being is *I* and also *you* under certain circumstances but not under others. In *late yesterday* the adjective *late* seems to be an essentially predeterminative modifier of *yesterday*, somewhat as in *southern France* the adjective *southern* is an essentially predeterminative modifier of *France*. Units such as *tomorrow afternoon* and *yesterday morning* are syntactically much like phrasal-proper-name units such as *Earlham College*; units such as *this morning* and *the next afternoon* are made particular in application by their determiner modifiers, as are units such as *last week*. *Noon* and *midnight* often have the syntax of proper nouns. The names of meals are sometimes pluralizers (as in *we had a good supper*), sometimes quantifiables (as in *we didn't have much supper*), and sometimes apparently proper nouns (as in *we have company today, and supper will be late*). Uncapitalized units such as *page 10* and *line 7* seem to require classification as phrasal proper names just as truly as capitalized *Act IV* and *Room 301* do. But units such as *the tenth* *page*, with ordinary determinatives making them particular, do not. The problem of classification is often a difficult one with such words as *mankind, christendom, society, fate*, and *nature*.

> *Mankind* has come a long way.
> *Society* is indebted to those who rebel against it.
> *Nature* is indeed cruel.

In uses such as these, proper-noun classification seems reasonable. Finally, the names of more or less organized bodies of thought— *Christianity, Buddhism, Islam*—raise problems. Probably they are best classified as proper nouns. Perhaps such nouns as *labor* and *management*, applied to social groupings, are best regarded as proper nouns also. Words spoken of as words often acquire the syntax of proper nouns.

> *Urbane* is a word I would avoid.

Proper names are readily made into pluralizers under various circumstances.

the Johnsons	another linguistic Copernicus
three Georges	the Miltons of the world
a Roosevelt	the Brooklyn of Whitman's day
the first Samuel Butler	the young Edison

In *where's Johnson?* the family name *Johnson* is a true proper noun; in *where are the Johnsons?* it is a pluralizer. In *there are three Georges in the class* the effective individual content of *George* as a true proper name is absent; in *the Miltons of the world* there is a generalizing of true proper-name content. It is natural that the honorific capital letters should be retained in cases such as these. They are also retained when a man's name is applied to his work or to products for which he has major responsibility.

> It's a Van Gogh.
> Bring your Jespersens to class.
> This is the third Ford we've owned.
> I'd like to hear some Beethoven.
> I haven't read much Dickens, I'm afraid.

Here *Beethoven* and *Dickens* have become quantifiables. In *Hollywood occasionally gets a good idea, but they wear it out very soon* the proper noun *Hollywood* has acquired collective force and is referred to by *they*.

Capitalization which begins as honorific marking of proper names is thus carried outside the category of proper names. It is carried still farther. Thus the pluralizer nouns *Londoner* and *Ohioan* have initial capitals simply because *London* and *Ohio* do, and words like *English, Cuban, Christian,* and *Wagnerian* (whether adjectives or nouns) have initial capitals for similar reasons. Even in verbs such as *Americanize* and *Anglicize* the capitals hang on. Sometimes they do get dropped. Thus they have disappeared, in some uses at least, in such words as *biblical, china, lynch, pasteurize, platonic, romance, sadism, sandwich, satanic, solon, vulcanize,* and *watt*. But trade names such as *Kodak* and *Kleenex* are given capitals even though their syntax is clearly that of the pluralizers and the quantifiables. Whether or not initial capitals are assigned to a word is of course not a criterion for classifying it as a proper noun or as something else. The category of proper nouns is a syntactic one, not an orthographical one.

Characteristic uses of nouns.—As has been said, the functions characteristically performed by nouns—the nounal functions—are as follows.

1. Subject, as in *paper isn't strong enough*.
2. Complement of a transitive verb, as in *we've used paper*.
3. Head in a nounal headed unit, as in *this paper isn't strong*.
4. Principal in a nounal apposed unit, as in *that's enough, George old fellow*.
5. Appositive in a nounal apposed unit, as in *my friend George was along*.
6. Object of a preposition as in *I went with George*.
7. Coordinate within a nounal multiple unit as in *George and I were there*.

But these are by no means the only functions nouns perform. For the possessive forms of nouns, performance of nonnounal functions is usual. For the common-case forms, it is frequent.

The possessive forms.—Inflection of nouns to form possessives is by the addition, to common-case forms, of an inflectional ending which in the written language is represented by an apostrophe and *s*. The addition of this ending generally does not involve increase in the number of syllables in the spoken forms.

boy 's	dog 's	Shaw 's	livestock 's
child 's	hero 's	winter 's	Rip 's
company 's	Malraux 's	woman 's	Robert 's
conservative 's	man 's	death 's	thief 's
country 's	Mary 's	Kate 's	wife 's

When the addition of this ending does increase the number of syllables, the written language still represents the form by *'s*.

| Alice 's | Fitch 's | Louise 's | witness 's |
| Fish 's | judge 's | waitress 's | wretch 's |

Common-case plurals that do not end in the inflectional *s* of plurality add the inflectional ending represented by *'s*.

| alumnae 's | children 's | men 's | sheep 's |
| alumni 's | Englishmen 's | people 's | women 's |

But common-case plurals that do end in the inflectional *s* of plurality are used as possessives unchanged except for the addition of an apostrophe in the written language.

boys '	heroes '	Richardsons '	wives '
conservatives '	judges '	weeks '	wretches '
countries '	pilots '	witnesses '	Youngs '

Some basic forms ending in /s/ or /z/ have considerable use as possessives without change in the spoken language and with the addition only of an apostrophe in the written. Nouns treated in this way are usually names of people, less often names of places.

Charles' answer	Fields' death
Dolores' room	Hendrix' family
Frances' father	Langston Hughes' best work
Gladys' new house	Mr. Jones' home
Mrs. Adkins' car	Mr. Mathews' permission
Robert Bridges' poetry	Mr. Sanchez' office
Willis' views	Mrs. Watts' notions
Dickens' novels	Texas' submerged lands

In careful and formal styles possessives employing a spoken syllabic ending and the written *'s* are commonly preferred for names like these. But the same considerations that operate against plurals like the *Bridgeses* and the *Battses* operate against possessives like *Robert Bridges's* and *Langston Hughes's*, and operate even more strongly. There is a feeling that the possessive of *Robert Bridges* should be made like the possessive of *these judges*, and that the possessive of *Langston Hughes* should be made like the possessive of *the Jews*, without the addition of another /z/. Possessives made without the addition of a syllabic suffix are well established for names ending in /s/ or /z/ and associated in the main with the distant past.

Achilles'	Erasmus'	Laertes'	Socrates'
Cervantes'	Heraclitus'	Moses'	Ulysses'
Copernicus'	Jesus'	Polonius'	Xerxes'

They are established also in a few fixed phrasings.

for goodness' sake   for conscience' sake

The written-language apostrophe is often omitted when possessives occur within phrasal proper names.

Martins Ferry   the Citizens Savings Bank
Pikes Peak   Columbia Teachers College
                       the Ex-Students Association

Apostrophes are not used in a number of compounds.

beeswax   bridesmaid   hogshead   swordsman

But in hyphenated units such as *bull's-eye* and *cat's-paw* they are kept.

The written language has four distinct forms for the great majority of pluralizers. Examples follow, with *C.* representing *common case* and *P.* representing *possessive*.

Written Singulars

C.	week	judge	hero	country	thief	man	alumnus
P.	week's	judge's	hero's	country's	thief's	man's	alumnus's

Written Plurals

C.	weeks	judges	heroes	countries	thieves	men	alumni
P.	weeks'	judges'	heroes'	countries'	thieves'	men's	alumni's

Week, judge, hero, and *country* are regular pluralizers, the last two involved in complexities of spelling when *s* is added but not when *'s* is added. In the spoken language these four words have only two forms: a basic form which functions as a common-case singular, and an inflected form which functions as a possessive-case singular and also as an indifferent-case plural. Thus in the spoken language

week's, weeks, and *weeks'* are all one form. *Thief* has three forms in
the spoken language; *man* and *alumnus* have four. Such a family
name as *Bridges* can have two forms in the written language but
only a single form in the spoken.

Mr. Bridges	the Bridges
Mr. Bridges'	the Bridges'

But a more conservative practice would have four written forms
here, representing two spoken forms.

Mr. Bridges	the Bridgeses
Mr. Bridges's	the Bridgeses'

Use of possessives as determiners.—The function most characteristically performed by possessives is the pronounal function of
determiner within nounal headed units. Used as determiners, possessives indicate that identification is specific and complete. Sometimes they identify on the basis of ownership. *Jack's car* may be
the only car Jack owns. *Jack's tie* is probably not the only tie
Jack owns, but it is the only one that attracts attention at the
moment of speaking or writing. Often possessives are concerned
with relationships distinct from simple ownership and yet not
wholly unrelated to it. In *Jack's hand* the hand is hardly "owned";
it is a part of the possessor. In *Mary's room at the William Penn
Hotel* the possessive *Mary's* indicates temporary possession, not
real ownership. In *Whitman's poetry* the possessive indicates au-
thorship, which is a kind of ownership too (as copyright laws
suggest) and may even be felt as an ownership that continues
after death. In *Japan's exports* the situation is not greatly different.
In *Mary's picture* the possessive can indicate (1) that Mary owns
the picture, or (2) that she made it, or (3) that she is the subject of
it. If she made it or is the subject of it, she has something of the
right to it that the author has to a book. If she is the subject of
the picture, something like *that picture of Mary* might be preferred
to *Mary's picture.* In *Jack's brother* there is no ownership of course,
but family relationships involve a kind of mutual possessing which
the verb *have* can also indicate, as in *Jack has one brother and two
sisters. Jack's friends* is much like *Jack's brother; Jack's enemies*
and *Jack's neighbors* are also similar. So are *Jack's inferiors*, where

the relationship is likely to be much less close. The relationships are personal ones in constructions such as these where possessives function as determiners of identification based on relationships involving "possession" of various kinds distinct from ownership. Sometimes possessives really indicate no more than strong interest. Thus in *there goes one of Bill's "beautiful morons,"* all the possessive may mean is that Bill shows considerable interest in women of a type here labeled beautiful morons. Sometimes the possessive indicates only that there has been a kind of dedication, at least in theory: for example, in *St. George's Church* and in *the People's National Bank*.

Sometimes determining possessives have relationships to nounal heads much like the relationships subjects have to predicators.

> He needs *his friends' help*.
> We advanced the date at *John's suggestion*.
> Every child needs *a mother's love*.
> *John's mistake* was in trusting Harrison.
> I hadn't heard about *Hugh's trip*.
> We came here shortly after *Roosevelt's death*.

His friends' help is much like *his friends help him* in meaning relationships; but *his friends' help* is a nounal headed unit, not a clause. *Hugh's trip* is like *Hugh traveled*, and *Roosevelt's death* like *Roosevelt died*. The possessives are like passive subjects in the italicized units which follow.

> *Germany's defeat* was inevitable.
> Have you heard about *John's promotion?*
> *MacArthur's dismissal* changed the situation.

Here *Germany's defeat* is like *Germany was defeated*. Nouns expressing meanings of occurrence have no passive forms; but this does not prevent frequent reversal in a kind of direction of predication.

MacArthur's dismissal: MacArthur was dismissed
Truman's dismissal of MacArthur: Truman dismissed MacArthur

But possessives paralleling passive subjects are often not usable. Thus *Latin's study* must give way to *the study of Latin*.

Nouns and nounal units marked by possessive inflection sometimes function as determiners of quantity.

two weeks' notice   *half an hour's* sleep
five years' experience   *a month's* rent
a few minutes' thought   *an evening's* entertainment
a hard day's work   *thousands of dollars'* worth
two weeks' vacation   *three hours'* credit

The construction seems to be of this type in such units as at *arm's
length, a stone's throw, a moment's pause,* and *a long day's drive,*
in spite of the fact that the head nouns here are probably felt as
pluralizers rather than quantifiables. Common-case construction
is generally preferred to possessive construction for meanings comparable to these when the heads are pluralizers.

a *three-day* trip   a *four-year* course
a *two-hour* walk   a *five-cent* charge
a *one-day* job   a *ten-dollar* bill
a *ten-minute* nap   a *three-cent* stamp

In prepositive positions within nounal headed units possessive
determiners are full determiners. The same possessives also occur
in postpositive positions, as objects of *of,* with determiner force
lost.

> It's an old grammar *of Addison Clark's.*
> We took some friends *of Mary's* along.
> It's no business *of Joe's.*
> That artificial English *of Hugh's* is very painful.
> The play *of Galsworthy's* that I like best is "Justice."
> Students *of Hudson's* express the same view.

Full determiners are superimposed in all of these sentences except
the last, in which the subject is undetermined. Postponed possessives are limited in occurrence.

Except for the determiners of quantity, possessive determiners
are generally nouns or nounal units of very limited types. They
are likely to be used of people; or of animals, dolls, and the like
thought of as having personality; or of divinities, natural phenomena, and the like that have been thought of similarly.

a child's mind   *the cat's* eyes
my parents' home   *Big Sister's* bed

Thor's beard	*death's* door
nature's freaks	*the sun's* rays

Or of groupings of people such as are commonly given proper names.

the nation's history	*the Army's* methods
England's destiny	*the University's* investments
labor's aims	*the jury's* verdict
the company's assets	*the government's* policy
the city's policy	*the Tribune's* editorial
the island's problems	*the Philharmonic's* new director

Or of units of time.

last year's model	*today's* paper
this semester's schedule	*New Year's* Eve

Uses of possessive inflection in fixed phrasings carry it farther.

at *his wit's* end	out of *harm's* way
to *his heart's* content	for *goodness'* sake
in *my mind's* eye	thought for *thought's* sake

Occasionally possessives are seen in units such as *the kitchen's pots, the play's title, the water's edge,* and *the box's top.* They are not very natural in such uses. Possessive determiners are generally applied to "possessors" of one kind or another, and possessors tend to be either human beings or enough like human beings, in one way or another, to deserve proper names. The relationships expressed are intimate ones.

Common-case modifiers sometimes compete with possessives.

the students' newspaper	the *student* newspaper
the family's car	the *family* car
Hoover's administration	the *Hoover* administration

Here the meanings are about the same, but the use of possessives relates the modifiers and the heads in a more personal way. Common-case nouns do not function as determiners, so that, though *Hoover's administration* is determined, *Hoover administration* requires a determiner. Sometimes a distinction in case in the modifier indicates a difference in meaning relationships.

the Negro's problem	the *Negro* problem
the mother's cat	the *mother* cat

The Negro's problem means "the problem the Negro faces": the point of view is the intimate, internal one of the Negro himself. *The Negro problem* very probably means "the problem the Negro produces for others": the point of view is external and perhaps unfriendly. In *the mother's cat* the cat belongs to the mother; in *the mother cat* the cat itself is the mother.

Prepositional units begun by *of* often compete with possessive determiners. In *the grave, scratchy voice of President Truman* the prepositional unit is perhaps preferred for rhetorical reasons: *President Truman's grave, scratchy voice* gets a good deal in front of the head *voice*. *The rise of Hitler* may seem to have a special effectiveness that *Hitler's rise* lacks. *The eyes of Mary* is not possible; *Mary's eyes* is the only locution for a relationship as intimate as this. *People's favorite sports* is normal; *the favorite sports of the people of Chile* avoids the possessive because *of Chile* follows *people*. Postpositive prepositional units, again, cannot function as determiners, so that *the* is used before *favorite sports*.

Hitler's rise	*the* rise of Hitler
the Negro's problem	*the* problem of the Negro

Use of possessives as nondeterminative modifiers.—Sometimes possessives used as prepositive modifiers in nounal headed units do not have determiner force.

bachelors' degrees	another *boys'* school
children's books	a *hornets'* nest
women's dresses	a *ladies'* man
teachers' colleges	a *man's* umbrella

The units given in the first column above are undetermined. *Bachelors' degrees* is as undetermined as *graduate degrees*, and *women's dresses* is as undetermined as *party dresses*. The units given in the second column are determined, but not by the possessives. Modifiers that would follow determiners can precede nondeterminative possessives.

> a *respectable* bachelor's degree
> no *very satisfactory* children's books
> a *somewhat unsuccessful* ladies' man

Nondeterminative possessives conflict with the central patterning of modern English, and they are of limited occurrence for this reason. *Several women's dresses* can be ambiguous: it can be equivalent to either *the dresses belonging to several women* or *several dresses for women*. The pull is toward the first meaning. *My favorite girl's name* can be similarly ambiguous, meaning *the name of my favorite girl* or *my favorite name for a girl*. A *wooden dressmaker's form* is unambiguous only because it is obvious that what is wooden is a form and not a dressmaker. *Her woman's guile* is unambiguous only when it is clear that what is "hers" is not a woman but feminine guile. The spoken language can reduce ambiguities through distinctions in intonation, but this solution is less than satisfactory. Modern English prefers to use uninflected basic forms of nouns, not possessives, as nondeterminative prepositive modifiers—when it lets nouns perform this adjectival function at all.

graduate degrees   the *Hoover* administration
business colleges   the *child* mind

Possessives without following heads.—Possessives are usable rather freely as representative forms which have assimilated both the meanings and the functions of what would be their heads in full phrasings.

Mary's old friends don't have much in common with *John's.*
Boys' clothes cost less than *girls'.*
My parents were stricter than *Bill's,* who were perhaps too uninterested in discipline.

Here *John's* represents *John's old friends;* the obviously parallel *Mary's old friends* assures this. *Girls'* will similarly be taken to represent *girls' clothes*—even in the spoken language, where *girls'* is not distinguishable from the common-case plural form. *Bill's* will be taken to represent *Bill's parents,* to whom the following *who* clearly refers. It is noteworthy that possessives without following heads can have singular, plural, or quantitative force.

Hugh's excuses were thin, but *Joe's was* thinner.
Hugh's excuses were thin, but *Joe's were* thinner.
Hugh's work was poor, but *Joe's was* worse.

Some possessives without following heads are usable even when there are no parallel full constructions in the immediate context.

> Susan spent three months at *her grandmother's*.
> We had supper at *the Carrolls'*.
> We had been shopping at *Macy's*.
> Jack is at *the dentist's*.
> We walked up Fifth Avenue to *St. Bartholemew's*.
> How shall we celebrate *New Year's?*
> He took his *master's* at Columbia.

Home, home, store, office, church, Eve, and *degree* are suggested by the possessives themselves here. This type of construction is sharply limited in occurrence.

Possessives used as subjects in gerundial clauses.—As has been said, possessive inflection often is given to subjects in gerundial clauses. The function of subject is of course nounal and is elsewhere assigned (when nouns perform it) to the common case.

> *Herbert's* marrying that silly girl is just too much.
> Instead of *the teacher's* wearing herself out reading compositions, the students could criticize each other's work.
> We didn't mind *the cover's* being torn.

This use of possessive inflection is not a comfortable one. In informal styles the tendency is to leave subjects of gerundials unmarked by possessive inflection, like subjects of other verb forms. In all styles the gerundial-clause pattern is often avoided because of distaste for possessive inflection on subjects.

Phrasal attachment of possessive inflection.—Very commonly possessive inflectional endings indicate relationships for preceding multiword nounal units rather than for the single words to which they are attached. These units may be headed units, apposed units, or multiple units. The normal place for possessive inflection is at the end of whole units in all such cases.

> *The poor girl's* husband has lost his job.
> The umbrella is *the new secretary's*.
> I don't understand *our friend Jack's* letting us down.
> *An hour and a half's* work is too much.

If the nounal unit is a headed one terminating in its head, what results is not unlike what results when such a unit is made plural: *the poor girl's* is obviously similar to *the poor girls*. If the nounal unit is an apposed one terminating in the appositive, what results is exceptional from the point of view of the older Indo-European grammar: in *our friend Jack's,* for example, the principal is not possessive but the appositive apparently is. In multiple units such as *an hour and a half's* the construction is strange too: the head word in the first coordinate is a common-case noun here, but the head word in the second apparently is a possessive. The key to the matter, of course, is the fact that in all of these units possessive inflectional endings belong not just to the words they are attached to but to the whole units. Possessive inflections terminate units much as prepositions begin them. *The Republican Party's candidate* and *the candidate of the Republican Party* employ *'s* and *of* in very similar ways.

When nounal units end in postpositive modifiers, possessive inflections are generally not appended in formal styles: other constructions are preferred instead. In careful styles possessive inflections are added more frequently.

> *someone else's* seat
> *thousands of dollars'* worth
> *the Wife of Bath's* marriages
> *the Dean of Student Life's* help
> *the Institute of International Education's* policies

Else is an adverb, but it clearly modifies *someone* and it has come to accept possessive inflection readily. In the last three examples given above, the capital letters help to outline the possessive units in the written language, and intonation takes care of the matter in the spoken. In informal styles, and especially in conversation, possessive inflection is added to units of still other types.

> *each of them's* interest in cats
> *the children across the street's* dog
> *the boy you met's* father
> *the girl he goes with's* mother
> at *a friend of mine's*

In the unit *a friend of mine's,* for *a friend of mine's home,* two layers of possessive inflection have been added to already-possessive *my,* but the outermost layer really belongs to the whole unit. In the spoken language intonation serves to outline the italicized units given above, but in the written language there are greater difficulties. Even in the most informal spoken use there are limits to what can be handled satisfactorily as possessive units. The italicized units which follow are certainly not very acceptable ones.

> *one of our friends' car*
> *the man that bought our house's wife*

Coordination of possessives occurs but is sometimes awkward.

> That was during *Harding's* or *Coolidge's* administration.
> Nearby is some of *Switzerland's* and *the world's* best scenery.
> This is either *Jim's* or *Marvin's*.

Possessives do fairly well as half coordinates where there is an effect of afterthought.

> *The hat is Jack's—or Bill's.*

They occur as modifiers within larger possessives, sometimes awkwardly.

> We're going in *Jane's father's* car.
> We're going over to *Jane's sister's*.

Nonnounal uses of common-case nouns and nounal units.—Nouns do not function as predicators, but nounal units with verbs in them sometimes do.

> She *sort of laughed*.

Here the verb *laughed* has been reduced to the status of object of a preposition within the total predicator. The style is informal.

Nounal complements of *be* sometimes approach the essentially adjectival function of complement of a copulative verb.

> It's *no use* to warn him.
> The buckle is *silver*.
> Hugh just isn't *your type*, little girl.
> *What color* are the baby's eyes?
> It's *tops*.

In *George is now thirty-five years of age* the situation is similar; the nounal complement has the force of adjectival *thirty-five years old*. Nounal complements are sometimes found after oblique verbs also.

> We went *home* at ten.
> We went *places* then.
> We came *north* a year later.

Nounal adjuncts are very common.

Come here, *George*.
That was on Sunday, *my only free day*.
I saw him *Tuesday*.
The moment he saw us, he rushed over to welcome us.
I'll do better *next time*.
We traveled *all afternoon*.
What way did you come?
We drove *north*.
She came back *three times*.
I *half* believed him.
We went to England *second class*.
He came back from the war *a new man*.
MacArthur or no MacArthur, the situation was desperate.
Wonder of wonders, we got his signature.
No doubt she meant it.
He's bought *his wife* another car.
She struck him *a hard blow*.

In spite of their variety, nounal adjuncts—direct address excepted—occur only in a very limited way. Thus though *I saw him Tuesday* is normal *I saw him noon* and *I saw him February* are not. Prepositions can easily be supplied for many nounal adjuncts, so that the nounal constructions can be regarded as syntactically reduced; but this is not always true. Adjuncts of direct address, for example, can hardly be supplied with prepositions; they are like subjects and many complements in having no relation-indicating words of this kind. Half-appositive relationships make nounal construction natural in such sentences as *that was on Sunday, my only free day*, and perhaps in such sentences as *he came back from the war a new man*.

Nouns and nounal units are used quite extensively as contained modifiers within headed units. They occur most often as prepositive modifiers within nounal headed units.

apartment hotels	*automobile* insur-	*old-age* security
brick houses	ance	an *open-air* meeting
chance acquaint-	*chewing* gum	a *fifty-mile* drive
ance	*danger* point	a *no-account* loafer
country towns	*farming* country	some *teen-age* girls
east winds	*football* players	a *wild-goose* chase
Ford cars	*history* courses	a *two-story* house

giant corporations	*sea* level	a *fire-insurance* com-pany
Judge Henderson	*Sunday* schools	
living wage	*telephone* books	his *mama's-boy* ways
night trains	*vacuum* cleaners	a *matter-of-fact* person
pet rabbits	*waiting* rooms	*middle-of-the-road* ideas

Country towns can be replaced by *rural towns*, in which an adjective is used as a modifier; but *rural* has less warmth than *country*, and perhaps too much of a sociological flavor. *Giant corporations* can be replaced by *gigantic corporations* with only a slight loss of forcefulness. *You'll break your fool neck* is stronger than *you'll break your foolish neck*. But there is no adjective that quite matches the *night* of *night trains*, and none that quite matches the *pet* of *pet rabbits* or the *university* of *university students*. Nouns and nounal units are used as predeterminative and postpositive modifiers in nounal units less often, but they are used in both these ways.

half the morning	the people *next door*
three times the usual number	a house *the size of a hospital*
the meeting *yesterday*	hair *the color of good coffee*
the trip *home*	eight hours *a day*

Nouns and nounal units occur also as contained modifiers within adjectival and adverbial headed units.

world famous	*six years* old	*fur*-lined coat
knee high	*ten pounds* heavier	*peace*-loving nations
girl crazy	*all night* long	*church*-going people
dirt cheap	*a great deal* worse	*a week* ago
raving mad	*machine*-made belts	once *a year*
boiling hot	*insect*-borne diseases	how *the devil*

Occasionally nouns function as appositives in adverbial apposed units.

up *front*   down *south*   back *home*

CHAPTER XI

ADJECTIVES

Inflectional forms of the adjectives.—The only inflection of adjectives which occurs in modern English is that which normally serves to indicate that an explicitly comparative view of the characteristic named is being taken and that this characteristic is thought to exist, in the instances or circumstances on which attention is centered, in other degrees than in the instances or circumstances with which comparison is made. Two types of inflected forms perform this function: comparative forms and superlative forms.

> Marietta is *older* than the other cities of the area.
> Marietta is the *oldest* city in the area.

Old has *older* and *oldest* as one-word inflected forms. *Conscientious* has *more conscientious* and *most conscientious* as what can most conveniently be called inflected forms too—phrasal in type, like the verb form *will play*. If *more conscientious* and *most conscientious* are classified as phrasal inflected forms of *conscientious*, it will be difficult to deny such classification to *less conscientious* and *least conscientious*. From the point of view of syntax, the reason for classifying *more conscientious*, *most conscientious*, *less conscientious*, and *least conscientious* with *older* and *oldest* is the fact that, like *older* and *oldest*, phrasal units of these four types are usable as heads in nounal headed units with a degree of freedom not at all possible for the basic forms.

> Of the two girls, the *older* is the *more conscientious*.
> Of the three boys, the *oldest* is the *least conscientious*.
> Of the two girls, the *younger* is the *less conscientious*.
> Of the three boys, the *youngest* is the *most conscientious*.

251

Modern English does not permit such a phrasing as *the young is the conscientious*. Such forms as *older* and *more conscientious* can be called plus comparatives; such forms as *less conscientious* can be called minus comparatives. Such forms as *oldest* and *most conscientious* can be called plus superlatives; such forms as *least conscientious* can be called minus superlatives. *More*, *most*, *less*, and *least* can be considered pronoun forms used as auxiliaries within phrasal adjective forms.

Explicit comparison is quite possible without the use of comparative and superlative forms. This is true even where judgements of inequality result.

> Marietta is very old in comparison with most cities of the Middle West.
> Marietta is not as old as Philadelphia, of course.

Where judgements of equality result, basic forms are normal.

> Marietta is as old as many cities farther east.

Regular inflected forms.—With exceptions to be noted later, adjectives with monosyllabic basic forms make comparative forms of plus type by adding an inflectional ending which in the written language is represented by *er* and make superlative forms by adding an inflectional ending written *est*. Complexities of spelling appear.

clean er	clean est	hard er	hard est
dri er	dri est	lat er	lat est
fin er	fin est	neat er	neat est
fre er	fre est	sadd er	sadd est

Some adjectives whose basic forms have two syllables make plus comparative and superlative forms in the same way. Common dissyllabic adjectives terminating in the suffix *y* do so most consistently.

| funni er | funni est | lucki er | lucki est |

Though not clearly divisible as *funny* and *lucky* are, *holy*, *pretty*, and *silly* follow the same pattern of inflection. Some other common dissyllabic adjectives with unstressed or weakly stressed second syllables—notably adjectives whose basic forms terminate in the suffix *ly*—employ the endings *er* and *est* less consistently, but do employ them.

able	friendly	mellow	simple
common	gentle	narrow	sober
crooked	handsome	noble	stupid
cruel	homely	pleasant	tender
deadly	kindly	quiet	wicked

Comparative and superlative forms employing the auxiliary pronoun forms *more* and *most* compete here but are perhaps less forceful: *he's the stupidest man I know,* for example, is more forceful than *he's the most stupid man I know. Polite* sometimes employs the endings *er* and *est* in spite of the fact that its second syllable is stressed. A few other dissyllabic adjectives whose basic forms have stressed second syllables employ the superlative suffix *est* in more or less fixed phrasings.

in the *minutest* detail   not the *remotest* notion

For most adjectives whose basic forms have two syllables, plus comparative forms are made only with the aid of auxiliary *more* and plus superlatives only with the aid of auxiliary *most.* This is almost always the case for adjectives whose second syllables are stressed. It is generally the case for adjectives whose basic forms end in *al, ant, ed, en, ern, ful, ic, ing, ish, ive, less, ous, some,* and *ward.* It is the case for other adjectives of miscellaneous types.

absurd	childish	fatal	skilled
active	comic	flippant	solemn
afraid	complete	futile	spacious
alert	content	gifted	splendid
amorous	cunning	gruesome	stylish
ancient	damning	hopeless	thoughtful
awkward	direct	hostile	thoughtless
backward	distinct	human	tired
basic	docile	humane	tiresome
brutal	dormant	monstrous	useful
candid	eager	proper	useless
careless	earnest	prudent	valid
certain	exact	rigid	vicious
charming	famous	selfish	vocal

For adjectives whose basic forms have more than two syllables, plus comparative and superlative forms require the use of the auxiliaries *more* and *most.*

leisurely, more leisurely, most leisurely
satisfactory, more satisfactory, most satisfactory

In general, phrasal adjectives such as *cold-blooded* employ the auxiliaries *more* and *most* when they form plus comparatives and superlatives.

cold-blooded, more cold-blooded, most cold-blooded.

It is possible, of course, to inflect contained adjectives rather than the larger phrasal ones, producing such forms as *colder-blooded* and *coldest-blooded;* but these are generally avoided except where the contained adjective is *good* or *bad*.

good-hearted, better-hearted, best-hearted
bad-tempered, worse-tempered, worst-tempered

Adjectives which begin with prefixes are likely to employ *more* and *most* whatever the corresponding adjectives without prefixes would do, though practice varies on this point.

unsafe, more unsafe, most unsafe
unhappy, more unhappy, most unhappy

Even adjectives whose plus comparatives and superlatives are ordinarily made with the aid of the endings *er* and *est* occasionally employ *more* and *most* in special situations to be noted later.

I guess I'm *more lazy* than sick.
You've been *most kind*.

The two methods of forming plus comparatives and superlatives are quite different in some respects. The inflectional endings cannot be used without the forms to which they attach. The auxiliary pronouns, on the other hand, can be used repeatedly without repetition of their head words, and can be used with the adverb *so* substituted for head words that will be clearly understood from context or situation.

It's harder and harder to save any money.
It's more and more difficult to save any money.
Their last secretary was erratic, but this one is more so.

All minus comparatives and superlatives are formed regularly, following a single pattern: the auxiliary pronoun forms *less* and *least* are placed before the basic forms.

free, less free, least free
happy, less happy, least happy
satisfactory, less satisfactory, least satisfactory

Irregularities in inflection.—Irregularly compared adjectives
are few. The most important are *bad* and *good*, with originally unrelated plus comparatives and superlatives.

bad, worse, worst   good, better, best

Little should be classified as an adjective when it expresses meanings of small size or of unimportance or unimpressiveness. Its plus
inflection is quite irregular.

little, less, least

Worse and *less* are unique among one-word comparatives in not
terminating in *r*. *Less* and *least* rarely express meanings of small
size now: *the least child* is archaic phrasing. But meanings of unimportance or unimpressiveness are expressed by *less* and *least* in
such locutions as *no less a person than the Dean, not the least
objection,* and *the least of my worries. Lesser* is a second comparative
of *little* which is not usable with clauses marked by *than* but occasionally occurs in such locutions as *the lesser of two evils* and *all
lesser institutions. Far* has irregular inflected forms.

far, farther, farthest

Further and *furthest* occur as variants of *farther* and *farthest. Elder*
and *eldest* are archaic as inflected forms of *old;* and *elder,* like *lesser,*
is not usable with clauses subordinated by *than.* In almost all
situations *old* is now regular. *Late* has *latter* as a comparative in
such phrasings as *the latter part of the nineteenth century;* but usually
late is regular.

At least one basic-form adjective has a regular superlative but
no comparative.

mere, merest

A few other basic-form adjectives have irregular superlatives but
no commonly used comparatives with the same meanings.

fore, foremost   northern, northernmost
hind, hindmost   southern, southernmost
eastern, easternmost   western, westernmost

Superlatives in *most* are now felt as compounds in which a modifying auxiliary pronoun has been united, postpositively, with a basic-form adjective head. Regular comparatives of such adjectives of direction as *western* occur occasionally, as in *Colorado is more Western than California;* but in literal directional meanings other constructions are preferred, as in *California is farther west than Colorado.* Several forms that are best classified as irregular superlative adjectives are based on adverbs.

inmost, innermost   uppermost
outmost, outermost   utmost, uttermost

At least one superlative in *most* is based on a noun.

topmost

Comparative forms not usable with *than* clauses exist alongside some of these superlatives. *Inner, outer, upper,* and *utter* are such forms. *Further* is a comparative in the process of detaching itself from *far* when it means *additional. Former* is now distinct from *fore* and *foremost;* it is best regarded as an adjective when it is used with the meaning of *earlier,* as in *a former resident.*

Some adjectives rarely or never compare. This is true of a considerable number of gerundial and participial forms whose classification as adjectives is somewhat arbitrary.

a *growing* child   an *educated* person
an *increasing* tendency   a *grown* man
his *suffering* hearers   an *organized* effort

But many other adjectives of gerundial and participial origin do compare: for example, *convincing, fattening, surprising, bored, complicated,* and *tired.* Such adjectives as the following do not compare.

hourly, daily, weekly   sole, lone
four-legged, triangular   chief, main, principal
bearded, striped   extinct, incurable

Right and *wrong* are generally not compared, though *correct* is.

It would help if his English were *less correct.*

True is compared, but *false* is not likely to be. *Bad* is compared, but *evil* generally is not, and *ill* is not. Adjectives of color, nationality, religion, and the like are compared.

> She has the *reddest* hair you ever saw.
> She's *more Irish* than necessary.

But *er* and *est* are avoided, even with monosyllabic adjectives such as *Scotch* and *French*. Such words as *perfect, final* and *dead* are compared with relative freedom, at least in some applications.

> I'm afraid his pronunciation is *more perfect* than ever.
> The decision was *less final* than was believed.
> It was the *deadest* party I ever got into.

In general, adjectives which do not compare are not modified by such degree modifiers as *very, too, as,* and *so.* But *alone* compares in such sentences as *she's more alone than ever,* and yet seems to reject *very* and *too,* if not *as* and *so;* and *little* as an adjective concerned with size is rarely compared and yet accepts *very, too, as,* and *so* quite readily. *Little* is a special case, of course: in *less children* it will be taken as the pronoun, with *less* pushing out *fewer,* rather than the adjective equivalent to *smaller.*

Meanings are clearly responsible for the absence of comparative and superlative forms for such adjectives as *hourly.* Most adjectives cannot be pegged to absolute meanings which forbid comparison uncompromisingly, but if *hourly* is to mean anything at all, it has such a meaning. It is harder to see why the *growing* of a *growing child* and the *grown* of a *grown man* should reject comparison. *More* and *most* can modify the verb *grow* as in *both the children are growing more this year,* though *very* and *too* cannot function as degree modifiers of verbs.

The uses of comparative forms.—Comparative forms of adjectives have their most characteristic use when clauses of comparison subordinated by *than* modify them.

> Mexico City is *higher* than is really comfortable.
> The city is *more cosmopolitan* than most cities in the States.
> The vegetation is *less tropical* than at lower altitudes.
> Boston is three centuries old, but Mexico City is an *older* city than that.
> Mexico City offers a *more stimulating* intellectual life than most cities do.

Definite determinatives of identity, such as *the,* cannot easily be superimposed on comparatives modified by *than* clauses; but indefinite determinatives, such as *a*, can. It is often possible, and even desirable, to leave the *than* clause implied rather than stated.

> Housing was expensive when we came, but the situation is *better* now.
> There must be *less complicated* ways of convincing him.
> You'll live *longer* if you don't worry.
> Gray is becoming *more malicious* year by year.
> We'd *better* have our brakes checked.

It is generally not desirable to use the forms of direct comparison where it is not clear what is being compared.

In the characteristic use with a *than* clause expressed or implied, the comparative of such an adjective as *fond* normally requires two completers. Thus in *he's fond of good music* the prepositional unit *of good music* is a completing modifier of *fond*, and in *he's fonder of good music than of good food* a second completing modifier, *than of good food*, is added to satisfy the special needs of the comparative.

Sometimes there is comparison of the degrees to which two qualities exist in a particular situation. If the *than* clause is reduced, the comparative form must employ *more* even in the case of an adjective that usually employs the ending *er* in forming its comparative.

> We were *more dead* than alive.
> She's *more sick* than lazy.

But when the *than* clause is not reduced, a comparative in *er* is usable.

> It's *thicker* than it is wide.
> Her typing is *neater* than it is accurate.

Comparatives modified by *the* are used in pairs, as has been said, to mark relationships of proportionate variation.

> The *smaller* the town, the *friendlier* the people.

The is a modifier of difference when it modifies comparatives in this way, not a determiner. *So much* could be substituted, though the result would be less natural. Comparatives used in pairs with *the* are concerned with highly relative, comparative ratings; but it is not possible to supply *than* completers.

Comparative forms of adjectives have another use, in which they are preceded by *the* or other definite determinatives and cannot be modified by *than* clauses. In this use comparative forms have the characteristic syntax of superlative forms, in essence, rather than the usual syntax of comparative forms. Comparative forms are usable with the syntax of superlatives only when the total number of instances, or groups of instances, is two. In careful and formal styles they are normally preferred to superlatives under such circumstances.

The *older* of the two boys is in college.
The *less studious* twin became a salesman.
About half the students were from Asia, and these were the *more industrious*.

There is a suggestion of two instances or groupings in such phrasings as the following, though it may not be very obvious.

his *better* judgement	the *older* generation
the *lower* grades	the *upper* middle class
the *newer* houses	the *better* features of the system

In *higher education* the comparative has this kind of force even though there is no determinative.

Comparative forms used with the syntax of superlatives tend to be crowded out by superlatives in many situations, especially in informal styles.

Which route is the *shortest?*
Joe always sits by the *best* lamp and leaves his wife the other one.
I got the *worst* of the argument.

In informal styles it would seem overprecise to ask which route is the *shorter* when only two routes are under consideration or to speak of the *better* lamp when there are only two lamps. The superlative forms used when there are more than two tend to be more natural also when there are only two. But where division into two is always present in the nature of things, superlative forms are not likely to be used.

Her *upper* teeth have to be pulled.
It is biological nonsense to call women the *weaker* sex.

Only the metaphorical meaning of *foot* makes a superlative possible in the following sentence.

A good politician always puts his *best* foot in his mouth.

Comparatives are well established also in such phrasings as *the better homes* and *the lower grades*, where *best* and *lowest*, lacking the suggestion of division into two presumably not very unequal groupings, would seem to refer to smaller numbers of homes and grades, at somewhat extreme positions in the scale.

Comparatives are sometimes given exceptional uses ın which they have *so much the* and, especially in doubtfully standard styles, *all the* as modifiers of differences.

So much the *better*.
That makes it all the *more doubtful*.
Is that all the *later* it is?

Minus comparatives are much less frequent than plus comparatives. Adjectives that do not employ the auxiliary pronoun *more* in forming plus comparatives do not often form minus comparatives. Other patterns are preferred.

His new office is not as big as his old one.
His new office is smaller than his old one.

Less big would seem unnatural here. Even adjectives that employ the auxiliary pronoun form *more* often avoid the companion form *less*.

His new office is not as convenient as his old one.

But *less convenient* is quite possible here.

The uses of superlative forms.—With respect to meaning, superlative forms of adjectives are not greatly different from comparative. *Marietta is the oldest city in the area* (or *Marietta is the oldest of the cities of the area*) is not unlike *Marietta is older than the other cities of the area* in content. The contrast may be a little stronger when comparatives are used: *Marietta is older than the other cities of the area* puts Marietta in isolation on one side and the remaining cities of the area on the other, whereas if *oldest* is used instead of *older* the resulting construction leaves Marietta in the same grouping as the other cities, even though it is still differentiated from them. From the point of view of syntax, there is more difference. Superlative forms cannot be modified by *than* clauses. In addition, they have a strong affinity for definite determinatives of identification, such as *the*.

> Cider is the *best* drink available.
> Cider is the *best* of the available drinks.
> Tom is our *least industrious* student.

With determiner modifiers, notably *the*, superlatives have considerable use in nounal constructions.

> Only *the most studious* passed.
> We left *the hardest* till last.

The is likely to be used even where the resulting unit is used as an adjunct and it seems preferable to avoid *the*.

> Which do you like *the best?*
> The students from Asia work *the hardest*.

Enthusiasm, pretended enthusiasm, surprise, and irritation all lead at times to the use of superlatives without much respect for accuracy but also without syntactic strangeness.

> They have the *prettiest* baby you ever saw.
> That's the *most ridiculous* thing I ever heard of.
> That's the *worst* yet.

Sometimes explicit comparison is pretty well lost sight of. This is true, for example, in polite *we had the best time!* spoken by departing female guests.

When indefinite determinatives combine with superlatives the result is syntactically exceptional. Sometimes there is an unusual type of superimposing.

> There's always a *worst* student.
> Everyone has a *best* friend.

These sentences are convenient equivalents of *there's always a student who is the worst student in the class* and *everyone has a friend who is his best friend*. *Most* superlatives following indefinite determinatives are generally a very different matter.

> He's a *most obliging* fellow.
> It was a *most delightful* occasion.

Here again explicit comparison is not really present. *Most* may seem elegant in this use: such modifiers as *extremely* are generally preferred, or no modifiers at all.

Superlatives have considerable use as complements of copulative verbs and as adjuncts (and as heads and coordinates in such complements and adjuncts) without preceding determinatives.

> It seems *best* to try another method.
> It's *hardest* of all to understand him when he's eloquent.
> She's *least accommodating* when she's having troubles.
> The vegetation is *most impressive* in the valleys.
> She always stays *longest* when we're busy.

Most superlatives again have occasional use where clear and specific comparison is not implied.

> You've been *most kind*.
> It was *most embarrassing*.

Phrasings such as *very kind* and *extremely embarrassing* are generally preferred. It is noteworthy that *you've been kindest* always involves specific comparison: context or situation must suggest a completing modifier such as, for example, *among our hosts here*.

Exceptional character of comparatives and superlatives. —Most basic-form adjectives accept *very*, *too*, *so*, and *as* as modifiers of degree. Neither comparatives nor superlatives accept these words. But comparatives accept such pronouns as *much*, as well as nounal units of various types, as modifiers of difference; and superlatives are often accompanied by similar modifiers in predeterminative uses when the superlatives function as heads in nounal units. Basic-form adjectives do not ordinarily accept these.

very old	very considerate
much older	a great deal more considerate
much the oldest	a great deal the most considerate

Comparatives also take the article *the* as a modifier of difference, in a construction quite distinct from those in which it functions as a determiner.

> *The* harder I try, *the* worse I do.

And superlatives take ordinal numerals and *next*.

Popocatepetl is not the highest volcano in Mexico but the *second* highest.

This room is the *next* most satisfactory.

In addition, comparative and superlative forms of adjectives are usable as head words in nounal units with a degree of freedom unknown to their basic forms. They do not often take other adjectives as modifiers as nouns do, but they take determiners and postpositive clauses and prepositional units, often even where the force of the units they head seems more adjectival than nounal.

She's looking *her best*.

She's *the healthiest she's ever been*.

The subjects on which Williamson is *the least dogmatic* are naturally those on which he is *the least ignorant*.

It is noteworthy that comparative and superlative forms are sometimes weaker in force than the basic forms to which they correspond. This is the reason sentences such as the following occur.

I wouldn't call Tom a *good* student, but he's the *best* in the class.

Tom certainly isn't a *good* student, but he's *better* than his classmates.

One day can be warmer than another without being warm, and one child can be older than another without being old. The basic forms are applicable only when certain standards are met. These standards have been built up on the basis of long experience. Comparatives and superlatives sometimes ignore them, and simply put instances or sets of instances side by side. *Old* is usable with inflection and also with modifiers all along a scale on which without either modifiers or inflection it is much less broadly usable. Carol can be seven years old, and older than Janet, and the oldest of her group, without being *old*. If such words as *still* and *even* are used with comparatives, established standards for corresponding basic forms are ordinarily not ignored. Thus *Jack's French is even better than his Spanish* implies that Jack's French and his Spanish are both good, in the judgement of the speaker or writer. And for many adjectives comparative and superlative forms never ignore the established standards for the basic forms. Thus if one person is said to be more obstinate than another, the implication is that both are obstinate.

Syntactically exceptional uses of adjectives.—Adjectives have considerable use in nonadjectival constructions. Their use as predicators is of course highly exceptional, but in informal styles *had* is sometimes dropped in such sentences as *we better be careful* and the comparative adjective *better* may be felt as the main predicator. The use of adjectives as subjects occurs in such formulas as *easy does it* and occasionally in contexts where an unstated head is suggested by what immediately precedes.

> Where European manners were rigid and punctilious, *American* were flexible and careless.

Other phrasings are generally preferred. The use of adjectives as complements of transitive verbs is quite limited.

> She knows *better*.
> We didn't spend *long* there.
> She isn't even pretty, let alone *beautiful*.

The use of adjectives and adjectival units as adjuncts is very considerable. Sometimes there is no corresponding adverb.

> You see the country *best* from busses.
> He certainly talks *big*.
> They carried him out *bodily*.
> The paper is delivered *daily*.
> We got home *early*.
> As *far* as I know, that's right.
> I read the paper *too fast*.
> We haven't waited *long*.
> *Prior to publication* certain changes will be necessary.
> Jack did the job *unaided*.

Sometimes corresponding adverbs exist, but adjectives are used as adjuncts because the adverbs have different secondary relationships or would even express different meanings.

> They ate the chicken *cold*.
> His lawyer got him off *easy*.
> They'll let the children in *free*.
> Jack tries *hard*.
> George has been getting to his classes *late*.
> It costs two thousand dollars *new*.
> I pushed the door *open*.
> We left him *very sad*.
> They beat him *unconscious*.

In *they ate the chicken cold* the adjective *cold* is an adjunct of manner or circumstance and a half modifier of the complement *the chicken*. In *they ate the chicken coldly* the adverb *coldly* is an adjunct of manner or circumstance and a half modifier of the subject *they*. The coldness which is related to the chicken is physical, that which is related to "they" is emotional. In *George has been getting to his classes late* the adjective *late* is an adjunct of manner or circumstance expressing the meaning *after the proper time*. In *George has been getting to his classes lately* the adverb *lately* is an adjunct of time equivalent in meaning to *recently*. Sometimes corresponding adverbs exist and are entirely usable but the simpler adjectives tend to be preferred, as more forceful, in informal styles when sentences are short and somewhat emotional. The adjectives used in this way are short, common ones.

> It hurts *bad.*
> Take it *easy.*
> He doesn't play *fair.*
> You're doing *fine.*
> She talks too *loud.*
> Go *slow.*
> *Sure* I like it.
> Hold *tight!*
> He's done it *wrong* again.

The line between adjectival adjuncts and adjectival complements is sometimes very hard to draw. Adjunct classification in the following sentences is not wholly satisfying.

> The principle still holds *true.*
> The door has banged *shut.*

Loose adjuncts are often adjectival in form.

Contrary to the general belief, the older form is not *sewn* but *sewed.*

Effective the first of November, the library will close at eleven.

Strange to say, the word has completely different meanings in the two languages.

Unknown to Griselda, the Marquis sent the two children to a sister.

Unknown in his home city, Findlay is known among classicists throughout the nation.

Within nounal headed units adjectives sometimes have exceptional uses. *Double* is a predeterminative modifier in *double the true value*. *Poor* precedes a determinative in *his poor first wife*. Postpositive adjective modifiers occur in a few more or less fixed phrasings.

mother *dear*   the university *proper*
the president *elect*   a battle *royal*
time *immemorial*   the first person *singular*

Verbal force is apparently responsible for the postpositive position of some adjectives: postpositive position is normal for clausal modifiers.

the best solution *imaginable*
a consciousness of questions *unsolved*

Postpositive position is often natural for adjectival units which themselves contain postpositive modifiers of their own and even for some which contain only prepositive modifiers.

applicants *desirous of personal interviews*
rooms *large enough*
a wall *six feet high*

Adjectives sometimes modify nounal heads as other nouns might modify them, not as adjectives ordinarily do. Thus *an insane asylum* is an asylum for the insane, not one which is insane, and *married life* is the life of the married.

Basic-form adjectives function as heads, with determiner modifiers, in headed units of nounal types under various sets of circumstances. Sometimes the adjectives are used of people, usually with categorical *the* but sometimes with other determiners. The force is almost always plural.

The *French* do these things well.
The *living* may have less to say to us than the *dead*.
The *old* require interesting occupations too.
Mexico does not forget her *poor*.
It's our own *dead* that matter.

Among nationality adjectives only a few—*English, Welsh, Scotch, Irish, Dutch,* and *French*—are usable as categorical plurals. It is quite exceptional for adjectives with determiners to be used of people with singular force.

> She'll bring her *intended* along.

In another exceptional use an adjective with a determiner is used of animals with indifferent-number force.

> Almost any animal will defend its *young*.

Sometimes adjectives modified by the definite article are used with neuter force as names of qualities or of embodiments of qualities. often in more or less fixed phrasings.

> They have no patience with the *mediocre*.
> He's always on the *defensive*.
> Humor celebrated the *ludicrous*.
> He has no real belief in the *supernatural*.
> We're in the *thick* of it.

In *all of a sudden* an adjective modified by an indefinite article is used similarly. Sometimes adjectives become heads because of unwillingness to repeat a word or longer unit just given prominent expression.

> We prefer the old furniture to the *new*.

Since *furniture* is quantifiable, substitute *one* cannot represent it after *new*. The adjective *new* has taken on the meaning and syntax of a head which is left unexpressed. In *he is a true conservative* this same kind of thing has taken place, but *conservative* has gone a step farther and become a noun with a readiness to accept adjectives as prepositive modifiers—and with an *s* plural.

Adjectives have limited use as modifiers of pronouns, as in *a great many* and *at long last* and as in *far more*. They have limited use also as modifiers of other adjectives, chiefly but not entirely gerundial and participial adjectives.

a *clear*-cut victory	a *new*-born child
deathly pale	*plain* silly
far better	*ready*-made clothes
a *full*-grown man	*Roman* Catholic schools
good looking	a *smooth*-talking salesman
the *idle* rich	*sound* asleep
ill-advised	the *very* best
late Victorian	*wide* open

Sometimes they modify adverbs.

better off	*far* ahead
clear through	*long* before
close by	*straight* ahead

Sometimes they modify prepositional units.

deep in her heart	*full* in the face
early in the year	*long* before noon
far beyond our needs	*straight* out main street

In *Paraguay is farther west* the adjective *farther* modifies a noun with the value of the prepositional unit *to the west*.

Adjectives function as objects of prepositions under various circumstances.

> She's sort of *pretty*.
> She's anything but *considerate*.
> It's nothing short of *scandalous*.
> George was the most reasonable by *far*.
> In *general*, they prove very satisfactory.
> I won't be gone for *long*.
> We picked them at *random*.
> I regarded him as *dependable*.
> I remember her as *small and delicate*.
> We took his co-operation for *granted*.
> She drives like *mad*.

Upside-down constructions and modifiers of exception, addition, and the like are often highly exceptional in construction. *For, like,* and (especially) *as* sometimes serve as copulative prepositions with adjectival objects which have half-modifier relationships with what precedes.

As coordinates, adjectives sometimes combine to perform functions they would hardly perform singly.

> *Slow and steady* wins the race.
> The program pleased *young and old*.
> The elephants are hunting *high and low* for Arthur.
> They stuck together through *thick and thin*.

CHAPTER XII

ADVERBS

Miscellaneousness of the category of adverbs.—The adverbs make up the most miscellaneous of the part-of-speech categories and follow highly individualistic patterns of behavior to a greater extent than words of other types do. The category could be broken up into several part-of-speech categories of less miscellaneous nature, but some of these would be quite small (and two or three of them would be closed as well), and they would not be syntactically as distinct as parts of speech should be. Only an extensive "grammar of words" can give adequate notice to the syntactic behavior of the words here grouped together as adverbs. Something can be said here, however, about the behavior of several important subcategories among them.

Adjective-like adverbs in ly.—The largest subcategory among the adverbs is made up of words formed by adding the suffix *ly* to adjectives. The basic forms of most adjectives (including gerundial, participial, and phrasal adjectives) can be transformed into adverbs by the addition of *ly*.

adequate ly	dul ly	loud ly	ridiculous ly
affirmative ly	good-natured ly	maddening ly	satisfactori ly
bad ly	hard ly	mere ly	seeming ly
bare ly	humane ly	miraculous ly	selfish ly
charming ly	hurried ly	mistaken ly	sole ly
chief ly	late ly	noisi ly	stern ly
cold-blooded ly	laughing ly	repeated ly	unceasing ly

Complexities of the spelling system appear. *Formerly* and *utterly* are exceptional in that *ly* has been added to old comparative forms. The adverb *especially* is more widely used than the adverb *specially*, though the adjective *special* is used more than the adjective

269

especial. Forms such as *ably, basically, fatally,* and *supposedly* show complexities in formation to be noted later. Not all adjectives have corresponding adverbs in *ly,* by any means. Such common mono-syllables as *big, fast, long, old, small,* and *young* have none. *Good* has *well* as the corresponding adverb: *goodly* is a slightly archaic adjective, not an adverb. Adjectives which themselves employ the suffix *ly* have no corresponding adverbs with a second *ly.* This is true of such adjectives as *bodily, early, hourly,* and *kindly,* which are usable as adjuncts without change, and of such adjectives as *deadly, friendly, leisurely, lonely, manly,* and *stately,* which are gen-erally regarded as not satisfactorily usable as adjuncts. Other ad-jectives of miscellaneous types seem not to form corresponding adverbs. This is true, for example, of *difficult, eastern, extinct, French, funny, foreign, grown, parallel, silly, skilled,* and *superior.*

Some more or less adjective-like adverbs in *ly* are made by the addition of *ly* to nouns, pronouns, and even other adverbs. This is true of *namely, partly, purposely, only, secondly, mostly,* and *nearly.*

Adjective-like adverbs in *ly* function most characteristically as adjuncts of predicators. Meaning relationships are varied.

> He does his work *thoroughly.*
> *Unfortunately* a little tact is needed.
> George has been coming to his classes *lately.*
> We *occasionally* see George at the beach.
> We *barely* finished.

Here relationships of manner, attitude, time, general frequency, and near negation are expressed. Manner is probably the rela-tionship most often expressed by adverb adjuncts in *ly.*

Adjective-like adverbs in *ly* function as complements occasion-ally.

> He treats his wife *badly.*

Occasionally they function as predeterminative and postpositive modifiers within nounal headed units.

nearly a year	advancement *professionally*
exactly the right amount	his behavior *socially*

They function as contained modifiers in nonnounal headed units with much greater frequency. They modify adjectives, most often as modifiers of degree but sometimes as modifiers of attitude, respect, or even manner.

absolutely impossible   *openly* critical
a *badly* managed affair   *painfully* correct
curiously silent   a *rapidly* growing city
decidedly better   *strikingly* beautiful
deeply grieved   *surprisingly* complex
doubly responsible   *terribly* expensive
easily obtainable   *typographically* superior
encouragingly simple   *understandably* hesitant
extremely pleasant   *utterly* hopeless
numerically equal   *wholly* inadequate
obviously sincere

They modify adverbs, though generally not other adverbs in *ly*.

exactly how   *practically* there   *entirely* too big

They modify prepositional units.

exactly in the middle   *decidedly* above it   *desperately* in love

They even modify pronouns

hardly anyone   *almost* none   *only* three

Only has an extraordinary range of uses.

> We were *only* trying to help.
> She's an *only* child.
> She's *only* a child.
> The program is for children *only*.
> There were *only* three of us.
> It was *only* then that he consented.

Adjective-like adverbs in *ly* commonly accept degree modifiers of various types, and sometimes modifiers of other kinds.

> He does his work *very* thoroughly.
> He does his work *as* thoroughly *as anyone does*.
> She needs to do something independently *of her family*.

Most of them can be compared with the aid of the auxiliary pronoun forms *more* and *most* and *less* and *least*, except that the adjective forms *worse* and *worst* serve as comparative and superlative for *badly* as well as for *bad*, just as the adjective forms *better* and *best* serve as comparative and superlative for both the adjective *good* and the adverb *well*. In informal styles, comparative and superlative adjective forms sometimes push out established comparative and superlative adverb forms as in the following sentences.

> You can live *cheaper* in the smaller towns.
> They can be glued together *easier*.

Clause-marker adverbs.—Clause-marker adverbs form a limited group which is of particular interest to syntax. These include the words which share with verbs and pronouns the function of marking main- and subordinate-interrogative clauses. Clause-marker adverbs have been listed previously, as clause patterns have been noted. Most clause-marker adverbs are always clause-markers; this is true of *where* except in its uses within compounds such as *somewhere*. But *however* and *though* are sometimes subordinating clause markers, as in the first two sentences that follow, and sometimes simple conjunctive adjuncts, as in the last two.

> We won't please him *however* we do the job.
> He acts as *though* he's suffering.
> We finally gave up, *however*.
> We decided, *though*, that we'd try again.

Once and *only* are sometimes subordinating clause markers but more often adjuncts of more ordinary types.

> *Once* you get to know him, you'll like him.
> The food is excellent, *only* they serve too much pie.
> I've talked to him *once* or twice.
> There are *only* a few afternoon classes.

As is an adverb with a remarkable variety of uses. Often it is used twice in a single sentence, first as a head word to which a clause of comparison later in the sentence is attached, then as the marker within the clause of comparison.

> *As* many students read Shakespeare now *as* did when I was in college.

Clauses marked by *as* are of course not always clauses of comparison. Sometimes *as* also serves as a preposition, as will be noted later. *While* is generally a clause marker of the subordinator variety, but it is sometimes a noun as in *for a long while* and sometimes a verb as in *we whiled away the hours*.

Clause-marker adverbs such as these are in general not pegged tightly to single meanings. Thus *if* occurs in adjuncts of different types in the following sentences.

If George hears about this, he'll be irritated.
Uruguay is the best-organized country in South America *if* not the largest or most powerful.
If your eyes are hurting, why don't you have them examined?

In the first of these sentences the clause begun by *if* is a true adjunct of condition. In the second, however, *if* begins an adjunct of concession, and *although* is usable, though *if* makes concessions a little less explicitly and so a little more delicately; and in the third *if* begins an adjunct of circumstance, and *when* is usable. *How* has a remarkable range of uses. As a complement with copulatives it can call for responses of ordinarily adjectival types.

> *How* is Mr. Hayes today?
> *How* was the movie?
> *How* does the coffee taste?
> *How* does the new dress look?

As an adjunct of manner, *how* calls for adverbial responses.

> *How* can we repair it?

As a contained modifier of pronouns, adjectives, and adverbs, marker *how* serves to inquire into number, quantity, price, duration, frequency, and matters of many other kinds. Its meaning is roughly that of *to what degree?*

> *How* many questions will there be?
> *How* much time will they take?
> *How* much are eggs?
> *How* long will the concert last?
> *How* often will the committee meet?
> *How* many times will the committee meet?
> *How* large is the auditorium?
> *How* well does she type?

But *how* cannot help to elicit such a response as *the third*, for *Jefferson was the third president*, where English has no really satisfactory way of phrasing the question. And in assertives *how* often gives way to the pronoun *what* even where *how* seems syntactically more appropriate.

What a large auditorium!

How is used as a marker in subordinate-interrogative clauses exactly as it is used in main-interrogative clauses except that it is not usable in clauses used as adjuncts, though *however* is.

> *How* does she do "Curfew Shall Not Ring Tonight"?
> I wonder *how* she does it.
> "Curfew Shall Not Ring Tonight" sounds terrible *as* she does it.
> "Curfew Shall Not Ring Tonight" sounds terrible *however* you do it.

The coordinators.—The basic coordinators *and, but, or,* and *nor* involve the kind of reference to what has just preceded that the demonstrative pronouns, or the personal pronouns of the third person, often involve, though when the coordinators are used this reference is made quite inconspicuously. *And,* for example, has pretty much the meaning of *in addition to this* in its most characteristic uses.

> Your knowledge of grammar will be greatly increased if you study Latin, *and* you will acquire background for English vocabulary study.

Here *and* ties back to the whole main clause which precedes it. But *and* often goes a little farther than simple addition.

> Puerto Ricans live close together, *and* they know what is going on.
> Smith has done everything he could for his wife, *and* she doesn't appreciate it.

In these two sentences *and* approaches *therefore* and *yet* in meaning, but not explicitly. *Therefore* and *yet* can be placed after *and* in these sentences, somewhat as *also* can be placed after *and* in the sentence given just before these two. In titles such as *Students and Religion* the meaning of *and* is not far from that of *in relation to.* The coordinators, of course, relate not simply clauses but also nonclausal units of almost every kind.

The precoordinators *both, either,* and *neither* are pronouns. *Not,* however, is a precoordinator adverb in sentences such as *it should have been said not once but several times.*

Conjunctive adverbs.—Some adverbs link without either subordinating what they begin or explicitly coordinating it. Classification as conjunctive adverbs must be given such words as *also*, *too* when it is equivalent to *also* in meaning, *furthermore, nevertheless, however* when it is equivalent to *nevertheless* in meaning, *still* with the same meaning, *else, therefore, hence, so* when it means *hence* and when it means *also*, and *accordingly*. These have essentially the meanings of such phrasings as *in addition to this, in spite of this,* and *because of this*; but they can refer to nucleuses and clauses more unmistakably than the demonstrative pronouns can.

> When it's too hot for coats, ties are uncomfortable *also*.
> He lived in a world of his own, and *yet* he was a part of the adult world *too*.

Conjunctive adverbs can refer to nonclausal units as well as to clausal.

> The house is luxurious but *nevertheless* unpretentious.

Here *nevertheless* can be said to relate the two adjectives *luxurious* and *unpretentious* somewhat as *but* does, though *nevertheless* can hardly mark the adjectives as participants in a multiple complement as the coordinator *but* does.

Conjunctive adverbs, too, display complex patterns of use of highly individual kinds. *Else* and *so* are of particular interest. *Else* is used as an adjunct reinforcing the coordinator *or*.

> The Hortons will be in Acapulco, or *else* in Cuernavaca.

Here its behavior is much like that of the pronoun *either* which reinforces second negated constructions.

> The Hortons won't be in Mexico City, and you won't find them in Cuernavaca *either*.

Else is also used as a contained modifier of nounal compound pronouns such as *anyone* and *something* and of similarly formed adverbs such as *anywhere*, of clause-marker pronouns and adverbs such as *who* and *where*, and of the determinative pronouns *much* and *little*.

> There was nothing *else* to say.
> It's somewhere *else*.

> Who *else* will be there?
> There isn't much *else* to do.

Here *else* is much like *other* in behavior.

> There was one *other* thing to say.
> What *other* people will be there?

So tends to have extremitive force.

> Growing old doesn't seem *so* bad when you consider the alternative.
> I didn't realize it was *so* late.
> Your dress is *so* pretty!

In the first two sentences *so* is conjunctive if it refers to something just said. It can also point to what seems obvious though unstated. *So* has lost conjunctive force in the last sentence, where it is simply equivalent to *extremely* in meaning. The use of *so* in the sense of *also* produces assertive clause patterning in such sentences as the following, in spite of the fact that *so* has no real extremitive force here.

> The mountains are very beautiful, and *so* is the sea.

So is sometimes simply a substitute word, comparable to the personal-pronoun forms of the third person.

> If planes are dangerous, cars are much more *so*.
> I'm afraid *so*.
> I suppose *so*.

Here *so* represents first an adjective—*dangerous*, which has been expressed prominently just before—and then two declarative clauses whose content would be clear in the situations in which the sentences were framed. The use of *so* to represent subordinate-declarative clauses is quite limited: *I'm afraid so* but *I'm sure of it*; *I suppose so* (or *think so*, or *will tell him so*) but *I know that*. *So* is often coordinated with nounal units in such phrasings as *a month or so*.

Among the conjunctive adverbs *so* looks now to what has preceded, as the coordinators do, and now to what is to follow, as the precoordinators do.

> The Hortons are friendly people with plenty of time and money, *so* they do a great deal of entertaining.

Classes are now *so* big that any close relationship between teachers and students is impossible.

We went half an hour early *so* that we would have good seats.

In the first of these sentences *so* is a conjunctive adjunct within the second main clause in a multiple sentence and links that main clause to the first one. *And* is quite usable with this *so*. In the second sentence *so* is the head word in a contained modifier, and itself has as a completing modifier the declarative clause which begins with subordinator *that*. In the third sentence *so* is the head word in an adjunct and has as a completing modifier the declarative clause which follows it immediately. *So* can be regarded as a conjunctive where it looks ahead to a completing modifier, as in the second and third of these sentences, as well as where it looks back.

Prepositional adverbs.—Words which normally take nounal completers in some or most of their uses, and which are clearly not classifiable as verbs, can conveniently be grouped together as prepositional adverbs. A list would include the following.

aboard	below	into	since
about	beneath	less	through
above	beside	like	throughout
across	between	minus	till
after	beyond	near	to
against	but	notwithstanding	toward
along	by	of	under
alongside	despite	off	underneath
amid	down	on	unlike
among	due	onto	up
around	during	opposite	upon
as	for	outside	with
at	from	over	within
before	in	past	without
behind	inside	plus	worth

Near is one of the few adverbs that have comparative and superlative forms made by adding *er* and *est*. *Amid* has a variant *amidst*, *around* has what is now felt as a short variant *round*, *beside* has a variant *besides* (used where the meaning is that of addition), *between* has a variant *betwixt*, and *till* has a long variant *until*. Literary words such as *atop* and *astride*, and the archaic *O* of

direct address, can be added to the list; so can *per, versus,* and *via.*
It does not seem wise to regard forms of living verbs as prepositional. In *the lot adjoining ours* it seems best to regard *adjoining*
as the predicator in a gerundial clause modifying the head noun
lot just as the relative clause *which adjoins ours* would modify it,
not as a preposition like the *beside* of *the lot beside ours.* Similarly in
all except three it seems best to regard *except three* as (for modern
English) an imperative clause used as a contained modifier of *all,*
not as a prepositional unit like the *but three* of *all but three. During*
and *notwithstanding* are another matter: *dure* is no longer a living
verb, and certainly *notwithstand* is not a verb.

Some of the prepositional adverbs listed require other part-of-
speech classifications also. *Despite* is sometimes a noun, *down* is
sometimes a noun and sometimes a verb, *due* is best regarded as an
adjective when it has no nounal completer expressed or implied,
inside is sometimes a noun, *less* is a pronoun much more often than
(as in *seven less four is three*) it is a prepositional adverb, *opposite*
is sometimes a noun, *past* is often a noun, *worth* is a noun in such
phrasings as *a dollar's worth.*

Prepositional adverbs are sometimes used with objects clearly
implied but not stated.

> The street was busy, but I finally got *across.*
> Come *in!*
> I haven't seen him *since.*
> Of course he wants *to.*
> That's something *like!*

This kind of thing is of limited occurrence except in subordinate
clauses. It is very frequent in subordinate clauses.

> The house we were looking *at* was much too big.
> It's worth looking *into.*
> We have other problems to think *of.*
> That's the man we came *with.*

At, into, of, and *with* are not likely to be used without expressed
objects in corresponding main clauses.

Some prepositional adverbs have uses in which they are best not
regarded as prepositions at all. Thus though *about* is a preposition
in *we were talking about the election,* it is a nonprepositional modifier

of what follows (like the equivalent *approximately*) in *there were about twenty* and in *I was about to ask.* Though *along* is a preposition in *we drove along the seashore for several miles*, it is not at all clearly so in *we get along well together. But* is a coordinator oftener than it is prepositional, and sometimes it is merely a contained modifier equivalent to *only*, as in *it was but a step to absolute ruin. Down* is a preposition in *farther down the mountain* but hardly so in *I lay down for half an hour* or in *he let me down when I was depending on him. In* is hardly a preposition in *we handed our papers in. Off* is a preposition in *I washed the dirt off the car*, but hardly in *did you turn the lights off?* The *on* of position or movement in contact with a line is a preposition in *on the coast* and in *on the road to Toledo*, but not very clearly so in *after lunch we drove on* or in *I kept on studying* where the line is a metaphorical line of effort. *Up* is a preposition in *he went up the stairs two at a time*, but hardly in *I looked up and saw what had happened* or in *she tore the letter up.*

As has been noted, a few prepositions sometimes have copulative force and so are used with adjectival objects. *As* functions in this way most often.

> They've always regarded him *as* essentially helpless.
> The proposal struck me *as* unrealistic.
> We gave it up *as* hopeless.

For is copulative in *we took it for granted* and *like* in *the furniture was like new.*

A few adverbs which are commonly used as one-word prepositions are also used as head words in phrasal prepositions. Thus *alongside of, inside of,* and *outside of* occur alongside the one-word prepositions without *of*, which are generally preferred. *Nearer to* and *nearest to* are probably commoner than the one-word prepositions without *to*.

> They're a little *nearer to* the campus than they were.

Though generally avoided in careful and formal styles, *off of* occurs alongside *off*, especially when there is no following object.

> Here's the bottle that lid came *off of.*
> Which bus did he get *off of?*

The use of prepositions is highly arbitrary. Some verbs take nounal complements, some take prepositional ones.

> He was watching *us*.
> He was looking *at us*.

Some adjunct relationships lack satisfactory prepositions.

> That's right, *George*.
> I reminded him *three times*.

Nouns and adjectives ordinarily do not take clearly nounal completing modifiers: prepositional units are normal here. Thus *he respects women* is matched by *his respect for women* and *he is respectful toward women* with the prepositions *for* and *toward* used with the noun *respect* and the adjective *respectful*. Where prepositions are required, choice among them is determined by conventions that are often hard to understand. Two prepositions are even involved in the distinction between two and more than two that is made with such pronouns as *both* and *all* and with comparative and superlative adjective forms in such phrasings as *the younger of the two* and *the youngest of the three*.

> We'll divide the profit *between* the two of us.
> We'll divide the profit *among* the three of us.

Between is used where division into two parts is made for numbers larger than two.

> There are excellent roads *between* Guadalajara and the other important cities of the region.

As has been said, contemporary English is reluctant to accept many possible combinations of prepositions and completing clauses. Among the subordinate-clause patterns employed in contemporary English, four can be called basically nounal: those of declaratives, imperatives, assertives, and infinitival verbids. Two other patterns are partly nounal in essence and partly adjectival-adverbial: that of interrogative clauses and that of gerundial verbid clauses. Gerundial clauses are rather freely usable as objects of prepositions.

> She is quite capable *of* decorating the truth.
> Frank isn't *past* being taken in by pretty girls.

Interrogative clauses are less freely usable as objects of prepositions, which often drop out before them.

> I've been thinking *about* what you said.
> I wasn't sure who it was.
> I don't care what he did.

Declarative clauses can complete only a very few one-word prepositions and a few reduced phrasal prepositions.

> Stevens was Chairman *until* he died.
> He must have loved her dearly, *for* he ruined himself for her.
> He married her *because* he loved her.

Here *because he loved her* is paralleled by *because of his love for her*. Infinitival verbid clauses complete only a few prepositions. Infinitival clauses without expressed subjects of their own have an extraordinary affinity for *to*; those with subjects have a similar affinity for *for . . . to*.

The *to* which is used with infinitives has a remarkably broad range of uses. It occurs not only where it would also be used with nonclausal objects, but also in many situations where other prepositions would be used—especially prepositions expressing relationships of respect, purpose, and end.

don't care *about* meeting him	decided *on* a change
don't care *to* meet him	decided *to* change
serves *as* an explanation	consented *to* a delay
serves *to* explain	consented *to* wait
shocked *at* his appearance	invited him *to* supper
shocked *to* see him	invited him *to* stay
stopped *for* a look	inclined *toward* the view
stopped *to* look	inclined *to* think
forced him *into* marriage	lived *until* he was ninety
forced him *to* marry	lived *to* be ninety
the honor *of* presenting	satisfied *with* his answer
the honor *to* present	satisfied *to* know this

In some of its uses a preposition usable before a noun or pronoun does not suggest itself immediately.

> *To* tell the truth, we all want comfort.
> Who is he *to* ask such favors?

Sometimes *to*, used of what lies ahead in time, takes on some of the force of the future auxiliary *will*.

These days are passing rapidly, never *to* return.
In time manifestations of provincialism, like Currier and Ives
    prints, were *to* become collectors' items.
If prices were *to* rise further, the government would have to
    take action.
We can look for real improvement in years *to* come.

Often *to* takes on meanings of constraint and possibility, as what
is thought of as lying ahead (or probably lying ahead) is seen, in
prospect, as compelling or as inviting.

We have work *to* do.
We're *to* bring sandwiches and fruit.
The novel *to* be read is *Passage to India*.
He has no relatives *to* turn to.
He has a new car in which *to* see Puerto Rico.
I don't know how *to* explain it.

Often *to* is used with infinitives where the occurrence of a preposition is syntactically exceptional. *To* is likely to add something of
abstractedness, or separation from strictest reality, in constructions
of this kind: the predication is viewed as a prospect, or an idea,
rather than as an actuality.

To be a bully seemed contemptible.
It takes a low bush *to* stand in a hard wind.
We wanted *to* be here.
He asks nothing except *to* be let alone.

Sometimes it is hard to see that *to* really makes a contribution.

We used *to* see Eugene oftener.
On Saturdays Jerry works in his yard till about ten and then
    begins *to* read his mail.

In the sentence just given, if *stops* is substituted for *begins* the
preposition *to* expresses purpose and begins an adjunct rather than
a complement. The *to* which occurs within an infinitival clause,
between an expressed subject and the infinitival predicator, is
best regarded as a preposition placed inside its clausal object.

We wanted you *to* be there.

Sometimes infinitival clauses with subjects of their own are made
objects of the prepositional apposed units *for . . . to*, with *for*
preceding the clause and with its appositive, *to*, inside the clause.

We're waiting *for* the main picture *to* end.
One way of finding Jerry would be *for* you *to* inquire at all the bars.

Two of the few prepositions that are usable with subordinate-declarative clauses as objects tend under certain circumstances to unite more closely with what follows them, becoming clause markers within subordinate-interrogative clauses rather than prepositions with clausal objects.

> Surely there isn't a mother *but* faces this problem.
> We need houses *like* were built in the last century.
> He looks *like* he looked twenty years ago.

Careful styles tend to avoid this kind of thing, and formal styles avoid it with *like* though they may accept it with *but*. The other prepositional adverbs that are usable with declarative-clause objects do not unite with such objects except as prepositions normally unite with their objects. Thus in *Stevens was Chairman until he died* the preposition *until* has in the clause *he died* an object that completes it just as the nounal headed unit *his death* would complete it, and in *he married her because he loved her* the preposition *because* has in the clause *he loved her* an object that completes it just as the nounal unit *his love for her* would complete the unshortened phrasal preposition *because of*.

As is prepositional much less than it is nonprepositional, and is best thought of as nonprepositional in such sentences as *you're as bright as me*, where *me* is simply the strong form of *I* used as subject in the reduced adverbial clause *as me* in which *as* is complement and marker. In less characteristically informal styles *as I am* would be preferred to *as me* here. Somewhat formal styles might employ *as I*. *Than* is best regarded as always a subordinator adverb employed in adverbial clauses, never prepositional. The two sentences which follow, both of them informal in style, are quite distinct in syntax.

> They got there earlier than us.
> They got there before us.

Here *than us* is an adverbial clause, like *than we did* and formal *than we*; and *than* is an adjunct and marker in this clause. *Before us*, on the contrary, is a prepositional unit in which *before* is the preposition and *us* is its object. *Before we did* is a prepositional unit also, and *we did* is the object of *before*. *They got there before we* is not acceptable: the strong prepositional force of *before* prevents it.

Other adverbs.—Other adverbs remain. There are adjective-like adverbs without *ly*. *Soon* is one and has the comparative and superlative forms *sooner* and *soonest*. *Rather* is a comparative adverb without a living basic form. It has a remarkable variety of characteristic uses.

> He opened the door—or *rather*, he started to open it.
> I'd *rather* not tell him.
> *Rather* than disappoint us, George went ahead with the arrangements.
> It was a careless action *rather* than a calculated one.
> It's *rather* late.

As a contained modifier equivalent to *somewhat* in meaning (*it's somewhat late*), *rather* loses comparative force. *Doubtless* must now be classified as an adverb, though the suffix *less* normally terminates adjectives. *Quite* is an adverb used chiefly in negated clauses (and so tending to reinforce the negation) and as a predeterminative contained modifier in nounal headed units.

> I didn't *quite* finish.
> That isn't *quite* right.
> He's *quite* a boy.

Very and *pretty*, and informal *real* and *awful* (and less often *mighty*), are best classified as adverbs when they function as contained modifiers of degree. *Awfully* tends to be preferred to the simpler adverb form without *ly*, even as degree modifier.

> *very* late   *real* late   *awful* late
> *pretty* late   *mighty* late   *awfully* late

Postpositive *galore* and the *alias* and *nee* which precede proper names are less clearly adjective-like adverbs. *Well* is an adjective-like adverb that is involved in notable competition with the corresponding adjective, *good*. When the interest is in people's health, *well* is used as the complement of copulatives, where adjectives are normal.

I'm afraid John isn't *well*.
He seems *well*, but he is really very weak.

Where the interest is in appearance from the point of view of attractiveness rather than of health, there is some confusion, and both *good* and *well* are often avoided.

Yellow isn't a very good color for Mary.

In somewhat formal styles *well* completes *be* in sentences such as *it is well to be prepared for disappointments*. In adjunct uses, *well* is the systematically normal word, but *good* has considerable use in informal styles.

I can't see very *good* without glasses.

The semantic range of *well* is remarkable, as the following sentences indicate.

This may *well* be true.
I can *well* understand it.
He's lived in Detroit as *well* as Chicago.
I prefer steak *well* done.
He's *well* on his way by now.
George isn't *well* today.
It would be *well* to consider other possibilities.
Well, I guess it's time for some coffee.

In the last of these sentences *well* is an adjunct that is no more than introductory in force.

There are pronoun-like adverbs which neither mark clauses as *when* does nor function as conjunctive adverbs as *else* does. The *why* which serves as a mild introductory adjunct is commonly distinguished from clause-marker *why* (and *what* and *which*) by its loss of the sound /h/.

Why, I suppose I can.

Adverbs such as *sometime, anyhow*, and *everywhere* are markedly like such pronouns as *someone, anybody*, and *nothing* in formation, meanings, and even syntax. Adverbs such as *now, here, then*, and *there* have obvious relationships to the demonstrative pronouns *this* and *that*. The relationship is less clear, perhaps, for such adverbs as the *still* which means *as late as this* and the *already* which means *as early as this*.

George is *still* in his office.
George is in his office *already*.

Ever is obviously much like the pronoun *any* in behavior and reinforces questioning, negation, and condition very similarly.

They won't *ever* admit it.
They won't admit it under *any* circumstances.

Once and *twice* are clearly related to the numeral pronouns *one* and *two*. Such adverbs as *seldom, sometimes, often,* and *always* have a great deal in common with such determinative pronouns of number as *few, some, many,* and *all*. In *sometimes,* as in *indoors,* an *s* plural appears among the adverbs, in a nounal component in a compound. *Often* has a comparative in *er* and a superlative in *est*. As has been noted, some "adjective-like" adverbs in *ly* are based on pronouns.

There are adverbs which are made up of old prepositions and their objects. In such adverbs as *aback, abreast, afield, afresh, ahead, anew, aside,* and *away* the old preposition is no longer a known component. *Akin, alike, alive,* and *awake* are similarly formed complexes for which classification as adjectives rather than as adverbs may seem desirable; but because of their prepositional-unit origin they are not usable as prepositive modifiers within nounal headed units and are most conveniently classified simply as adverbs. Other adverbs that were once prepositional phrases include *indeed, indoors, perhaps, percent,* and (with exceptional apostrophe) *o'clock*. *Percent* and *o'clock* are characteristically limited to uses as postpositive modifiers of numeral pronouns. Occasionally *percent* is treated as a noun, but *percentage* (as in *a certain percentage*) is preferred in such uses. Such adverbs as *hereafter* and *thereupon* have their prepositional component following its adverb object, as do clause-marker adverbs such as *whereby* and *whereupon*.

Adverbs of still other types remain. *Maybe* and *ago* are verbal in origin. As has been said, *ago* is quite exceptional in the types of modifiers it takes.

a year *ago*   long *ago*   two weeks *ago* yesterday

Awhile is composed of an article and its head noun—normally kept separate after prepositions, as in *for a while*.

Finally, there is *not*, whose use as a clause negator affects clause structure strikingly, as has been noted.

Performance of nonadverbial functions by adverbs and prepositional units.—The functions characteristically performed by adverbs can be regarded as the adverbial functions. Almost all of them are performed by prepositional units also, since the syntax of prepositional units is determined by the prepositions and these are adverbs in part of speech. The adverbial functions are as follows:

1. Complement of an oblique verb, as in *she looked up* and *she looked at us.*
2. Second complement, as in *she's put the checkers away* and *she's put the checkers in their box.*
3. Adjunct, as in *he isn't happy here* and *he isn't happy in Chicago.*
4. Head in an adverbial headed unit, as in *he did it rather badly* and in *he did it entirely without help.*
5. Prepositive modifier in an adjectival or adverbial headed unit, as in *it was surprisingly good* and *he behaved very obstinately.*
6. Predeterminative modifier in a nounal headed unit, as in *it irritates even his best friends* and *nearly a year went by.*
7. Postpositive modifier in a headed unit, as in *the people here, the best murder mystery yet, the people of Chapel Hill, parallel to the railroad,* and *independently of his family.*
8. Principal in an adverbial apposed unit, as in *we expect to spend the summer out in Utah.*
9. Appositive in an adverbial apposed unit, as in *we'll be out there in August* and *we'll be back in Pennsylvania in August.*
10. Coordinate in an adverbial multiple unit, as in *he talked slowly and without emphasis.*

Prepositional units are normally used as postpositive modifiers rather than as prepositive ones, but in *if he's at all dependent* and in *for at least an hour* prepositional units function first as the prepositive modifier of an adjective and then as the predeterminative modifier of a noun. Prepositional units can often be coordinated with adjectives as well as with adverbs.

He is honest and without malice.

Adverbs and adverbial units, including prepositional units, have considerable use in nonadverbial functions. They occur as subjects.

Once is enough.
After eleven will be too late.
To neglect the basic economic problem would be to court disaster.
From Miami to San Juan is a thousand miles.
As has been said, a few prepositions sometimes have copulative force.
It took longer *than* seemed necessary.
There isn't a child *but* has to rebel against its parents.
We need houses *like* were built in the last century.

They occur as complements of transitive verbs.

We'd better let *well enough* alone.
They left *here* at ten.
I think *so.*
I've never seen *but one scorpion.*
He's hard to see except *in the morning.*

As complements of copulative verbs.

He isn't *well.*
How does the coffee taste?

As heads in nounal units.

by the *by*	*now* that you mention it
everywhere I go	every *now and then*
the *hereafter*	this *once*
the *like*	every *so often*

As adjective-like prepositive modifiers in nounal units.

in *after* years	the *off* season
an *after-dinner* speech	his *only* argument
a *by* product	more *on-the-job* training
an *in-between* coloring	the *opposite* side
the *down* payment	an *outside* room
people of *like* minds	an *over-all* reorganization
a *minus* sign	a *through* train
a *near* collision	the *up* button

As determinative modifiers in nounal units.

between forty and fifty students
from ten to fifteen minutes

As objects of prepositions.

till *afterwards*	from *nowhere*
until *a short time ago*	at *once*

since *before the war*	until *recently*
from *behind the counter*	kind of *roughly*
in *between the extremes*	since *then*
from *here*	near *there*
by *now*	nothing like *as well*
between *now and then*	*where* are you from?

In coordination with words and multiword units of nonadverbial types.

> passports, visas, *and so forth*
> my one *and only* chance
> an *up*-and-coming salesman

Actually a rather small number of words, and a rather small number of situations, account for most of the uses of adverbs in nonadverbial functions. Subordinator *as* and *than* function as subjects, as complements of verbs of various types, and even (as in the following sentence) as objects of prepositions.

> Conditions such *as* his family lives in are a disgrace.

But and *like* have similar syntactically exceptional uses when they enter subordinate clauses and do not merely act as prepositions outside them. Such words as *once, now,* and *here* are convenient brief equivalents of such units as *one time, the present,* and *this place.* Adjuncts of addition and exception (such as *except in the morning*), upside-down constructions (such as *kind of roughly*), and series terminators (such as *and so forth*) are allowed great syntactic freedom. In the main the use of adverbs in nonadverbial constructions is quite limited. At some points limits are sometimes set in too arbitrary a fashion. Thus the use of *where* with the prepositions *at* and *to* is commonly condemned, on the grounds that these prepositions are redundant with *where;* but in sentences such as the following *to* seems highly desirable.

> Where in the world has John run off to now?
> Where to?

CHAPTER XIII

FULL DETERMINATIVES
OF IDENTIFICATION

As has been said, determinative pronouns are characteristically used in two ways:

1. As determiner modifiers of nounal heads.
2. As forms which have assimilated both the meanings and the syntactic functions of what would be their nounal heads in unreduced construction.

Full determinatives of identification can combine with singular forms of pluralizer nouns to form units usable in nounal functions where undetermined singulars of pluralizers normally are not usable. The full determinatives of identification are *this*, demonstrative *that, the, a, some, any, either, every, each, no, neither, what, which, whatever,* and *whichever.* Of these, *the, a,* and *every* are exceptional in not being usable in nounal functions: they require expressed heads.

***Demonstrative* this *and* that.**—The demonstratives *this* and *that* identify by pointing of one kind or another, whether physical or not. *This* implies relative nearness in whatever dimension. *This pen* is a pen probably in the speaker or writer's hand. *This gloomy old house* is a gloomy old house that the speaker or writer is probably in or near at the moment. *This morning, this noon, this afternoon,* and *this evening* are parts of the day in which they are spoken or written; *this spring, this summer, this fall,* and *this winter* are in process, not too far ahead, or in the immediate past. *Today* and *tonight* replace *this day* and *this night* unless modifiers are added as in *this day of surprises, to this very day,* and *this beautiful night.* In informal styles, *this* sometimes simply implies prominence in the speaker or writer's thinking.

Then I got *this* letter from Grace.
The story begins with Ryabovich attending *this* party.

That implies relative remoteness. *That pen* is a pen perhaps in the hand of the person addressed, or perhaps at a distance or even no longer in existence; but it can also be a pen in the speaker's hand, looked at with a certain detachment or perspective, or perhaps even with some special emotion, for whatever reason. *That week* is a week in the past or the future, neither the present week nor the week before it (*last week*) or after it (*next week*); *that day* is a day in the past or the future, neither the present day nor the day before it (*yesterday*) nor the day after it (*tomorrow*).

As determinative modifiers both *this* and *that* are applicable to people but sometimes a certain amount of delicacy is necessary in using them—and especially in using *that*.

> Who is *that* woman in the red dress?
> *This* little boy is our neighbor.

The woman in the red dress is apparently out of hearing, and the little boy is quite young. The use of the demonstratives in the following sentences is emotional.

> We've tried *this* doctor and *that*.
> *Those* neighbors!
> She's one of *those* big, helpless women.
> Have you provided for *those* children of yours and *that* little wife?

Emotional demonstratives are of course not confined to applications to people.

> He's parked *that* Buick of his in front of our drive again.

The *that* of *close that door!* is often emotional, used where *the* would be adequate. The *that* of *he has that natural, unpretentious manner which marks the Westerner* has a less obvious emotional value.

In doubtfully standard informal use *this* and *that* are sometimes made plural in upside-down nounal units in which they modify *kind*.

> *Those* kind of chairs are very comfortable.

Here *chairs of that kind* has been turned upside down. The plural force of the whole subject unit seems to make substitution of *those* for *that* natural. But if either *sort* or *type* is used instead of *kind*, there is less tendency to make the demonstrative plural.

The demonstratives have very considerable nounal use.

> *This* is fun.
> I haven't seen him from that day to *this*.
> *Those* are very comfortable-looking shoes.
> I've been doing *this* and *that* all morning.
> What's *that?*
> Who's *that?*
> *This* is Mary Jones.

This is Mary Jones employs the normal, unemotional formula for identification of the speaker over the telephone and of others in introductions. But demonstratives used nounally of people can be emotional also.

> *That*'s a good fellow!
> Surely she didn't marry *that?*

Demonstratives used nounally often refer to occurrences, nucleuses, clauses, sentences, and series of sentences.

> Look at *that!* The baby's walking.
> You may be right at *that*.
> There was little building and not much repairing, and *that* at a time when the community was growing rapidly.
> When work is done inefficiently, people like to excuse *this* by blaming the climate.
> Pennsylvania is a very beautiful state. *That* is, the parts of it you will spend your time in are very beautiful.
> Joe means well—*that*'s the best you can say for him.
> We see him when he comes to town, but *that* isn't often.
> We saw snow only once during the winter, and *that* was when the mountains high above the city were covered with it.
> *That*'s how matters stood.
> I tried to tell her *that*.

The use of demonstratives to refer to occurrences, nucleuses, and the like is sometimes criticized, and is perhaps best kept at a minimum in careful and formal styles; but sometimes the construction is much neater than the alternatives. *That* is commoner than *this* in this use, but *this* can refer to what the speaker or writer is about to say and *that* cannot.

> I'll say *this:* he's strictly honest.

Sometimes demonstratives used nounally refer to adjectives, numeral pronouns, and miscellaneous expressions of number and quantity.

"Is he boring?" "I wouldn't call him *that.*"
It's hot now, but it will be hotter than *this* after April.
"There are five vacant rooms." "*That*'s too many."
Judy's eight now, and she seems older than *that.*
The first test failed half the class, but the second failed more than *that.*

In the last sentence *that* will be taken to refer to *half the class* and *that one* would be taken to refer to *the first test*, as *it* would.

This is a very useful word for referring to antecedents late in immediately preceding main clauses.

His speech was concerned chiefly with *the subject of land ownership. This* was a very delicate matter, since many of those present were plantation owners.
The universities get *some of the young people who come to New York*, but *these* form only a small part of the total number who come.
Grades are not to be recorded on the *enrollment cards. These* are to be kept for the teacher's own records.

The personals would depend less on nearness and more on the type of syntactic prominence that subjects have, and are not usable in place of *this* in these sentences. *That* is not usable to refer to earlier possible antecedents as *this* refers to later; there is no paralleling of *this* and *that* as *the latter* and *the former* are paralleled.

That is often used nounally with the value of a form of the definite article *the* and an implied head to which postpositive modifiers are attached.

Morally and socially his world was not very different from *that* inhabited by his parents.
We picked the coolest apartment among *those* available.
The English spoken in rural Georgia is quite different from *that* spoken in rural Indiana.
The happiest people are *those* whose work interests them.
There are *those* who disagree.

Basic-form *that* cannot refer to people in this use, though plural *those* can. Combinations of *the* and substitute *one* compete with nounal *that* in some situations. The meanings are the same, but the syntax is not.

The demonstratives *this* and *that* modify both pluralizers and quantifiables. When they modify plurals, alone among determiner modifiers they themselves show number.

this girl	that day	this lettuce	that advice
these girls	those days		

Both *this* and *that* have considerable use as modifiers of degree attaching to adjectives, adverbs, and pronouns, as adverbs do.

this big   that badly   that many

Demonstratives are not repeatable as the personals are. Thus in *let go of that before you break it* the demonstrative is used only once and is then replaced by *it*.

The definite article the.—In origin the definite article *the* is an unstressed variant of the demonstrative *that*. From the point of view of meaning it functions as a less forceful equivalent of *this* as well as *that*.

How do you like *the* weather?
How do you like *this* weather?
What did you think of *the* speech last night?
What did you think of *that* speech last night?

The element of pointing is normally weaker with *the* than with the demonstratives. There is a similar directing of the attention; but there is more dependence on obviousness and less on selection by means of pointing of one kind or another. In this respect determinative *the* is a great deal like nounal *he* and *it*. Characteristically *the* indicates that identification seems complete on the basis of conspicuousness in the particular situation or context.

I'm afraid *the* milk is sour.
Mary's in *the* garage.
Where's *the* paper?
We drove out into *the* country.
When Juanita went to confession, she told *the* priest what had happened.
The President is speaking tonight.
Before *the* drought was over, many farmers were ruined.
Sophomores who read Chaucer find *the* English very difficult.

Sometimes *the* implies obviousness on a basis broader than particular situations in the usual sense.

> *The* sun makes life possible, but it can also kill.
> Our ancestors blamed *the* devil for these things.

Somewhat exceptional uses of the definite article include the categorical use modifying plural nouns and adjectives used nounally (of people) with plural force.

> *The* Spaniards brought Negro slaves into their Caribbean possessions.
> *The* Lutherans have their own schools too.
> *The* steelworkers are on strike.
> *The* women make their influence felt in politics now.
> *The* French still have important Caribbean possessions.
> Even *the* very young and *the* very old need interesting things to do.

The difference between the categorical plural with *the* and the general plural without determiners is not always clearly felt, but it is basically significant. *The Germans have had trouble with all their neighbors* is a statement about a national grouping and implies nothing about individual Germans. *Germans are good workers* is a statement about individual Germans, looked at in general but as individuals nevertheless. It does not imply that every German is a good worker; allowance for exceptions is understood.

The use of the definite article to mark representative singulars is contrary to its ordinary patterning in modern English, but it is frequent nevertheless.

> I never try to work much in *the* morning.
> It's always pleasant here in *the* winter.
> Carol plays *the* violin exceptionally well
> He buys ties by *the* dozen.
> Smoking is certainly bad for *the* throat.
> *The* automobile has changed American life.
> *The* American husband is willing to help with the dishes.
> As far as *the* eye could see, the land was empty.
> Writing with *the* left hand creates problems in school.
> This book will interest *the* teacher most.
> *The* enemy attacked the next day.
> He's playing *the* fool as usual.

What should perhaps be considered representative plurals and quantifiables are much less frequent.

> Warm salt water is good for *the* nerves.
> Everyone should get in *the* water in the summer.
> Those who live in *the* country deserve good medicine too.

Representative singulars with *the* are best established, perhaps, with names of the major divisions of the day (the morning, the afternoon, the evening, the night) and of the year (the spring, the summer, the fall, the winter), with names of units of measurement (the pound, the yard, the dozen) used with *by*, and with names of musical instruments such as the piano and the violin. These are oddly limited uses. Though it is normal to say *she plays the piano* and mean the typical piano, it is not usual to say *she drives the automobile* and mean the typical automobile. Similarly, though it is usual to say *we buy tea by the pound*, the use of *the* immediately after the naming of the price (as in *green tea is now two dollars the pound*) belongs to genteel usage, and *a* is usually preferred. Applied to people and their institutions, the representative singular with *the* gives an effect of detachment.

> In terms of patterns of behavior, *the* Negro is not a single human type in the British islands, the French islands, Puerto Rico, Cuba, and Haiti.

Here *the Negro* is a sociological abstraction, like *the American husband, the city*, and *the home* in some uses.

Definite articles are common with names of parts of the body in some situations where possessives of personals might be expected. This is true following a complement to which a possessive personal would refer if one were used.

grabbed George by *the* arm	took the child by *the* hand
chilled us to *the* bone	shot him through *the* heart
looked me in *the* eye	look a gift horse in *the* mouth

The is kept in corresponding passives, and sometimes in other constructions where a possessive would have the subject as antecedent.

> He was shot through *the* heart.
> He was red in *the* face.
> I was feeling weak in *the* legs.

But for parts of the body *the* often gives a somewhat impersonal effect.

Those of the natives that have had comfortable lives are beautiful people. *The* features are fine, and *the* eyes large and bright.

Metaphorical locutions sometimes employ this *the*.

I'm feeling a little down in *the* mouth right now.
We'll pay through *the* nose.
He gives me a pain in *the* neck.

The use of the definite article with proper names is a matter of some complexity. True proper nouns ordinarily have no article. A few quite exceptional place names employ *the* with what otherwise seem like true proper nouns: for example, *the Argentine, the Netherlands, the Bronx, the Crimea, the Hague*. Such old titles of books as *the Bible, the Koran*, and *the Iliad* do similarly. Ordinarily the use of honorifics before names of people does not involve the addition of articles: for example, in *Mr. Hayes, Dr. Gaston, President Luckey, General Lee, Bishop Manning, Sr. Collazo*. But *the* is often regarded as desirable before the adjective honorifics *Reverend* and *Honorable*, when these are used with people's names; and it is used with a few exotic honorifics, as in *the Emperor Maximilian* and *the Metropolitan Sergius*. When *the* is used before an honorific, another construction is approached: the apposed-unit construction of *the prophet Isaiah* and *the Spaniard Serrano*.

Names of oceans, seas, rivers, groups of islands, mountain ranges, deserts, ships, trains, planes, and hotels normally have *the*.

the Atlantic	the West Indies	the *Queen Elizabeth*
the Caribbean	the Appalachians	the *Ozarker*
the Ohio	the Sahara	the Taft

Ohio and *Mississippi* are states; *the Ohio* and *the Mississippi* are rivers. *Queen Elizabeth* is the name of a queen; *the Queen Elizabeth* is the name of a ship.

Articles and adjectives together seem to modify true proper nouns in such phrasings as *the indefatigable Poutsma* and *the late Senator Norris*. But in such phrasings as *the Dorothy Lucker we know, the first Roosevelt*, and *the seventeenth-century Samuel Butler* proper names have become pluralizers. Probably this is what has happened also in *the new Puerto Rico*, where the island is thought of as a cluster of variants—one Puerto Rico in 1900, another in 1930, another now.

For phrasal proper names with head words that are pluralizers rather than true proper nouns, the normal pattern calls for use of *the*.

the Appalachian Mountains	the Great Lakes
the Atlantic Ocean	the Gulf of Mexico
the Butler Museum of Art	the Middle Ages
the Canal Zone	the Modern Language Association
the City of New York	
the College of William and Mary	the Ohio Hotel
	the Pan-American Highway
the Dead Sea	the Republic of Panama
the First Methodist Church	the Statue of Liberty
the General Electric Company	the University of Utah

But *the* is not used in some phrasal proper names in which pluralizer nouns are heads. This is normally true of names of islands, bays, lakes, mountains, counties, forts, cities, streets, and parks.

Mustang Island	Mahoning County	Wick Avenue
Hudson Bay	Mexico City	Washington Boulevard
Lookout Mountain	Main Street	Mill Creek Park
Mount Everest	Lake Erie	Fort McHenry

It is true of names of colleges, universities, and other educational institutions, and sometimes of names of buildings used by such institutions, when the pluralizer head word is preceded by a proper noun or other relatively specific word or phrase.

Houghton College	California Institute of Technology
Ohio State University	
Southern Methodist University	Taliaferro Hall
	Gould Gymnasium

In formal institutional use, *the* is sometimes placed before such a name as *Ohio State University*.

Sometimes *the* has semantic value like that of *the best*, *the correct*, or *the true*.

That's not *the* way for an adult with a positive I.Q. to learn a foreign language.

Mustaches were quite *the* thing in those days.
From the historical point of view the Orthodox Church also
can argue that it is *the* Church.

In such phrasings as *the other day*, as in *I saw Helen downtown the
other day*, there is an offhand quality to *the* and no real idea of conspicuousness. *The other day* means about what *on a recent day* would
mean.

Like the demonstratives, the definite article *the* modifies both
pluralizers and quantifiables, but unlike the demonstratives it does
not inflect for number. It has adverbial uses in which it modifies
comparative adjectives, adverbs, and pronouns.

Joe looks *the* worse for wear.
The sooner we get there, *the* better it will be.

The indefinite article a.—The characteristic use of the indefinite article *a* is to identify simply by placing in a category. The
a new hobby of *Edgar needs a new hobby* has for the singular almost
the same force that the *new hobbies* of *Edgar needs new hobbies* has
for the plural. In most constructions singular forms of pluralizers
must have determiners. *A* is their minimum determiner. Often
what is identified by *a* has not had previous mention in the context
but continues to be important after the first mention. Once identification is established, however inexactly, *a* becomes unusable.
Sometimes what *a* identifies is of no more than momentary consequence, as is the case in *I got a cup of coffee at nine and then worked
till eleven*. Sometimes the identification marked by the use of *a* is no
more than an additional classification of what is known to speaker
or writer and to hearer or reader from another point of view.

I learned yesterday that Professor Hidalgo is *a* Mason.
Harris is *a* sensitive, imaginative person.

Though it identifies only in terms of membership in a category—
for example, as in the last sentence above, the category of sensitive,
imaginative people—*a* is a full determinative in its syntax, not a
partial one. *A new car* is as fully determined syntactically as *that
new car* or *Jack's new car*. But the determinative pronouns *such,
what*, and *many* are used with *a* and precede it; and extremitive
adjectival modifiers containing *how, so, as, too, however*, and *that*
precede it also.

I hadn't realized what *a* long trip we would have.
Many *a* man has tried.
He's so stern *a* father that his children sometimes have to
  ask twice for things they shouldn't have.
However low *a* price he paid, he wasted his money.

Like general *one* and substitute *one*, the indefinite article originally developed from the numeral *one*. In its most characteristic
uses *a* is now concerned with identification more than with number.
In *I wanted an A in the course* the unit *an A* and the unit *the course*
are alike singular, and singular number is unemphasized in the two
units alike. In *I wanted one A in the course* the use of the numeral
one gives number central importance. But in some uses the indefinite article *a* is still semantically very close to the numeral *one*.

> I'll be back in *a* day or two.
> She wastes *a* third of her time.
> We were for the change, to *a* man.

One third of her time suggests a more accurate estimate than *a third
of her time*, just as *one hundred dollars* suggests a more careful
count than *a hundred dollars*.

In negated clauses, main interrogatives, and subordinate interrogatives with question or condition force, the indefinite article *a*
is often semantically close to the numeral *one* but to some extent
parallels *any* also.

> Does he have *a* wife?
> I didn't bring *a* camera.
> I don't know *a* thing.
> I didn't say *a* word.
> He doesn't have *a* friend in the world.
> If he's ever read *a* major work in the field, he shows no signs
>   of it.

A often suggests that what is thought of as a reasonable allotment
is a single specimen: one wife, one camera at hand. Thus *does he
have a wife?* contrasts with *does he have any children?* But sometimes *a* is used (often with *single* and other reinforcing locutions)
where *any* might be expected, as in *he doesn't have a friend in the
world.*

The indefinite article *a* approaches *each* in meaning when it
modifies names of units of measurement (of time, distance, size,

weight, etc.) and unites with them to form postpositive modifiers in units naming cost and frequency. There is historical objection to calling this *a* the article, but there is no doubt that it is now felt as the article.

> forty dollars *a* month three times *a* day
> a dollar *a* pound twice *an* hour

Like the definite article *the*, the indefinite article sometimes marks representative singulars. *A* lacks the effect of detachment that *the* has in this use. *A* approaches *any* here, but *any* is more sweeping and leaves no room for exceptions.

> *A* good house is warm in winter and cool in summer.
> *A* cat is a relatively independent pet.
> Shopping is hard on *a* man.

The indefinite article is variable in form, in both the spoken language and the written. Before vowel sounds it terminates in an /n/ which it does not have before consonant sounds.

> a good job a Ph.D. an only child
> a one-man job an adequate job an M.A.

Before words beginning with unstressed syllables in which initial *h* may or may not be pronounced, *a* seems to have an uneasy preference over *an*.

> a habitual drunkard a historical novel
> a hallucination a hysterical woman

The indefinite article normally modifies only singular pluralizers. It often modifies nounal units which are plural in form but singular in force, as in *she gave me a bad thirty minutes*. In such units as *a little* and *a great many* it modifies other determinative pronouns.

Indefinite some.—*Some* is much like the indefinite article *a* in some of its uses but has a wider variety of uses than *a* does and modifies plurals and quantifiables as well as singulars. Syntactically *some* is most like *a* when it modifies singular pluralizers.

> *Some* student has been trying to reach you.
> You'll have to find *some* other good excuse.
> Surely there's *some* way to stop him.
> I'll come to your house *some* day next week.

Here, as with *a* in its most characteristic uses, there is identification only to the extent of classification. *Some* differs from *a* in making more of a point of the inexact character of such identification. Sometimes it carries a suggestion of emotion.

> Phyllis learned to talk like that in *some* Speech course.
> *Some* girl friend of George's has his car today.

Where there is contrast, *some*, like numeral *one* but less often, serves as a replacement for the article *a*.

> For *some* reason or other, there's no need to lock doors here.

When *some* modifies plurals, it expresses indefiniteness with respect to both identification and number.

> *Some* visitors came by while you were out.
> The orchestra played *some* lively Mexican pieces.
> Elena has *some* remarkable silver pins on sale.

Some is here a great deal like an indefinite article for the plural, and it is significant that in the sentences given above *a* will ordinarily replace *some* if the number of the head is changed to singular. But *some* is often not used with plurals after *be* and *as* where *a* is needed with singulars.

> The brothers are good mechanics.
> Everyone regards the brothers as good mechanics.

Some is used with plural heads where there is contrast or a suggestion of contrast.

> *Some* English teachers have sensible sets of linguistic prejudices, but most of them do not.
> *Some* people just don't understand George.

Some also occurs where the meaning of *an appreciable number* is implied.

> We stayed there for *some* years.

Some occasionally precedes a numeral pronoun on which it is superimposed. Here it is semantically close to *approximately*.

> Jenny has accumulated *some* thirty absences.

When *some* modifies quantifiables, it expresses indefiniteness with respect to both identification and quantity.

> *Some* furniture for the porch would help.
> I could eat *some* more chicken.
> Horton will give you *some* impressive bad advice.

Some is found, as with plurals, where there is contrast or a suggestion of contrast and where the meaning of *appreciable* is implied.

> *Some* porch furniture is comfortable, and *some* isn't.
> *Some* milk is still unpasteurized.
> I waited *some* little time.
> The college is at *some* distance from the town.
> He's a man of *some* importance.

In informal styles *some* occasionally takes on a good deal of the force of the adjective *phenomenal*, as a modifier of singulars, plurals, and quantifiables.

> It's *some* town!
> Those were *some* parties!
> It was *some* fun!

A touch of this force is evident in the compound *somebody* used as in *he wants to be somebody*.

Like most determinative pronouns (but unlike *a*), *some* has nounal uses. Here it is always either plural or quantifiable in force.

> *Some* of the visitors had been here before.
> *Some* of his advice was good.
> *Some* of us went swimming.
> The war brought misery to *some* but wealth to others.
> If there's any coffee, I'll take *some*.

Some of them and *some of it* are often preferred to *some* alone.

> We ate Mexican dishes constantly, and *some of them* were wonderful.
> We drank cider all along the road, and *some of it* was wonderful.

Some does not often occur in negated clauses—except main interrogatives and subordinate interrogatives with question or condition force. The sweeping, all-inclusive force of *any* makes *any* very popular as a negative reinforcer. In main interrogatives and in subordinate interrogatives with question or condition force—whether negated or not—*some* is used as well as *any*, but with different force.

Will you have *some* soup?
Why should we put *some* more money into that old car?
Doesn't she have *some* rooms to rent?
I wonder whether I've said *something* unwise.
If you've had *some* experience, you won't find the work hard.

In general, in sentences such as these *some* suggests appreciable
amounts or numbers and/or expectation of positive replies. For
this reason *will you have some soup?* has a more generous quality
to it than *will you have any soup?* where *any* has some of the force
of *the least bit* and does not suggest a positive answer.

Some tends to be replaced by *somewhat* in adverbial uses, but it
does occur in them.

> The medicine helped me *some.*

Indifferent **any** *and* **either.**—When *any* and *either* are used as
determiner modifiers of singular forms of pluralizers, they have
pretty much the semantic content of the indefinite article *a* with
it doesn't matter which added as a loose adjunct. *Any* expresses
indifference to identity within groups with three or more members;
either expresses the same meaning within groups with only two
members.

> Hilda will marry *any* man with a bank account.
> Bill can write with *either* hand.

Either normally modifies only singulars. *Any* modifies singulars
where singular number seems appropriate and plurals where plural
number seems appropriate.

> *Any* good mechanic could repair that.
> The state university trains more lawyers than *any* other insti-
> tution in the area.
> I shall appreciate *any* suggestions you care to make.

When *any* modifies plurals it normally expresses indifference to
number as well as to identity.

In such a sentence as *Frank can get excited about any pretty girl
that comes along* the meaning of *any* is not far from that of *every* or
that of *all.* But often the meaning of *any* is close to that of the *one*
to which it is related in origin, and even to the determinative *no* of
zero (only a short step from *one*), rather than to that of *every* and
all at the opposite extreme of universality and totality.

Students who have failed *any* grade twice cannot remain in school.

Andrew has hardly *any* close friends.

Any errors that appear will be called to your attention.

Here *any grade* is semantically close to *a single grade*, and *hardly any close friends* is not far from *almost no close friends*. *Any errors* involves an implication that it is doubtful that errors, or at least an appreciable number of errors, will appear. It is a curiosity of semantics that the meaning of *it doesn't matter which* is equally compatible with meanings close to that of *every* and with meanings close to that of *no*.

Any is a favored word for giving a sweeping quality to negated clauses, main interrogatives, and subordinate interrogatives with question or condition force. *Have you heard any complaints?* is a sweeping open question; *have you heard a complaint?* and *have you heard complaints?* (or *some complaints?*) are questions framed in expectation of particular replies—*yes, I've heard one* and *yes, I've heard some*. If *any* is given dominant stress in uses of this kind, its old relationship to *one*—next door to zero—can make itself very strongly felt. *Does he have any good qualities?* with dominant stress on *any* means about the same thing as *does he have even one good quality?* A negative answer is pretty clearly expected here. But *any* is a slippery word, and understatement and hyperbole are of course frequent. Where the context or situation indicates what is intended, *any* is usable even in negated clauses, main interrogatives, and subordinate interrogatives with question or condition force, with the meaning which approaches that of *every*.

Surely you don't believe *any* fanciful story Jack tells you.

The *any* which approaches *every* in meaning accepts *almost* as a prepositive modifier. The *any* which approaches determinative *no* accepts near-negative *hardly* and *scarcely*.

I used to be able to eat *almost any* fried foods.

Hardly any fried foods agree with me now.

In negated clauses, main interrogatives, and subordinate interrogatives with question or condition force *any* ordinarily modifies plurals in preference to singular forms of pluralizers.

> The Jacksons don't have *any* children.
> Have you seen *any* ants in the kitchen?
> If we have *any* visitors, we'll make lemonade.

But sometimes plurals would suggest plurality where it seems unsuitable. *Any* can modify singular forms of pluralizers in such a situation, though it will sometimes seem a little emotional and *a* may be preferred to it.

> There isn't *any* kitchen in the apartment.
> Does Allen have *a* wife?
> If we had *an* automobile, we'd take you home.

As determiner modifiers of pluralizers, both *any* and *either* take on special meanings at times. In *he'll be here any day* the meaning of *any day* is roughly equivalent to *today or soon*. He'll be here *some day* puts the incompletely identified day into the future more indefinitely. In *I warned him any number of times* the meaning of *any* is roughly equivalent to that of *a very great*. *Either* is occasionally used where *each* is usually preferred, as in *on either side of the door stood a huge urn.*

Any is used as a determiner modifier of quantifiables also, and in this use it expresses indifference to quantity as well as to identity. Here *any* is semantically close now to *all* and now to *the least bit*.

> *Any* money she earns goes to charity.
> *Any* advice will be appreciated.
> I doubt that she speaks *any* Italian.
> There isn't *any* flour in the house.
> Is there *any* malaria in the area?
> If we had *any* time left, we'd go on to Martinique.

Both *any* and *either* have nounal uses.

> *Any* of the neighbors would be glad to help.
> They served hash once a week, but I never ate *any*.
> *Either* of your parents can fill out the form.
> I hadn't met *either* of the girls before.

In many situations *of them* or *of it* is appended to *any*, and *of them* to *either*, or substitute *one* is employed as a head, in preference to using *any* and *either* nounally without modifiers of the whole.

> There are about a dozen seats left, but hardly *any of them* are
> satisfactory.
> There are two newspapers, but we don't take *either one*.

Any has considerable use in adverbial constructions, (1) as a modifier of comparatives and of the *too* of excess and (2) as an adjunct, though here *at all* tends to be preferred.

> I couldn't finish *any* sooner.
> Henriette doesn't come *any* more.
> I'm afraid I didn't explain *any* too well.
> I didn't sleep *any* last night.

Either has considerable use as an adjunct, and as a modifier of head constructions of varied types, when it is used in the second of two negated clauses or smaller units as *too* is used where there is no negation.

> The food wasn't very expensive, but it wasn't very good *either*.
> Unfortunately Phyllis isn't rich or pretty *either*.

As a precoordinator, *either* is sometimes an adjunct and sometimes a contained modifier attaching to a head of practically any kind.

> *Either* you'll let Hawkins have his way or you'll have trouble.
> He's *either* insensitive or cruel.

As a precoordinator *either* can be used when there are more than two coordinates.

> *Either* the subject matter of such courses is no longer of wide interest, or the teaching is poor, or the students are forced into other courses.

Universal *every* and *each*.—*Every* and *each* are full determinatives of universality, which they come at through representative singulars. *Every* is preferable to *each* where large numbers are involved and individual members of the category are not as clearly in mind.

> After 1932 all over the world *every* Jew carried a heavy burden of fear and horror.
> *Every* college in the country teaches something it calls English.
> *Every* moment of our stay in New York was pleasant.
> Garbage is collected *every* third day.
> We have *every* reason to hope for improvement.

In the last of these sentences the use of *every* suggests a considerable number of reasons, perhaps in optimistic overstatement. Even where relatively small numbers are involved, *every* is preferable to *each* if a sweeping universality without too much attention to individual members of the category is wanted.

> *Every* window in the room was broken.

Every accepts modifiers such as the adverbs *almost* and *absolutely* to form phrasal determiners, whereas *each* does not.

> We had a test *almost every* week.
> *Absolutely every* egg in the dozen was bad.

Each often seems preferable to *every* where small definite numbers are involved and more attention to the individual members of the category seems desirable. Where the number involved is two, *every* is not usable.

> Susan was carrying a jellyfish in *each* hand.

Every and *each* modify only heads with singular force, never plurals or true quantifiables. *Every* often modifies phrasal heads whose form is plural though their force is singular.

> We stopped *every few miles* to rest.

Every accepts various adverbial units as heads in exceptional nounal headed units used as adjuncts of predicators.

> *every* now and then   *every* once in a while
> *every* so often

Every is occasionally preceded by possessive determiners.

> his *every* gesture   whose *every* mood

Every is like *the* and *a* in having no nounal use. It has considerable use with substitute *one* as head where nounal use might be expected.

> We went to half a dozen British movies, and *every one* was good.

Each is quite usable in nounal constructions, or *one* can be added.

> My father always brought *each* of us children a present when he came home from his trips.
> There are a dozen of us in the group, and *each* has his special interest.

Every and *each* express universality, but in most of their uses there are limits, whether clearly or vaguely defined, within which universality is visualized. Thus in *everyone goes without a coat in summer* there is—not to mention inaccuracy—a tacit limitation to an area or a city or perhaps a smaller social segment, such as a school or an office. Universality and totality are closely related concepts, or perhaps the same concept looked at in different ways. Hence *every* and *each* compete with *all*. Representative singular *every student* and *each student*—the first quite sweeping, the second more painstaking in its interest in individual students—compete with plural *all students* and *all the students*.

Negative no and neither.—When *no* and *neither* are used as determiner modifiers of singulars, they express meanings of *a* (or the numeral *one*, or even *any*) and *not* together.

> *No* human being is completely unaffected by flattery.
> *Neither* parent should administer all the punishment.

No expresses this meaning when groups with three or more members are involved; *neither* expresses it when groups with only two members are involved. *Neither* normally modifies singulars—not plurals, and not true quantifiables. *No* has a stronger affinity for plurals than for singulars.

> There are *no* churches in our section of town.
> Judy has had *no* cavities so far.
> *No* women were present.
> *No* classes are meeting today.

The meaning, in the end, is that of zero. The pull is toward the plural because determiners of number in general have plural heads. But where singulars seem clearly more suitable *no* is used with singulars.

> He really has *no* home.
> The trouble is that George is *no* diplomat.

No is used as a determiner modifier of quantifiables as well as of pluralizers. Here it is semantically equivalent to *not a bit of*.

> There's *no* mustard left in the bottle.
> It's *no* fun to hear Shakespeare chopped up like that.

In nounal use *no* is replaced by its long variant *none*. Usually a modifier of the whole begun by *of* follows. Where the reference is to pluralizers, the unit is generally felt to have plural force.

> *None* of the stores are open on Sundays.
> *None* of the snapshots were very good.
> *None* of us are going.

Occasionally *none* has clear singular force where it refers to pluralizers.

> It was *none* other than the Congregational minister.

None is also used, like *no*, with reference to quantifiables.

> *None* of the food was aesthetically satisfying.
> At bottom Edgar had *none* of the assurance that appeared on the surface.
> It's *none* of his business.

None has some nounal use without modifiers of the whole, especially in highly reduced answers to questions but also in some other situations.

> "How much coffee do we have?" "*None*, I'm afraid."
> One is better than *none*.

Neither has nounal uses too, especially when modifiers of the whole follow. The reference is always to pluralizers, and the group in point always has two members. In careful and formal styles the unit is treated as singular in force.

> *Neither* of the boys likes it.
> *Neither* of them is really to blame.

In informal styles such units are sometimes treated as plural, like similar units with *none*. There is a strong tendency to employ *one* as a head with *neither* in preference to using *neither* nounally.

> *Neither one* of the boys likes it.
> We bought two watermelons, but *neither one* was good.

No, *none*, and *neither* all perform adverbial functions. *No* sometimes functions as an adjunct beginning gerundial clauses.

> There's *no* understanding Joan.

No sometimes modifies comparatives and *none* sometimes modifies *too*.

> I'm a little older but *no* wiser.
> The instructions are *none* too clear.

Neither has considerable use as an adjunct in the second of two negated clauses.

> I didn't go, and *neither* did Bill.

In its use as precoordinator, *neither* functions as adjunct and as contained modifier of heads of varied types.

> *Neither* taking courses nor writing a thesis interests Hudson now.
> She's *neither* rich nor pretty.

Clause-marker what.—Among the clause-marker pronouns *what* and *which* and *whatever* and *whichever* are basically determinative in type. *What* is used as a determiner in main interrogatives asking for identification where there is a feeling that the number of possibilities is great.

> *What* name have they given the baby?
> *What* teachers did you have last semester?
> *What* furniture will we need?

What has considerable nounal use in interrogatives.

> *What* have they named the baby?
> *What* will we need?
> *What's* the best way to get rid of ants?
> *What* in the world can we do in Buffalo?
> *What* does Garner want now?

As a subject, nounal *what* always has singular force with relation to its predicator.

> *What* has *made* the city grow so fast?
> *What* circumstances have *made* the city grow so fast?

In general, nounal *what* is not usable when words referring to people are implied as heads for it. Thus *what did you have in French?* cannot mean *what teachers did you have in French?* But as a complement, *what* sometimes asks for classification of people by such things as profession, religion, and college class, with the context indicating the precise type of classification wanted.

> Jim is a Methodist, but *what* is his wife?

In reduced constructions asking for repetition of a word or phrase, *what* occasionally functions as a kind of head word preceded by other determinatives, and occasionally as a predicator or as head word in a predicator.

> A *what?*   Some *what?*
> He *what?*   They've *what?*

What is used as a marker in assertives. Here it has pretty much the semantic content of the adjective *phenomenal.*

> *What* a name they've given that poor baby!
> *What* a view! *What* lobsters! *What* weather!
> You can't imagine *what* a mess I've made.

When extremitive *what* modifies singular forms of pluralizers, the article *a* is also employed and follows it. Often *what* occurs where the marker adverb *how* would seem syntactically more appropriate. *What a beautiful view!* is semantically more or less equivalent to *it's a phenomenally beautiful view,* but the syntax of *what* is quite different from that of *phenomenally.*

What is used in subordinate-interrogative clauses that have true question force much as it is used in main interrogatives, and in subordinate assertives much as it is used in main assertives.

> I don't know *what* name they've given the baby.
> Renfrew is an engineer, but I'm not sure *what* Robertson is.
> It's astonishing *what* a good husband Jerry is.

In subordinate interrogatives *what* can have the meaning *what kind of person.*

> You know well enough *what* Garner is.

What has considerable use in subordinate-interrogative clauses with the force of nounal heads and modifying clauses together.

> *What* Eugene needs is new interests and new friends.
> This weather isn't *what* is considered typical here.
> *What* we got was another stuffed shirt.
> *What* trips we take are relatively uninteresting.

What trips we take is felt as equivalent to *the trips that we take* in number force. Used nounally as subject in interrogative clauses, *what* can have plural force with relation to its own predicator if a clear plural reference has been established.

> The stores aren't numerous, but *what* are to be found are excellent.

What is not usable in interrogative clauses following head words to which the markers in the interrogative clauses refer, as *that* is used in *we already knew everything that he said.*

What occasionally functions as an adjunct.

> *What* does Joan care about cost?
> *What* does it matter to you?

In informal styles it sometimes replaces clause-marker *that* in subordinate-declarative clauses made objects of the preposition *but.*

> He's not so obstinate but *what* he'll listen.
> Who knows but *what* we'll get to Hawaii next?

***Clause-marker* which.**—*Which* is used as a determiner in main interrogatives asking for identification where there is a feeling that the number of possibilities is small.

> *Which* seats shall we take?
> *Which* daughter married the congressman?

Which has a considerable nounal use in main interrogatives.

> *Which* of your courses takes the most time?
> *Which* is it—too big or too small?

Substitute *one* has considerable use as a head word for *which*. In this use *one* serves as a clear indicator of number.

> We're giving the kittens away now. *Which one* would you like?
> I don't have time for all the stories in the collection. *Which ones* would you recommend especially?

Which is used in subordinate-interrogative clauses that have true question force, much as it is used in main interrogatives.

> I wonder *which* daughter married first.
> Let me know *which ones* you'd like.

In careful and formal styles *which* is sometimes used as a determiner modifier in interrogative clauses which follow words or multiword units—often whole nucleuses—to which *which* refers.

The license expires at the end of the second year, at *which* time it will be necessary to procure another.

In the thirties many Puerto Ricans blamed United States economic policies for the depression, for *which* reason desire for independence became very strong.

The upper classes may continue to block reforms, in *which* case we must expect the use of violence.

Much more commonly *which* is used in nounal constructions in interrogative clauses which follow nounal units to which *which* refers.

He always ends with the argument *which* seems most impressive to him.

He always ends with the arguments *which* seem most impressive to him.

In informal styles this nounal *which* sometimes refers to whole nucleuses.

When I go to work there are no places to park, *which* means that I have a real problem.

Nounal *which* is rarely used with reference to people as individuals, but it is quite usable with reference to groupings of people and with reference to abstractions of human types.

He was related to a family named *Fitton*, which in turn was related to the Houghtons of Lancashire.

Joe acted like a fanatic—*which* he is.

Which is not a clause marker at all in the locution *every which way.* *Which* does not inflect for number. It does borrow a possessive from *who*, however, for use in interrogative clauses which follow nounal units to which *whose* refers.

This is an age of problems *whose* solution is made more difficult by modern ideas.

Alternatives to *whose solution* are *the solution of which* and *of which the solution*, both of them relatively awkward. Often, however, it seems advisable to look for phrasings of other kinds. Such verbs as *have* and *belong*, and such prepositional adverbs as *of* and *with*, obviously can come at the meanings expressed by possessive inflection.

Clause-marker whatever *and* whichever.—The compounds *whatever* and *whichever* do not often occur in main interrogatives, where such units as *what in the world* are preferred.

> *Whatever* happened?
> *What in the world* happened?

They have considerable use in subordinate-interrogative clauses that have the force of nounal heads and modifying clauses together.

> We used *whatever* boxes we could find.
> I'll take *whichever one* you give me.
> *Whatever* he does is done well.

Here *ever* is semantically equivalent to *any*, despite the differences in syntactic structures.

> We used any boxes that we could find.
> I'll take any one you give me.
> Anything that he does is done well.

Whatever and *whichever* also have considerable use in subordinate-interrogative clauses used as adjuncts of indifference, where larger constructions begun by *no matter* compete.

> *Whatever* reasons he gave, the truth is that he's afraid to get involved.
> *Whatever* you do, don't trust him.
> I'll be satisfied *whichever* way it goes.

Whatever and otherwise-archaic *whatsoever* have uses as postpositive modifiers of nounal heads. Here they reinforce meanings of negation, question, and condition, and are not clause markers.

> George used no judgement *whatever*.
> If he had any judgement *whatsoever*, he wouldn't be in the trouble he's in.

CHAPTER XIV

OTHER DETERMINATIVES

Like the full determinatives of identification, the partial determinatives of identification and the determinatives of number and
quantity are characteristically used both as determiner modifiers
of nounal heads and as forms which have assimilated the meanings
and the syntactic functions of what would be their nounal heads
in unreduced constructions. Full determinatives can be superimposed freely on most of them, as in *that same day*, in *his third
job*, in *my next visit*, in *the three boys*, and in *his many friends*; but
full determinatives are not likely to be superimposed on such determinatives of number and quantity as *enough* and *all*. The partial
determinatives of identification are *same, such, other*, the ordinal
numerals, *last, next, former, latter*, and *own*; the determinatives of
number and quantity are the cardinal numerals, *few, little, several,
enough, many, much, all*, and *both*.

The determinative of identity: same,—The pronoun *same*
has essentially the meaning also expressed by the adjective *identical*. *Same* is most characteristically used as a partial determiner
within nounal units, and modifies singulars, plurals, and quantifiables.

> Jerry and I went to the *same* college.
> The *same* two salesmen came by yesterday.
> George always uses the very *same* excuses.
> He'll give you the *same* advice again.

Same has nounal uses of various types.

> It's all the *same* to me.
> Things never look the *same* after a long absence.
> The *same* to you!

In standard usage, *same* is normally preceded by a full determiner. *Same* normally requires completing modifiers, expressed or

implied. When expressed, these are generally interrogative clauses subordinated by *as* or *that*.

> Things never look the same after a long absence as they looked before.
> The same two salesmen that came here before came by again yesterday.

Same often serves as head in adjunct constructions, especially in informal styles.

> Hodges lacked support, but he went ahead *just the same*.
> Teachers want security *the same as everyone else*.

The determinative of type: such.—*Such* varies in meaning from equivalence with locutions such as *of this kind* almost to equivalence with *the* or *that*.

> Some *such* arrangement was necessary.
> We're usually at home at *such* times.
> The invitations went to *such* guests as seemed likely to interest the guest of honor.
> There isn't any *such* street.

In the last of these sentences *any such* has practically the semantic value of *any that*, which is not an accepted combination.

Such tends to have emotional force. This may be mild: in effect, only a clear hint of favorable or unfavorable attitudes. The meaning still varies from that of *of this kind* to that of *the* and *that*.

> I never heard of *such* a method.
> You never saw *such* weather.
> *Such* clothes as we had were not appropriate.

The multiple-unit determinative *such-and-such* is semantically an emotional equivalent of *some*.

> They'll hire *such-and-such* a man from outside, and he'll do what they won't let the local men do.

The emotional force of *such* is sometimes very strong, and *such*, like *what*, comes to be involved in meanings the adjective *phenomenal* expresses.

> *Such* an idea!
> Did you ever see *such* waves!
> There was music—and *such* music!

When *such* is superimposed on units made up of adjectives and
nounal heads, it takes on the semantic force of an extremitive
modifier of the adjectives, though syntactically it is best regarded
as a modifier of the nounal heads.

Such a big house would be hard to heat.
It isn't wise to use *such* picturesque language.
We had *such* a nice time!
They really aren't *such* high prices if you want quality.

Here *such* has replaced the semantically related adverb *so*. *Such*
cannot do this when no nounal head follows the adjectives, and it
cannot do it with the pronouns *few, little, many,* and *much.*

The prices really aren't *so* high if you want quality.
I didn't realize that there was *so* little time.

Like *same, such* normally requires completing modifiers, expressed or implied. These are generally interrogative clauses
marked by *as* or declarative clauses.

Some *such* arrangement *as this* was necessary.
We always take *such* things *as flashlight, blankets, and mos-
quito netting.*
I never heard of *such* a method *as that.*
Such a big house *as that one is* would be hard to heat.
The children were having *such* a good time *that their mother
hated to call them in.*

Expressed completing clauses are often reduced. Sometimes, as in
the second sentence above, they amount to lists which *such* marks
as not complete. Sometimes *as to* infinitival clauses complete *such.*
Sometimes its completers pull *such* to postpositive position, as in
some arrangement such as this was necessary. Sometimes as *such* is
used in informal styles it is hard to formulate satisfactory completers of even reduced types.

In standard usage *such* occurs in nounal constructions relatively little.

He's a wonderful husband. There aren't many *such.*
The fury of the storm was *such* as to leave few houses un-
damaged.
Such were the conditions which brought on the revolt.

Such is often the head word in loose adjuncts which are also half
appositives of preceding nouns or nounal units.

Phyllis was bored by her husband's attentions, *such as they were.*

They lived on small game, *such as rabbits and quail.*

The determinative of difference: other.—The pronoun *other* is applied to members of a category already prominently represented by one or more members. As a determiner modifier *other* modifies singulars, plurals, and quantifiables.

Wednesday will be all right, or any *other* day this week.
Who are those *other* people?
I left my *other* glasses at home.
Where are the *other* two schools?
Other opportunities will turn up.
I liked the *other* furniture better.
Was there any *other* mail?

The indefinite article *a* merges with *other* to form *another*, which has the full-determinative force of *a.*

We saw *another* British movie.

After *the* the commonest uses of *other* occur where there is a twofold division.

One of the brothers is very serious, but the *other* is a playboy.
We wasted five days of the six, but the *sixth* was wonderful.

But in a few offhand phrases such as *the other day, other* means no more than *recent* and *the* no more than indefinite *a.* After *every* quite often *other* still has its ancient meaning of *second.*

Milk is delivered every *other* day.

Often *other* is simply equivalent to *additional.*

Bert wanted *another* hamburger, of course.

It is noteworthy that if a numeral were substituted for *an* here *other* would be replaced by *more*, which is primarily concerned with number and quantity and so takes on the meaning of *additional* more naturally.

Other has considerable nounal use.

Dudley was wearing one shoe and carrying the *other.*
It won't work, for one reason or *another.*

In contrast with *some* the basic form *other* is used where the compound *another* might be expected.

> It won't work, for some reason or *other*.

The inflected plural form *others* appears in nounal use.

> Some students have a taste for grammar, and *others* don't.
> I liked the first poem but not the *others*.

Like *same* and *such*, *other* normally requires a completing modifier, expressed or implied. Expressed completers take the form of interrogative clauses of comparison subordinated by *than*, and sometimes pull *other* to postpositive positions.

> We have no problems *other than expense*.

Occasionally a unit with *other* as head functions as an adjunct, and occasionally *other* is coordinated with the adverbs *somewhere* and *somehow*.

> I've never known the Buckners to entertain *other than lavishly*.
> We'll get the job done *somehow or other*.

The ordinal numerals.—The ordinal numerals are based on the cardinals and make up a series which can be extended indefinitely. Most ordinals are formed by adding a suffix written *th* to the corresponding cardinals, whether these are single words or phrasal units.

> sixth   twenty-sixth   three hundred and sixth

Where the cardinal ends in the suffix *ty*, a syllabic variant of *th* written *eth* is added, as in *twentieth*. *First, second, third, fifth, eighth,* and *ninth* are irregular, *eighth* and *ninth* in spelling only; phrasal ordinals such as *twenty-third* extend these irregularities. *First* and *second* originally had no relationship to *one* and *two*. *One hundredth, one thousandth,* and *one millionth* are generally simplified by the omission of *one*. *Nth* occurs in *to the nth degree*. Number ideographs are sometimes combined with ordinal suffixes in the written language, notably in such street names as *116th Street*.

The ordinal numerals identify on the basis of position within sequences. The sequences are of varied types, involving positions in time, space, importance, and relationships of still other kinds.

The *twenty-first* century should be a peaceful one.
Clara is Henry's *third* wife.
The Hortons live in the *fourth* house from the corner.
Fentress is the *second* vice president now.
Mary is a *second* cousin.

Nounal uses of ordinal pronouns are frequent.

We got to Marietta on the *fifth* of November.
Let me be the *first* to congratulate you.
Let me be among the *first* to congratulate you.
Our second thoughts are generally better than our *first*.
We were unduly suspicious at *first*.

The ordinals have very considerable use as adjuncts and some use as modifiers of superlative adjectives.

Let's investigate other possibilities *first*.
I came out *second* best.

Other determinatives of sequence: last, next, former, latter.—*Last* and *next* identify on the basis of position in sequences, like the ordinals; but they are not involved in counting. *Last* is sometimes applied to the member or members of a series with which the series is terminated.

The Tempest was Shakespeare's *last* play.
We spent the *last* days of our stay shopping.

In this sense *last* contrasts with *first*. But often *last* contrasts with *next* rather than with *first: last* and *next* identify in terms of proximity, *last* immediately before the central point, and *next* immediately after it.

The *next* town will be larger than the *last* two, won't it?

Last and *next* were originally related to the adjective *latest* and the adverb *nearest*, and the line separating the determinative pronouns from the superlative adjective and adverb is not a very rigid one. But the nearest town need not be the next town on a route. In *Moore's latest attack on the Administration* the adjective *latest* is concerned with recentness, just as it is in *the latest fashions*. In *the last session of the legislature* the pronoun *last* is concerned with position in a series of sessions. *Last* and *next* become full determiners in such units as *last week* and *next year*, where they are used with relation to the time of speaking or writing. Used in very similar units with relation to other times, they are partial determiners.

> I'll see you *next* Saturday.
> We were in Evanston on Christmas Day, and we spent *the next* Saturday in Chicago.

Last and *next* have nounal uses also.

> Jack would be the *last* to deny it.
> We were in Marietta the week before *last*.

They have considerable use as adjuncts and as heads in adjunct units, and *next* sometimes modifies superlative adjectives.

> What shall we do *next?*
> *Next to losing our baggage*, that was the worst thing that happened.
> Monday is the best day, and Tuesday is *next* best.

Former and *latter* are determinative pronouns which distinguish between two more or less parallel references in terms of the order in which they have just been mentioned.

> Uruguay and Paraguay have had completely different histories, and the *former* is now one of the most advanced countries in the world in its political and social organization while the *latter* is not.

Such words as *first, second,* and *last* replace *former* and *latter* where there are more than two possible references.

The determinative pronoun of possession: own.—The partial determinative *own* is always used with a superimposed possessive which it reinforces semantically much as an intensive *self* form of a personal pronoun reinforces a noun or pronoun. *Own* most often reinforces possessive pronouns which refer to subjects or complements in the clauses.

> George brought his own boat.
> We took George for a ride in his own boat.

Own is usable with possessive pronouns in such sentences as *it was my own fault*, but it is not usable in such sentences as *I have your copy.* It is quite usable with possessives of nouns, as in *that's Judy's own doll.* Occasionally *own* marks a more permanent relationship than might be indicated by a possessive without *own.*

> When I passed out the pencils, one boy said his wouldn't work.
> When I passed out the pencils, one boy asked whether he might use his *own.*

Usually, however, *own* simply accentuates what the possessive which precedes it would indicate in any case. Where accentuation is out of place, *own* is out of place. Thus *George picks his ties recklessly* should have *own* after *his* only in certain contexts: for example, after something has been said about how other people choose ties for him, or about how he chooses ties for other people.

As a determiner modifier *own* attaches to singulars, plurals, and quantifiables.

> Gray is his *own* worst enemy.
> Clara makes her *own* clothes.
> Use your *own* judgement.

In *Clara makes her own clothes* the use of *own* implies a feeling that *her* needs accentuation: it is not a usual thing for women to make their clothes themselves. *Clara arranges her own hair badly* would be usable with *own* only in special contexts: for example, after something had been said about how her beauty parlor arranges her hair or about how she arranges other people's hair.

Own is also used as a nounal head modified by preceding possessives. It does not inflect for number.

> George's ties are loud, but my *own* aren't much quieter.
> She's been holding her *own* but not gaining.
> I did it on my *own.*
> The university has no hospital of its *own.*
> She would like children of her *own.*

The cardinal numerals.—Including the phrasal forms, the cardinal numerals make up a series which can be extended indefinitely. The nonphrasal cardinals are few. The first ten numerals set a pattern which is incorporated in every succeeding ten, though with noticeable modifications in the second ten.

one	eleven	twenty-one	one hundred and one
two	twelve	twenty-two	one hundred and two
three	thirteen	twenty-three	one hundred and three
four	fourteen	twenty-four	one hundred and four
five	fifteen	twenty-five	one hundred and five
six	sixteen	twenty-six	one hundred and six
seven	seventeen	twenty-seven	one hundred and seven
eight	eighteen	twenty-eight	one hundred and eight
nine	nineteen	twenty-nine	one hundred and nine
ten	twenty	thirty	one hundred and ten

Eleven and *twelve* are special cases. The teens show variants of *three* in *thirteen* and of *five* in *fifteen,* and a written *t* is lost in *eighteen.* In the names of the tens which terminate in *ty* the series *two* to *nine* appears again.

two	twenty	six	sixty
three	thirty	seven	seventy
four	forty	eight	eighty
five	fifty	nine	ninety

Variants of *two, three, four, five,* and *eight* appear in the names of the tens. Such words as *hundred, thousand, million,* and *billion* continue the system of cardinal numerals. *Dozen* is a numeral outside the decimal system but useful for many purposes because it is divisible by two, three, four, and six whereas ten is divisible only by two and five. In such a phrasal numeral as *five thousand four hundred and twenty-three* the relation of the parts is fairly complex. There are three coordinates here: *five thousand* is one, *four hundred* is a second, *twenty-three* is the third. *Five* is a modifier of *thousand,* and *four* a modifier of *hundred. Twenty-three* is a multiple unit within the larger multiple unit. The whole phrasal numeral can modify a noun head: this is of course its normal use. Or it can be given nounal uses.

There is no true numeral pronoun for zero. *No* is the closest thing to one, as has been said. There are also such nounal pronouns as *nothing* and little-used *nil* and *naught.* The word *zero* is a noun, not a pronoun: it has many uses in connection with temperatures, grades, and other phenomena rated on numerical scales. The ideograph is variously read as *zero,* as *naught,* and even (where there is not counting but naming, as in *I'll be in Room 204* and in *my phone number is 29063*) as though it were the letter *o.* Hybrid forms occur in which numerals and other determinatives of number combine in phrasal units.

> *Several hundred* tickets were sold.
> Let's take *a few dozen* of those doughnuts along.
> There were about *a hundred* students in the class.

Like determinative pronouns of other types, the cardinal numerals have use as determiner modifiers in nounal units as their most characteristic function but are also used nounally.

> We bought *two* watches from Mr. Frank.
> *Three hundred thousand* people live in the city now.
> We needed one watch, but we bought *two.*
> The next *two* we buy will be steel ones.
> We'd better take along *two dozen* of the big doughnuts George likes.

In nounal uses *dozen, hundred, thousand, million,* and *billion* add *s* when they have plural force and are not preceded by another pronoun of number, but ordinarily do not add *s* when another pronoun of number precedes them.

> There were thousands of birds.
> There were several hundred of us.

Remarkable reduction is present in uses such as occur in *I'll be back at ten* and *David's ten now,* and in *seventy-five isn't a very good grade* and *seventy-five is an ideal temperature.*

The cardinal numerals have considerable use in identifying on the basis of position in sequences of various types. Here they compete with the ordinals. Unlike the ordinals, however, the cardinals tend to be used in units with the force of phrasal proper names: names of years, of hours, of buildings (as identified by street numbers), of rooms, of volumes and other major divisions in lengthy works, of chapters, of acts and scenes in plays, of pages, of telephone numbers, etc.

> Hoover became President in *1928.*
> We arrived at *five in the morning.*
> The address is *625 Oxford Avenue.*
> The class meets in *Room 315.*
> I finished *Volume III* yesterday.
> I stopped at *page 75.*

When cardinal numerals are used to identify, they are not always spoken as they are when they are used as counting words. Thus *1928* as the name of the year is usually spoken as *nineteen twenty-eight* but in counting is likely to be *one thousand nine hundred and twenty-eight*. The form *nineteen hundred and twenty-eight* is possible in both situations. When cardinals are used to identify, the last two digits are often spoken as one unit and what precedes as another. What precedes often indicates the number of the century (though not directly, since 1928 was not in the nineteenth century), the number of a block, or the number of a floor. In some proper-name uses the letters of the alphabet compete with the cardinal numerals, or supplement them: for example, in *Appendix B* and in *Apartment D*.

The cardinal numerals are also used in an abstract way in mathematical calculations.

> *Six* divided by *two* is *three*.

One requires particular notice. As has been said, both general *one* (meaning *a person*) and substitute *one* (as in *a green tie and a gray one*) developed from the numeral, as did the indefinite article *a*. General *one* has a *self* form like those of the personals; substitute *one* has an *s* plural; the indefinite article *a* is quite distinct from the numeral *one* in form, though it is not very distinct in syntax and not at all distinct in meaning at some points. What remains as the pattern of uses of the numeral *one* is still rather complex.

As is true of the other numerals, numeral *one* is normally concerned entirely or at least primarily with number.

> The newsstand usually buys *one* copy of *Harper's* and three of the *New Yorker*.
> It's the *one* course you shouldn't miss.

In nounal uses also, numeral *one* is often concerned entirely or at least primarily with number.

> "How many tennis balls are left?" "Just *one*."
> No *one* of the available buildings is adequate.

Numeral *one* is sometimes concerned with identity as much as with number or even more, so that it is semantically a stressed indefinite article in effect. This is notably true where there is contrast, where there is selection from within a group, and where *one* refers to a period of time in the past as *some* would to a period of time in the future.

> Students have difficulty in transferring from *one* institution to another.
> The whole class liked phonemics. *One* student said the exercises were like a game.
> Willie bought a gun, and *one* day he shot at something in his corn.

This article-like numeral *one* is also used in nounal constructions where the article *a* cannot be used.

> *One* of these buildings is used as a museum, and another houses laboratories.
> They have a comfortable house, but they would like *one* in a newer part of town.
> It's a dog, but it doesn't look like *one*.
> I'm not *one* to object to a little noise.

The determinatives of small number and quantity: **few, little, several.**—There are two determinatives of indefinitely small number, *few* and *several*, and one determinative of indefinitely small quantity, *little*. *Few* and *little* are very flexible words. *Few students* will suggest one range of numbers in one school or in one situation, and another range in another. *Little money* is similarly flexible. *Several* is more nearly fixed: the range is from three to seven or eight or thereabouts.

Except when it is modified by *a*, *few* has near-negative force: there is a feeling of approach to the *no* of zero. It is used as a determiner with nounal heads and as a nounal form.

> On the *few* occasions when Williamson has been right, he has been right for highly irrational reasons.
> We have very *few* problems with the boys.
> Very *few* of us are really satisfied.
> *Few* will disagree with this judgement.
> His needs are *few*.

Phrasal *a few* normally lacks the near-negative force of *few* without *a*. There is a feeling of approach to *some* rather than to *no*.

Like *few*, phrasal *a few* is used both as a determiner with nounal heads and nounally.

> We'd like to buy *a few* things in New York.
> We have quite *a few* problems with the boys.
> We had been in Puerto Rico only *a few* months.
> *A few* of the neighbors have dogs.
> We caught a great many fish, but we kept only *a few*.

Quite a few means *an appreciable number*, and is very different in force from *very few*. *Only a few* and *just a few* have much the same force as *few* alone, and are often preferred to the single word. Adjectival modifiers of *few* are occasionally incorporated in *a few*, but only in a very limited way.

> *A favored few* always get first choice.

Like many adjectives and a few adverbs, *few* has a comparative form in *er* and a superlative in *est*. Both *fewer* and *fewest* are used as determiners and nounally.

> We have *fewer* free days than we used to have.
> We have some free days, but *fewer* than usual.
> Johnny's paper has the *fewest* errors.
> Johnny made some errors, but the *fewest* so far.

Both forms require completing modifiers, expressed or implied, like comparatives and superlatives in general. Both forms are near-negative in force.

Near-negative *few* (without *a*) and its inflected forms *fewer* and *fewest* are most characteristically used in careful and formal styles. In informal styles, and to some extent even in careful styles, combinations of *many* and *not* are generally preferred.

> We don't have many problems with the boys.
> We don't have as many free days as we used to.

Also *less* and *least* tend to replace *fewer* and *fewest*.

Several has nothing of the near-negative force of *few*. It is used both as a determiner and nounally.

> We waited *several* days.
> *Several* of us stayed.

Several is best regarded as an adjective where it stresses variety and distinctness rather than number, as in *we went our several ways.*

Like *few*, except when *a* is used with it *little* has near-negative force: there is a feeling of approach to the *no* of zero. *Little* is used as a determiner and nounally.

> There is *little* doubt that English teachers are confused.
> You're welcome to what *little* coffee there is.
> *Little* remains of the work of the Shakers.
> She had *little* or nothing to say.
> Things got better *little* by *little*.

Phrasal *a little* normally lacks the near-negative force of *little* without *a*. It occurs both as a determiner and in nounal uses.

> We usually eat *a little* fruit.
> The boys were having *a little* fun in their way.
> There's quite *a little* milk in the refrigerator.
> If there's any coffee, I'll take *a little*.
> I'll be back after *a little*.

Like *few*, *little* has a comparative form, *less*, and a superlative form, *least*. Both occur as determiners and also in nounal uses, with near-negative force.

> I have *less* time than I used to have.
> A little *less* uncertainty is desirable.
> The *less* said, the better.
> This room has the *least* space.
> The *least* we can do is pay for repairs.

In informal styles near-negative *little* (without *a*) and its inflected forms *less* and *least* tend to be avoided, like near-negative *few*.

> There isn't much doubt that English teachers are confused.
> I don't have as much time as I used to.

But *less* is much better established than *fewer*, and indeed tends to replace *fewer*, and to serve as a comparative for both *few* and *little* as *more* does for both *many* and *much*. *Less* replaces *fewer* most often when a modifier of comparison follows immediately.

> As late as the sixteenth century English was spoken by *less* than five million people.

Between 1604 and 1755 no *less* than twenty English dictionaries appeared.
There are now *less* than one hundred strong verbs in the language.
Less than half the entering freshmen will get degrees in the end.

Less also replaces *fewer* in constructions in which no modifier of comparison follows.

Please answer in twenty-five words or *less*.
There were a dozen of us, more or *less*.

These uses of *less* must be regarded as standard. *Fewer* is also quite usable, and is commonly preferred for careful and formal styles. *Least* shows less tendency to replace *fewest*, except that the fixed phrasing *at least* does not distinguish number from quantity at all.

Four dozen diapers are the *least* you can get along with.
There were at *least* five students from Maine.

Little (and *a little*), *less*, and *least* all have considerable use as adjuncts and as heads in adjunct constructions. *Little* and *a little* modify comparatives, the *too* of excess, some basic-form adjectives and adverbs (generally with *too* implied), and prepositional units; *less* and *least* perform some of these functions and are of course used as modifiers of basic-form adjectives and adverbs in phrasal comparatives and superlatives.

Little did we realize that we would never see Louise again.
Phil discouraged us *less*.
She likes her history course *least*.
It's *a little* better.
It's *a little* too big.
She's *a little* young.
He's *a little* to the right in his thinking.
He's *less* like his father now.
He likes to display *little*-known information.

As has been said, *little* is often an adjective concerned with size, as in *a little girl*.

The determinative of sufficiency: enough.—*Enough* is the determinative of sufficiency, semantically equivalent to the adjective *sufficient*. The concept of sufficiency is of course a highly flexible one much of the time, involving estimates that are not subject to accurate measurement. *Enough* functions as a determiner modifying both plurals and quantifiables.

> Janet certainly has *enough* friends.
> Frank doesn't give *enough* time to his family.

It functions in nounal uses, with both plural and quantitative force.

> There are some envelopes, but hardly *enough*.
> That's *enough* from you!
> *Enough* of the letters are here to keep us busy.
> *Enough* of the correspondence is here to keep us busy.

It is used as an adjunct and as a modifier of adjectives and adverbs, both basic-form and comparative, and of *more* and *less*. When it modifies basic-form adjectives and adverbs, it follows them.

> The children aren't at home *enough*.
> The town isn't big *enough*.
> He didn't go slowly *enough*.
> It isn't *enough* better.
> That isn't *enough* more.

Determinatives of large number and quantity: many and much.—*Many* and *much* are companion determinatives, like *few* and *little: many* expresses large number, and *much* large quantity. Like *few*, *little*, and *enough*, *many* and *much* are very flexible words in application.

Many is used as a determiner with nounal heads, and in nounal uses.

> She has *many* reasons to distrust us.
> There aren't *many* towns along the road.
> George's *many* friends will miss him.
> There aren't *many* of us around now.
> The *many* do not really need the leadership of the few.

Especially in informal styles, *many* and the determinative unit *very many* tend to be used chiefly in negated clauses, main interrogatives, and subordinate interrogatives with question or condition force. Elsewhere *a good many* tends to replace simple *many* and *a great many* to replace *very many*. (And of course *a lot* and *lots* compete.)

> There weren't *many* meetings after Easter.
> There were *a good many* meetings before Easter.
> There aren't *very many* children here.
> There are *a great many* children here.

As many, so many, and *too many* occur in both types of situations.

As complement in assertives, as predeterminative modifier before *a,* and (with *too*) as postpositive modifier, determinative *many* has exceptional relationships to singulars.

> *Many's* the time I've heard him say it.
> *Many* a man has tried and failed.
> One excuse too *many* has been given.

Much is used as a determiner with nounal heads, and in nounal uses.

> We didn't waste *much* time.
> There isn't *much* wood in the building.
> *Much* of the time was wasted.
> They don't have *much* in common.
> He doesn't know *much* about Puerto Rico.
> I thought as *much*.
> How *much* do those Japanese cameras cost?

Upside-down construction is involved in some of the uses of *much,* and in others—especially after *be*—remarkable syntactic and semantic extensions are apparent.

> He isn't *much* of a teacher.
> The flowers weren't *much*, but it was nice to have them.
> Judson isn't *much* to look at.
> How *much* are eggs?
> The children were too *much* for us.

Much has a great deal of use in adverbial functions. It is used as an adjunct and as a modifier of comparatives, superlatives with determiners, *too,* prepositional units, etc. In upside-down construction *much* even serves as head in predicators and predicator-and-complement sequences.

> I didn't sleep *much* last night.
> I don't *much* like the idea.
> The last book wasn't *much* better.
> Carter talks *much* more convincingly.
> The coat isn't *much* too big.

It's *much* the worst time to go to New Orleans.
Much to my surprise, June decided to come along.
They aren't *much* alike.
The situation was *much* the same when we got back.
The first play was *much* the best.
Harriet as *much* as admits that she married for money.

Unmodified *much* is largely confined to negated clauses, main interrogatives, and subordinate interrogatives with question or condition force. Such nounal units as *a great deal*, *a good deal*, informal *a lot*, and informal *lots* are generally preferred to *much* where negation, interrogation, and condition are not involved.

He didn't have *much* fun.
He had *a great deal* of fun.

Very much tends to be restricted as *much* alone is.

There isn't *very much* of the cake left.
There's *a great deal* of the cake left.

More serves as comparative for both *many* and *much*. *More* functions as a determiner modifying both plurals and quantifiables.

There will be *more* tourists next month.
Are there any *more* questions?
Let's wait a few *more* days.
We need *more* space.
Have some *more* coffee.

It functions in nounal uses, with both plural and quantifiable force.

We have two cats, and we don't need any *more*.
Williamson had very little patience in those days, and I doubt
that he has *more* now.
I have a little *more* to do.

Upside-down construction extends the use of *more*.

Harry is *more* of a teacher than George is.
He was *more* than kind.

Preceded by the numeral *one*, *more* can modify singular forms of pluralizers.

We need one *more* chair.
I'll take one *more* piece.

The phrasal determiner *more than one* also modifies singulars.

> *More than one* reason has been given.

Sometimes *more* follows its head.

> I need two weeks *more*.

Like comparatives in general, *more* requires completing modifiers, expressed or implied. Its normal completers are interrogative clauses of comparison. These are often separated from it.

> There will be *more* tourists next month *than there are now*.

Like comparatives in general, *more* is often weaker in force than its basic forms *many* and *much*.

> There aren't *many* tourists now, but there are *more* than there were last month.

More combines with basic-form adjectives and adverbs to form phrasal comparatives, as has been noted. It also functions as adjunct and as head in phrasal adjuncts, and it modifies prepositional units.

> We drive the car *more than we should*.
> Don't you feel *more* at home now?

The combination *any more* has considerable use in negated clauses, main interrogatives, and subordinate interrogatives with question or condition force.

> We don't watch TV *any more*.
> If the baby cries *any more*, pick him up.

In upside-down construction *more*, like *much*, acts as head in predicators and predicator-and-complement sequences.

> The Democrats have *more* than recovered their losses.

There is no tendency to confine the use of *more* to clauses in which there is negation, question, or condition. In this respect *more* is unlike its two basic forms, *many* and *much*.

Most is the superlative for both *many* and *much*. It functions as a determiner modifying both plurals and quantifiables, and is used nounally.

Who made the *most* mistakes?
The oldest child gets the *most* attention.
We've all had literature courses, but Mary's had the *most*.
We made the *most* of our opportunity.

In both these uses *most*, like superlatives in general, tends to be preceded by superimposed *the*. But it is also used without *the*.

Most is used very commonly with the meaning *the majority* or *the largest part*. In this sense too it is concerned with both number and quantity.

> *Most* children like pets.
> *Most* of our students come from middle-class families.
> *Most* restaurant coffee is poor.
> *Most* of the rice eaten in the States is dull.

The is normally not used with *most* in this use. Thus *George eats the most desserts* is likely to mean *George eats more desserts than the rest of us do*, but *George eats most desserts* is likely to mean that George eats more kinds of desserts than he refuses.

Most combines with basic-form adjectives and adverbs to form phrasal superlatives, as has been noted. It also functions as an adjunct.

> The third candidate's manner impressed us *most*.

The determinatives of totality: all and both.—*All* is the pronoun of totality where groups with three or more members are involved, and also where quantifiables are involved. *Both* is the pronoun of totality where groups with only two members are involved.

All functions as a determiner modifying both plurals and quantifiables.

> *All* big cities have traffic problems now.
> Bring Henry along, by *all* means.
> *All* salt water stings when it gets in your eyes.
> *All* poetry is artificial.
> The appropriation is inadequate, beyond *all* doubt.

It functions in nounal uses, with both plural and quantifiable force.

> *All* but three of the boys are going.
> There wasn't room for *all* of us.
> Death comes to *all*.
> Almost *all* of that enormous cake was eaten.

In apposition with *you, all* is sometimes applied to groups of two in the southern United States.

> When are you *all* coming over to see us?

All competes with the representative-singular determinative of universality *every.*

> *All* virtues can become vices.
> *Every* virtue can become a vice.

Quantitative nounal *all* is semantically very close to *everything* in such sentences as the following.

> Is that *all?*
> She knows *all* about it.

It is semantically close to *everything* in a number of more or less fixed phrasings where it is entrenched.

above *all*	best of *all*	in *all*
after *all*	for *all* I know	once and for *all*
at *all*	for *all* of me	when *all* is said and done

Sometimes nounal *all* implies that the totality it represents is small.

> That's *all* we ask.
> *All* that was visible was the hair, forehead, and eyes.
> He's the owner, for *all* I know.

Ironic use is sometimes made of this *all.*

> *All* Barbara wants is a big house in town and another in the country, and two or three Cadillacs, and a yacht, and enough money to operate this equipment.
> *All* Neely wants is everything.

All has many adverbial uses. It functions as a predeterminer modifier of noun heads, as most determinatives of number and quantity cannot.

| all the boys | all morning |
| all the milk | all England |

Here *all morning* is equivalent to *all the morning,* and the proper noun *England* has the force of determiner and head noun together. In *all the boys* totality within a particular group of boys is expressed by *all;* in *all boys* totality is not limited to any particular group.

All of the boys exists alongside *all the boys* and is syntactically like *none of the boys, few of the boys,* etc. *All* is often used as an adjunct with half-appositive relationships.

> We're *all* going.
> We've *all* been given the same answer.

All has strikingly varied adverbial uses as contained modifier.

> *all* too soon   *all* of a sudden   *all* right
> *all* the better   *all* through the war   *all* up

All has syntactically exceptional uses as head word in upside-down predicators or predicator-and-complement sequences.

> It's *all* but ruined him.

In informal styles *all* occurs as a coordinate terminating series where its use is highly exceptional.

> Meanwhile Judy had graduated and *all*.
> She's pretty and clever and *all*.

Both is used with reference to pairs. It functions both as a determiner in nounal units and nounally.

> You'll need *both* hands.
> *Both* of us heard it.
> We liked them *both*.

Both emphasizes joint participation. Where joint participation is clear without *both*, the word is generally avoided: *the two* is likely to be used, or there is no such word.

One of the two procedures is certain to be satisfactory.
It is difficult to see many similarities between the two languages.
The two get on each other's nerves.
Paul and Babbitt belonged to the same club.

Like *all*, *both* often functions as predeterminer modifier of noun heads, though such units as *both the boys* are really not different in meaning from such units as *both boys*. Like *all*, *both* is often used as an adjunct with half-appositive relationships, as in *we were both disappointed*. In addition, as a precoordinator *both* attaches to a wide variety of heads.

> He's *both* encouraged us and interfered with us.
> He drinks coffee *both* with meals and between them.

CHAPTER XV

PERSONAL PRONOUNS

The nounal pronouns differ from the determinative pronouns in not being used, except in the possessive, as determiner modifiers. Thus nounal *she* is not used as determinative *that* is used in *who is that girl?* though it is used as determinative *that* is used in *who is that?* Among the nounal pronouns, the set of personal pronouns— *I, you, he, she, it, we, they,* and their "inflected" forms—is of exceptional syntactic importance.

The personal pronouns of the first and second persons.— *I* is the personal pronoun of the first person singular. *I* is every person's name for himself. It is not the name a person uses in identifying himself or in signing a letter; and it is not a name by which people can be addressed. But *I* is the name every person uses of himself when he can. *I* is for people, without regard to sex, age, or social class; but it is put in the mouths and thoughts of animals, dolls, and anything else that is treated personally and endowed with language as in children's play. Often the hearer knows no other name for the speaker who refers to himself as *I*.

We is the personal pronoun of the first person plural. *We* is not the plural of *I* in the sense that *boys* is the plural of *boy:* for every human being, there is only one *I*. *We* is simply a plural in which *I* is included.

> If you and I can agree, *we* can get somewhere.
> When Wilson and I try, *we* can usually agree.
> You and Wilson and I can get together if *we* try.
> Iowans are just Middle Westerners. *We* aren't spectacular in any way.

We often refers to nouns or nounal units prominent in what has just been said, as in the examples above; it is also used without them, with prominence in the situation fixing the reference. In formal styles a postpositive modifier occasionally helps to fix the reference.

> *We who have known him* are fully aware of the range of his powers.

In rather formal styles *we* is sometimes a modest substitute for *I*.

> *We* have distinguished between what Byron wrote glibly and what he took some pains with.

Perhaps this *we* is intended to suggest inclusion of the reader. In journalistic use this *we* sometimes hints at inclusion of fellow journalists: the opinions expressed are to be taken as those of the staff or of spokesmen for the staff. Sometimes *we* is simply whimsical.

> A red-haired woman cornered *us* at a cocktail party last week to tell us about a peculiar habit her husband has picked up.

We is occasionally an equivalent of *you*.

> Now it's time for *our* medicine.

Sometimes *we* is roughly equivalent to *a person* or *people* or general *one*, though it includes the speaker or writer more explicitly.

> *We* become more and more impatient of interruptions as the years go by.

Smaller *we*'s are sometimes referred to within larger ones.

> Some of us felt that *we* were being outmaneuvered.

You is the personal pronoun of the second person singular as well as of the second person plural. *You* is everyone's name for a person to whom he is speaking or writing, though it is not a good name for use in attracting attention. Like *I*, *you* is for people, without regard to sex, age, or social class, and is also applied to animals, dolls, and the like when they are treated like people. Occasionally *you* is actually the speaker or writer.

> It was from here that *your* father used to set out for the mines, none of his family knowing whether he would ever return. And *you* hope *your* present days here will help to bring him back to *you* as he was when young.

Much more frequently *you* is a typical person.

> If *you* have health and a little money and a few friends, nothing else matters very much.
> Bashfulness is a quality *you* don't expect to find in a man like Judson.
> *You* have to be careful in *your* dealings with Thompson.

The language has no completely satisfactory way of referring to the typical person. In informal styles, *you* is clearly the most-used pronounal method, in spite of the fact that it can be ambiguous.

In earlier centuries *you* was always plural, but when the old singular *thou* became emotional and delicate—often contemptuous, though also often affectionate and, as still applied to God in prayer, even reverent—*you* became singular and plural alike, with only its *self* form indicating number. The situation generally makes clear just what the reference of *you* is. Occasionally, both in formal styles and in very informal ones, a postpositive modifier helps to fix reference.

> *You of the student body* have responsibilities too.
> *You with the sandwiches!*

Sometimes its number force is indicated elsewhere in the sentence.

> You're a real diplomat.
> You're real diplomats.
> Aren't you coming along, George?
> You people should come to see us.
> We hope you two can come.

You plural is used with reference to nouns or nounal units prominent in what has just been said, and (much more often) with the situation itself indicating the reference.

> *Virginians* are sometimes hard to put up with. *You*'re much too proud of your ancestors.
> It's good to see *you* again.

The fact that *you* can be taken as either singular or plural has advantages when, for example, Christmas cards are printed with such phrasings as *wishing you a Merry Christmas*.

Third-person-singular he and she.—*He, she,* and *it* are the personal pronouns of the third person singular. *He* and *she* are like *I* and *you* in being designations normally applied to people. *He* and

she are applicable to everyone as a subject of conversation or writing. Usually *he* and *she* are substitutes which take the place of
other designations already prominently expressed.

> *May* will come along if *she* can.
> *The man who was sitting across from me* looked as though *he*
> wanted a chance to escape.

The great virtue of *he* and *she* is their usual inconspicuousness,
which makes it possible to repeat them over and over again. But
they are so well established as substitute words that even relatively
bulky forms of them are commonly required where nouns would
otherwise be repeated close together.

> *May* has invited *herself* to come along again.

Sometimes *he* and *she* are substitutes not for what has been said
but for what will be said prominently in what follows immediately.

> When *he* was just beginning to write plays, *Shakespeare* used
> a great deal of rhyme.

In informal conversation the reference of *he* and *she* is sometimes
indicated by such means as gestures.

> Who's *he?*
> Well, *she's* pretty at least.

Here *he* may be equivalent to *that man at the next table*, and *she* to
our waitress. In formal styles, and in a few fixed phrasings, the
reference of *he* and *she* is sometimes indicated by a following modifier.

> All things come to *him who waits.*
> *He who hesitates* is lost.

But in most situations this kind of thing is avoided. *Who's she with
the big red car?* seems quite unnatural, for example.

He and *she* are primarily for people, divided into male and female. Thus a man named *Warren* is referred to as *he* and a woman
named *Warren* as *she*, whether or not such honorifics as *Mr.* and
Miss are used with the name, while a city given the same name
will not ordinarily be so referred to. When *your date* is used of a
person, it is referred to by *he* or *she;* when it refers to an occasion
by *it. He* and *she* are also applied to anything that is regarded as

having personality, including dolls and toy animals, for example. Where the feeling about personality is strong, *he* and *she* are sometimes used without much regard for precise sex classifications. Thus a kitten or a goldfish may be referred to as *he* (or *she*) quite mistakenly, just as it may be given the name *Oswald* (or *Flora*) on the basis of the wrong guess about its sex. God is referred to as *he*, and when *he* refers to God, as when it refers to Christ, an honorific capital letter often begins it. Death is sometimes referred to by *he*, but only somewhat poetically. Nature is more often referred to by *she*, and may even be called Mother Nature; sometimes fortune is also *she*. Countries can be referred to, a little emotionally, as *she*, though this is hardly true when the name used is an old plural such as *the United States*. Ships are commonly *she;* planes, automobiles, and trains are less likely to be thought of in terms of personality and femininity. No other pronouns take sex into account, though such nouns as *boy*, *waitress*, *William*, and *Susan* normally do.

He is sometimes made to serve as an equivalent to *he or she.*

Some student left *his* notebook in the reading room.
If *your child* is given plenty of time to eat, dress, and get ready for school, *he* will begin *his* day's work in a good frame of mind.
Surely *whoever told Mary* didn't know how much unhappiness *he* was causing.

He is not really a satisfactory equivalent for *he or she: he* is too definitely male in most of its uses. *He or she* is awkward, and in informal styles *they* is usually substituted. The shift in number makes this an objectionable substitution for careful and formal styles, which either hold to *he* or resort to rephrasings that avoid the problem. *He* is sometimes impossible where the reference is to representative *everyone* or *everybody*.

Everyone treats Mary well, but she treats *him* badly.

Third-person-singular it.—*It* is for what is felt as lacking personality. *It* can represent not only pluralizers and proper names but also quantifiables.

I parked *the car* where *it* would be in the shade.

New York still draws young men of talent from all over the
country, just as *it* always has.
Practically everyone likes *milk* better when *it's* cold.

It is entirely usable for animals, though it gives way to *he* and *she*
when they are regarded as personalities, or when sex is mentioned.
A rooster can be referred to as *it* in complete disregard of obvious
sex classification, if there is no interest in the rooster as a personality. *It* is quite usable for human babies, though the family and
the friends of the family would certainly use *he* or *she*. *It* is even
usable of human beings generally, without regard either to sex or
to number, as a subject in identifications which are begun vaguely.

Who was that? I thought *it* was your sister.
If anyone needs help, *it's* George.
A young woman came to the door when we knocked. *It* was
the new secretary.

It often represents sentences and even sequences of sentences,
especially when it is used as complement of such verbs as *know,
mean, believe, doubt, say, admit,* and *deny.*

I just don't believe *it.*

It can represent main divisions of multiple sentences, and main
nucleuses.

She's pretty, and she knows *it.*
You'll be in trouble before you know *it.*
Why won't he admit an error? Is *it* because he lacks self-
confidence?

It represents subordinate clauses with great frequency. Most
commonly these are used as delayed appositives to *it* in a construction which permits postponement of the subordinate clauses while
it represents them in the positions which would otherwise be normal for them.

It's unfortunate *that Mary isn't here.*
It doesn't matter *what he thinks.*
I'll leave *it* to you *which route we take.*
It was the women *who filled home-town papers with accounts of
their presentation at the Court of St. James.*
It was then *that Marie's mother decided that Marie was no
longer an innocent little dove.*

In main interrogatives this *it* is sometimes thrown directly in front of clausal appositives, as in *why is it that we can't get together?* Sometimes even in declaratives *it* precedes declarative-clause appositives directly, and acts as a kind of buffer for them after predicators and prepositions that do not accept them as completers.

> I resent it *that such a charge is added.*
> I'll see to *it that a good typewriter is available.*
> You can depend on *it that Hugh will make trouble.*

It often represents subordinate clauses, or nucleuses of subordinate clauses, which are hardly in apposition with it.

> I'm sure *he's been mistreated*, but he shouldn't take *it* out on us.
> *It* might help *if we talked to the Dean.*
> Smith can't help *it if he likes company.*
> *It* makes him unhappy *when people think he's unfriendly.*

It often represents prepositional units. Most often the preposition is *to* or *for* . . . *to* and its object is an infinitival clause. The whole unit is a delayed appositive to *it*, as subordinate clauses often are.

> *It* isn't easy *to be bored in New York.*
> *It*'s important *for Jones to be satisfied.*

It also represents other prepositional units, chiefly ones expressing meanings of duration and distance. These units, again, are used as delayed appositives to *it*.

> *It*'s only sixty miles *to Cleveland.*
> *It*'s three years *since he's had a real vacation.*
> *It* doesn't matter *about the horses.*

Less frequently, *it* represents adjectives and adjectival units.

> She's *intelligent*, but she doesn't look *it*.

It sometimes represents headed-unit delayed appositives which parallel clauses in their content, even when these appositives themselves are plural in force.

> *It*'s incredible *the chances Hudson takes.*

The paralleling clause here is *what chances Hudson takes.*

It has considerable use without expressed reference in the context. As a subject, *it* sometimes seems to be a name for natural forces beyond personality and sex, somewhat as *I* is a name for speaker or writer.

> *It*'s snowing.

Volition of a stubborn kind is attributed to this *it* in such sentences as *if it would only rain!* Sometimes *it* is equivalent to *the surroundings, the time, the situation,* or to such general nouns as *things* or *matters.*

> *It*'s very pretty here.
> *It*'s ten thirty.
> *It*'s winter now in Uruguay.
> If *it* weren't for the heat, we'd go shopping.
> How goes *it?*
> We'll have to make the best of *it.*
> May's making *it* hot for us.
> When *it* comes to irritating people, he's phenomenal.
> Take *it* easy, boy.
> I had *it* out with him.

Sometimes *it* is equivalent to *the running, the point,* or *the goal.*

> The food here isn't in *it* with that at the Commons.
> *It* isn't that I distrust him.
> Out with *it!*
> We'll have to run for *it.*

Sometimes *it* expresses ideas of hostility or trouble.

> She has *it* in for us.
> He'll catch *it* when his wife finds out.
> I'm afraid I'm up against *it.*

Sometimes *it* has no clear semantic content and yet is an integral part of the phrasing.

> Joe likes to lord *it* over people.
> I've gone *it* alone long enough.
> George has no taste for roughing *it.*
> The boys are whooping *it* up again.

Sometimes *it* refers to something prominent in the particular situation, much as the demonstratives *this* and *that* do.

> *It*'s a tough life.
> Stop *it!*

***Third-person-plural* they.**—*They* is the personal pronoun of the third person plural. It serves as plural for *he, she,* and *it*; but unlike these singulars, it is wholly indifferent to sex and personality and the absence of them. Being plural, *they* is not applicable to true quantifiables such as *fun* and *furniture. They* is generally a substitute word used with obvious reference. Sometimes, like the other personal pronouns, it is used with its reference made clear by the prominence in the situation of what it refers to.

Who are they?

Here *they* can be equivalent to *those women who just came in.* In sentences such as the following the context clarifies the reference somewhat less directly.

> We had expected to lose several hours at the Border, but *they* hardly looked at our baggage.
> When I started banking here, *they* gave me a bankbook that I've never used.

Especially in informal styles, *they* is sometimes equivalent to *people,* and so is very similar to general *you* and *we,* though it suggests that speaker and spoken-to are apart from the general group represented.

They say we won't have any classes Tuesday.

As has been noted, in informal styles *they* is often used as a substitute for awkward *he or she.*

> If you see Robert or Ruby, tell *them* I'll be in Washington in December.

Inflection of the personal pronouns.—Many nouns—especially proper nouns—have distinct common-case and possessive forms. The matter of case is more complicated for the personal pronouns. All the personal pronouns have common-case forms compounded with *self* in addition to basic common-case forms or their equivalents. Actually only *you* and *it* have basic common-case forms: most of the personal pronouns have distinct nominative and objective forms dividing the functions performed for nouns by common-case forms. Finally, most of the personal pronouns have two possessive forms, a short form and a long one, dividing the functions performed for nouns by single possessive forms. Only *his* and *its* function in as many situations as the possessives of nouns. Paradigms can be made as follows.

	Basic Common	Nominative	Objective	*Self* Common	Possessive Indifferent	Possessive Short	Possessive Long
1 sg.		I	me	myself		my	mine
2 sg.	you			yourself		your	yours
3 sg.		he	him	himself	his		
3 sg.		she	her	herself		her	hers
3 sg.	it			itself	its		
1 pl.		we	us	ourselves		our	ours
2 pl.	you			yourselves		your	yours
3 pl.		they	them	themselves		their	theirs

The nominative and basic-common-case forms are usually regarded as the basic forms. As between the nominatives and the objectives, however, the objectives are now the stronger forms, and in second-person *you* an old objective has completely displaced an old nominative—the *ye* of the biblical *ye shall know the truth, and the truth shall make you free.* From the point of view of simplicity of system, it is unfortunate that in standard American English there has not been a general displacement of nominatives by objectives, as in popular Jamaican, where *him talk* is equivalent to standard American *he talks.* The relationships of the inflected forms to the basic forms are obviously highly individualistic: only listings of one-word forms of some of the irregular verbs (notably *be*) and, in a smaller way, plurals for such nouns as *woman* and *person* and comparatives and superlatives for such adjectives as *good* and *bad,* are comparable in irregularity. Even possessives are made irregularly for personal pronouns. The *s* ending used in possessive forms of nouns appears also in the indifferent possessives *his* and *its* and in all the long possessives except *mine,* but all the short possessives except *my* employ an ending written *r,* though only *your* and *their* can be said to add it to the basic forms. Possessives of personal pronouns, like the possessive of *who,* are not marked in the written language by the apostrophe which is prescribed for possessives of nouns. The *self* forms are obviously compounds. In some *self* forms the first component is a possessive, in others an objective, in *herself* modern-English *her* could be either. It is highly exceptional that for syntactic reasons clear compounds require classification as inflected forms.

The uses of the nominative and objective forms.—The nominative forms of the personal pronouns are normal in all styles as subjects of expressed verbs in the common and subjunctive modes.

> *She* doesn't often get to New York now.
> What would *he* do if he found it out?

In formal styles nominative forms of the personal pronouns are used as subjects when common-mode or subjunctive verb forms are implied but not expressed.

> Others were closer to the President than *he*.
> No one else was as uncompromising as *they*.

In formal styles nominative forms of personals are also used as subjects in gerundial clauses used as loose adjuncts.

> Harkins had drawn up a plan of organization, *he* to be director.

In formal styles nominative forms of personals are used as complements of common-mode and subjunctive forms of the verb *be*.

> It was *he* who drafted the plan for "Universities for the People" which was published in 1853.

In formal styles nominative forms of personals are used as complements of infinitival forms of the verb *be* where the main subjects stand in relation to these complements as they would stand if *be* were the main verb.

> It is said to have been *he* who brought about the change.
> It may not have been *she*.

In formal styles nominative forms of personals occur, finally, in adjuncts which are also half appositives of subjects.

> They never disagreed on anything basic, *he* and his friends.

In what must be described as careless nonstandard use nominative forms sometimes occur as coordinates where both long-established principles of syntax and the present trend of the language support objective forms.

> Someone will bring you and *I* back.

Such a unit as *you and George* is usable in all nounal functions without change; it is not surprising that such a unit as *you and I* should occasionally be so used also, even though *I* is a weaker form in general than *me*.

As head words, principals, and coordinates, nominative forms are normal where they would be normal if a personal pronoun alone replaced the total headed, apposed, or multiple unit.

> *He* who hesitates is lost.
> *We* children were generally left at home.
> Joan and *I* can bring the food.

Especially in informal styles, *he* and *she* have some use as modifiers and heads where such adjective-nouns as *male* and *female* would be syntactically more normal.

> a *he* man   It's a *he*.
> a *she* goat   It's a *she*.

The objective forms of the personal pronouns are normal in all styles as subjects in infinitival clauses and in gerundial clauses used as objects of the preposition *with*.

> We wanted *him* to wait a little longer.
> *Him* be diplomatic?
> It's hard to work with *him* talking all the time.

They are normal in all styles as first complements of transitive verbs and as second complements preceding first complements.

> They brought *us* home.
> They didn't give *her* a chance.

They are normal in all styles as objects of prepositions.

> There's a package for *him*.

The objective *me* has no competition from the nominative *I* in the isolate *dear me!* though the possessive *my* is usable, without an adjective, as an isolate.

In informal styles objective forms are preferred to nominatives as subjects in clauses in which common-mode or subjunctive verbs are implied but not expressed.

> You haven't lived here as long as *her*.
> Who'd pay the bill? *Me?*

In informal styles the preference for objective forms rather than nominatives extends to subjects in gerundial clauses not used as objects of the preposition *with*.

We had to wade across the street—and *me* in my best suit.

In informal styles objective forms occur in apposition with expletive *there* in divided apposed-unit subjects.

There used to be three of us, but now there's only *me*.

In informal styles objective forms are preferred to nominatives as complements of the verb *be* as of all other verbs.

That's *him* coming up the drive now.
It must have been *us*.

As head words, principals, and coordinates, objective forms, like nominatives, are normal where they would be normal if a personal pronoun alone replaced the total headed, apposed, or multiple unit.

Informal styles restrict nominative forms of personal pronouns to use as subjects of expressed common-mode and subjunctive verb forms. Careful styles tend to restrict nominative forms of personals in the same way, but to avoid using objective forms where formal styles reject them. Thus informal *you haven't lived here as long as her* is likely to be matched in careful styles by *you haven't lived here as long as she has* and informal *that's him coming up the drive now* is likely to be matched by *that's Benson coming up the drive now*. There is nothing stiff about these less markedly informal patterns: they are quite usable in face-to-face spoken English, where the formal patterns would generally be out of place.

The basic common-case forms *you* and *it* are of course usable like both the nominatives and the objectives of the other personal pronouns. The common-case form of *you* is also usable in direct address, like the common-case forms of nouns.

I'm sorry for you, *you* poor little thing.

The uses of the self forms.—The *self* forms of the personal pronouns replace the nominative and objective (or basic common-case) forms in two types of situations. They function, first, as reflexives. As reflexives they most often refer back to the subjects

of the clauses in which they occur. They function as first complements of transitive verbs (occasionally including *be*), as second
complements preceding first complements, as objects of prepositions, as adjuncts of benefit, and (exceptionally) as subjects in
reduced infinitival clauses.

> You've hurt *yourself*.
> Marian just isn't *herself* today.
> He always gives *himself* the benefit of the doubt.
> We bought billfolds for *ourselves*.
> We bought *ourselves* billfolds.
> She wants *herself* included.
> She considers *herself* mistreated.

Reflexives also function as coordinates in multiple units used in
these ways.

> He always gives *himself* and his friends the benefit of the
> doubt.

Often the subject to which a reflexive refers is implied rather than
stated.

> Be *yourself*.
> Take care of *yourself*.
> It isn't easy to rid *yourself* of such people.

As reflexives following nounal complements *self* forms often refer
to these complements.

> We left him to *himself*.
> No one tells her the unpleasant truth about *herself*.

Within nounal headed units reflexives sometimes refer to preceding possessives.

> Something has destroyed Mary's faith in *herself*.

As reflexives *self* forms generally make the same kind of syntactic contribution to their clauses that nouns and other pronouns
make.

> His wife threatens to kill *him* if he leaves her.
> His wife threatens to kill *herself* if he leaves her.

Enjoy takes reflexive complements which are in effect empty: *ourselves* in *we've enjoyed ourselves* makes no such contribution to its
clause as *our visit* does in *we've enjoyed our visit*. This is a highly

exceptional use of reflexives in English. But English has a number of verbs (and meanings of verbs) which apparently are now used only with reflexive complements. This is true of *absent, avail, bestir, betake, bethink, busy, conduct* ("behave"), *plume, pride,* and *resign* (in the sense of "reconcile").

> I should bestir *myself* and get this thing finished.
> We'll have to resign *ourselves* to the situation.

Reflexive complements are left unexpressed after many verbs.

> Don't bother me.
> Don't bother.
> The police hurried us on our way.
> The police hurried on their way.

Sometimes there is a choice between expressing reflexive complements and not expressing them, with little if any difference in force.

> I can't keep myself cool now.
> I can't keep cool now.
> We'd better get ourselves ready.
> We'd better get ready.

Sometimes if the reflexive is expressed there is more of a feeling of effort or achievement, or of responsibility.

> He shaves himself.
> He shaves.
> Benson has got himself into hot water again.
> Benson has got into hot water again.
> She's starving herself to death.
> She's starving to death.

After many verbs where they would seem syntactically normal but are not used, the absence of reflexives is not likely to be felt.

> We *set* to work the next morning.
> We *put* up at a small hotel.
> We finally *got* rid of the ants.

But many reflexive complements cannot be left out.

> The new Greek teacher introduced *himself*.
> It would be sad if Williamson confined *himself* to the dull topics he knows something about.
> Restrain *yourself*, Morton.
> Help *yourself* to some peanuts.

Objective and basic-common-case forms of personals, rather than *self* forms, are used as objects of prepositions in many units which follow nounal complements when the reference is to the subjects rather than to the complements.

> Do you have a pen with *you?*
> Ben has a lot of mischief in *him.*
> Jack never takes us with *him.*
> Joan has the Dean against *her.*

In constructions of this kind, if the prepositional unit is moved forward objective and basic-common-case forms are still used.

> I had with *me* a letter of introduction from my bank.

Sometimes objective and basic-common-case forms are preferred even though there is no complement that would interfere with *self* forms.

> Look behind *you!*

In informal styles objective and basic-common-case forms sometimes replace *self* forms as reflexive adjuncts of benefit preceding complements.

> I've bought *me* a new car.

In addition to serving as reflexives, the *self* forms of the personal pronouns function also as what are usually called intensives. As intensives they stand in apposition or half apposition to the words or longer units they refer to. *Self* forms used as intensive appositives are italicized in the following sentences.

> You'd better talk to the manager *himself.*
> Christ *himself* had a traitor among his followers.
> I *myself* am inclined to agree.

Intensives characteristically stress identity. They tend to be somewhat emotional, and, like emotional constructions in general, can produce more or less opposite effects. In the second of the sentences given, *Christ himself* is like *even Christ* in force. The implication is that the example is an extreme one. In the third sentence *myself* adds, or can add, an effect of modesty to *I*. The *self* forms are half appositives in the following sentences.

He's taught Spanish *himself*.
She made the dress *herself*.
You're inclined to postpone things *yourselves*.
George asked Louise to come *himself*.
George asked Louise to come *herself*.

The half principals in all these sentences are the subjects of the clauses in which the *self* forms are adjuncts and half appositives. In *George asked Louise to come herself* the adjunct *herself* modifies the predicator *come*. No half principal for *herself* is expressed: the implied subject of *come*, suggested by the first complement (*Louise*) in the main clause, would serve as half principal if it were expressed. Half-appositive intensives characteristically refer to subjects and are half-appositives to them, and it is not unusual for the subjects to be implied rather than stated—as, for example, in *do it yourself*.

Self forms of personal pronouns sometimes replace nominative, objective, and basic-common-case forms in multiple units where the construction does not require *self* forms.

They invited my wife and *myself*.

Here *myself* may seem more modest than the more direct form *me*, as well as more similar to the first coordinate *my wife* in composition and bulk. Such uses of the *self* forms meet with criticism, and from the point of view of simplicity of syntactic system they seem undesirable.

The uses of the possessive forms.—Short possessive forms of personal pronouns characteristically perform only two syntactic functions. First, they act as determiner modifiers in nounal headed units. As determiner modifiers they are generally concerned with the same relationships that possessive forms of nouns are concerned with.

The boys have torn *their* clothes.
I'm in *your* way.
I hope *my* Spanish won't seem too bad.
We never located *our* man.
No one understands *her* treatment of her husband.
Hitler was able to maintain control until *his* final defeat.

Determiner possessives of personal pronouns are a normal way of identifying parts of the body, aspects of the psyche, education, clothes, and intimate possessions in general.

> The children raised *their* hands.
> I have a right to change *my* mind.
> She did *her* master's at Columbia.
> You can take off *your* coat.

But prepositional units, together with *the*, replace such possessives in various fixed phrasings.

> I can't for the life *of me* see why he did it.
> From the look *of them*, they aren't healthy.

In the *my dear sir* of direct address the possessive *my* has a somewhat formal honorific quality. This *my* easily becomes ironic or condescending, as it is likely to be in *my boy*, for example.

Short possessives of personal pronouns function also as subjects in gerundial clauses used as subjects, complements of transitive verbs, and objects of prepositions other than *with*.

> I hope you don't mind *my* asking this.
> Is there a chance of *our* having to do it?

As subjects in gerundial clauses, possessives of personal pronouns are more generally acceptable than possessives of nouns. They are not usable, however, where multiword subjects of gerundials merely happen to terminate in personal pronouns.

> May resents the idea of a man like *him* marrying her sister.

The short possessive *my* has highly exceptional use as an emotional isolate.

Long possessive forms always perform nounal functions but generally do so by virtue of reduction, just as possessives of nouns often do.

> Jack's idea was silly, but not as silly as *ours*.
> *Hers* is an old-fashioned home.

Here *ours* and *hers* represent *our idea* and *her home*.

Long possessive forms of personal pronouns have a second use as objects of *of* in postpositive modifiers within nounal units. Here they have lost determiner status.

Some friends of *ours* are coming by.
That husband of *hers* will keep her in line.
It's no business of *mine*.

The indifferent possessives *his* and *its* are used like both the short possessives of the other personal pronouns and their long possessives. *It*, of course, generally refers to what is felt as lacking personality, and the relationships expressed by possessives generally involve personality. But *its* is used a great deal more than the possessives of nouns to which *it* can refer. Thus *the play was approaching its end* is quite normal, whereas *we left at the play's end* is not, and would generally be replaced by *we left at the end of the play*.

CHAPTER XVI

OTHER NOUNAL PRONOUNS

In addition to the personal pronouns, a somewhat miscellaneous group of other nounal pronouns must be recognized. Included in this group are the phrasal reciprocal *each other*, expletive *there*, general *one*, substitute *one*, the compounds of the *someone* type, and the clause markers *that, who,* and *whoever.*

The reciprocal.—Reflexives and reciprocals are closely related semantically, and they perform the same syntactic functions. They differ in that there is a crossing of relationships when a reciprocal is used and not when a reflexive is used.

The bride and groom seem pleased with each other.
The bride and groom seem pleased with themselves.

Reciprocals can refer only to plural nouns, pronouns, or nounal units; reflexives can refer to singulars as well. With reciprocals the crossing of relationships sometimes becomes complex.

We five children were always quarreling with each other.

There is no one-word reciprocal pronoun in modern English. Phrasal *each other* is now felt as composed of a head *other* and a determiner modifier *each.* In the parent construction *each* is a half appositive of the plural to which phrasal *each other* refers, and *other* functions quite separately.

They seem pleased each with the other.

Each other is not affected in form by the person of its antecedent, and in this respect is quite unlike the *self* forms. It has a regularly formed possessive.

We must keep *each other's* respect.
Mary and Roberta have a low view of *each other's* husbands.

When *each other's* modifies a pluralizer, the plural form of the pluralizer is normal in spite of the fact that *each other's* is a singular form.

Like reflexives, reciprocals are often implied rather than expressed.

> The McPhersons *met* at the University.
> The two families hardly *speak* now.

The somewhat archaic phrasal reciprocal *one another* is used as *each other* is used, except that it is generally used only to refer to plurals naming groups with at least three members.

The expletive.—Expletive *there* is a highly exceptional pronoun characteristically used as principal in apposed-unit subjects. It occurs most typically when the verb is *be* and the mode of the verb is common or subjunctive.

> *There* isn't time for much reading nowadays.
> *There's* something wrong.
> *There's* no one at home.
> *There's* always George to think about.
> If *there* weren't any good doctors in the village, we wouldn't
>   want to live there.

Occasionally *there* occurs with infinitival and gerundial forms of *be*.

> It isn't right for *there* to be so many uncertainties.
> *There* being no further business, the meeting was adjourned.

There is also used very commonly with verbs completed by infinitival clauses, or by prepositional units in which *to* is used with infinitival clauses, where *be* is the infinitive.

> *There* are said to be many errors.
> *There* had better be enough.
> *There* happen to be three possibilities.
> *There* seems to be a discrepancy.
> *There* must be some mistake.
> *There* may not be any other solution.

After *let* in somewhat formal styles *there* is used in first complements where infinitival clauses with *be* as predicator serve as second complements.

> Let *there* be no mistake.

The semantic resemblance to syntactically distinct *may there be no mistake* makes the use of *there* after *let* seem natural.

Be expresses meanings of existence, occurrence, and availability in such sentences as have been given. *There* is used as principal in apposed-unit subjects with other verbs where meanings of somewhat similar types are expressed.

With his honesty *there* was mingled an unfortunate blindness to reality.
There comes a time for decision.

In standard usage the expletive pronoun *there* does not determine the number force of apposed-unit subjects in which it is the principal: the appositives do this. Even when appositives are implied rather than stated, they determine number force. This accounts for the forms of the verbs in the questions which follow.

"There aren't any seats." "*Aren't there?*"
"There isn't any room." "*Isn't there?*"

It is possible, however, that the use of expletive *there* is partially responsible for the use of singular verb forms in such sentences as the following.

There *is*, besides Athens and Rome, Copan and Cuzco to be taken into account.
At Christmas there *is* special food which is eaten at no other time, special songs, and a great deal of visiting.
There *was* a present tense and a past.
There *is* no industry and no farming.
All afternoon there *was* sunshine and rain by turn.

General **one.**—General *one* is semantically equivalent ordinarily to *a person* or *people*. As has been noted, *you*, *we*, and *they* are all semantically equivalent to *a person* and *people* at times; but *one* is the favored pronoun for this use in formal styles, and it is likely to be preferred to the three personals even in careful styles. *One* is unique among the pronouns outside the personal subcategory in being indefinitely repeatable, like the personals.

In the course of *one's* life, *one* may make a dozen real friends if *one* is lucky.
One tries to avoid unpleasantness, doesn't *one?*

It is possible to employ personal pronouns rather than repetitions of *one*.

> In the course of *his* life, *one* may make a dozen real friends if *he* is lucky.

But repetition of *one* is likely to be preferred, especially in formal styles. Like *you, we,* and *they,* general *one* is indifferent to sex, and this is an advantage. *He* is never convincingly indifferent to sex. Sometimes, of course, *one* is "a person" of a single sex, and the substitution of a personal pronoun is less unsatisfactory.

> One can hope to keep *her* figure indefinitely if *she* is careful about *her* diet.

Sometimes *one* is really a mask for *I* or even for *you*.

> *One* noticed the high percentage of charming women that evening.
> *One* should be careful in dealing with Williamson.

General *one* does not accept modifiers. But the *one* which sometimes precedes people's names—commonly with a somewhat disparaging effect, as in *then we had to see one Theodore White, brother-in-law of our congressman*—is best regarded as general *one* used as principal in apposed units in which proper names function as appositives.

The basic form *one* is a common-case form, like *you* and *it*. A possessive is made as for singular nouns. There is also a *self* form, as for the personals and no other pronouns, usable both as a reflexive and as an intensive.

> *One* can take *oneself* too seriously in these matters.
> *One* should develop one's pictures *oneself*.

General *one* has no plural forms. Other uses of *one* are more important; but general *one* is useful, and it is unfortunate that it has not established itself in informal styles.

Substitute one.—The characteristic use of substitute *one* is to provide a substitute for a noun or nounal unit prominent in the context, to which prepositive modifiers (accompanied by postpositive modifiers or not) can be attached to form nounal units with pronoun heads.

She made two big loaves and one small *one*.
The newer books for children are better illustrated than the older *ones*.

Here the italicized *one* of the first sentence is clearly a substitute for *loaf* and is modified by the determiner *one* and by the adjective *small*. The italicized *ones* of the second sentence is as clearly a substitute for *books for children* and is modified by the determiner *the* and the adjective *older*. Substitute *one* is like the personal pronouns of the third person in that it serves as a way of avoiding the repetition of ordinarily bulkier nouns and nounal units: it is unlike the personal pronouns in its ready acceptance of modifiers. Substitute *one* is derived from numeral *one*, and it has not lost all number force. For this reason it can represent only pluralizers, never quantifiables.

We need two chairs, and we want sturdy *ones*.
We need some furniture, and we want it to be sturdy.

Substitute *one* inflects both for number and for possessive case.

An indolent mother may be preferable to a fussy *one*.
Indolent mothers may be preferable to fussy *ones*.
An indolent mother's household may be more peaceful than a fussy *one's*.

Substitute *one* is readily preceded by modifiers of relatively simple descriptive types.

This street is the *main* one.
His other car is an *imported* one.
Is the train a *through* one?
Wicker chairs are no more comfortable than *metal* ones.
He has a three-hour course and two *two-hour* ones.
When we have prizes, Jane always gets the *best* one.

Superlatives ordinarily cannot be followed by substitute *one*, however, when modifiers of the whole begun by *of* come next, as in *the largest of the apartments*. Substitute *one* is not usable after many modifiers with somewhat exceptional relationships to their heads: repetition or reduction is necessary instead.

He's a woman hater and she's a *man hater*.
There were two English teachers and a *history teacher*.

The Methodist Church is not greatly different from the
   Baptist.
There's a grade school on one corner and a *high school* on the
   other.

Some determiner modifiers can precede substitute *one* directly
and some cannot. Possessives cannot, and neither can determinative pronouns of number.

> Sarah's friends are less picturesque than *Jane's.*
> I had three pens but lost *two.*
> Pens become expensive if you lose *many.*

A few determinative pronouns of identification ordinarily do not
precede substitute *one* directly. This is true of *some, such, former,
latter,* and *own.* The indefinite article *a* is well established directly
before substitute *one* only where an adjective has been pulled in
front of *a.*

We got an answer, but not as clear *a* one as we had hoped for.

In dubiously standard informal use, *a* precedes *one* more often.

We expected to find jellyfish, but we haven't seen *a* one.

When the definite article *the* precedes substitute *one* directly, there
is usually a postpositive modifier attached to *one* also; but this is
not always the case.

> I'll take the one you leave.
> The ones with locks are the most useful.
> These just aren't the ones.

This and *that* can precede substitute *one* directly, though *these* and
those generally do not; so can most of the other determinative pronouns of identification.

> I didn't like his last letter, and *this* one is worse.
> *Either* one will be all right.
> She has two sons, but *neither* one is much good to her.
> I had no idea *which* ones he wanted.
> It's always the *same* ones that make the trouble.
> This chair looks nice, but the *other* one is more comfortable.
> I read the first chapter and skipped the *second* one.
> These pictures aren't as good as the *last* ones.

When other modifiers intervene, determiners of every kind can modify substitute *one*.

> Sarah's undramatic friends may be preferable in the end to *Jane's* picturesque ones.

Substitute *one* functions as a head for postpositive modifiers, but only when it has at least one prepositive modifier.

> We got some seats, but not *the* ones *we'd wanted*.

In *I have a good watch, but I need one with an alarm* it is best to regard *one* as the numeral, not the substitute. Expression of the implied noun *watch* would not result in loss of this *one:* there would only be a possible preference for its unstressed equivalent, the indefinite article.

> I have a good watch, but I need *a watch* (or *one watch*) with an alarm.

The *one* of *I need one with an alarm* is not a substitute: it is a determinative pronoun (not a nounal one) used without a stated head.

Generally the reference of substitute *one* is clear from the context. When substitute *one* stands for *person*, however, the help of context is sometimes relatively subtle.

> We aren't the *ones* to tell him.

Such locutions as *their loved ones* and *the little ones* are emotional. In *I heard a new one yesterday*, substitute *one* will be taken, without further context, to mean "joke" or "tricky piece of reasoning."

Formal styles have a tendency to reject substitute *one* where informal styles would want it.

> The proposal has its good points as well as its bad.

From the point of view of meaning such general nouns as *thing, matter, man,* and *person* are quite comparable to substitute *one* in some of their uses; but syntactic classifications cannot be made simply on the basis of meanings.

The compounds terminating in one, body, **and** thing.— The determinative pronouns *some, any, every,* and *no* combine with substitute *one* and the nouns *body* and *thing* to form compounds.

No one is written phrasally but is best grouped with the compounds nevertheless when it is used as *nobody* is used. In the compounds, *some, any, every,* and *no* have the meanings they have as uncompounded determinatives. *One* and *body* have essentially the common-sex meaning of *person. Thing,* of course, has a broad neuter meaning. The compounds in *one, body,* and *thing* are all singulars, and inflect only to form possessives.

The compounds in *one, body,* and *thing* are sometimes modified postpositively by adjectives which have been crowded out of the position they usually take between determiners and nounal heads.

> Anyone *interested* can apply.
> Something *new* has been added.

Where the pronoun *other* would be used in uncompounded equivalents, the adverb *else* is used postpositively with the compounds in *one, body,* and *thing.*

> Everyone *else* had left.
> Every *other* person had left.

The compounds accept some adverbs prepositively, as modifiers of predeterminer types.

> Almost *everyone* knows it.

Though the compounds in *thing* are basically neuter, they are sometimes applied to people.

> He's *nothing* to her.
> She's *something* special.

Upside-down constructions and the like employ them with some frequency.

> He was *anything* but pleased.
> He's *something* of a musician.
> I haven't seen *anything* of George lately.

They function as series enders where they are syntactically irregular.

> He hasn't apologized or *anything*.

The compounds in *one, body,* and *thing* cannot be modified by modifiers of the whole begun by *of.* Thus though *all of the students were present* is entirely possible, as is *everybody in the class was present*, it is not possible to say *everybody of the students was present*. Where modifiers of the whole begun by *of* are used, the uncompounded units *any one*, *every one* and *no one* are usable.

> *Every one* of my Latin teachers stressed grammar.

Unlike the corresponding compounds, uncompounded *any one* and *every one* are usable where the reference is to countable pluralizers other than people.

> *Any one* of my Latin courses taught me more English grammar than all my English courses.
> *Every one* of my English courses dealt with the British past.

The compound pronouns are syntactically notable in that personal pronouns sometimes refer to their second components.

> Nobody would become a coal miner if he could help it. People would go into almost any other kind of work first.

Here the *he* which in the first sentence has *nobody* as its antecedent is not itself negative. In the second sentence *people* is preferred to a *he* which would have *nobody* as its antecedent again. Actually such pronouns as *nobody* must often be classified as syntactically ununified mergings rather than true compounds.

Clause-marker **that.**—Among the clause-marker pronouns only *that*, *who*, and *whoever* are fundamentally nounal. Clause-marker *that* is distinct from demonstrative *that* in normally being unstressed and also in not inflecting for plural number. *That* is used as a clause marker both (1) in subordinate declaratives, imperatives, and assertives and (2) in subordinate interrogatives. In declaratives, imperatives, and assertives it always functions as an adjunct that contributes nothing except to mark its clause: nothing equivalent to it occurs in corresponding main declaratives. In subordinate declaratives marker *that* can be expressed or omitted at will in many situations.

> I had no idea *that* it was so late.
> I had no idea it was so late.
> They have so much money *that* they can't spend it all.
> They have so much money they can't spend it all.

That is likely to be needed in situations that occur chiefly in somewhat formal styles.

> They admit *that* other procedures are possible.
> Our representative in the area was fully aware *that* a revision of policy was necessary.

It is often desirable also after *be*.

> It isn't *that* he's lazy.
> The truth is *that* I don't understand him.

Often it helps to clarify construction.

> Miss Kirchwey told the Attorney General *that* some months ago she was informed that the government had a file on her.
> James How believed *that* Falder had committed a grave crime, and *that* for this reason he should receive no mercy.

That is not usable where a subordinate-declarative clause is reduced to *not*. In such situations *not* is treated as the substitute adverb *so* is treated.

> I guess *not*.
> I'm afraid *not*.

And, as has been said, *that* is likely not to be usable in declaratives used as objects of prepositions.

> We got home before the rain began.

In subordinate imperatives and assertives, marker *that* is normally expressed.

> No one has proposed *that* new negotiations be begun.
> Don't forget *that* here we are.

That is usable as a marker in subordinate interrogatives only when these follow heads that *that* refers to. In interrogatives *that* performs most nounal functions and takes the place of words and multiword units that would be employed if the interrogatives were made into corresponding main declaratives. Marker *that* is indifferent to what is felt as personality or the absence of personality, so that it competes with both *who* and *which*. Wherever it is hard to decide between *who* and *which*, *that* has an advantage.

> The courses and teachers *that* have impressed him are few.
> I didn't hear the quartet *that* sang last night.

Where the reference is to designations of people not regarded in terms of individual personality, *that* is likely to be preferred to *who*.

> He isn't the hero *that* I thought he was.
> Fool *that* I was, I believed him.

That is preferred to *who* and *which* after superlatives and *only*.

> The student was the best husband *that* the Wife of Bath ever had.
> He is the most dramatic pianist *that* has played here in years.
> This is the only room *that* is available.

That is likely to be preferred to both *who* and *which* when other pronouns, excepting the personals, are referred to.

> Who *that* you know would like a cat?
> Nothing *that* I said seemed right.
> There isn't much *that* I can do.
> That's all *that* was said.

That has no possessive. Though it is indifferent to number in form, it transmits the number force of what it refers to.

> We'd better replace the box *that is* seriously damaged.
> We'd better replace the boxes *that are* seriously damaged.

That differs from *who* and *which* in rejecting use in subordinate interrogatives functioning as loose adjuncts. Thus it is not possible to replace *who* and *which* with *that* in the following sentences.

> We missed McPherson, *who* was in France at the time.
> We went on to Trinidad, *which* was very different.

That also differs from *who* and *which* in not being usable as object of preceding prepositions. But prepositions can often be left in normal declarative positions and *that* can be moved to the front alone.

> There's the man *that* you were looking for.

And prepositions can simply be dropped after a few head nouns such as *day, year, time, place, way, rate,* and *reason*, and after such adverb heads as *now* and *everywhere*, leaving *that* performing adverbial functions.

> That was the day *that* we arrived in San Francisco.
> The hours *that* I waited seemed interminable.

He didn't say a word all the time *that* I was there.
The last time *that* I saw her, she was married to a musician.
That's the place *that* we bought the typewriter.
She cooks kid the way *that* they cook it in northern Mexico.
At the rate *that* he's growing, he'll be bigger than his father in
another year.
The reason *that* Miami has so many amusement places is ob-
vious.
Now *that* you know the truth, you can understand our feel-
ings.
We see him everywhere *that* we go.

Prepositions have dropped out before *that* also in interrogative
clauses such as the following, in which *that* functions as adjunct.

It was then *that* I understood.
It was there *that* we met.
Why is it *that* he worries so much?

In these three sentences *that* functions as *then, there,* and *therefore*
would function in main declaratives corresponding to the interrogatives that *that* begins here.

As has been said, in informal and even in careful styles clause-
marker *that* is commonly not expressed in subordinate-interrogative clauses for which it does not function as subject.

The house *we lived in* had almost no wood in it.
He isn't the man *we thought was coming.*
We want the best *there is.*
Rents were high the year *we were there.*

Clause-marker who.—*Who* is used as a clause marker both in
main and subordinate interrogatives. It almost always has reference to people.

Who parked that car in front of our drive?
The person *who* parked that car has no manners at all.

Stories about animals occasionally use *who* as a way of making the
characters seem human.

Once there was a polite little polar bear *who* lived in the
frozen regions of the far north.

But this is unusual. *Who* sometimes seems hardly usable even for
babies, so that *the last three babies that were born in this hospital* is

likely to seem better with *that* than it would with *who*. *Who* is a common-sex pronoun, like *you* rather than *he* and *she*. Both *he* and *she* can refer to *who*.

> *Who* left his pipe on the table?
> I wonder *who* left her purse on the table?
> I'm looking for the girl *who* left her purse on the table.

Who has three case forms: nominative *who*, objective *whom*, possessive *whose*. In all styles the nominative form is used as subject.

> *Who*'d like to go downtown with me?
> I wonder *who* owns the land.
> The men *who* fought alongside Madero and Carranza and Zapata are no longer young.

The nominative is also used as complement of *be* in all styles.

> *Who* is that man?
> Let's find out *who* that man is.

In informal styles, and to some extent even in careful styles, in main interrogatives and in subordinate interrogatives that do not follow something *who* refers to, nominative *who* is used as complement of all verbs, and as object of prepositions not brought to the front of their clauses with it.

> *Who* will the Republicans nominate?
> Hedda didn't care *who* she married.
> *Who* were you talking to when I came in?
> I am not sure *who* this letter should be addressed to.
> He's always drinking beer with heaven knows *who*.
> It's hard to remember who is in love with *who*.
> You saw *who?*

In subordinate interrogatives that do follow something *who* refers to, nominative *who* is generally avoided as complement of transitive verbs other than *be* and as object of prepositions. Objective *whom* is employed, or another phrasing is used.

> The man *whom* Hedda married was no match for her.
> The man *that* Hedda married was no match for her.
> The man Hedda married was no match for her.
> The people for *whom* Juarez struggled have not forgotten him.
> The people *that* Juarez struggled for have not forgotten him.

The people Juarez struggled for have not forgotten him.

Louise has announced her engagement to George Hancock, *whom* I believe you know.

Louise has announced her engagement to a man I believe you know—George Hancock.

The old man has two sons, one of *whom* is a doctor.

The old man has two sons, one of them a doctor.

The old man has two sons. One of them is a doctor.

Jesse Owens, *whom* many call the greatest athlete of our times, once held three world records in three different events.

Harris is the man to *whom* to speak.

Harris is the man to speak to.

Harris is the man you should speak to.

The objective form *whom* is usual as complement of transitive verbs other than *be* in formal styles and to some extent in careful styles.

Whom did the American revere? *Whom* did he condemn? No one knows *whom* the President will select.

Whom is used as object of prepositions in formal styles, and to some extent in careful styles, and the prepositions are likely to be brought to the front of their clauses along with *whom*.

To *whom* were these communications directed?

The use of *whom* as subject of a verb from which it is separated by such a sequence as the *you think* of the following sentence can be described as genteel nonstandard.

I am noting here qualifications for members and suggest that you list for us any persons *whom* you think will qualify.

The use of the objective form *whom* in face-to-face relationships is likely to seem affected. *Whom* tends to seem quite formal, and to be avoided in most constructions even in careful styles. Clause markers usually come early in their clauses, in what is felt as subject territory; and the object form *whom* has consequently come to seem inappropriate.

The possessive form *whose*, like the possessives of personal pronouns, is not given an apostrophe in the written language, which distinguishes the merged *who's* of *who's coming?* and *who's been here?* from the possessive *whose* of *whose car is that? Whose*, like *his* and the possessives of nouns, is used both as a determinative modifier and in nounal constructions.

> *Whose* car is that?
> I wonder *whose* car that is.
> *Whose* is that?
> I have no idea *whose* it is.
> Granting that Gillis' classes are the most interesting, *whose* are the most informative?
> The man *whose* ladder we borrowed lives at the corner.

In form, *who* is indifferent to number.

> Who is that girl?
> Who are those girls?

When it functions as subject without something before it that it refers to, *who* normally is used with singular verb forms in preference to plural, even where *who* clearly anticipates a plural reply.

> Who's *eating* at the Club this year?
> Who's *been invited* to the reception?
> Who *was* at the party?

All can be attached to *who* in these questions without affecting the number of the verb. In many questions, of course, there is no certainty of the number of the designation which *who* calls for.

> Who wants coffee, and who wants tea?

When *who* follows something it refers to, it transmits the number force of what it refers to.

> The people *who live* next door are musicians.
> The girl *who lives* next door is a musician.

Clause-marker whoever.—The compound *whoever* is rarely used in main interrogatives in contemporary American English, but it does occur.

> *Whoever* told you that?
> *Who in the world* told you that?

Whoever is used in subordinate-interrogative clauses that have the force of nounal heads and modifying clauses together. Uncompounded *who* is not usable in this way in contemporary English.

Whoever left the key will probably be back soon.
The person who left the key will probably be back soon.

Often *whoever* expresses indifference to identity in a way that relates it semantically to *anyone* and *no matter*.

He votes for *whoever* gets the Republican nomination.
He votes for anyone who gets the Republican nomination.
Whoever did it, it wasn't a good job.
No matter who did it, it wasn't a good job.

Whoever has an objective form *whomever* and a possessive form *whosever*. Both are avoided in informal and even in careful styles.

Whoever he marries will have to tolerate a lot.
He bores *whoever* he talks to.
We'll have to take care of the duck *whoever* it belongs to.

Often prepositions simply cannot move to the front with *whoever*; *he bores to whomever he talks* is hardly possible, being too much like *he talks to whoever* (or formal *whomever*) *he sees*, where the preposition is not a part of the interrogative clause but rather has the clause as its object. Sentences like *we'll have to take care of the dog whosever it is* are possible but infrequent.

The longer compound *whosoever* is now rarely used.

CHAPTER XVII

SIMPLEXES, REPETITIVES, COMPOUNDS

Written-language assignment of word status.—The central subject matter of grammar is the behavior of words in sentences. Sentences are of various types. Alongside single clausal sentences of many degrees of complexity—some of them clausal units within which other clausal units are contained—there are multiple sentences, split sentences, and nonclausal sentences. In speech, sentence structure is often quite careless: the more deliberate practices of the written language are a safer guide to what native users of contemporary English regard as satisfactory sentences. Words are of various types too. Written-language practice is our best guide as to what are commonly regarded as "words" and what are regarded, on the one hand, as formatives without word status (such as the *tele* of *telegraph*, the *orn* of *adorn*, the *un* of *untrue*, and the *an* of *Chilean*) and, on the other hand, as phrasal units. For the literate—for whom grammars are made—words are units that are commonly written with spacing before and after them but not inside them. The written language both expresses and helps to shape the popular view of what combinations of sounds and of letters are words and what are not.

From the point of view of grammatical analysis, written-language assignment of word status seems entirely reasonable when word status is given to minimal readily separable units. In such a sentence as *the Republicans are unhappy at the moment* the sequence of written-language words can be interrupted between successive words with comparative ease. We can put *conservative* after *the*, *certainly* after *Republicans*, *very* after *are*, *again* after *unhappy*, *exactly* after *at* (especially if we also put *present* after *the*), and *present* after *the*. Actually we can separate *Republican* and *s* by inserting *leader*, and *un* and *happy* by inserting *usually*, producing *the Republican leaders are unusually happy at the moment*. But *Republicans* is best regarded as only an inflected form of *Republican*, as *are* is of *be*; and *un* is normally bound tightly to what follows it, so that though *we met uneven terms* is phonemically very similar to *we met on even terms* we can put such words as *very* and *genuinely* between *on* and *even* but not between *un* and *even*.

Republican, *happy*, and *moment* are divisible into components whose uses in modern English are not confined to these complexes. A sophisticated analysis might recognize in these words the *re* of *real*, the *publ* of *publish*, the *ic* of *Arabic*, the *an* of *Chilean*, the *hap* of *mishap*, the *y* of *lucky*, the formative which in *movement* appears as *move* and in *motion* and *motive* as *mot*, and the *ment* of *movement*. An unsophisticated analysis might not divide these three words, since *Republican*, *republic*, and *public* are fairly distinct in their common meanings, the *hap* of *happy* is commonly distinct from that of *mishap* and *happen* in meaning, and the *mo* of *moment* is not likely to be recognized by either meaning or internal form though the *mo* of *momentum* might be recognized. *Republicans*, *unhappy*, and *moment* are "words," like *the*, *are*, and *at*, because they are clear units that are not easily interruptible but usually are readily separable from what precedes and follows them. Similarly *conform* is one word in *I conform* but *can farm* is two words in *I can farm*, where we can easily put *always* between *can* and *farm*.

Difficulties presented by written-language words.—From the point of view of grammatical analysis, written-language words are least satisfactory where there has been merging of what elsewhere are words, without development of syntactic unity. Merged forms into which, in informal styles, a number of common verbs enter freely must be treated in grammatical analysis exactly as their unmerged equivalents are treated: they must be broken apart. The *we're* of *sometimes we're wrong* may be phonemically indistinguishable from the *were* of *some times were wrong*, but *we're* is subject and predicator together here. *We're* is easily interruptible too, as in *sometimes we certainly are wrong*. The *aren't* of *we aren't here to ask favors* is main predicator and negator adjunct together, and the negator *not* really negates not the predicator *are* or even the nucleus *we are here* but *we are here to ask favors*, the focus of negation being on the adjunct of purpose *to ask favors*. (*We are here, but not to ask favors.*) The *let's* of *let's go* must be analyzed like the *let us* of *let us pray* and the *make him* of *make him stop*. Syntactically ununified forms in which verbs do not participate are less conspicuous, but occasionally their lack of syntactic unity is noteworthy. Thus the *nothing* of *nothing that I do pleases him* is really not referred to by the *that* of *that I do: that I do* is not a transform of *I do nothing*. In the main subject *nothing that I do* actually the determiner *no* has as its head the sequence *thing that I do*, and *that* refers to *thing* rather than to *nothing*. *Another* is syntactically like *the other* and *a second*, not like *other* alone. *Another boy* is usable as a subject, like *the other boy; other boy* is not. In *inasmuch* and *insofar*, *as* and *so* maintain their special relationship to following modifiers, which commonly begin with *as*.

Written-language words are also unsatisfactory where part-of-speech classification must be assigned to written-language phrases, hyphenated or unhyphenated. Thus phrasal-verb status must be assigned the following.

ad-lib	double-park
blue-pencil	dry-clean
cold-shoulder	hand-pick
court-martial	soft-soap
cross-index	window-shop

Here hyphenation indicates a relationship which stops just short of the compounding which has occurred in such verbs as *browbeat* and *daydream*, and is much closer than that of adjuncts to predicators.

Phrasal nouns fall into rather distinct subcategories. Phrases of foreign origin sometimes have noun status in English.

coup d'etat	status quo
non sequitur	Puerto Rico
sine qua non	Viet Nam

Another subcategory of phrasal nouns is made up of English words in combinations that are syntactically anomalous in nounal uses.

an about-face	too much make-believe
an also-ran	another merry-go-round

no cure-alls	those ne'er-do-wells
a free-for-all	a once-over
a good-for-nothing	their say-so
some hand-me-downs	the old so-and-so
a pitiful has-been	some stay-at-homes
no in-betweens	a great to-do
our in-laws	several ten-year-olds

Where verb-and-adverb combinations such as *blowout, setup, showdown,* and *turnover* acquire noun status, it is generally as compounds now. But when the adverb is *in* or *to,* and also when the verb looks light in comparison with the adverb, written-language-phrase status is sometimes preferred to compound status: for example, in a *run-in,* a *lean-to,* a *set-to,* and a *go-between. Have-not* and *know-how* are generally written as phrases, as in *too many have-nots* and *not enough know-how.* A third subcategory of phrasal nouns has nounal heads followed by modifiers within the phrasal units. At least in careful and formal styles, plural inflection occurs at the end of the nounal head words.

hangers-on	talkings-to	editors-in-chief
goings-on	runners-up	mothers-in-law

But this internal position for plural inflection is not a comfortable one. In informal styles phrasal nouns terminating in *in-law* are often given plural inflection at the end, as in *both my brother-in-laws are engineers.* Such a phrasal noun as *Jack-of-all-trades* will not often be pluralized. Where letters serve as nounal heads, plural inflection falls on postpositive modifiers in all styles.

three A-minuses   several B-flats

In a fourth subcategory of phrasal nouns, affixes combine with multiword units of various kinds, rather than with single words.

New Yorker	ex-world champion
Puerto Rican	submachine gun
North Carolinian	stick-to-itiveness

It is obvious that a New Yorker is not a Yorker who is new but an "er" from New York, just as an islander is an "er" from an island.

Most phrasal adjectives are syntactically similar to the phrasal nouns in which affixes combine with phrases rather than with the single words to which they attach.

| big-hearted | single-minded | uncalled-for |
| old-fashioned | thick-skinned | unheard-of |

A few phrases of foreign origin must be classified as phrasal adjectives in English.

a-la-carte   bona fide

Matter-of-fact and *spick-and-span* are phrasal adjectives of other types.

Phrasal pronouns include such ordinals as *two hundred and fourth*, the reciprocal *each other*, and the *no one* which requires classification with *nothing* and *anybody*.

Part-of-speech classification of multiword units is best avoided wherever possible. Certainly units which are hyphenated only when they are used as prepositive modifiers of nounal heads need not be classified as phrasal adjectives.

a well-educated person	a little-known fact
our better-informed citizens	some much-needed rest
an easy-going wife	a longed-for visit
old-age security	a no-account loafer

Here the hyphenated sequences are simply modifier-and-head units used as prepositive modifiers within larger units. Hyphenation is a way of showing relationships where otherwise they might not be clear in the written language. In *modern-language teaching* what is modern is the languages; in *modern language teaching* what is modern, if we can depend on the absence of hyphenation, is the teaching of languages.

Words often combine in fixed longer units which, like the words themselves, are not readily interruptible. Sometimes the words which compose such units are not readily definable individually: this is true, for example, in *hard up* and *spick-and-span*. In such units as *at once* and *French doors* the meanings of the individual words are clearer but the combinations have a fixed quality nonetheless. Phrasal proper names are units that are not easily interruptible. *Henry Bamford Parkes, the Republican Party*, and *the University of New Mexico* are all rather tightly bound units. But the words which compose fixed units such as *hard up, at once,* and *Henry Bamford Parkes* are clear and in other uses are readily separable from what precedes and follows them. Moreover writing many sequences such as these without spacing would be visually unsatisfactory. Modern English tends to avoid long and complicated words—just as at the other extreme it avoids nonsyllabic words, writing *Jack's* as one word, not as *Jack s*, even when *Jack's* is subject and predicator together or, as in *Jack's building a boat*, subject and beginning of predicator.

Written-language compounds are relatively fixed combinations of what elsewhere are words, somewhat as phrasal proper names are; but compounds are written as words rather than as phrases. Often they exist alongside phrasal units whose structure is indistinguishable. Thus *high school* and *short cut* are written as phrases but *highway* and *shortcake* are written as compound "words." If we follow written-language distinctions here, we will treat the relationships binding *high* and *school* and *short* and *cut* as matters of sentence structure and those binding *high* and *way* and *short* and *cake* as matters of word formation, in spite of the obvious inconsistency. Our simplest course will be to accept written-language distinctions in our analysis just as we do in our writing. Sometimes, of course, practice is divided: at the moment, for example, *air lines* and *airlines* both occur.

The problem of "sames."—When we ask whether two occurrences of a particular combination of sounds or of letters constitute occurrences of the same word or formative, we raise a question not to be answered without taking history into account. The evidence of history warrants our regarding the italicized words in the following pairs as "sames" in spite of the differences in meanings.

We rode in the day *coach*.
We went with the football *coach*.

A *free* press would help.
A *free* meal would help.

A mountain *range* divides the state.
An electric *range* occupies the corner.

It *took* time to convince George.
My last vaccination *took*.

Benson made me a good offer, so I took him *up*.
Benson wanted to see Montreal, so I took him *up*.

The historical evidence does not warrant our regarding the italicized words in the following pairs as sames.

> It's another *case* of measles.
> It's another *case* of beer.

> Roberts was elected in a close *race*.
> Germs are still dangerous enemies of the human *race*.

> Harriet's roast beef is always *rare*.
> Not all these books are *rare*.

> We *sounded* Russell out.
> Russell *sounded* favorable.

Similarly the evidence of history warrants our regarding the *pass* of *passive* and that of *passion* as the same, but it does not warrant our regarding the *ped* of *pedagogue* and that of *biped* as the same.

History of course includes more than origins. The following words look like clear word-plus-word compounds but in original composition were not what they seem.

> cockroach   goodby   outrage   shamefaced

Complete analysis cannot ignore origins, but the view of the structure of such words as these which now suggests itself has made itself felt in their forms and is perhaps more significant than their original composition. In *goodby*, for example, it is very hard to take the first syllable as a variant form of the word *God* now, with both its present form and the existence of such locutions as *good morning* and *good night* pulling in another direction; and the existence of *by-and-by* inevitably influences the interpretation of the second syllable of *goodby*. Such forms as *mushroom* and *shamrock* are another matter. In origin *mushroom* and *shamrock* are not combinations of the English words *mush* and *room* and *sham* and *rock*, and the meanings of *mush* and *room* and *sham* and *rock* are irrelevant to the meanings of *mushroom* and *shamrock*. Accidents of internal form are not enough to justify viewing *mushroom* and *shamrock* as anything but simplexes.

The study of the history of words and formatives is tremendously complex, and grammatical analysis obviously cannot presuppose thorough knowledge of it. Most identifications of words as "sames" in different uses are somewhat tentative. Differences in spellings are commonly relied on as indications of differences in histories, and rightly so. Thus *rain* and *rein* and *reign* are seen at once as three distinct words in spite of their identity in pronunciation. *Block* and *bloc*, *metal* and *mettle* and *plain* and *plane* are seen as separate words, in spite of identical ultimate origins, because of the differences in spellings and meanings. Minor fashions in spelling such as alone distinguish *favor* from *favour*, *theater* from *theatre*, and *dialogue* from *dialog* are of course to be dismissed as insignificant. There must be much less reliance on pronunciation than on spelling: regional differences alone would make this inevitable. Pronunciation, spelling, and meaning often unite in causing what was once a single word to be regarded as two words now. Thus *elect* and *elite*, *gentle* and *genteel*, *grammar* and *glamour*, *native* and *naive*, *prove* and *probe*, *tradition* and *treason*, *ticket* and *etiquette*, and *triumph* and *trump* are now universally regarded as separate words. Meanings are untrustworthy guides, since many words take on strange collections of them; but meanings must inevitably be taken into account. After all, it is as representatives of meanings that words exist. Meanings suggest, for example, that the *tick* which is used of the noise made by clocks and that which is used of mattress covers and that which is used of small living creatures are different words, and historical fact supports the guess.

Variant forms must be recognized, both for words and for formatives without word status. An exceptionally variable word is *will*, as the following sentences show.

> You'*ll* be here, *won*'t you?
> You *won*'t be here, *will* you?

Is and *has* include among their variants forms that in the spoken language assimilate to what precedes them, as /z/ and /s/, exactly as various inflectional endings do.

> Bill'*s* trying hard.
> Jack'*s* tried hard.

The negative prefix *in* is an exceptionally variable formative, as the following words illustrate.

ignoble	inaccurate
illegal	incomplete
impolite	irrational

History, meanings, and clear patterns of use support recognition of clusters of variants in cases like these. *Will* can replace *ll* and *wo:* the difference will be in style, or in emphasis, with word order involved in the change from *won't you?* to *will you not?* The *in* of *inaccurate* cannot replace, for example, the *ir* of *irrational*, but there is a clear pattern of use here: the variant employed in any complex is determined by the nature of the phoneme that begins the following component, just as for the indefinite article choice between the variants *a* and *an* is determined by the phoneme that begins the following word and *a usual complaint* and *an unusual complaint* occur side by side.

We had better classify all inflected forms as variants of their basic forms. As has been noted, "inflection" is of various kinds. What is actually compounding is best regarded as inflection in the case of the *self* forms of the personal pronouns and general *one*; if we are to regard considerations of syntax as of first importance, we will want to classify *himself* as an inflected variant of *he*. What were originally distinct words, as their internal forms still show, are used to fill out inflectional patterns when, for example, *went* is made a past for *go*, *people* a plural for *person*, *worse* a comparative for *bad*, and *her* a possessive for *she*. Changes within basic forms provide a more important type of inflection. Thus the past of *win* is *won* and the plural of *foot* is *feet*. The addition of inflectional endings is the commonest type of inflection in English. Thus what the written language represents by *s* is added to *destroy* to make a third person singular and to *boy* to make a plural. Sometimes the addition of inflectional endings is accompanied by changes in the forms to which the endings are added, as when in *bought* a variant of the ending usually written *ed* has been added to a variant of *buy*. One-word "inflected" forms of all these types are best regarded merely as syntactic variants of their basic forms. When auxiliaries are employed, phrasal inflected forms result. Thus *has gone* is a phrasal inflected form of *go*.

Often groups of related forms must be recognized where lack of clear patterning will hardly allow us to speak of clusters of variants. Thus though we can describe *sang* and *bled* as inflected variants of *sing* and *bleed*, we had better regard *song* and *sing* and *blood* and *bleed* simply as related words; and though we can describe the plural noun *thieves* as a variant of *thief*, we had better consider that the noun *thief* and the verb *thieve* are merely related words. In the case of *stop* and *look*, on the other hand, we had better consider that single words function both as nouns and as verbs.

Categories of words on the basis of their internal structure.—On the basis of their internal structure English words (apart from syntactically ununified mergings such as *I'm, aren't, let's,* and *another*) can be classified in four categories: simplexes, repetitives, compounds, and complexes. Subcategories of the compounds and the complexes will require notice. One-word inflected forms of words of all these varieties are of course to be classified exactly as the corresponding basic forms are classified.

The simplexes.—The category of simplexes is made up of words which do not contain components readily recognizable either as words themselves or as formatives which lack word status but, like words, have their own relationships to meanings, however tenuous these relationships may become in particular uses.

Classification as simplexes had better be assigned to practically all monosyllables except (1) such syntactically ununified merged forms as *we're, aren't,* and *let's;* (2) such monosyllabic complexes employing nonsyllabic suffixes as *truth* and *fourth;* and (3) shortened words such as *trig* and *prof*, which are used alongside unshortened *trigonometry* and *professor*, and which when analyzed would reflect the analysis given their unshortened variants.

Simplexes are not to be thought of as not divisible through historical analysis. Such words as *as, lone, lord, preach, square,* and *twit* were compounds or complexes within historic times, but their history is irrelevant to our classification here: they are now felt as simplexes. The concept of groups of simplexes sharing a common ancestry and alike marked by it need not be regarded as a contradiction in terms. The relationships between *may* and *main* need not affect classifications here, or those between *gloom* and *glum*, or between *grow* and *green*, or between *no* and *not*, or between *ride* and *road*, or between *twice* and *twin*, or between *which* and *where*, or even (as has been said) between *song* and *sing*. All such words can be classified as simplexes in terms of their place in the word stock of contemporary English, and the "meaningful fractions" seen, for example, in *twice* and *twin* can be left to the history of the language for treatment.

Many words of two or more syllables must be regarded as simplexes in modern English too. This is true of such words as the following.

barbecue	chocolate	harvest	pilgrim
borrow	either	hundred	shampoo
bottom	flabbergast	hurricane	stirrup
cannibal	fuel	Massachusetts	yellow

The feeling for syllable-sized units is strong in modern English, and acceptance of such words as these as simplexes is uneasy. From the point of view of historical analysis many such words are undoubtedly divisible. *Fuel*, for example, is composed historically of a variant of the *foc* of *focus* and a variant of the suffix *al*. In form *fuel* is not less like *focus* than *bought* is like *buy*, but *bought* and *buy* have the special relationship of inflected variant and basic form. The relationship of *fuel* to *focus* belongs to the history of the language. Similarly *vowel*, with the same Latin ancestry as *vocal*, is most naturally regarded as a simplex in modern English; but here the semantic-historical relationship of *vocalic* to *vowel* complicates the matter and makes it convenient to classify the *vocal* of *vocalic* as a variant of *vowel*.

The repetitives.—The category of repetitives is small, but it deserves notice. It includes, first of all, a few words with components repeated without change. *Poohpooh, tomtom, goodygoody*, and *hushhush* are repetitives of this kind. Much more often, repeated components are varied in the repetition. Commonly there is variation in vowels, as in *crisscross*, or in consonants, as in *hobnob*. Some components obviously have word status themselves, others do not. The repetitives have histories of varied types: whatever their histories, words such as these form a special category. Included are verbs.

crisscross	heehaw	pitterpatter	seesaw
dillydally	hobnob	poohpooh	shillyshally
flimflam	kowtow	powwow	zigzag

Nouns.

claptrap	honkytonk	mumbojumbo	singsong
hocuspocus	hubbub	picnic	tomtom
hodgepodge	knickknack	riffraff	voodoo

Adjectives.

harumscarum	hoitytoity	nambypamby	tiptop
helterskelter	humdrum	pellmell	topsyturvy
higgledypiggledy	hushhush	rolypoly	wishywashy

And at least one adverb: *willynilly*.

The taste for rhyme and alliteration which makes itself felt in many slogans, for example, is largely responsible for the existence and popularity of the repetitives. The relation between the components which make up repetitives seems to be essentially that of such repetitive coordinates as *better and better* and *tried and tried* and the *work, work, work* of *all we do is work, work, work*. But in many repetitives neither component alone can suggest the meaning of the combination. The longer repetitives are sometimes written as phrases, with hyphens.

The compounds.—The category of compounds is made up of words that are divisible into components all of which have the status in contemporary English of known words. Compounds are quite numerous. The relationships between component words are clear in the great majority of compounds, and are of very few types.

By far the largest subcategory among the compounds is made up of head-and-modifier combinations. In most compounds of this kind the head follows the modifier, but in some it precedes. Usually head-and-modifier compounds have the part-of-speech classifications of their heads. Sometimes they must be assigned other part-of-speech classifications in addition: *weekend*, for example, is a verb as well as a noun. Sometimes the head component is a verb and the modifying component is an adverb or, less typically, a noun or even an adjective.

backfire	outgrow	browbeat	typewrite
offset	underpay	proofread	foresee

In great numbers of compounds the head component is a noun and the modifying component is another noun or, less typically, an adjective, an adverb, or even a pronoun.

boathouse	playboy	blacklist	afterthought
bullfighter	shoplifter	deadline	insight
carload	shotgun	foreword	outskirts
folklore	thundershower	highbrow	underworld
honeymoon	tomcat	loudspeaker	uprising
housekeeping	weekend	shortcoming	tenpins

Noun heads precede the modifying adjective *full* in an exceptional variety of compounding.

carful   hatful   houseful   spoonful

In some compounds the head component is an adjective, sometimes gerundial or participial in origin, and the modifying component is an adverb, a noun, or even another adjective.

everlasting	underprivileged	homesick	workmanlike
ingrown	airtight	lifelike	newborn
outspoken	churchgoing	topheavy	thoroughgoing
overconfident	heartbroken	waterproof	widespread

In a few compounds the head component is an adverb and the modifying component is a pronoun.

altogether   nowhere   somehow

Adverb heads precede the modifying adverb *ever* in a few compounds.

however   whenever   wherever

In a few compounds the head component is a pronoun and the modifying component is another pronoun or even an adverb or a noun.

anyone   everyone   overmuch   selfsame

Pronoun heads precede the modifying adverb *ever* in a few compounds.

whatever   whichever   whoever

A considerable number of head-and-modifier compounds can hardly be assigned the part-of-speech classifications the heads ordinarily have. Thus heads which would ordinarily be classified as verbs often combine with modifiers to form nouns. Sometimes an adverb modifier precedes the verb head, as in *income* and *wel-*

fare. Much more commonly, especially in compounds which relatively formal styles tend to avoid, the verb head comes first.

blowout	giveaway	rakeoff	takeoff
buildup	handout	roundup	throwback
cutoff	hangover	sendoff	tossup
farewell	holdup	setback	touchdown
gadabout	letdown	shutdown	turnout
gettogether	makeup	stowaway	writeup

Comparison with verb-and-adverb sequences from which such compounds as these derive is instructive.

> Another tire blew out on the way back.
> They're building up another candidate for governor now.
> We'll have to cut the current off.

Verb heads sometimes combine with modifiers of noun, adjective, and pronoun types—most often complementary modifiers—to form noun compounds.

daredevil	spitfire	tattletale	standstill
killjoy	stopgap	diehard	cureall

Verb heads sometimes combine with complementary noun modifiers to form adjectives.

breakneck   telltale

In *maybe* the verb form *may* has combined with a complementary infinitive to form a compound adverb.

Noun heads sometimes combine with modifiers of varied types—adjectives, nouns, pronouns, adverbs—to form compounds that are not nouns. Sometimes such compounds must be classified as verbs.

shortchange

Sometimes as adjectives.

barefoot   secondhand   downtown   outside

Sometimes as adverbs.

likewise	anyway	sometime
sidewise	awhile	sometimes

Sometimes as pronouns.

anybody   everything   something   nobody

Adjective heads apparently occur in very few nonadjectival compounds, but *grownup* is a compound noun with a participial adjective as head, and *already* and *notwithstanding* are compound adverbs with adjectival heads. Pronoun heads occur in such compound adverbs as *almost* and *nevertheless*.

Preposition-and-object compounds make up a category much smaller than that of modifier-and-head compounds. Adverb status is of course syntactically normal for preposition-and-object compounds.

alongside   indeed   overboard   underfoot

In some compound adverbs of this kind the object component precedes the preposition component.

thereby   thereupon   wherein   wherewith

Some preposition-and-object compounds require classification as adjectives.

aboveboard   outdoor   underage   uphill
offhand   overnight   underground   upstairs

A few preposition-and-object compounds require classification as nouns.

afternoon   outdoors   overalls   tonight

Compounding almost always involves heads and modifiers or prepositions and objects, but in some compounds the components seem to be related in other ways and in some the nature of the relationship is not clear. In a few compounds the components seem to have the relationship of principal and appositive: for example, in the adverbs *roundabout* and *underneath*. In a few compounds the components seem to have the relationship of half head and half modifier which subjects and complements sometimes have: for example, in the noun *sundown* and in the adverb *headfirst*. In a few compounds the components seem to have the relationship of coordinates: for example, in such nouns of direction as *northeast*, in the adjective *bittersweet*, and in the adverb *henceforth*. In such nouns as *undergraduate, overtime,* and *godsend* the components are clear enough but their relationship seems less clear. This is the case also in such compound prepositional adverbs as *into* and *without* and in such exceptionally formed compound nouns as *whatnot, whereabouts,* and *wherewithal.* We must speak here of components in unanalyzed strings.

Sequences of capitalized initial letters from sequences of words sometimes form what can be regarded as compounds of an exceptional type. Examples are *IQ* and *TV*, in which the component letters are given their individual letter-name pronunciations, and UNESCO, which is pronounced as an ordinary word with such a spelling would be pronounced.

Compounding of exceptional types has inevitably received disproportionate attention here: the great majority of compounds are of head-and-modifier type, and the head components are most often nouns. Written-language compounding occurs in oddly restricted ways. Modifying nouns combine with following head nouns, as in *roommate* for example, much more freely than modifying adjectives do. Thus *high school, real estate,* and *sweet potato* are written as phrases, not as compounds. It is especially uncommon for modifiers of gerundial origin to be joined with noun heads as is done in *mockingbird.* Modifying nouns are not likely to be joined with head nouns when the total number of syllables is as high as four, so that though *bathroom* is treated as a compound *reference room* is not likely to achieve similar status. Not many compounds have more than two words as components as *teaspoonful* and *nevertheless* do. Thus though *birthday* is compounded *birthday cake* is treated as a phrase, and phrasal status is maintained for combinations such as *forget-me-nots.* Phrasal status is maintained even for many noun-and-noun combinations of the type most likely to be compounded: for example, for *boy friend, room rent, safety pin,* and *summer school.* When compounding occurs, modifying nouns are usually basic forms. Sometimes they are basic forms ordinarily not used outside compounds, as in *ashtray, oatmeal,* and *scissortail.* But plural forms occur in such compounds as *clothesbrush, newspaper, teethridge,* and *thanksgiving*; and possessives (without apostrophes) occur in such compounds as *beeswax, bridesmaid, doomsday,* and *townspeople.* Precise semantic relationships between modifiers and heads are quite varied. An armchair is a chair with arms, a mailbox is a box for mail, a taxpayer is a payer of taxes, a tomcat is a cat whose sex would make the name *Tom* appropriate. *Heartsick* means "sick at heart," *homesick* means "sick for home." Many compounds are not easily rephrased. Some compounds can offer visual difficulties. Thus *nowhere* looks like a combination of *now* and *here* as well as one of *no* and *where*, and compounds such as *beefeater, forestage, tosspot,* and *towhead* can be puzzling in the written language. *Bedraggled* has been pronounced on television, quite seriously, as though it were a combination of *bed* and *raggled.* Compounding is sometimes avoided because of visual difficulties it would produce. Thus *no one* is written as two words, though *nobody* and *someone* are written as compounds; and though *setup* is commonly treated as a compound, *run-in* is hyphenated. For such items as *awhile* and *anyway* decision between compound status and phrase status is made quite arbitrarily. *A while* is written as two words when used in nounal constructions, as in *for a while*; and such items as *all right, any more, every place, some day,* and *any time* are written as phrases rather than compounds by those who are careful of the niceties of current usage. *Awhile,* of course, is readily interruptible: *I waited a long while* is common alongside *I waited awhile. Indeed* is compounded, but *in fact, in spite (of),* and *in order (to)* are written as phrases.

When words unite in compounds, in general they keep their shapes about as well as they do in other uses. Some phonological merging does occur. *Cupboard* is a striking example of exceptional spoken-language merging; *lapboard* follows the usual pattern. *Eurasia* and *partake* are old merged compounds. Lewis Carroll's *chortle,* uniting *chuckle* and *snort,* is a merged form of somewhat different type. Commercial and journalistic English produces striking merged compounds that in the main appear to be no more than tricks to catch attention. Thus standard *service center* becomes commercial *servicenter.* Even a national association of teachers of English has employed the merged compound *counciletter* issue after issue. *Motel,* for *motor hotel,* seems to have passed into general use; *brunch,* for *breakfast-lunch,* is more restricted in use. Merged compounds differ from such merged forms as *I'm* in that they are syntactically unified.

CHAPTER XVIII

COMPLEXES

The complexes.—The category of complexes is made up of words among whose components are noninflectional formatives which do not have word status but which are recognizable, more or less readily, as meaning-conveying entities in themselves even though their contributions to the meanings of particular combinations are not always obvious. Sometimes among the components which make up complexes there are items which elsewhere have word status. This is the case in *untrue, island, raspberry, biochemistry, Chilean,* and *seventh,* where *true, land, berry, chemistry, Chile,* and *seven* are immediately recognized as words themselves in other uses, though *un,* this *is,* this *rasp, bio,* this *an,* and *th* apparently have no status as words. In some complexes all the components are formatives which lack word status. This is true in *reject, captor, bigamous, chronology,* and *omnivorous.*

Two groups of affixes—prefixes and suffixes—are commonly set up among the formatives. Classification as affixes is most often assigned to formatives which combine with numbers of English words. Such affixes can of course combine with other formatives as well as with English words. Thus the negative prefix *im* of *immovable* occurs also in *immense.* Several affixes can be employed in a single complex, but practically every complex contains at least one formative that is not an affix. Shortened words such as *semipro,* for *semiprofessional,* constitute a natural exception to this rule: such a word as *insuperable* is exceptional in a more fundamental way.

Prefixes.—Adverb-like formatives that combine with following words are most likely to be classified as prefixes. A list of prefixes widely used in the central, nontechnical body of the language might well include the following.

1. *A*, as in *afloat, alive, asleep, across, away, anew, apiece.*
2. *Ad*, as in *adjoin, administer.*
3. *Anti*, as in *anticlimax, antifreeze, antisocial.*
4. *Be*, as in *befriend, befuddle, belittle, because, below, beside.*
5. *Co*, as in *coexist, co-operate, coeducation, coworker.*
6. *De*, as in *decentralize, decode, defrost, detour, debunk, denominate, devote.*
7. *Dis*, as in *disagree, dislike, disown, disbelief, dishonest, disinterested.*
8. *En*, as in *enact, endear, enliven.*
9. *Ex*, as in *ex-president, ex-student, exchange, excommunicate, explain, exterminate.*
10. *Extra*, as in *extracurricular, extramarital.*
11. *Hyper*, as in *hypercritical, hypersensitive.*
12. *In*, as in *indigestion, inequality, inadequate, indefinite, invaluable.*
13. *Inter*, as in *interact, intermarry, intermeddle, inter-American, intercollegiate.*
14. *Mis*, as in *misinterpret, misprint, misspell, misadventure, mishap, mistake.*
15. *Non*, as in *nonaggression, nonconductor, nonsense, nonexistent, nonintoxicating, nonpartisan.*
16. *Post*, as in *postdate, postscript, postgraduate.*
17. *Pre*, as in *prearrange, prepay, prerequisite, preview, pre-Christian, prehistoric, prenatal.*
18. *Pro*, as in *pro-British, prolabor, pronoun, proportion.*
19. *Re*, as in *reelect, reprint, recommend, remark, remove.*
20. *Sub*, as in *subdivide, sublease, subcommittee, subhead, subway, subconscious, subnormal.*
21. *Super*, as in *superimpose, supersaturate, superstructure, superman, supernatural.*
22. *Trans*, as in *transplant, transship, transatlantic.*
23. *Ultra*, as in *ultraconservative, ultrafashionable.*
24. *Un*, as in *unbelief, unrest, uneasy, uneducated, unexciting, unfriendly, unlike, unwell,* and as in *unbutton, uncover, unlock.*

Only a few of the prefixes listed above are native in origin: *a, be,* in part *mis,* and *un. A* originated as an unstressed variant of several prepositions, *be* as an unstressed variant of *by,* and *mis* (to the extent that it is native in origin) as an unstressed variant of the *miss* of *amiss.* Some complexes beginning with *a* often seem archaic or literary: *on foot* is now commoner than *afoot,* and *in bed* than *abed.* A curiosity of word formation is the literary *a-borning* of

what then was the theme of the play that thus died a-borning? Negative
un is apparently both the most used of all English prefixes and the
one farthest from word status. Clear word-and-word compounds
such as *overeat* and *outdo* have been much more characteristic of
English word formation than prefix-and-word complexes.

Many complexes made up of nonnative prefixes and English
words were formed outside English. In general, the nonnative prefixes listed above have word status in the languages from which
they were acquired, and some of them are used in English in
borrowed phrases such as *ad hoc, de facto, non sequitur,* and *sub rosa.*
Pro and *con* acquire word status in *the pros and cons; ad, con, pro,*
and *sub* are sometimes used as shortenings of *advertisement, confidence* (in *con man*) and *convict, professional,* and *submarine.* Exceptional uses of prefixes with implied following components occur.

There are cold drinks available, alcoholic and non-.

Extra is an English adjective in *an extra shirt* and in informal *extra
big.* The distinction between the "prefix" *en* of *endear* and the word
in of *income* and *inflame* is obviously arbitrary. A number of the
nonnative prefixes listed have variants which deserve notice. Such
variants occur in *accompany, affirm, agglutinate, allocate, ammuni-
tion, annul, approximate, arrange, assure, attune,* and *abase*; in
collateral, commission, condescend, correlate; in *diffusion*; in *em-
bitter, impart, irradiate*; in *evocation, efface*; in *ignoble, illegal, im-
patient, irresponsible*; in *suffix, suppress*; in *surcharge.* Many of the
complexes in which nonnative prefixes occur have the flavor of
careful and formal styles.

Under certain circumstances, hyphens separate prefixes from the
components with which they unite. The hyphens in *non-Catholic,
pre-Christian,* and *pro-British* simply permit the retention of capital
letters: *transatlantic* and *unchristian* are exceptional in dropping
the capitals. *Co-op* and *co-ed* would offer exceptional visual difficulties if they were written unhyphenated. Hyphens are sometimes
employed in such a complex as *re-form* to indicate that the combination is a fresh one: *re-form* means simply "form again," whereas
reform generally implies improvement. *Ex* is a special case: when
it has the meaning of "former" it is followed by a hyphen regularly,
when it has other meanings it is not.

The negative prefixes deserve special notice. As has been said, negation is concerned with meanings of dissent or difference. *Un* is the most widely used of the negative prefixes, but *non* enters into new complexes more freely than *un* does, though *non* also tends to seem a little formal perhaps. Native *un* is used alongside *dis*, *mis*, and (most of all) *in* in related complexes.

unable	inability	undigested	indigestion
uncivil	incivility	unequal	inequality
uncomfortable	discomfort	unfortunate	misfortune
uncompleted	incomplete	ungrateful	ingratitude
uncomprehending	incomprehension	unsanitary	insane
undecided	indecision	unstable	instability

Words terminating in *ing, ed, able*, and *ful* are likely to be made negative by *un*. In general, the use of nonnative terminations is likely to be accompanied by the use of nonnative negative prefixes rather than *un*. It is noteworthy that negative prefixes are sometimes attached to forms that are rarely used without the prefixes.

ungainly   unprecedented   unspeakable

Here the negated complexes have simply proved more useful than the corresponding unnegated forms. In *unloosen* and *disgruntle* there is not really negation of the components which follow the prefixes; rather, there is intensification perhaps.

It is possible to set up a small subcategory of prefixes characteristically used not with English words but with other formatives. The following adverblike formatives—some of them with variant forms not noted here—would be included in such a subcategory.

1. *A*, as in *apathy* (and *amoral*).
2. *Ab*, as in *abominate* (and *abnormal*).
3. *Ana*, as in *analogy*.
4. *Ante*, as in *antecedent* (and *anteroom*).
5. *Apo*, as in *apology*.
6. *Cata*, as in *catalogue*.
7. *Circum*, as in *circumference* (and *circumlocution*).
8. *Dia*, as in *diagonal*.
9. *Epi*, as in *episode*.
10. *Hypo*, as in *hypochondria*.
11. *Intra*, as in *intravenous* (and *intramural*).
12. *Meta*, as in *metabolism* (and *metaphysics*).
13. *Ob*, as in *object*.

14. *Para*, as in *paragon*.
15. *Retro*, as in *retrospection* (and *retroactive*).
16. *Se*, as in *segregate*.
17. *Per*, as in *perfect* (and *perform*).
18. *Syn*, as in *synchronize*.

It is also possible to include among the prefixes formatives of numeral and adjectival types: for example, the *bi* of *bifocal* and the *mono* of *monotone*. But formatives of these types frequently combine with suffixes, as in *binary* and *monism;* and prefixes of less dubious types normally combine only with words and non-affixal formatives.

Suffixes.—Classification as suffixes is most often assigned to formatives, themselves without word status, which follow numbers of English words and combine with them to form complexes. Suffixes commonly determine part-of-speech classifications for the complexes they terminate. A few commonly terminate verbs.

1. *Ate*, as in *authenticate, captivate, motivate*.
2. *En*, as in *blacken, quicken, weaken, frighten, strengthen, lessen*.
3. *Er*, as in *waver, patter*.
4. *Ize*, as in *centralize, nationalize, characterize, pasteurize, scandalize, revolutionize*.
5. *Le*, as in *crackle, crumble, snuggle, fondle*.

From the point of view of history, verb forms terminating in *ate* are perhaps best seen simply as variants of forms without this *ate*, as *illuminate*, going back to a Latin past-participial stem, is in origin a variant of *illumine*, going back to the corresponding Latin infinitival stem; but in modern English where pairs such as *captive* and *captivate* exist it seems reasonable to regard *ate* as a verb-making suffix. The suffix *en* which terminates verbs is comparable in internal form with the suffix which terminates such adjectives as *wooden* and with the inflectional endings employed in such plurals as *oxen*, such participles as *fallen, thrown*, and *done*, and such pronoun forms as *mine* and *none*. It is strikingly like the prefix *en* of *endear* in both meaning and form, so that in *enliven*, as compared with *deaden* and *endear*, there seems to be repetition both of form and of meaning. Frequentative-diminutive *er* and *le* are not likely to be noticed except in fairly sophisticated analysis, but they are felt.

A list of suffixes which commonly terminate nouns will have to be longer.

6. *Ade*, as in *blockade, escapade, lemonade.*
7. *Age*, as in *breakage, postage, shortage, percentage.*
8. *Al*, as in *refusal, rental, trial.*
9. *An*, as in *Ohioan, Tennesseean, Chilean.*
10. *Ance*, as in *allowance, clearance, forbearance, utterance.*
11. *Ant*, as in *assistant, claimant, disinfectant.*
12. *Ard*, as in *drunkard, dullard, laggard.*
13. *Cy*, as in *bankruptcy, captaincy.*
14. *Dom*, as in *boredom, freedom, officialdom.*
15. *Ee*, as in *absentee, draftee, employee.*
3. *Er*, as in *patter.*
16. *Er*, as in *baker, burner, reader, islander, officer, Vermonter, goner, outsider.*
17. *Ery*, as in *bakery, distillery, machinery, scenery, snobbery.*
18. *Ese*, as in *Japanese, journalese.*
19. *Ess*, as in *hostess, stewardess.*
20. *Ette*, as in *kitchenette, statuette.*
21. *Hood*, as in *childhood, neighborhood, falsehood.*
22. *Ice*, as in *cowardice, justice, notice, service.*
23. *Ing*, as in *shirting, inning.*
24. *Ion*, as in *rebellion, action, confession.*
25. *Ism*, as in *determinism, alcoholism, egoism, idealism, Lutheranism.*
26. *Ist*, as in *tourist, typist, faddist, novelist, idealist, defeatist.*
27. *Itis*, as in *sinusitis, tonsilitis.*
28. *Ity*, as in *conformity, absurdity, oddity.*
5. *Le*, as in *ripple, sparkle, sniffle, speckle.*
29. *Let*, as in *booklet, cutlet, ringlet.*
30. *Ling*, as in *duckling, yearling, hireling, underling.*
31. *Ment*, as in *abandonment, amazement, befuddlement, merriment.*
32. *Ness*, as in *clumsiness, meanness, naturalness, sameness.*
33. *Ship*, as in *courtship, dictatorship, instructorship, salesmanship, hardship, membership, township.*
34. *Ster*, as in *gangster, teamster, youngster.*
35. *Th*, as in *growth, warmth.*
36. *Ude*, as in *solicitude, quietude.*
37. *Ure*, as in *architecture, composure, failure.*
38. *Y*, as in *assembly, destiny, flattery, warranty.*
39. *Y*, as in *Billy, dolly, sonny.*

Variant forms of some of these suffixes require notice. Thus for modern English the *ence* of *adherence, correspondence,* and *occur-*

rence is best regarded as a variant of *ance,* and the *ent* of *corre-spondent* and *superintendent* and the *ante* of *vigilante* as variants of *ant.* The *art* of *braggart* is a variant of *ard.* The *aire* of *concessionaire,* the *ar* of *liar,* the *eer* of *mountaineer,* the *ier* of *cashier,* the *or* of *governor,* and the *yer* of *lawyer* are most conveniently regarded as variants of an *er* suffix which, like the prefix *mis,* is partly native and partly nonnative in origin. The *ry* of *jewelry* and *chemistry* and the *ary* of *dictionary* and *tributary* can be regarded as variants of *ery.* The *et* of *islet* and *couplet* is a variant of *ette,* the *ty* of *cruelty* and *safety* and the *te* of *naivete* are variants of *ity,* the *t* of *height* is a variant of the *th* of *growth,* and the *ie* of *Annie* and *Charlie* is a variant of the *y* of *Billy.* The suffixes *er* of *patter, er* of *baker,* and *ing* of *shirting* are identical in their internal forms with the in-flectional endings of *bigger* and *playing. Stranger* can be either an inflected adjective or a noun complex.

> Jack's point of view seems *stranger* than ever.
> You're almost a *stranger* here.

A number of suffixes commonly terminate adjectives.

40. *Able,* as in *likable, commendable, comfortable, objectionable, perishable, marriageable, peaceable, suitable, personable.*
8. *Al,* as in *conditional, clinical, tidal, continual.*
9. *An,* as in *Chilean, Lutheran, Roman, republican.*
11. *Ant,* as in *buoyant, pliant.*
17. *Ary,* as in *customary dietary, revolutionary, secondary.*
1. *Ate,* as in *considerate, affectionate, compassionate.*
41. *Ed,* as in *talented, moneyed, bigoted.*
42. *En,* as in *golden, silken, wooden.*
43. *Ern,* as in *eastern, northern.*
18. *Ese,* as in *Japanese, Siamese.*
44. *Ful,* as in *beautiful, hopeful, forgetful, resentful.*
45. *Ic,* as in *basic, choleric, scenic.*
46. *Ish,* as in *bookish, Danish, selfish, outlandish, youngish, reddish, offish.*
47. *Ive,* as in *active, constructive, defective, plaintive.*
48. *Less,* as in *tireless, aimless, coatless, mannerless.*
49. *Ly,* as in *bodily, disorderly, monthly, deadly, likely, lonely, sickly, leisurely, scholarly.*
50. *Ous,* as in *dangerous, cavernous, famous, murderous, con-tinuous, solicitous.*
51. *Some,* as in *troublesome, meddlesome, venturesome, lonesome, tiresome.*

52. *Ward*, as in *homeward, wayward, backward, forward.*
53. *Y*, as in *bony, slippery, windy, sticky, folksy.*

Here again variant forms of some of the suffixes listed require notice. Thus the *ible* of *contemptible, digestible, gullible,* and *sensible* occurs alongside the *able* of *comfortable*; the *ar* of *consular, polar,* and *linear* and the *ile* of *infantile* and *servile* occur alongside the *al* of *continual* and *lineal, ar* occurring especially after *l*; the *ent* of *absorbent* and *different* occurs alongside the *ant* of *buoyant*; the *ory* of *conciliatory* and *supervisory* occurs alongside the *ary* of *customary*; the *ite* of *composite* and *definite* occurs alongside the *ate* of *considerate*; and the *ose* of *verbose* occurs alongside the *ous* of *famous.* Some adjectives employ both *ic* and *al* where a single suffix would seem sufficient: this is the case in *alphabetical, methodical, nonsensical,* and *spherical*; *economical* generally differs from *economic* in meaning. The suffix *ed* of *moneyed* is of course identical in internal form with the inflectional ending *ed* of *played.*

A few suffixes commonly terminate adverbs.

49. *Ly*, as in *happily, longingly, heatedly, partly, namely, mostly, overly.*
52. *Ward*, as in *afterward, toward.*

When *ly* is added to adjectives ending in the suffix *ic*, the suffix *al* is normally interposed in the written language (though it may not appear in the spoken), as in *authentically, basically, diplomatically, dramatically,* and *heroically. Publicly* has no *al.*

A few suffixes commonly terminate pronouns.

54. *Teen*, as in *fourteen, sixteen.*
55. *Th*, as in *fourth, hundredth, nth.*
56. *Ty*, as in *sixty, seventy.*

Eth occurs as a variant of *th* used after the suffix *ty*, in such complexes as *twentieth* and *sixtieth.* The *th* of *fourth* is of course identical in internal form with the *th* of *growth.*

About half of the suffixes listed above are native in origin. The language has long used suffixes much more extensively than prefixes. Problems in classification of course occur. *Able* and *full* are adjectives with meanings not very different from those most often expressed by the "suffixes" *able* and *ful: blamable* and *careful* can be regarded as word-and-word compounds comparable to *blame-*

worthy, *carefree*, and *carful*. The occasional use of *ism* and *teens* as nouns is obviously derived from their use as suffixes, and is clearly of minor importance among the uses made of these items. The *ly* of such adverbs as *rapidly* could be regarded as an inflectional ending added to many adjectives when these are used in the functions commonly described as adverbial, just as a possessive ending is added to many nouns when these are used as determiners. It seems wise to follow the tradition in matters such as these. Another problem arises from the circumstance that Latin and Greek word formation employed formatives commonly called "stems" where modern English word formation has words. It is not always clear where such stems end and suffixes begin. But precise historical accuracy in this matter is not of primary importance to the grammar of contemporary English. Whenever it is possible to do so, word formation in English can most conveniently be thought of as conforming to the pattern which most simply describes genuinely native word formation. Thus *notable* is best thought of as a complex made up of the verb *note* and the suffix *able*, in the same way that *likable* is made up of the verb *like* and the suffix *able*. Whether the original stem was *not* or *nota*, and the original suffix the Latin precursor of *able* or simply of *ble* (as the existence of *digestible* and *soluble* suggests) is hardly relevant for modern English. Similarly *dedication* is most conveniently regarded, in modern English, as a complex made up of the verb *dedicate* and the suffix *ion*.

The association of particular suffixes with particular parts of speech is by no means exclusive. Thus *blockade*, *package*, *spiral*, *engineer*, *service*, and *station* must all be classified as verbs as well as nouns, though they end in fundamentally nounal suffixes. *Doubtless* is an adverb now rather than an adjective, as comparison of *doubtless leaders are needed* and *fearless leaders are needed* shows. *Favorite* is a noun, not an adjective; hence the insistence on *favorites* rather than *favorite* in *these songs are favorites now*. *Music* is a noun, not an adjective; *directive* and *weekly* are nouns as well as adjectives, and *directive* seems to be used as a noun more than as an adjective. Complexes terminating in suffixes have their individual histories and consequently their individual ranges of use, just as other words do. Complexes are sometimes so far from the meanings of their components that relationships are likely to remain unsuspected. Thus the complexes *embrace* and *bracelet* are not now likely to be thought of as related to the noun and verb *brace*, and the complex *steady* is not likely to be related to the second component of the compound *bedstead*. *Emergency* is far from *emergence* in its usual meanings, and *hospitality* from *hospital*. *Objective* and *objection* seem quite distinct in their common meanings; so, for that matter, do the noun *object* and the verb *object*. *Traction* and *tract* have very different meanings.

Suffixes tend to unite with words belonging to particular parts of speech. Thus *ful* and *less* generally unite with nouns, as in *hopeful* and *hopeless*, and *ness* generally unites with adjectives, as in *sadness* and *hopelessness*. The *ly* which terminates adjectives unites with nouns ordinarily, as in *leisurely* and *monthly*; and generally the *ly* that terminates adverbs unites with adjectives, as in *sadly* and *hopefully*. But untypical combinations are frequent. Thus *forgetful*, *resentful*, and *tireless* have verbs as first components, and *sameness* has a pronoun as first component. The adjective complexes *deadly* and *sickly* have adjectives as first components, not nouns; and the adverb complexes *partly*, *mostly*, and *overly* have noun, pronoun, and adverb first components.

It is possible to recognize a small subcategory of suffixes which characteristically combine not with words but with other formatives. The following formatives might well be included in this subcategory.

1. *And*, as in *multiplicand*.
2. *Esce*, as in *effervesce*.
3. *Id*, as in *humid*.
4. *Ine*, as in *genuine*.
5. *Ish*, as in *finish*.
6. *Mony*, as in *matrimony*.
7. *Oid*, as in *anthropoid*.
8. *Or*, as in *humor*.
9. *Osis*, as in *psychosis*.

Indication of sex, nationality, smallness, direction of predication.—The *ess* of *hostess* is the only suffix used in a significant number of nouns to indicate sex, and the use even of *ess* is not really very extensive. The "gender" of English nouns is ordinarily not indicated by their internal forms at all. *That boy* is referred to as *he*, and *that toy* as *it*. *Harry* is normally referred to as *he*, and

Mary as *she*. *That cat* can be referred to as *he*, *she*, or *it*, depending partly on the sex of the cat and partly on whether the cat is regarded as a personality or not. Actually *Harry* would be referred to as *she* if the name were given seriously to a girl, and *Mary* as *he* if this name were given seriously to a boy—though if, for example, the name *Mary* were applied to a boy sarcastically, the pronoun *she* would probably refer to it, continuing the sarcasm. It remains true that English has categories of nouns that are characteristically limited in their application by considerations of sex. Nouns with applications of various kinds are ordinarily thus limited.

Most given names of people, and of pets, dolls, and toy animals, indicate sex, real or fictitious. Mostly, as has been said, this is not a matter of any common internal form: it is a matter of the usual assignment of some names to males and others to females. But such terminations as the *ine* of *Pauline* and *Josephine* and the *ette* of *Henriette* do sometimes serve to distinguish feminine forms from masculine. Sometimes sex is indicated in the written language and not in the spoken, as when *Francis*, *Billy*, and *Joe* are used for boys and *Frances*, *Billie*, and *Jo* for girls.

Words used in direct address, both in face-to-face communication and in letters, and words used as honorific modifiers of proper names often indicate sex. The *sir* and *gentlemen* of direct address are for men, the *ma'am*, *madam*, and *ladies* for women. The commonest honorific modifiers of proper names—*Mr.*, *Miss*, and *Mrs.* —indicate sex; *Miss* and *Mrs.* indicate marital status also, though less dependably. Ecclesiastical honorifics such as *Brother*, *Sister*, and *Father* indicate sex; so do such ancient honorifics as *King* and *Queen*, and such family honorifics as the *Uncle* of *Uncle Carl* and the *Aunt* of *Aunt Mary*. Sex is indicated twice in such a designation as *Aunt Mary*, where the honorific is used with a given name; it is indicated only in the honorific in such a designation as *Mrs. James M. Whitney*, which would name a different person if the honorific were dropped. Some honorifics used with proper names, such as *doctor*, are usable without reference to sex.

Nouns applied to people in their relationships to home, family, marriage, courtship, and similar intimate aspects of life commonly indicate sex clearly. This is true of *father, husband, brother, son, grandfather, grandson, uncle, nephew, lover, bridegroom, bachelor, widower,* and *host;* and of the feminine counterparts of these words. But *parent, child, grandparent, cousin, relative, friend,* and *guest* are applied freely to members of both sexes. In such pairs as *fiancé* and *fiancée* there is distinction in the written language but not in the spoken. *Widower* is grammatically exceptional in giving a distinguishing suffix not to the form applied to the female but to that applied to the male. *Blonde* and *ingénue* are used only of women.

A few nationality nouns indicate sex. This is true of the compounds *Dutchman, Englishman, Frenchman, Irishman, Scotchman,* and *Welshman.* Corresponding feminine compounds such as *Englishwoman* are likely to be avoided.

Nouns applied to divinities and quasi-divinities, and those applied to holders of positions in social and ecclesiastical hierarchies coming down from the medieval and earlier past, or to those engaged in activities of a supernatural or at least extraordinary character, commonly indicate sex. This is true of *god, devil, pope, emperor, king, prince, lord, duke, bishop, count, knight, sir, gentleman, rector, priest, monk, master, heir, godfather, wizard,* and *hero;* and of their feminine equivalents where there are such. But *saint* and *peasant* can be applied to members of either sex.

Nouns applied to people as members of occupational and social groupings characteristic of present-day life sometimes indicate sex. In *man, boy, woman,* and *girl* sex is of course of central interest; *person, child,* and *baby* ignore it. Compounds ending in *man* and *master* and the feminine equivalents show sex: examples are *congressman, laundryman, milkman, policeman, salesman,* and *postmaster;* and *congresswoman, policewoman, washerwoman,* and *postmistress.* Such nouns as *actor, alumnus, farmer, landlord, masseur,* and *waiter* are normally applied only to men, though *actor* and *farmer* are sometimes applied also to women. *Actress, alumna, landlady, masseuse, salesgirl, waitress, co-ed, housewife,* and *seamstress* are applied only to women. Two-word designations such as *delivery boy, chorus girl,* and *repair man* are applicable only to members of a single sex. The modern tendency in English is to ignore sex in designations of members of occupational groupings and the like. There is no sex limitation for such words as *architect, artist, author, clerk, cook, dancer, doctor, editor, instructor, judge, librarian, manager, minister, musician, patient, pianist, preacher, president, principal, professor, student, reporter,* and *teacher.* Even a few compounds terminating in *man* have become applicable to members of both sexes: for example, *chairman, freshman,* and *spokesman.* Forms such as *poetess* and *aviatrix* are avoided.

Some nouns which are applied to animals are applicable only to those of a single sex. Thus *stallion* and *gelding, bull* and *steer* and *ox, ram* and *wether, boar, tomcat, rooster* and *cock, drake,* and *gander* can be applied only to males; and *mare, cow, ewe, sow,* and *hen* can be applied only to females. Words applied to the young are generally indifferent to sex: this is true of *colt, calf, lamb, duckling, gosling, kitten,* and *chick.* Most nouns applied to wild animals ignore sex: for example, *deer, lion, tiger, elephant, wolf, squirrel,* and *rabbit. Buck* is applicable only to males; *doe, lioness,* and *tigress* only to females. *Horse, cattle, sheep, pig* and *hog, cat, chicken, duck, goose, dog,* and *goat* are all applicable to males and females alike. Increasing urbanization is of course causing decreasing interest in sex distinctions in nonhuman forms of life; city people are likely not to know what a drake, for example, is.

There is considerable use of modifying words to indicate sex: for example, in *boy friend, woman doctor,* and *female kitten.*

The formation of adjectives and nouns of nationality deserves notice. The favored pattern employs the suffix *an* to form complexes which are both nouns applied to people and adjectives. All New World nationalities have words employing this suffix, united more often than not with a formative which is a variant of the name of the country, as in *Brazilian* and *Cuban. Argentinian* is in competition with *Argentine,* which seems to have wider use. Many adjectives and nouns of nationality for other parts of the world employ *an* also: for example, *Australian, Egyptian, Italian, Norwegian,* and *Russian. Arabian* is an adjective; the corresponding noun applied to people is *Arab.* The noun *Spaniard* employs the suffix *ard,* which is derogatory in most of its uses but is not so felt in *Spaniard.* Various adjectives and nouns of nationality employ the suffix *ese:* for example, *Chinese, Japanese,* and *Portuguese.* The adjective *Icelandic* employs *ic,* and such adjectives as *Danish, English, Finnish, Polish, Spanish,* and *Turkish* employ *ish.* The nouns of nationality are distinct here—*Icelander, Dane, English-man* (for males), *Finn, Pole, Spaniard, Swede,* and *Turk*—but the adjectives are also used as names of languages. Adjectives and nouns based on names of continents characteristically employ *an:* for example, *African, Asian, European,* and phrasal *South American.* Nouns applied to natives, and sometimes to residents, of states within the United States most often employ the suffix *an:* for example, *Californian, Ohioan,* and *Texan. Vermonter* and *New Yorker* employ *er. New Yorker* is also applied to natives and residents of New York City. Other cities in the United States seem not to have equally well established nouns to apply to their natives and residents, though various Old World cities have adjectives and nouns in *an,* such as *Athenian, Parisian, Roman,* and *Venetian.* Regional nouns in *er* include *Southerner* and such phrasal nouns as *Middle Westerner* and *New Englander.* Adjectives and nouns for religious groups are often in *an:* for example, *Christian, Confucian, Episcopalian, Lutheran,* and *Mohammedan. Protestant, Quaker,* and *Methodist* illustrate the use of other suffixes in adjectives and nouns. *Jewish* is an adjective only. Adjectives in *an* are sometimes based on the names of those who have influenced the world in fields other than religion: for example, *Aristotelian, Darwinian, Elizabethan, Freudian, Marxian, Rabelaisian,* and *Shakespearean. Marxian* competes with *Marxist,* which seems to be established as an adjective as well as a noun; *Napoleonic* employs *ic.* Adjectives and nouns for political parties sometimes employ *an,* as in *Republican,* and sometimes *ist,* as in *Socialist. Democratic,* in *ic,* is an adjective only.

Names of languages are generally quantifiable nouns identical in form with corresponding adjectives of nationality: for example, *Italian, Chinese, Icelandic, English,* and *Dutch. Arabic* is commonly used for the language of the Arabs, not *Arabian.*

There is much less feeling for diminutives in English than there is in, for example, Spanish. A number of diminutive suffixes are employed, however: notably the *ette* of *kitchenette,* the *le* of *sparkle,* the *let* of *booklet,* the *ling* of *duckling,* and the *y* of *sonny.* The *y* of *sonny* belongs largely to the language of children. Diminutives, of course, can easily be made derogatory in force. *Underling, hireling*, and *weakling* are generally derogatory, and *sonny* can be given similar emotional force. The *ard* of *drunkard* and *laggard* seems to be the only rather consistently derogatory suffix.

Something essentially the same as the direction of predication of verbs is notable in many noun and adjective complexes and, in part at least, seems to center in the suffixes. Complexes terminating in the *er* of *baker* tend to have common-voice force: a baker bakes, an employer employs. Complexes terminating in the *ee* of *employee* tend to have passive force: an employee is employed, a trainee is trained. Complexes terminating in the *able* of *commendable* tend to have passive force: what is commendable can be commended, what is endurable can be endured. Sometimes pairs of complexes seem to differ in a kind of incorporated direction of predication. A contemptuous person expresses contempt, a contemptible person receives it. A respectful person expresses respect, a respectable person is the object of respect. But once again, every complex has its own history and its own set of uses. Some complexes have common-voice force in one use and passive in another. A hopeful person hopes, a hopeful situation is the object of hope. Readers read when they are people, are read when they are books. Employees are employed, but absentees absent themselves. What is commendable can be commended, but what is suitable suits. Tourists tour, but defeatists are defeated or feel that they are. The complexes must be known as wholes.

It is a curiosity of English word formation that often nonnative adjectives occur alongside native nouns where native adjective complexes might be expected. Examples follow.

island, insular   sea, marine
lip, labial   water, aqueous
moon, lunar   will, voluntary

Watery and *willful* exist, of course, but are often emotional. Native *nightly* exists alongside *night*, but is commonly frequentative in force whereas nonnative *nocturnal* is not. *Old* and *age* are an exceptional pair in that the adjective is native and the noun not.

Nonaffixal formatives.—In addition to the formatives which are conveniently grouped as prefixes and suffixes, English employs great numbers of formatives not ordinarily so grouped. Many of

these are clearly variants of English words in origin. The complex
numerals terminating in *teen, ty,* and *th* include obvious examples
at the heart of the ancient native vocabulary.

two		twen ty	
three	thir teen	thir ty	thir d
four		for ty	
five	fif teen	fif ty	fif th
eight	eigh teen	eigh ty	eigh th
nine			nin th
twelve			twelf th

Noun complexes terminating in nonsyllabic *th* provide further
examples of the use of formatives which are clearly variants of
common native words.

bear	bir th	long	leng th
broad	bread th	slow	slo th
dead	dea th	strong	streng th
deep	dep th	wide	wid th
foul	fil th	young	you th

New World adjectives and nouns of nationality provide examples
of the use of formatives which are variants of words belonging to a
more recently acquired vocabulary.

Americ an	Canadi an	Ecuadori an	Nicaragu an
Argentini an	Columbi an	Guatemal an	Panamani an
Bolivi an	Costa Ric an	Hondur an	Peruvi an
Brazili an	Cub an	Mexic an	Venezuel an

Most of the formatives which are readily seen as variants of
English words are not native in origin. Various circumstances
account for their existence. The union of suffixes and words of
foreign origin which terminate in foreign inflectional endings is
normally accompanied by loss of the foreign inflectional endings.

asphyxi ate	deliri ous	mor al	phenomen al
bacteri al	epitom ize	nucle ar	seri al
catastroph ic	fin al	odi ous	skelet al
cosm ic	foc al	optim ist	stimul ant
crani al	minim ize	orchestr al	vacu ous

Modern developments of old inflectional endings, and terminations
felt as equivalent to these, are similarly dropped.

| Buddh ist | Cub an | pian ist | Puerto Ric an |
| Chin ese | Mexic an | punctili ous | Tex an |

This is of course not typical English word formation: fundamentally it is Latin and Greek word formation, manipulating stems rather than words, carried into English. But in such a complex as *tropical*, which is best related to *tropics* rather than *tropic*, the native inflectional ending *s* can be said to be dropped.

Rather similar differences between words and the corresponding formatives used before suffixes appear where *le* and *y* disappear in compounding. When adjectives terminating in *le* unite with the suffix *ly*, what is most conveniently regarded as loss of *le* occurs.

| ab ly | feeb ly | peaceab ly | subt ly |
| doub ly | gent ly | sing ly | understandab ly |

Such a native adjective as *fickle* may tend to refuse union with *ly*. What from the point of view of English is best regarded as loss of *y* before a suffix occurs in complexes following patterns not native in origin.

anarch ist	biolog ist	econom ize	iron ic
bigam ous	calor ic	geograph er	occup ant
biograph er	colon ist	harmon ize	tyrann ous

A great number of variant forms appear before suffixes because of the use in Latin word formation of two verb stems, one of them conveniently derived from the infinitive and the other from the past participle. Latin past-participial stems are commonly marked, in written English, by the use of either the letter *t* or the letter *s*, somewhat as participial forms of English verbs are commonly marked by the use of *ed* and *t*. Sometimes both infinitival stems and participial stems have in effect become English words, with written forms either still close to those of Latin or altered because of use in French. In the following pairs the Latin infinitival stems have provided English with verbs and the Latin participial stems with nouns or adjectives. The Latin "stems" are here complex.

applaud, applause	exceed, excess
conceive, concept	expand, expanse
consider, considerate	extend, extent
despair, desperate	impel, impulse
determine, determinate	impinge, impact

offend, offense
pretend, pretense
proceed, process
produce, product
pursue, pursuit

recur, recourse
resolve, resolute
revert, reverse
succeed, success
transcribe, transcript

In the following pairs both stems have provided English with verbs.

confound, confuse
construe, construct
convince, convict
deduce, deduct
design, designate
dissemble, dissimulate
esteem, estimate

illumine, illuminate
imply, implicate
oblige, obligate
pursue, prosecute
repel, repulse
require, request
restrain, restrict

Sometimes English has Latin past-participial stems as words but does not give the corresponding infinitival stems equivalent status. The following English verbs, some of them also nouns or adjectives, are in effect Latin past-participial stems.

abominate	delete	exact	pollute
appreciate	deliberate	execute	prevent
attract	deviate	exhibit	radiate
attribute	dominate	exhilarate	respect
celebrate	educate	expedite	select
collect	effect	impress	separate
communicate	eject	instigate	stimulate
compensate	elect	instruct	subtract
confess	elongate	intoxicate	supervise
confiscate	equate	object	terminate
constitute	erect	palpitate	tolerate
correct	erupt	penetrate	unite

Sometimes English has Latin infinitival stems as words but not Latin past-participial stems. The following English verbs are in effect Latin infinitival stems, most of them complex in structure.

absorb	conserve	imagine	prolong
acquire	console	infringe	provide
adapt	contend	introduce	publish
affirm	converse	inveigh	reconcile
apply	deify	invoke	repeat
coalesce	derive	move	retain
compare	destroy	permit	reveal
compel	exclude	prepare	satisfy
compete	glorify	present	solve

Some suffixes of Latin origin are often combined with Latin
infinitival stems which lack word status in English though the
corresponding past-participial stems have such status. This is true
of *ant* (and its variant *ent*) in particular; it is also true of *able* (and
its variant *ible*).

abomin able	corrig ible	exig ent	separ able
appreci able	educ able	expedi ent	stimul ant
celebr ant	effici ent	intoxic ant	termin able
communic ant	elig ible	penetr able	toler able
constitu ent	exhilar ant	radi ant	toler ant

Other suffixes of Latin origin are often combined with past-participial stems which lack word status in English though the corresponding infinitival stems have such status. This is true of *ion* and
ive in particular; it is also true of *or* and *ory*.

absorpt ive	conservat ive	imaginat ive	prolongat ion
acquisit ion	consolat ory	infract ion	provis ion
adaptat ion	content ion	introduct ory	publicat ion
affirmat ive	conversat ion	invect ive	reconciliat ion
applicat ion	deificat ion	invocat ion	repetit ive
coalit ion	derivat ive	mot or	retent ive
comparat ive	destruct ive	permiss ive	revelat ory
competit or	exclus ive	preparat ory	satisfact ion
compuls ive	glorificat ion	presentat ion	solut ion

It is noteworthy that though the verbs *convince* and *convict* now
express rather distinct meanings ordinarily, the noun *conviction*
serves as a semantic companion to both. The relation of *revolution*
to *revolve* and *revolt* is similar.

Stems of Latin past-participial type are developed for new verbs
such as *pasteurize* (as in *pasteurization*), and have even been invented for *starve* (in *starvation*) and *talk* (in *talkative*). From the
point of view of English word formation, stems of Latin infinitival
and Latin past-participial types are frequently best regarded
simply as variants.

Changes which took place in French sometimes add to the number of variant past-participial and infinitival stems of Latin origin.
Thus four stems appear in the group of words which includes *receive, recipient, receipt,* and *reception*. Three stems appear in the
group which includes *despise, despicable,* and *despite. Obey* and

obedient show variant forms of the same infinitival stem; so do *pertain* and *pertinent*. *Memoir* and *remember* show two French variants of the Latin stem of *memorable*.

Variations in noun and adjective stems from Latin and Greek also complicate word formation for modern English. Here again histories of use in French add to the complexity which is found, and the tendency to make new words on Latin and Greek models adds also. Quite often there is simply what the written language represents as the addition of a vowel before a suffix, to what without this addition has word status in English.

actu al	commerci al	gase ous	rebelli ous
adverbi al	contemptu ous	grammari an	ritu al
artifici al	courte ous	habitu al	savi or
avarici ous	dictatori al	musici an	spaci ous
Christi an	equatori al	Parisi an	Spani ard
circumstanci al	ethere al	presidenti al	spiritu al
civili an	eventu al	proverbi al	textu al
collegi ate	financi al	raci al	vici ous

Sometimes written *ti* replaces *ce* rather than *t* before suffixes: for example, in *conscientious, essential,* and *preferential,* which in English will be related to *conscience, essence,* and *preference.*

Variations of other types occur in noun and adjective stems from Latin and Greek.

accurac y	decenc y	hypnot ic	messeng er
agenc y	degenerac y	idioc y	numer al
analyt ic	emphat ic	idiomat ic	parochi al
apologet ic	enm ity	inim ical	stigmat ize
aristocrac y	frequenc y	intimac y	syntact ic
buoyanc y	genet ic	jocul ar	systemat ic
contr ary	grammat ical	judici al	tubul ar
crimin al	humil ity	mechan ic	volumin ous

Differences in form are sometimes very considerable.

cross, crusade	people, popular
devil, diabolic	point, punctual
double, duplicity	poor, poverty
fierce, ferocious	rule, regular
market, mercantile	saint, sanctity

Differences in meanings often accompany differences in forms.

lieu, local   noun, nominal
master, magisterial   pilgrim, peregrination

Nonaffixal formatives which can hardly be regarded as variants of English words are numerous also. Examples are italicized in the following pairs of words.

misanthropic, anthropocentric   orthodox, orthography
biology, microbe   patient, passion
capable, capture   repeat, petition
carnage, carnivorous   pedal, centipede
isochronal, chronometer   anglophile, philology
homicide, suicide   police, metropolis
democrat, democracy   polygon, polyp
crescent, increase   potable, potation
culpable, exculpate   deride, risible
equal, equivalent   sacrament, sacrilege
feminism, effeminate   sequence, consecutive
prefer, coniferous   preside, session
professorship, confess   resist, insistence
infringe, fraction   associate, sociology
polygamous, gamogenesis   sophism, philosopher
geometry, perigee   respond, sponsor
hexagon, trigonometry   destroy, construction
gregarious, segregate   stupor, stupefy
exhilarate, hilarious   dissuade, persuasion
iatric, psychiatrist   assume, resumption
liquid, liquefy   tenable, detain
monolithic, lithography   polytheism, theology
logic, philology   toxic, antitoxin
delude, illusion   protrude, intrusion
immanent, remain   intuition, tutor
mental, demented   unanimous, unison
remit, mission   urbanization, suburb
monism, monopoly   pervade, evasive
announce, denunciation   very, verify
omniscient, omnipresent   invincible, evict
adorn, ornament   revive, vivisection
anonymous, onomatopoetic   devour, omnivorous

But English continues to make new words from Latin and Greek stems, especially in scientific and technical applications. Thus the *aud* of *audible* now has word status in technical use, as well as the *audit* of *audition* and *auditory*, which has long had word status.

Phot is established in technical use, though the *photo* of *photograph* is very much more widely known. *Neon* is well known, but difference in meanings is likely to prevent it from being related to the *neo* of *neolithic*.

Grammatical relationships binding the components of complexes.—It is possible to extend analysis of syntactic type into complexes, noting that their components are often clearly related as modifiers and heads, or as principals and appositives, or as prepositions and objects, or as coordinates. Prefixes commonly seem to function as modifiers of what follows them: for example, in *coexist, dislike, ex-president, hypercritical, indigestion, interact, misprint, nonaggression, prearrange, reelect, subdivide, superimpose, transplant, ultraconservative,* and *unhappy.* Sometimes prefixes seem to function as prepositions, and the following components as their objects: for example, in *afoot, antifreeze, because, postwar, pro-British,* and *transatlantic.* Much less frequently prefixes may seem to act as heads for what follows them. Thus *endear* and *enrich* have the value of *make dear* and *make rich,* and *dear* and *rich* can be viewed as complementary modifiers of *en* as of *make.* Though there are arguments against assigning head status to affixes, suffixes very commonly can be viewed as heads modified by the components which precede them. Thus in *colds always weaken me* the *en* of *weaken* functions essentially as the *make* of *colds always make me weak* functions: *weak* can be viewed as a complementary modifier of *en* and *make* alike. An Ohioan is an "an" from Ohio, just as an Ohio farmer is a farmer from Ohio; and though *Ohio* is a proper noun, *Ohioan* is a pluralizer. Some suffixes seem more like modifiers of what precedes them: thus the *ette* of *kitchenette* seems to relate to *kitchen* as the *small* of *small kitchen* does. Some suffixes seem to have a relation to what precedes them like that of prepositions to their objects: thus the *ed* of *talented* and the *less* of *coatless* may be felt as structurally much like the *with* of *a pianist with talent* and the *without* of *he was without a coat.* The *teen* of *sixteen,* in origin a variant of *ten,* is in a coordinate relationship with the component which precedes it: sixteen is six and ten.

Complexes containing more than two clear components sometimes raise the problem of precisely what has combined with what. In such a complex as *luckily* this problem does not exist: it is clear that the suffix *ly* has combined with the adjective *lucky*, within which the suffix *y* has combined with the noun *luck*. In *unluckily* the matter is not quite so simple: the complex can be viewed as a combination of *un* and *luckily* or as a combination of *unlucky* and *ly*. In *deodorizer* the problem is still worse: the complex is obviously a combination of *deodorize* and *er*, but *deodorize* is hardly divisible satisfactorily into either *deodor* and *ize* or *de* and *odorize*. A somewhat different problem faces us when we look at such a pair of complexes as *coextend* and *coextension*. It seems best to consider here that *coextension* is a combination of the suffix *ion* and the complex formative *coextens*, which is a variant of *coextend*. *Coextend* is obviously made up of the prefix *co* and *extend*; *extend*, in turn, is made up of *ex* and *tend*. But it is possible to ignore the existence of *coextend* and describe *coextension* as a combination of *co* and *extension*, and then to ignore the existence of *extend* and describe *extension* as a combination of *ex* and *tension*.

We often encounter difficult problems when we attempt careful analysis of the composition of complex words. We react to the presence of meaningful "fractions" that we have trouble identifying with certainty, since we tend to learn words as wholes. In such a slogan as *think or thwim*, obviously paralleling *sink or swim*, the *thwim* carries meaning. Pretty clearly the *ash* of such a set of words as *bash*, *dash*, *gash*, *lash*, *splash*, *clash*, and *mash* carries meaning. It seems best not to attempt division of such words as these. Even complexes which are clearly divisible into generally recognized components, without leftovers, are commonly best regarded simply as unit strings of components whose precise relationships are left unanalyzed.

CHAPTER XIX

VOWELS AND CONSONANTS

Everything that is put into English—in thought, speech (or song), or writing—is composed of clauses and clause equivalents which can be broken up into predicators, subjects, complements, isolates, and adjuncts, and then (where sentence structure is not extremely simple) into syntactic units of varied types within these major divisions. Everything that is put into English is also composed of words, and many words can be divided into components that are recognized by the linguistically sophisticated and sometimes even by the linguistically naive. Finally, everything that is put into spoken (or sung) English is composed of sounds, and everything that is put into written English is composed of letters, ideographs, and marks of punctuation.

Spoken language has a longer history than written language; and even yet, unless they are deaf, children learn to hear and talk before they learn to read and write. The written language is based on the spoken and ordinarily should not be studied apart from the spoken. But the subject matter of grammar is the sets of molds and patterns which languages employ in the formulation and communication of thought. For the study of the syntax and word formation of standard contemporary American English, the ordinary written forms give reasonably adequate representation to what must be taken into account. The structures employed in written English are the same as those employed in spoken; spoken English simply employs them less cautiously, leaving many unfinished and others curiously combined. But when analysis of the distinctive sounds of the language and their written representations is attempted, obviously a clear distinction between spoken English and written English becomes necessary.

The sounds employed in contemporary American English can receive only very superficial treatment here. Like the work of the linguistic historians and the lexicographers, the highly specialized work that has been done on the sounds of contemporary English requires separate treatment: there is no possibility of doing it justice in a one-volume grammar. Spelling and punctuation are another matter. The written language ordinarily ignores differences in dialect and gives relatively little attention to differences in emotional attitudes which in the spoken language affect pitches, stresses, and pauses very considerably. Thus in the written language a single representation of a bit of poetry serves for innumerable spoken versions, varying tremendously from speaker to speaker and, for a single speaker, from occasion to occasion: the reader makes his own version, which may well be more effective unspoken than as he would speak it.

> Music I heard with you was more than music,
> And bread I broke with you was more than bread.
> Now that I am without you, all is desolate.
> All that was once so beautiful is dead.

Finally, the spelling and punctuation of the written language are commonly taught in schools, whereas the system of vowel and consonant sounds, pitches, stresses, and pauses of the spoken language is best mastered unanalytically, by children, as gestures and mannerisms are learned—though it is true that when the language is learned after childhood even intonation is likely to be approached analytically.

Both the ordinary written form of the language and the currently usual varieties of phonemic transcription represent the distinctive vowel and consonant sounds of contemporary English as units occurring one after another in uninterrupted or interrupted sequences. The evidence of the laboratories makes it clear that the stream of sound is not as sharply segmented as such representations suggest. Sounds blend into neighboring sounds; some, indeed, are heard primarily because of the way they alter neighboring sounds. The vowel and consonant sounds usually recognized as significant are bundles of phonetic characteristics, so that the stream of sound is capable of analysis of very different types. But the traditional type of analysis continues to be useful, and it has great advantages where there is an interest in relating sounds and established spellings. The significant vowel and consonant sounds, or phonemes, are abstractions: the /t/ of *ten*, for example, is notably different in phonetic characteristics from the /t/ of *forty*. But all our units are abstractions.

  The stressed vowel sounds.—Especially if we are interested in relating sounds and spellings, the significant vowel sounds of English can conveniently be divided into stressed sounds and unstressed ones. The stressed vowel sounds can be further subdivided into long vowel sounds and short ones. In what seems to be the commonest practice in American English, six long vowel sounds and six short ones are distinguished in stressed syllables. These are commonly identified by the characteristic positions of concentration of the arching tongue.

	Long	*Short*
High-front	/i/ of *bead*	/ɪ/ of *bid*
Mid-front	/e/ of *laid*	/ɛ/ of *led*
Low-front		/æ/ of *lad*
Low-back	/ɔ/ of *laud*	/ɑ/ of *rod, calm*
Mid-back	/o/ of *load*	
High-back	/u/ of *food*	/ʊ/ of *good*
Mid-central	/ɜ/ of *bird*	/ʌ/ of *bud*

For the long vowel sounds the tongue is characteristically held relatively tense; for the short vowel sounds it is held relatively lax, and the positions are a little lower than for the corresponding long sounds. The lips are characteristically rounded for all the back vowels except the low /ɑ/ of *rod* and *calm*. For mid-central /ɜ/ the tip of the tongue is characteristically pulled back and elevated slightly. The names "long" and "short" are traditional. In their favor is the fact that the "short" stressed vowel sounds rarely end words, and that it is when they end words at pauses that stressed vowel sounds take most time. Especially in slow speech, stressed vowel sounds tend to be notably impure in quality before voiced consonant sounds and at the end of words followed by pauses, so that it becomes possible to regard them as diphthongs. Comparison of stressed vowel sounds before voiceless /t/, before voiced /d/, and at the end of words that are spoken alone is of interest.

seat, seed, see	lit, lid
rate, raid, ray	let, led
	bat, bad, baa
sought, sawed, saw	sot, sod, ah
rote, road, roe	
moot, mood, moo	foot, hood
curt, curd, cur	butt, bud

Some of the complexities of English word formation and spelling have their basis in the fact that often the joining of a word and a noninflectional suffix results in the substitution of a short vowel sound for a long vowel sound or a diphthong, and that the spelling may or may not indicate the substitution.

abund ant	deprav ity	penal ty	south ern
appell ate	episod ic	pleas ant	speci al
athlet ic	fabul ous	profan ity	stat ic
brev ity	fac et	profund ity	tabl et
cav ity	fest ive	san ity	thrott le
clos et	inflamm able	schol ar	van ity
compos ite	metr ic	secret ary	volcan ic
cyclon ic	microscop ic	seren ity	zeal ous

It is noteworthy that in a number of inflected verb forms the addition of an inflectional ending is accompanied by the shortening of a vowel sound.

do, does, done	deal, dealt
flee, fled	leave, left
say, says, said	mean, meant
shoe, shod	drive, driven
keep, kept	write, written

In *holiday* the first vowel sound has been shortened in compounding. But in *studious* a long vowel sound has replaced the short sound of *study*.

The list of stressed vowel sounds given above is not adequate for all varieties of American English. In words like *rod* and *bother* some speakers use a slightly rounded short sound /ɒ/, which they distinguish from the /ɑ/ of *calm* and *father*. In words like *bath* and *dance* some speakers use a short sound /a/, between /æ/ and /ɑ/. In words like *bird* some speakers use a long sound /ɜ/, without "r coloring," instead of /ɝ/. In what follows, the existence of /ɒ/,

/a/, and /ɜ/ is ignored, except that the use of /a/ as the first sound in various diphthongs and triphthongs is noted.

The spellings of the stressed vowel sounds.—In what seems to be the commonest practice, then, twelve vowel sounds are distinguished in stressed syllables. The alphabet used in the ordinary written language provides only five vowel letters. The alphabet also provides three glide letters—*r*, *w*, and *y*—which have considerable use in the representation of vowel sounds as well as consonant sounds. But the glide letters and the vowel letters together would not be enough even if they were efficiently used. In this situation there has been an attempt, in effect, to assign the five single vowel letters to the six short vowel sounds—*u* being divided between the /ʌ/ of *cut* and the relatively little used /ʊ/ of *put*—and make two-letter representations basic for the long vowel sounds. The attempt has not been made consistently, but it has been made part of the time. In the two-letter representations of long vowel sounds, sometimes the first letter indicates the position of the tongue concentration and the second is little more than an indication that the sound is long, as is the case in *keen* and *toe*. But sometimes the two letters are about equally important in indicating tongue concentration, as is true in *say* and *saw* and *laid* and *laud*. The last letter, the glide letter *r*, indicates the position of the tongue in spellings given /ɜ/: for example, in the *ur*, *ir*, *er*, and *or* of *lurk*, *shirk*, *jerk*, and *work*. This *r* is doubled as some consonant letters are doubled, as in *furry*, *stirred*, and *conferring*. The last letter also indicates tongue position in two spellings of /u/: *eu* and *ew*, as in *rheumatism* and *blew*.

A number of spellings of both vowel and consonant sounds terminate in nonsyllabic *e*. In *scene, cane, tone,* and *rune* nonsyllabic *e* is delayed: it is written last but is part of the representation not of the final consonant sound /n/ but of the vowel sounds which precede /n/ in these words. In *see, toe,* and *rue* nonsyllabic *e* is part of the representation of the vowel sounds which terminate these words; in *bronze* and *shelve* it is part of the representation of the final consonant sounds. Sometimes a nonsyllabic *e* performs two functions: this is true of the *e* of *rage*, which is part of the representation of the vowel sound /e/ and is also part of the representation of the consonantal combination /dʒ/. Sometimes a nonsyllabic *e* has no real function and is genuinely "silent": this is true of the *e* of *cigarette*, for example, and of that of *come*. Syllabic final *e* is quite limited in occurrence, though some of the most frequently used words have it; it occurs usually (1) in words that are commonly unstressed, such as *he*, *she*, and *the*, and (2) in modern acquisitions from other languages, such as *simile*, *finale*, *café*, and *protégé*. Nonsyllabic final *e* is normally dropped before inflectional endings and noninflectional suffixes beginning with vowel letters, and before the glide-letter suffix *y*.

activ ity	cring es	favorit ism	rip est
admir ed	cring ing	fre ed	Rom an
admir ing	dabbl ed	fre er	rout ed
agre ed	dabbl er	fre est	rout ing
amaz es	dabbl ing	ho ed	sal able
amaz ing	danc er	lik able	scen ic
captiv ate	destin y	loos en	serv ice
coher ence	di ed	nois es	statu ette
collaps ible	dy ed	nois y	stor age
compos ure	engin eer	refug ee	su ing
constru ed	escap ade	refus al	Swed ish
constru ing	extrem ist	ridicul ous	trembl ed
continu al	ey ed	rip en	trembl ing
cring ed	ey ing	rip er	wast ing

When a suffix or inflectional ending beginning with a vowel letter is added to a word ending in an *le* representing syllabic /l̩/, and when the suffix *y* is added, the *e* is dropped according to rule and usually there is also a change from syllabic /l̩/ to nonsyllabic /l/ in the spoken forms, so that, for example, *dabbler*, *trembling*, and *bubbly* have no more syllables than *dabble*, *tremble*, and *bubble*. But when inflectional *ed* is added, syllabic /l̩/ is retained before /d/. Loss of nonsyllabic *e* when, for example, *ing* is added to *cringe*, *route*, and *waste* destroys distinctions made in the written basic forms: *cringing* and *wasting* look like rhymes for *bringing* and *lasting*, and *route* and *rout* become indistinguishable in their written past forms and gerundial forms.

Under certain circumstances nonsyllabic final *e* is kept before suffixes and inflectional endings beginning with vowel letters.

1. Words ending in *ee* and *oe* retain these spellings before vowel letters other than *e*, as in *agreeable, freeing, canoeing*, and *hoeing*.

2. Words ending in *ce* and *ge* retain these spellings before *a*, *o*, and *u*, as in *changeable, noticeable,* and *courageous.*

Dye and *singe* keep *e* before *ing,* so that *dyeing* and *singeing* are visually distinct from *dying* and *singing.* In such words as *die, lie,* and *tie* the spelling *ie* is replaced by the spelling *y* when *ing* is added. Nonsyllabic final *e* is dropped before consonants, irregularly, in *argument, awful, duly, ninth, truly, truth,* and *wholly.* The normal retention of this *e* before consonants is illustrated in *amazement, hopeful, freely,* and *solely.* Its normal retention in compounds, even before other vowel letters, is illustrated in *firearm,* as compared with *firing.* Loss in a compound occurs in *wherever.*

In some words whose basic forms end in *o* preceded by a consonant letter or a glide letter, when the inflectional ending *s* is added there is a substitution of *oe* for *o.* This is true whether *o* represents a stressed /o/ or an unstressed vowel sound. This substitution occurs in the following words.

doe s	goe s	mosquitoe s	potatoe s
dominoe s	heroe s	mulattoe s	tomatoe s
echoe s	innuendoe s	Negroe s	torpedoe s
embargoe s	jingoe s	noe s	vetoe s

In *does* the vowel sound is shortened. Most words ending in *o* retain this *o* unchanged when *s* is added, as in *dynamos* and *pianos.*

Though the basic representations of long vowel sounds employ two letters, one-letter representations must be described as regular for five of these sounds—all except /ɜ/—under certain circumstances. In regular spellings a single letter represents a long vowel sound—

1. When this letter is followed by a single consonant letter other than *x* and this consonant letter is followed by a vowel letter, a semivowel letter, or an *le* representing syllabic /l/, as in *famous, hatred,* and *enable.*
2. When this letter is followed by a vowel letter representing a vowel sound in the following syllable, as in *idea* and *ruin.*
3. When the vowel sound represented by this letter ends the spoken word, as in *he, no, few,* and *simile,* and also as in *debris, crochet, Utah,* and *apropos.*

It should be added that though a single letter can represent a long vowel sound at the end of the word (where short vowel sounds rarely appear), representations using a single letter are in fact exceptional here, and generally occur only in words that are commonly unstressed (such as *do*, *to*, *the*, *a*, *he* and *who*), in words like *few* where *e* represents consonantal /j/ and *w* represents long /u/, and in modern acquisitions from other languages (such as *ski*, *café*, *tomato*, and *menu*, as well as such words as *debris* and *crochet* where silent consonant letters follow).

Irregular uses of normal spellings of long vowel sounds must also be taken into account. These occur under the following circumstances.

1. When a single vowel letter represents a long vowel sound even though two consonant letters follow. This type of irregularity occurs notably in representations of /ɔ/ in such words as *ball*, *malt*, *walk*, *boss*, *coffee*, *cost*, *long*, *often*, and *cloth*, and in representations of /o/ in such words as *roll*, *jolt*, *bold*, and *folk*. It occurs also in such words as *truth* and *bathing*.
2. When a single vowel letter represents a long vowel sound before a single pronounced consonant letter which ends a word. This kind or irregularity occurs in such words as *control* and *extol*. It also occurs before inflectional *s* in such forms as *radios*, *skis*, *cafés*, and *menus*.
3. When two consonant letters separate a delayed *e* from its companion vowel letter, as in *ache*, *range*, *clothe*, and *butte*.

Tables of the spellings given the vowel sounds of contemporary English are complex things, even when (as here) they attempt only to relate these spellings to the pronunciations employed in a single somewhat-normalized variety of American speech. Some spellings occur only in a very few words, at least for the central nontechnical stream of the language: these can be left out of tables and noted separately. Rare spellings of this kind are not always contrary to the basic system, as the *u* of *busy* is, for example; sometimes, like the *ey* of *key* (which seems fully as normal for /i/ as the *ay* of *pay* seems for /e/), they are simply spellings that have been put to very little use. Spellings which are not rare, and for this reason require notice in tables, can be classified as primary, secondary, and anomalous. The primary spellings will be, in the main, native spellings which lie at the heart of the spelling system. These frequently involve uses of the Latin letters quite distinct from those found in other languages using these letters. The secondary spellings will be spellings which are notably distinct from the primary spellings but which nevertheless follow a pattern. Some secondary spellings will be nonnative, in general employing the Latin letters much more nearly as they are employed in other languages. Thus the *e-e* of *fete* is a nonnative secondary spelling, while the *a-e* of *fate* is a native primary spelling for the same sound. Other secondary spellings have other explanations. Thus the *w* of *few* is essentially a terminal spelling. A tendency to distinguish spellings used elsewhere from those used at the end of words is noteworthy at various points, and accounts for the use, among primary spellings of /e/, of *ai* in *maid* alongside *ay* in *may*, for example. The anomalous spellings listed in the tables which follow are spellings which conflict with the general patterning of English spellings and yet have considerable use. The *oo* of *good* and the *ea* of *sweat* are such spellings: the use of two-letter combinations for short vowel sounds makes this classification necessary. *Good* and *sweat* employ the spellings *oo* and *ea* anomalously, *food* and *heat* do not. The *ear* of *earn* is an anomalous spelling for the long vowel sound /ɜ/ which in *urn* is represented by a primary spelling, since in *earn* two vowel letters precede *r*. *Earn* and *yearn* employ the spelling *ear* anomalously, *ear* and *year* do not.

A table of spellings of the long stressed vowel sounds follows.

1. High-front /i/.
    Primary, *e* series: *ee, ea, ei, e-e, e.*
    feet, meat, ceiling, scene, genius
    Secondary, *i* series: *ie, i-e, i.*
    chief, machine, mosquito
2. Mid-front /e/.
    Primary, *a* series: *ai, ay, a-e, a.*
    aim, lay, lake, table
    Secondary, *e* series: *ee, ei, ey, e-e, e.*
    fiancée, feint, obey, crepe, bouquet
3. Low-back /ɔ/.
    Primary, *a* series: *au, aw, a.*
    sauce, lawn, hurrah
    Secondary, *o* series: *ou, o.*
    cough, long

4. Mid-back /o/.
    Primary, *o* series: *oa, ou, ow, oe, o-e, o.*
    load, dough, grow, toe, tone, noble
5. High-back /u/.
    Primary, *o* series: *oo, ou, o.*
    food, group, do
    Secondary, *u* series: *eu, ui, ue, u-e, u.*
    pseudonym, fruit, blue, rune, junior
    Secondary, *w* series: *ew, w.*
    flew, few
6. Mid-central /ɜ/.
    Primary, *r* series: *ur, urr, ir, irr, er, err, or.*
    burn, furry, first, stirring, verb, deterred, word
    Anomalous: *ear, our.*
    earth, journey

Rare spellings of the long vowel sounds can be illustrated as follows.

For /i/: minuti*ae*, qu*ay*, p*eo*ple, k*ey*, subp*oe*na.
For /e/: G*ae*lic, g*au*ge, gr*ea*t.
For /ɔ/: br*oa*d, g*o*ne.
For /o/: ch*au*ffeur, plat*eau*, y*eo*man, s*ew*.
For /u/: b*eau*ty, l*ieu*, sh*oe*, l*o*se.
For /ɜ/: connoiss*eur*, c*o*lonel, w*o*rry, m*yr*tle, m*yrr*h.

A table of spellings of the short stressed vowel sounds follows.

7. High-front /ɪ/.
    Primary, *i.*
    hint
    Secondary, *y.*
    hymn
8. Mid-front /ɛ/.
    Primary, *e.*
    bred
    Anomalous, *ea.*
    dead
9. Low-front /æ/.
    Primary, *a.*
    bad
10. Low-back /ɑ/.
    Primary, *o.*
    dollar
    Secondary, *a.*
    father

11. High-back /ʊ/.
    Primary, *u.*
    full
    Anomalous, *oo.*
    book
12. Mid-central /ʌ/.
    Primary, *u.*
    sun
    Secondary, *o.*
    wonder
    Anomalous, *ou.*
    young

Rare spellings of the short vowel sounds can be illustrated as follows.

>For /ɪ/: *E*nglish, b*ee*n, s*ie*ve, wom*e*n, b*u*sy, b*ui*ld.
>For /ɛ/: *a*ny, ag*ai*n, s*ay*s, h*ei*fer, j*eo*pardy, fri*e*nd,
>　　　*Oe*dipus.
>For /æ/: m*a*'*a*m, pl*ai*d, l*au*gh, mer*i*ngue.
>For /ɑ/: sal*aa*m, rend*e*zvous, bur*eau*cracy, bourge*oi*s,
>　　　kn*ow*ledge.
>For /ʊ/: w*o*lf, c*ou*ld.
>For /ʌ/: d*oe*s, n*o*ne, hors d'*oeu*vre, bl*oo*d.

The diphthongs and triphthongs.—In the commonest type of American English, stressed vocalic combinations include nine diphthongs.

	Front-rising	*Back-rising*	*Centering*
High-front			/ɪr/ of *mere*
Mid-front			/ɛr/ of *merit*
Low-front			/ær/ of *narrow*
Low-central	/aɪ/ of *line*	/aʊ/ of *noun*	
Low-back			/ɑr/ of *farm*
Low-back	/ɔɪ/ of *loin*		/ɔr/ of *form*
High-back			/ʊr/ of *poor*

And two triphthongs.

	Front-rising	*Back-rising*
Low-central	/aɪr/ of *tire*	/aʊr/ of *sour*

The triphthongs are obviously first front- and back-rising and then centering. The frequent absence of "*r* coloring" in some varieties of American English is ignored here. So is the existence, in some varieties of American English, of a mid-back centering diphthong /or/, whose users distinguish, for example, *hoarse* from *horse* and *wore* from *war*.

The diphthongs and triphthongs employ three vocalic glides, here represented by /ɪ/, /ʊ/, and /r/. Such long vowel sounds as the /e/ of *hay* and the /o/ of *hoe* are likely to end, especially when they occur at pauses, with sounds which are phonetically like the /ɪ/ of *high* and the /ʊ/ of *how;* and such short vowel sounds as the /æ/ of *sad* often end with a sound which is phonetically close to the /ə/ of *beard* when *beard* is spoken "without *r* coloring"—and sometimes, as in *hang* and *bag*, with a sound which is phonetically close to the /ɪ/ which terminates the diphthong of *hike*. But the vocalic glides of the diphthongs and triphthongs commonly have an indispensability which makes it seem necessary to give them notice in phonemic representations. A better system of phonemic representation would not assign the same symbol to the short /ɪ/ of *pin* and the vocalic glide of *line, loin,* and *tire;* nor would it assign the same symbol to the short /ʊ/ of *put* and the vocalic glide of *noun* and *sour;* nor would it assign the same symbol to the consonantal /r/ of *rod* and the vocalic glide of *farm.*

The spellings which represent the diphthongs and triphthongs are best described as units, without much effort to identify each letter with a particular component sound. Some of the spellings employed can of course be broken down into component letters which correspond quite normally to component sounds. The spellings of /aɪ/, however, suggest a long vowel sound like /i/ and /o/, not a diphthong. Thus the *i-e* of *line* employs a delayed *e* exactly as the *a-e* of *lane* and the *o-e* of *lone* do. Some of the spellings of the diphthongs terminating in /r/ suggest long opening sounds though the opening sounds actually used are short. Thus the *ea* of *fear* suggests the presence of the long /i/ of *feat* rather than of the short /ɪ/ of *fit,* and the *ai* of *pair* suggests the presence of the long /e/ of *pain* rather than of the short /ɛ/ of *pen.* Such spellings as occur in *tore* and *barring* suggest a consonantal /r/ comparable to the consonantal /n/ of *tone* and *banning;* but the consonantal /r/ of contemporary American English of the commonest type does not follow vowel sounds in the same syllables. The use of *y* to represent /aɪ/ and unstressed /ɪ/ at the end of words causes complications in spelling when inflectional endings and noninflectional suffixes are added. Before the *'s* of possessives and before *ing* and noninflectional suffixes beginning with *i,* this *y* remains; before the *s* of plural nouns and that of third-singular verb forms, it normally becomes *ie* (except that proper names retain *y,* as in *the Whitbys*); before other inflectional endings and noninflectional suffixes it normally becomes *i.*

family 's	familie s	dizzi ly	merci ful
fly ing	flie s	fli er	readi ly
imply ing	implie s	impli ed	silli est
lobby ist	lobbie s	lobbi ed	thirti eth

Exceptions occur, and usage is divided, where suffixes and inflectional endings are added to monosyllabic words such as *dry* and *shy*. *Y* is kept before *ward*, as in *cityward;* it is replaced by *e* in somewhat archaic *beauteous* and *plenteous*. In a considerable number of words the letter *i* alone represents the diphthong /aɪ/ before silent *gh*, as in *sigh*, *sight*, and *tightly;* in *sign* and *island* it does so before silent *g* and *s*.

A table of spellings of the front- and back-rising diphthongs follows.

> 13. Low-central /aɪ/.
>> Primary, *i* series: *ie, i-e, i*.
>> pie, pine, triumph
>> Secondary, *y* series: *y-e, y*.
>> style, dry
> 14. Low-back /ɔɪ/.
>> Primary, *o* series: *oi, oy*.
>> coin, coy
> 15. Low-central /aʊ/.
>> Primary, *o* series: *ou, ow*.
>> shout, cow

Rare spellings of these diphthongs can be illustrated as follows.

> For /aɪ/: *a*isle, bay*o*u, h*ei*ght, *eye*, c*o*yote, b*uy*, d*ye*.
> For /ɔɪ/: b*uoy*.
> For /aʊ/: sauerkr*au*t

A table of spellings of the centering diphthongs and the triphthongs follows.

> 16. High-front /ɪr/.
>> Primary, *e* series: *eer, ear, ere, er*.
>> queer, clear, here, period
>> Secondary, *i* series: *ier, ir, irr*.
>> cashier, spirit, irritate
>> Secondary, *yr*.
>> tyranny
> 17. Mid-front /ɛr/.
>> Primary, *a* series: *air, are, ar*.
>> stair, care, caring
>> Secondary, *e* series: *ear, er, err*.
>> wear, merit, errand
> 18. Low-front /ær/.
>> Primary, *a* series: *ar, arr*.
>> guarantee, arrogant

19. Low-back /ɑr/.
     Primary, *a* series: *ar, arr*.
     harm, barring
20. Low-back /ɔr/.
     Primary, *o* series: *oar, our, ore, or, orr*.
     roar, course, store, form, horrible
     Secondary, *a* series: *aur, ar, arr*.
     laurel, warm, quarrel
21. High-back /ʊr/.
     Primary, *o* series: *oor, our*.
     poor, tour
     Secondary, *u* series: *ure, ur*.
     sure, jury
22. Low-central /aɪr/.
     Primary, *i* series: *ire, ir*.
     tire, wiring
23. Low-central /aʊr/.
     Primary, *our*.
     sour

Rare spellings of the centering diphthongs and the triphthongs can be illustrated as follows.

For   /ɪr/: w*ei*rd.
For   /ɛr/: pr*ayer*, h*eir*, th*ere*, *eyr*ie, b*u*ry.
For   /ɑr/: baz*aar*, h*ear*t, s*er*geant, memo*ir*.
For   /ɔr/: dr*awer*, reserv*oir*, d*oor*, tow*ar*d.
For   /ʊr/: n*eur*al, potp*our*ri.
For   /aɪr/: p*y*rotechnic, l*yr*e.

Those who have a diphthong /or/ use this diphthong in preference to /ɔr/ where *oar, our,* and *ore* are written (as in *roar, course,* and *store*), and even in some words where *or* is written—in *fort,* for example, though not in *fork.* It must be noted also that /ær/ is widely used in preference to /ɛr/ where *air, are,* and *ear* are written, as in *stair, care,* and *wear.* Actually there are especially great regional variations in the pronunciation of the diphthongs and triphthongs in general.

   The vowel sounds of unstressed syllables.—Twelve single vowel sounds and eleven diphthongs and triphthongs commonly function as peaks in stressed syllables in American English. Almost all stressed syllables have vocalic peaks: exceptions occur in absolutes such as the *sh!* that is used in attempts to silence children.

In what are most conveniently regarded as unstressed syllables, discriminations are less exact. Only four vowel sounds function as peaks in such syllables, and there are no diphthongs or triphthongs.

24.	High-front	/ɪ/ of *exact, coffee*
25.	High-back	/ʊ/ of *situation, statue*
26.	Mid-central	/ɚ/ of *pursue, differ*
27.	Mid-central	/ə/ of *oppose, sofa*

A better system of phonemic representation, again, would not assign the same symbol to the short stressed /ɪ/ of *pit* and the unstressed /ɪ/ of *exact* and *coffee*, nor would it assign the same symbol to the short stressed /ʊ/ of *put* and the unstressed /ʊ/ of *situation* and *statue*. It seems reasonable, however, that the vocalic glides of diphthongs and triphthongs should be regarded as variants of the unstressed vowel sounds.

The unstressed vowel sounds exist in many subvarieties and shade into each other confusingly. Unstressed /ɪ/ is qualitatively like both the long stressed /i/ of *seek* and the short stressed /ɪ/ of *sick,* and unstressed /ʊ/ is qualitatively like both the long stressed /u/ of *food* and the short stressed /ʊ/ of *good*. The unstressed /ɪ/ of *coffee* is likely to sound like stressed /i/ if it occurs at a pause, as in *here's the coffee*, but like stressed /ɪ/ elsewhere, as in *the coffee's ready*. The unstressed *"r* colored" /ɚ/ of *pursue* and *differ* is qualitatively like the stressed /ɝ/ of *person* and *defer*. The unstressed /ə/, or schwa, of *oppose* and *sofa* commonly has a somewhat higher tongue position than the stressed /ʌ/ of *upper*, but is qualitatively much like it. It should be added that many unstressed syllables are without vocalic peaks. This is true when (occasionally) /m̩/ and /ŋ̍/ function as peaks, as in some pronunciations of the second syllables of *sophomore* and *baking powder*, and when (much more often) /l̩/ and /n̩/ function as peaks, as in the final syllables of *devil, idle, comparison*, and *sudden*.

The unstressed vowel sounds do not have a set of spellings of their own. In theory at least, all the spellings used to represent the vocalic parts of stressed syllables are also usable to represent the unstressed vowel sounds, so that the different distributions of stress and absence of stress in *telegraph* and *telegraphy*, for example, can alter all the vowel sounds without disturbing spelling. But even in unstressed syllables, particular spellings do tend to be associated with particular vowel sounds.

1. Unstressed /ɪ/ is commonly represented by spellings which in stressed syllables would suggest the high-front and mid-front sounds /i/, /ɪ/, /e/, and /ɛ/, or the front-rising diphthong /aɪ/.
2. Unstressed /ʊ/ is commonly represented by spellings which in stressed syllables would suggest long high-back /u/.
3. Unstressed /ɚ/ is commonly represented by spellings which in stressed syllables would suggest "*r* colored" /ɝ/ or the diphthongs and triphthongs terminating in /r/.
4. Unstressed /ə/, schwa, is most characteristically represented by spellings which in stressed syllables would suggest low-front /æ/, low-back /ɑ/ or /ɔ/, mid-back /o/, high-back /ʊ/, mid-central /ʌ/, or the diphthongs /aʊ/ and /ɔɪ/.

But schwa tends to replace /ɪ/ and /ʊ/. Schwa can be regarded as the true obscure vowel sound toward which unstressed syllables gravitate.

Unstressed /ɪ/ seems firmly established at the end of such words as *posse, coffee, money, spaghetti,* and *candy,* and before inflectional endings and noninflectional suffixes as in *worried, silliness,* and *odious.* It is well established in inflectional *ing,* though in inflectional *es* and *ed,* used as in *passes* and *hated,* /ə/ offers it strong competition. It is well established in various prefixes and suffixes.

be*f*riend	*i*llegal	wreck*a*ge	defeat*i*st
de*c*eive	*i*nclude	bankruptc*y*	saintl*y*
d*i*scover	m*i*sspell	bas*i*c	badl*y*
*e*ndear	pr*e*scribe	shirt*i*ng	sixt*y*
*e*xhibit	r*e*place	girl*i*sh	bon*y*

But schwa is often dominant where /ɪ/ might be expected, so that the *ent* of *dependent* and the *ant* of *determinant,* for example, are not distinguished in pronunciation.

Unstressed /ʊ/ occurs at the end of words and of syllables, and before inflectional endings and noninflectional suffixes. It is the most infrequent of the unstressed vowel sounds. Examples of unstressed /ʊ/ follow.

accent*ua*te	habit*ua*l	sens*ua*l	tiss*ue*
cas*ua*l	Hind*u*ism	silh*ou*ette	us*ua*l
Febr*ua*ry	iss*ue*	stat*ue*	virt*ue*
grad*ua*te	rit*ua*l	text*ua*l	vis*ua*l

In comfortable informal speech unstressed /ʊ/ followed by schwa tends to disappear. Thus such words as *casual* and *usual* come to have only two syllables, with schwa in the unstressed one.

Unstressed /ɚ/ is quite well established in most types of American English. Examples follow.

simil*ar*	nad*ir*	act*or*	s*ur*vive
theat*er*	cupb*oar*d	glam*our*	nat*ure*
past*eur*ize	whipp*oor*will	ac*re*	mart*yr*

Unstressed /ɚ/ has one spelling which is not used to represent the vocalic parts of stressed syllables: the spelling *re*, which occurs after /k/ and /g/ in such words as *acre*, *euchre*, and *ogre*, though not in *soccer* and *eager*, and which is also used quite exceptionally in the word *timbre*, meaning "tone," and sometimes in *theatre*, where it apparently is thought to have prestige value. Schwa shows little tendency to supplant /ɚ/. In most varieties of American English /ɚ/ gives way to schwa only when another /ɚ/ or an /r/ occurs in an immediately following syllable in the same word—as in *catercornered*, *governor*, *southerner*, and *surprise*, in each of which the first *r* is often ignored. In such words as *flatterer* and *caterer* there is what is conveniently regarded as two /ɚ/'s.

Obscure schwa, /ə/, is of course the commonest vowel sound in unstressed syllables. Widely varied spellings represent schwa.

*a*bove	defin*i*te	fam*ou*s
purch*a*se	ster*i*le	healthf*u*l
qu*i*et	bott*o*m	fort*u*ne
bur*eau*crat	madem*oi*selle	anal*y*sis

Obviously the ear offers especially inadequate guidance to the spellings that represent the vowel sounds of unstressed syllables. It is not surprising that such words as *definite* and *optimist* are very frequently misspelled.

The consonant sounds.—Distinctions in vowel sounds are characteristically produced by moving the tongue and the lower jaw to form variously shaped resonance chambers. Distinctions in consonant sounds are characteristically produced by employing various kinds of obstruction in the way of the flow of air through the mouth and lips. This obstruction can occur at the lips, as for the labials; at the front teeth, as for the interdentals; in the front of the mouth above the teeth, as for the alveolars; at the roof of the mouth toward the front, as for the palatals; in central areas of the mouth, as for central /r/; and at the back of the mouth, as for the velars. The aspirate /h/ is another matter, and can be regarded simply as an emphatic beginning for vowel sounds and the consonantal glides /j/ and /w/ as in *huge* and *whale*. For the labials and labiodentals the active obstructing agent is the lower lip; for the other consonant sounds, excepting the aspirate /h/, it is the tongue.

Twenty-two consonant sounds seem best regarded as monophthongal and represented in simple phonemic transcription by single symbols. They can be subdivided on the basis of the character of the obstruction which produces them. For six, the obstruction is complete and may be followed by explosive release: these are the stops. For eight, the obstruction is incomplete, so that the flow of air continues but friction is set up at the point of obstruction: these are the fricatives. For three, complete obstruction blocks the passage of air through the mouth and lips but passage is permitted through the nose: these are the nasals. For one, the flow of air passes along the side (or sides) of the tongue, with the point of the tongue making a light partial obstruction and the bulk of the tongue rather low in the mouth: this is the lateral /l/. Three consonant sounds are closely related to corresponding vowel sounds: these are the consonantal glides. The aspirate /h/ remains.

Fourteen of the consonant sounds characteristically involve a vibration of the vocal cords which is sometimes called voicing, and which is also involved in all vowel sounds. Eight consonant sounds are characteristically voiceless. These eight include aspirate /h/ and half the stops and fricatives, which occur in voiced-voiceless pairs. Since the stream of speech is dominated by voicing, the voiceless consonants represent relatively great departure from the normal characteristics of the stream and so are relatively energetic. Most energetic of all are the voiceless stops, which tend to acquire a noticeable aspiration when they precede vowel sounds in the same syllables. When they follow the vowel sounds of their syllables and are followed by unstressed vowel sounds, voiceless stops tend noticeably to acquire voice, so that, for example, *latter* may be indistinguishable from *ladder*. The distinction between voicing and absence of voice sometimes distinguishes verbs from nouns or adjectives. Spellings do not always indicate this distinction where it is made.

advise, advice	house, house
believe, belief	save, safe
diffuse, diffuse	sheathe, sheath
excuse, excuse	teethe, teeth
grieve, grief	use, use

Sometimes a combination of distinction between voiced and voiceless consonants and distinction between long and short stressed vowel sounds distinguishes verbs from nouns.

breathe, breath	graze, grass
bathe, bath	

Voicing of voiceless consonants in such plurals as *calves, oaths,* and *houses* is a similar phenomenon. So is voicing before suffixes.

grief, grievous	north, northern
mischief, mischievous	worth, worthy

In *southern* and *wizard* a shift to short vowel sounds accompanies this voicing. The influence of neighboring sounds often affects voicing. This is notably true when before the voiceless /t/ of *to* the voiced /z/ of *used, supposed,* and *has* becomes voiceless /s/ and the voiced /v/ of *have* becomes voiceless /f/.

The six stops are as follows:

	Voiceless	*Voiced*
Bilabial:	/p/ of *pore*	/b/ of *bore*
Alveolar:	/t/ of *tore*	/d/ of *door*
Velar:	/k/ of *core*	/g/ of *gore*

All of the stops have single consonant letters as their basic representations. But for two reasons consonant letters are doubled, in fact or in effect, in a great many words.

1. Sometimes doubling indicates that a preceding vowel letter represents a short stressed vowel sound. Doubled consonant letters which perform this function are generally followed by vowel letters, glide letters, or *le* representing syllabic /l̩/, as in *luggage, mattress,* and *nibble.* In addition, at the end of words *f, k, l, s,* and *z* are normally doubled after short stressed vowel sounds, though other consonant letters are not—so that *sniff, lock, bell, pass,* and *buzz* contrast with *snip, lob, bet, pan,* and *bug.*

2. In a great many complexes doubling occurs because of the coming together of two components which are no longer kept distinct in the spoken language. One of the repeated letters terminates the first written component, the other begins the second; there is no corresponding repetition of the consonant sound. If a single vowel letter representing a stressed vowel sound precedes, the vowel sound will normally be short, as in *annotate, attribution, suffix,* and *supplicate.* In compounds the components are usually kept distinct, and they are kept distinct in some complexes also. Thus in *headdress, roommate, greenness,* and *unnerved* if there is no actual doubling of consonant sounds, there is at least clear prolongation, and what results can be represented reasonably enough by /dd/, /mm/, and /nn/. This is a very different matter from the repeating of consonant letters where there is no repeating or clear prolonging of consonant sounds.

There is also a certain amount of doubling after unstressed vowel sounds for no reason that is clear in English: for example, in *staccato.* And in such words as *panicky, picnicking,* and *trafficked* the letter *c* is replaced by *ck* before inflectional endings and noninflectional suffixes beginning with *e, i,* and *y* to make it clear that the sound represented is the stop /k/ and not the fricative /s/. In pairs like *classical* and *classicism* and *authentic* and *authenticity, c* represents /s/ before *e* and *i.*

A great deal of doubling takes place when inflectional endings and noninflectional suffixes are joined to basic-form words. Doubling normally takes place when the following conditions are met:

1. The word with which the suffix or inflectional ending is combined ends in a single consonant letter other than *x* or *h,* or in the glide letter *r.*

2. A single vowel letter, or a single vowel letter preceded by the combination *qu* (as in *quit*), precedes this single consonant letter or *r*.
3. The vowel sound of the last syllable of this word (the only syllable if the word is monosyllabic) is stressed in the resulting form, as in *referring* as opposed to *reference*.
4. What is joined to the basic-form word is either a suffix *le* or *y* or a suffix or inflectional ending beginning with a vowel letter.

Examples of doubling when these conditions are met follow.

abhorr ence	controll ing	godd ess	ragg ed
bagg age	dabb le	handicapp ing	rebutt al
bagg ed	deterr ent	kidnapp er	shrubb ery
bagg ing	forgett able	lagg ard	starr ed
blott er	gladd en	mann ish	starr y
committ ee	gladd est	quizz es	zigzagg ed

There is no doubling or prolonging of sounds here. Except where *r* is involved (as in *deterrent, deterring, starred,* and *starry*) and except also for a few forms such as *controllable* and *controlling*, the doubling of letters normally serves to indicate that the preceding vowel letter represents a short stressed vowel sound, whether the stress on the vowel sound is primary stress as in *unforgettable* or secondary or weak stress as in *kidnapper* and *zigzagging*. Exceptional doubling occurs in such words as *excellence* in spite of the pattern of stress; the doubling in *excelling* is of course normal. Doubling is commonly absent before the suffixes *ic* and *ity*.

angel ic	symbol ic	abnormal ity	Christian ity
atom ic	method ical	avid ity	steril ity

But *metallic* shows regular doubling before *ic*. Absence of doubling results in irregular spellings in *benefited, benefiting, paralleled,* and *paralleling*, where secondary or weak stresses precede the inflectional endings, and in *chagrined*. Substitution of single-letter representation of consonant sounds for doubled sometimes occurs before suffixes where otherwise the same letter would be used three times in succession.

dul ly	ful ly	shril ly

In *dully* and *shrilly* there is what can be regarded as /ll/ in the spoken language; in more frequently used *fully* there is only a single /l/.

The doubling of consonant letters in such words as *wedding* is obviously not unlike the doubling of vowel letters in such words as *weeding*, and the doubling with variation in such words as *stricken* (which is to *strike* as *hidden* is to *hide*) is not unlike the use of two vowel letters in such words as *leading*. Like the doubling of vowel letters, the doubling of consonant letters is commonly a way of indicating vowel sounds.

It should be noted that vowel letters participate directly in a number of representations of consonant sounds. Several two- and three-letter representations of the velar stops include the vowel letter *u*, and when these combinations end words an *e* follows the *u*. In such words as *vague* the *e* participates in the representations both of the velar stop and of the long vowel sound which precedes it. The spelling *ed* for /t/ and /d/ serves, for great numbers of regular verbs, to make the verb inflectional ending visually if not aurally distinct from noninflectional /t/ and /d/. Thus *packed* is visually quite distinct from *pact*, *paced* from *paste*, *passed* from *past*, *sighed* from *side*, *barred* from *bard*, *mowed* from *mode*, *bowled* from *bold*, and *banned* from *band*. The verb inflection which is written *ed* is notably variable in the spoken language. It is pronounced /d/ after all voiced sounds except another /d/: for example, in *played*, *showed*, *robbed*, *loved*, *raised*, *rolled*, and *banged*. It is pronounced /t/ after all voiceless consonants except another /t/: for example, in *ripped*, *laughed*, *frothed*, *missed*, and *patched*. After /d/ and /t/ *ed* is pronounced /ɪd/ or /əd/: for example, in *waded* and *hated*. Sometimes this *ed* is also pronounced /ɪd/ or /əd/ when a noninflectional suffix follows it, as in *confessedly*, *markedly*, and *preparedness* where without such a suffix it is pronounced /d/ or /t/.

Like the stressed vowel sounds, the consonant sounds have some spellings which are employed in very few words and are best omitted from tables of the commoner spellings. The commoner spellings, again, can be classified as primary, secondary, and anomalous. Irregular uses of primary and secondary spellings occur under the following circumstances.

1. When a single consonant sound which does not follow a short stressed vowel sound is given doubled representation. This occurs (1) after long stressed vowel sounds, as in *butte, chauffeur, hall, office, poll,* and *toss;* (2) after unstressed vowel sounds, as in *abbreviate, raccoon, acknowledge, adduce, plaintiff, aggression, immoral, mayonnaise, supply, waitress,* and *dilettante;* and (3) when a consonant sound precedes, as in *vitally* and *basically* where *a* is silent before /l/ or /l/.

2. When final *d, g, n,* and *t* are given doubled representations after short stressed vowel sounds, as in *add, egg, inn,* and *butt;* and conversely when final *c, f, k, l, s,* and *z* are given undoubled representations after short stressed vowel sounds, as in *bloc, chef, trek, armful, yes,* and *whiz.*

3. When the *e* of such combinations as *ge, que,* and *ve* does not participate also in the representation of immediately preceding stressed vowel sounds, as in *garage, plaque,* and *love;* and conversely when the *e* of such combinations as *the,* in which two consonant letters are employed, does participate in the representation of immediately preceding stressed vowel sounds, as in *bathe* and *clothe.*

4. When a single vowel letter representing a short vowel sound is followed by a single consonant letter which is in turn followed by a vowel letter or a glide letter. Thus irregularly used single consonant letters in *study, coming, menace, metal, rabid, rapid, second, vigor,* and *condition* contrast with regularly used doubled consonant letters in *muddy, humming, pennant, mettle, rabbit, rapping, beckon, bigger,* and *commission.*

The last of these irregularities is the most frequent of the irregularities affecting the representation of vowel sounds. It occurs most often in words acquired from other languages, but is also found occasionally in native words. The irregularity is in the use of the single consonant letter, but the damage is done to the representation of the preceding short vowel sound, which becomes indistinguishable from a regular representation of a long vowel sound—in *study,* for example, as compared with *student.*

A table of spellings of the stops follows.

    28. Voiceless-bilabial /p/.
        Primary, *p* series: *p, pp.*
        drop, upper

29. Voiceless-alveolar /t/.
      Primary, *t* series: *t, tt.*
      bit, bitten
      Anomalous: *ed.*
      heaped
30. Voiceless-velar /k/.
      Primary, *k* series: *k, ck.*
      strike, stricken
      Secondary, *c* series: *c, cc.*
      cane, tobacco
      Secondary, *q* series: *q, qu, que.*
      quit, conquer, grotesque
      Anomalous: *ch.*
      character
31. Voiced-bilabial /b/.
      Primary, *b* series: *b, bb.*
      dab, rabbit
32. Voiced-alveolar /d/.
      Primary, *d* series: *d, dd.*
      mad, saddle
      Anomalous: *ed.*
      played
33. Voiced-velar /g/.
      Primary, *g* series: *g, gg, gu, gue.*
      longer, giggle, guard, rogue

Rare spellings of the stops can be illustrated as follows.

For /t/: vel*d*, *Th*omas, pi*zz*a.
For /k/: sa*cch*arine, a*c*quaint, *kh*aki, tre*kk*ing.
For /g/: *gh*astly.

The eight fricatives are as follows.

	Voiceless	*Voiced*
Labiodental:	/f/ of *thief*	/v/ of *thieve*
Interdental:	/θ/ of *wreath*	/ð/ of *wreathe*
Alveolar:	/s/ of *race*	/z/ of *raise*
Palatal:	/ʃ/ of *notion*	/ʒ/ of *erosion*

Except for its use in combination with /d/, the voiced palatal fricative /ʒ/ is the least used of all the consonant sounds, rarely beginning a word (though exotic *genre* and *gendarme* begin with it) and tending to give way to /dʒ/ at the end of words, as in *garage.*
Only four of the fricatives have single letters as basic representa-

tions: /f/, /v/, /s/, and /z/. The letter *v* is doubled in only a few words, most of them regarded as slang: *divvy, flivver, revved, savvy.* Moreover *v* is rarely allowed to end a word, though it does terminate *Slav* and *rev* at least. These restrictions on the use of the letter *v* make it impossible for the written language to distinguish, for example, *have* and *having* from *save* and *saving* as it distinguishes *can* and *canning* from *cane* and *caning.* Doubling occurs within certain representations of /ʃ/: notably in the *ssi* of *mission.* When *c* represents /s/ and (with *i*) /ʃ/, it is not doubled: thus *tacit* has a single *c* just as *facing* does, and *pernicious* has a single *c* just as *ferocious* does. Similarly *t* is not doubled in representations of /ʃ/, or *s* and *g* in representations of /ʒ/. The language has no representations of /ʒ/ employing two consonant letters, and so cannot represent /ʒ/ regularly after short stressed vowel sounds—for example, in *vision.* *S* is sometimes doubled in representations of /z/, as in *scissors* and *dissolve;* but usually, as in *risen* (which is to *rise* as *hidden* is to *hide*), it is not doubled.

The fricatives have a number of two- and three-letter representations terminating in *h, e,* and *i.* The consonant letter *h* is used in a few anomalous representations of velar stops (for example, in *stomach, khan,* and *ghetto*) and in an anomalous representation of the consonantal glide /r/ (as in *rhyme*), but normally its presence within two- and three-letter representations of single consonant sounds serves to mark these sounds as fricatives. When *e* is used with *c* and *g* it indicates that fricatives, not the stops /k/ and /g/, are being represented. When it is used with *v, s,* and *z,* it simply prevents these letters from being used at the end of words. The taboo against ending with *v* has been noted. There is a similar prejudice against a word's ending with a single *z,* though a few words such as *quiz* and *whiz* do. A final single *s* is usually inflectional, so that inflectional /s/ and /z/ are generally distinct in appearance if not in sound from noninflectional. Thus *lacks* is visually quite distinct from *lax, laps* from *lapse, patients* from *patience, crews* from *cruise,* and *sees* from *seize.* But *famous, crisis, gas, lens,* and *as* are examples from small categories of words that do end in noninflectional single *s.* The various inflectional endings which are written *s* and *'s,* like the inflectional ending of verbs that is written *ed,* are notably variable in the spoken language.

After all voiced sounds except /z/ and /ʒ/ they are pronounced /z/: for example, in *boys, buys, Mary's, comes, wives, roads, Bill's*, and *sags*. After all voiceless consonants except /s/ and /ʃ/ they are pronounced /s/: for example, in *rips, wife's, froths, bats*, and *cracks*. After /z/, /ʒ/, /s/, and /ʃ/ they are pronounced /ɪz/ or /əz/ and *es* is written for *s* though *'s* remains: for example, in *buzzes, mirages, badges, Cass's*, and *rushes*. The single noninflectional *s* of *as*, like the single *f* of *if*, the single *e* of *the*, and the single *o* of *to*, is employed in a word that is commonly unstressed. In the combination *the*, the letter *e* serves to mark the consonant sound as voiced. Quite often the *e* which functions as a part of the representation of a fricative functions also as a part of the representation of the preceding vowel sound: for example, in *base, bathe, Chinese, daze, drove, prestige*, and *spice*. Where *i* occurs in representations of the palatal fricatives /ʃ/ and /ʒ/, it represented /j/ after /s/ and /z/ in earlier pronunciations. Similarly *race you* still becomes /reʃə/ in the spoken language, and *raise you* still becomes /reʒə/.

A table of spellings of the fricatives follows.

34. Voiceless-labiodental /f/.
    Primary, *f* series: *f, ff*.
    stifle, stiff
    Secondary: *ph*.
    photograph
35. Voiceless-interdental /θ/.
    Primary: *th*.
    bath
36. Voiceless-alveolar /s/.
    Primary, *s* series: *s, ss, se*.
    sight, fuss, dense
    Secondary, *c* series: *c, ce, sc, sce*.
    cite, dance, scent, coalesce
37. Voiceless-palatal /ʃ/.
    Primary, *s* series: *sh, si, ssi*.
    short, expansion, passion
    Secondary, *c* series: *ch, ci, c*.
    machine, racial, associate
    Secondary, *t* series: *ti, t*.
    nation, negotiate
38. Voiced-labiodental /v/.
    Primary, *v* series: *v, ve*.
    over, cove

39. Voiced-interdental /ð/.
    Primary, *th* series: *th, the.*
        mother, wreathe
40. Voiced-alveolar /z/.
    Primary, *s* series: *s, se.*
        criticism, applause
    Secondary, *z* series: *z, zz, ze.*
        zero, quizzes, gauze
41. Voiced-palatal /ʒ/.
    Primary, *s* series: *si, s.*
        invasion, composure
    Secondary, *g* series: *g, ge.*
        regime, beige

Rare spellings of the fricatives can be illustrated as follows.

    For /f/: sa*pph*ire, rou*gh.*
    For /s/: quart*z.*
    For /ʃ/: o*c*ean, fu*ch*sia, fa*sc*ist, *sch*wa, con*sc*ious,
            cu*sh*ion, a*ss*ure, *s*ugar.
    For /v/: o*f*, Ste*ph*en, di*vv*y.
    For /z/: *Cz*ar, di*s*cern, di*ss*olve, *x*ylophone.
    For /ʒ/: equa*t*ion, sei*z*ure, bra*z*ier.

The nasals and the lateral are as follows.

	Voiced Nasals	*Voiced Lateral*
Bilabial:	/m/ of *rum*	
Alveolar:	/n/ of *run*	/l/ of *lull*
Velar:	/ŋ/ of *rung*	

After a stressed vowel sound in the same syllable—for example, in *feel, fail, foal, fool, fill,* and *full*—/l/ seems very close in quality to /əl/. The nasal /ŋ/ does not begin English words.

Two of the three nasals, /m/ and /n/, and the lateral /l/ have single letters as basic representations. These are doubled just as single-letter representations of the stops are doubled. The velar nasal /ŋ/ has *n* as a one-letter representation only when /ŋ/ occurs before the velar stops /k/ and /g/, as in *think* and *finger.* What was once /g/ after /ŋ/ is not pronounced in such words as *sing* and *long* (where it would end the words); and the letters *ng* together represent /ŋ/. In *longer* and *longest, stronger* and *strongest,* and *younger* and *youngest* the letters *ng* still represent /ŋg/, but in more typical *singer, hanger,* and *longing* they represent only /ŋ/.

A table of spellings of the nasals and the lateral follows.

> 42. Voiced-bilabial /m/.
>> Primary, *m* series: *m, mm*.
>> man, immigrate
> 43. Voiced-alveolar /n/.
>> Primary, *n* series: *n, nn*.
>> pun, annual
> 44. Voiced-velar /ŋ/.
>> Primary, *n* series: *n, ng*.
>> bank, bang
> 45. Voiced-alveolar /l/.
>> Primary, *l* series: *l, ll*.
>> pole, fell

Rare spellings can be illustrated as follows.

> For /n/: co*m*ptroller
> For /ŋ/: hara*ng*ued, to*ng*ue

The consonantal glides and the aspirate are as follows.

	Voiced	*Voiceless*
Front:	/j/ of *yea*	
Central:	/r/ of *ray*	
Back:	/w/ of *way*	

Aspirate: /h/ of *hay*

As has been said, the consonantal glides are closely related to the vocalic glides. The /j/ of *yacht* is much like the /ɪ/ of *tie*, and the /r/ and /w/ which begin *roar* and *wow* are much like the /r/ and /ʊ/ which terminate these words. The consonantal glides occur only before vowel sounds in their syllables, the vocalic glides occur only after other vowel sounds in their syllables. Glides which occur between stressed and unstressed vowel sounds can ordinarily be assumed to belong to the syllables of the stressed vowel sounds. Thus in *barometric, origin, tyranny,* and *various* the sound represented by *r* can be said to combine, as a vocalic glide, with the vowel sound that precedes it, whereas in *barometer, original, tyrannical,* and *variety* the sound represented by the same letter can be said to function as a consonantal glide beginning the syllables to which it belongs. The aspirate /h/ occurs only before vowel sounds in the same syllables and before /j/ as in *humid* and /w/ as in *whet*. The aspirate normally disappears in unstressed syllables: for example, in *prohibition* as compared with *prohibit* and in unstressed *his* (as in *Cox lost his hat*) as compared with stressed *his* (as in *the hat's his*). The consonantal glides do not disappear from unstressed syllables to any comparable extent, but in many situations they do tend to fall out or to be replaced in one way or another. Thus in the sentence *Jim will get you hundreds of them* comfortable pronunciations will tend to omit the /w/ of *will*, to combine the /j/ of *you* with the /t/ of *get* to produce /tʃ/, and to substitute /ɚ/ for /rə/ in *hundreds*.

A table of spellings of the consonantal glides and the aspirate follows.

    46. Voiced-front /j/.
        Primary: *y*.
          yes
        Secondary: *i*.
          million
        Secondary: *e*.
          feudal
    47. Voiced-central /r/.
        Primary: *r*.
          dream
        Anomalous: *rr, rh*.
          surround, rheumatism
    48. Voiced-back /w/.
        Primary: *w*.
          wear
        Secondary: *u*.
          equal
    49. Aspirate /h/.
        Primary: *h*.
          home

Rare spellings can be illustrated as follows.

        For /j/: vi*gn*ette, hallelu*j*ah.
        For /w/: *ch*oir.
        For /h/: mari*j*uana.

Consonant combinations.—Consonant combinations within syllables are much more numerous than vocalic combinations. Only five, however, are used both before and after the vowel sounds of the syllables in which they occur.

/tʃ/ of *choke, rich*   /sp/ of *spare, lisp*
/dʒ/ of *joke, ridge*   /st/ of *stair, list*
                               /sk/ of *scare, risk*

The exclusively prevocalic consonantal combinations that can be regarded as normal for contemporary English are of two types. One type terminates in the lateral /l/ or in one of the consonantal glides /j/, /r/, and /w/. The remainder of such a combination is a single consonant sound (as in *clean, cure, cream,* and *quick*) or two consonant sounds of which the first is the voiceless fricative /s/ (as in *skewer, sclerosis, scratch, squad, spew, splash, spread,* and *street*). The other normal prevocalic type begins with the voiceless fricative /s/ and has only a single consonant sound following this /s/. *Sphere, small,* and *snow* can serve as examples. Such words as *slow* and *sweet* can be said to belong to both types. Many possible combinations of the two established prevocalic types either do not occur or occur only in words of foreign origin and more or less exotic character, many of them names of people and places. Thus /pw/ and /bw/ are accepted in such place names as *Pueblo, Puerto Rico,* and *Buenos Aires,* but do not occur otherwise and cause difficulties in these names.

Prevocalic consonantal combinations of types that are not natural for contemporary English are accepted in such exotic words as *tsetse* and *Tlaxcala*. In such words as *Cnut, Dvorak, Gdynia,* and *tmesis* schwa is commonly inserted between the first two consonant sounds, so that an unstressed syllable is added to what the written language suggests. In a considerable number of words whose spellings suggest unusual consonant combinations, the spoken language simply ignores one of the written consonant letters. This is true of such words as *bdellium, gnaw, know, pneumonia, psychology, ptomaine,* and *write*.

The exclusively postvocalic consonantal combinations that can be regarded as normal within syllables in contemporary English are of two types very much like the two types of prevocalic combinations. One type begins with the lateral /l/ or one of the nasals /m/, /n/, and /ŋ/. The remainder of such a combination is a single consonant sound (as in *self, bump, ant,* and *ink*) or /tʃ/ or /dʒ/ (as in *squelch, bulge, lunch,* and *fringe*), or two consonant sounds of which the second is /s/ (as in *waltz, glimpse, chintz,* and *jinx).* The other type of normal postvocalic consonantal combination terminates in /s/ and has only a single consonant sound in front of this /s/. Such words as *mix, collapse,* and *quartz* can serve as examples. Such words as *false* and *dance* can be said to belong to both groups. Some possible combinations of the established postvocalic types do not occur. Thus /mb/, /mv/, /nð/, and /lg/ are not used. In such words as *rumble* and *assemble* /b/ pretty clearly belongs to the following syllable, not with /m/.

The number of postvocalic consonantal combinations in use in contemporary English has been increased by the development, in modern times, of the wholly consonantal inflectional endings written *s* and *ed,* and of the wholly consonantal noninflectional suffixes written *th.* The use of these terminations has resulted in a considerable number of consonantal combinations which cannot be called either "normal" or exotic. Examples follow.

/ðz/	of *bathes*	/kts/	of *facts*
/ndz/	of *bands*	/sks/	of *risks*
/gd/	of *dragged*	/pθs/	of *depths*
/ndʒd/	of *plunged*	/ksθs/	of *sixths*
/ŋkt/	of *thanked*		

The use of some combinations such as these goes beyond the situations in which the nonsyllabic consonantal suffixes and inflectional endings appear. Since /kt/ is accepted in *packed,* it is the more easily maintained in *fact;* and since /ŋkt/ is accepted in *thanked,* it is the more easily maintained in *adjunct.* But English is a language which refuses to pronounce the *p* of *psychology* or the *b* of *thumb,* though it insists on writing them. In comfortable speech, simplification of consonant combinations takes place very commonly. Thus *clothes* loses /ð/ and is pronounced like the verb *close. Bands* loses /d/ and is pronounced like *bans, sects* loses /t/ and becomes indistinguishable from *sex, priests* loses /t/ and rhymes with *niece, asked* loses /k/ and rhymes with *past.* Where it is clear (with the help of context) and usual, such simplification is not undesirable. Simplification is normal in sequences of spoken words when difficult combinations are thrown together at rapid tempos, though when the tempo is slowed simplification may seem slovenly. A common type of misspelling is the result of following the ear rather than the grammar where difficult combinations occur.

> I have to take three *advance* courses next semester.
> Yesterday everyone *seem* to agree.
> I hadn't *practice* the piece enough.
> Laurette was finally *ask* to leave.
> My brother *use* to room with me.

The participial endings in such combinations as *creamed chicken, iced tea, mashed potatoes,* and *whipped cream* are retained in standard written English, though *ice cream* and *roast beef* have no such endings. Writing is one thing, pronunciation is often quite another. It no longer seems reasonable to maintain the point of view which in the last century caused the McGuffey Readers, for example, to drill students on the careful pronunciation of such archaic consonant combinations as were represented by written *thank'd'st, help'd'st,* and *rob'd'st.* But sometimes simplification is not clear and usual, and difficult combinations must be got through. Thus *bathes, wasps,* and *risked* can hardly be simplified.

The spelling of the great majority of consonant combinations does not require special notice. The sounds which go to make up the combination /spr/ in such a word as *spray,* for example, are represented in the combination exactly as they are represented individually in such words as *say, pay,* and *ray.* The spellings given /tʃ/ and /dʒ/ require notice, however, and so do the uses to which the written language puts the letter *x.* The affricates /tʃ/ and /dʒ/ have spellings much like those of monophthongal palatal fricatives. The *ch* of *each* and the *tch* of *itch* may seem like a pair such as the *l* of *heel* and the *ll* of *hill,* but it is better to regard them simply as a spelling in which /t/ is not represented individually and one in which it is. The combination /dʒ/, however, has basic one-letter representations, and in the *dg* of *cadging* as compared with the *g* of *caging* there is true doubling comparable to that shown in the *ck* of *backing* alongside the *k* of *baking.* The letter *x* represents two consonant sounds normally, and a single vowel letter in front of it always represents a short vowel sound, as in *axle, lexicon, Dixie, boxing,* and *buxom.* The *ks* of *oaks* represents sound by sound what the *x* of *coax* represents together. Very commonly the two sounds represented by *x* are not in the same syllable.

The following table shows the spellings of /tʃ/ and /dʒ/, and the spellings which employ the letter *x*.

    50. Voiceless-affricate /tʃ/.
        Primary, *c* series: *ch, tch.*
        rich, witch
        Secondary, *t* series: *ti, t.*
        question, nature
    51. Voiced-affricate /dʒ/.
        Primary, *g* series: *g, dg, dge, ge, gi.*
        germ, fidget, badge, college, region
        Secondary, *j* series: *j, dj.*
        jerk, adjective
        Secondary, *d* series: *di, d.*
        cordial, verdure
    52. Voiceless-stop-and-fricative /ks/.
        Primary spellings requiring notice: *x, xc.*
        lax, excellent
    53. Voiced-stop-and-fricative /gz/.
        Primary spelling requiring notice: *x.*
        exact

Rare spellings of /tʃ/ and /dʒ/ can be illustrated as follows.

        For /tʃ/: *c*ello, *Cz*ech, righ*te*ous.
        For /dʒ/: exa*gg*erate.

X has the value of /kʃ/ in *sexual* and of /gʒ/ in *luxurious*. In *anxious* the combination *xi* has the value of /kʃ/.

    Unrepresented sounds, silent letters, reversals in order, exotic sounds.—Unrepresented sounds occur. Among the vowel sounds schwa is unrepresented before /m/ where *sm* and *thm* terminate words, as in *baptism* and *logarithm*. Unstressed /ɪ/ or schwa is unrepresented also in numerous possessive singulars of nouns: for example, in *boss's*. Among the consonant sounds /t/ is unrepresented in *eighth* and the consonantal glide /w/ in *one* and *once*. The most frequently unrepresented of all vowel and consonant sounds is the consonantal glide /j/, which occurs unrepresented in such words as *unit, music, futile, cute, human, cure, volume, genuine,* and *failure*. When /j/ occurs unrepresented, it is almost always before a sound, stressed or unstressed, represented by the letter *u* or a combination of letters begun with *u*. In some varieties of American English, unrepresented /j/ occurs, and in others it does not occur, after /θ/, /t/, /d/, and /n/ in the same syllable, in such words as *enthusiasm, Tuesday, dupe, nuisance, durable,* and *mature.* Pairs such as *youth* and *use, feudal* and *futile,* and *hew* and *hue* show /j/ represented by *y* and *e* alongside unrepresented /j/. Pairs such as *ooze* and *use, coo* and *cue,* and *poor* and *pure* put words not employing unrepresented /j/ alongside words employing it.

Abbreviations, of course, leave sounds unrepresented on a much larger scale: *Mr.* and *N. Y.* can serve as examples. A few abbreviations are commonly read in what amount to translations: *lb.* and *viz.,* for example, as *pound* and *namely.* Such interlingual symbols as the number ideographs disregard sounds completely, so that the symbol *5,* for example, is read as *cinco* in Spanish and *five* in English.

Silent letters are more frequent than unrepresented sounds. First of all, there is a category of words in which *e* occurs without function. A few common words of native origin are included in the category: *come, done, eye,* and *owe* are examples. Modern acquisitions, especially from French, make up a larger subcategory: *belle, caffeine, caste, cigarette, clientele, façade, locale, route,* and *silhouette* can serve as examples. Often a vowel letter is silent, and the number of syllables is reduced, where otherwise there would be two or three unstressed syllables in succession. In the following words pronunciation of a vowel sound where the italicized vowel letters occur might seem affected.

abom*i*nable	choc*o*late	*i*nterest	several
artist*i*cally	colonel	labor*a*tory	unpard*o*nable
bas*i*cally	di*a*mond	marr*i*age	vict*u*als
bus*i*ness	ev*e*ry	parl*i*ament	Wed*ne*sday
carr*i*age	fam*i*ly	reas*o*nable	wonderf*u*lly

The *o* of *iron* is silent even though pronouncing it would give the word only one unstressed syllable. In a large number of words, unstressed syllables disappear in rapid, comfortable speech but remain in careful speech. Finally, silent vowel letters occur, without reduction in number of syllables, in many words in which unstressed vowel sounds drop out before /l/ and /n/, and in some words in which they drop out before /m/ and /ŋ/; and these consonant sounds then function as peaks of syllables. Syllabic /l̩/ develops after most of the consonant sounds, but generally not after the fricatives /θ/, /ð/, /ʃ/, or /ʒ/, or after a consonantal glide or the aspirate /h/. The following words show silent vowel letters where syllabic /l̩/ occurs.

approval	channel	devil	idyl
baffle	desolate	docile	simultaneous

Syllabic /n̩/ usually develops only after the alveolars /t/, /d/, /s/, and /z/. The following words show silent vowel letters where syllabic /n̩/ occurs.

ardent   certain   comparison   medicine

Syllabic /m̩/ occurs infrequently, after labial /p/ and /b/ and labiodental /f/ and /v/; syllabic /ŋ̩/ occurs infrequently after velar /k/ and /g/.

Silent consonant letters are fairly common. The inconspicuous simplification normal for consonant clusters produced by the addition of consonantal inflectional endings has been noted. Simplification of essentially the same kind sometimes occurs when two words come together. Thus in *last night, must be, first grade,* and *best student* the first word in each pair is commonly pronounced without /t/. In addition, consonant letters that are silent without regard to preceding or following words occur with some frequency. Examples follow.

lamb	exhibit	mnemonic	soften
thumb	shepherd	solemn	bouquet
doubt	John	pneumonia	mortgage
bdellium	oh	psychology	postpone
indict	catarrh	ptomaine	asthma
yacht	know	cupboard	wrong
handsome	half	comptroller	sword
sign	calm	coup	two
might	talk	debris	who
thought	folk	island	faux pas
hour	should	fasten	rendezvous

In such words as *indict, sign, might, talk,* and *folk,* however, the consonant letters here described as silent can be regarded as parts of the representations of vowel sounds. It should be noted that consonant letters that are silent in particular words are sometimes pronounced in related words.

crumb, crumble	phlegm, phlegmatic
doubt, dubitative	prohibition, prohibit
malign, malignant	shepherd, cowherd
muscle, muscular	solemn, solemnity
schism, schizophrenia	corps, corpus
resign, resignation	receipt, reception

In such complexes as *fasten, moisten,* and *soften* the *t* is silent; in such corresponding simplexes as *fast, moist,* and *soft* it normally is not.

Letters representing successive sounds occasionally occur in reversed order. The consonantal combination /hw/ has *wh* as its normal representation, as in *which* and *whet.* The consonantal combination /nj/ is represented by *gn* in a few exotic words such as *lorgnette* and *vignette.* The presence, side by side, of the spellings *er* and *re* for the same unstressed vowel sound, and of the spellings *el* and *le* for the same syllabic consonant sound, as in *eager* and *ogre* and *libel* and *liable,* is a phenomenon of a somewhat different but related type.

Sounds outside the usual sets of vowel and consonant sounds occur in absolutes such as what is written as *tut, tut* (or *tsk, tsk,* or *tch, tch*). Sometimes exotic sounds are employed in words acquired from other languages, notably French: for example, in *rapprochement, milieu,* and *salon.* Obviously words which require the production of unfamiliar vowel and consonant sounds can have only limited usefulness. Similarly efforts to maintain accent marks on words which have become English leads only to trouble: our typewriters generally do not have accent marks. The dieresis which used to be employed in such words as *naive* and *cooperate* is equally impractical—and the cedilla of, for example, *facade.*

The stability of established spellings.—There is no doubt that the complexity of its spelling is a major defect of contemporary English. Entirely too much school time must be given to spelling, at the expense of subject matters of much greater fundamental importance. Where choice among recognized spellings is possible, spellings which conform to the patterning of the primary spellings should be preferred: *chaperone* rather than *chaperon,* for example, since the vowel sound of the last syllable is the stressed long /o/ of *bone* and *tone.* Where spellings are fixed but choice among recognized pronunciations is possible, decision again should be in favor of what conforms best to the primary patterns of the spelling system: /aɪ/ rather than /ɪ/ in *isolate*, for example, and /i/ rather than /ɛ/ in *economic*. But native speakers should not tamper very much with pronunciations they learned in childhood. Naturalness and absence of anything approaching affectation are highly desirable in spoken language, and regional variations add interest to it. Those who learn English past childhood should not be greatly concerned about traces of foreign accent. The British novelist Joseph Conrad learned English as a young man, and spoke with an accent all his life; but no one has written the language more effectively, and he was a brilliant conversationalist as well.

Once their precise composition has been established, the written forms of words are remarkably secure. Indeed, widespread literacy seems to have made them almost invulnerable: literate people will not tolerate alterations in familiar combinations of letters. Even such unfortunate bits of native spelling as the *gh* of, for example, *caught*, *taught*, and *brought* (and of *night* and *through*) seem quite secure. The tremendous borrowed vocabulary of modern English has generally paid much more attention to letters than to sounds. This is of course the reason English and Spanish so often relate identical or nearly identical combinations of letters—for example, in place names and in such very different words as *ideal*, *original*, *pasteurize*, and *chili*—to essentially identical aggregations of meanings, and yet employ very different combinations of sounds. Literate people seem to relate visual impressions to meanings somewhat less flexibly than they relate aural impressions to them. One who hears *Bible* pronounced almost as he pronounces *bobble* finds it much easier to accept the different pronunciation than he would to accept another spelling. Noah Webster's early effort to reform English spelling by introducing such spellings as *tung*, *crum*, *iland*, *fether*, and *wimmen* was doomed to failure and would doubtless have even less chance now. Clever respellings catch the eye and so are useful in advertising.

| Kash Karry | Your Wate and Fate |
| Rold Gold | Signs of All Kigns |

Such a chapter heading as *Liquor Is Quiquor* gets attention similarly. But this kind of thing is acceptable only in a very limited way. Such a slogan as *do right and fear no man, don't write and fear no woman* is amusing, but the written-language words are given their established spellings here: it will not do to confuse *right* and *write* and *rite* and *wright*. In most kinds of writing, "correct" spelling is obligatory. From the point of view of the spelling system the spelling r-a-i-n in *the rain of Henry VIII* is clearly preferable to the established spelling r-e-i-g-n, but the systematically preferable spelling is simply not acceptable here.

CHAPTER XX

STRESS, SYLLABIFICATION, INTONATION, AND PUNCTUATION

Stress in words.—Variations in what is commonly called stress are a notable characteristic of spoken English. The term "stress" is not an ideal one: "prominence" would be more satisfactory, and prominence is evidently produced largely by increasing duration and changing pitch. It is convenient to distinguish stressed syllables from unstressed ones, but syllables can be either stressed or unstressed in varying degrees. In *irreparable* only the second syllable is stressed. Among the three unstressed syllables following the stressed syllable, the last comes closest to stress and the first is farthest from it. There is a tendency to alternate stressed and unstressed syllables, and a sequence of three unstressed syllables is likely to seem troublesome, though such sequences occur in standard pronunciations of, for example, *communicable, despicable, disputable, evidently, formidable, hospitable, incomparable,* and *irrefutable.* In *‚polio‚mye'litis* there are four stressed syllables. Among the four the last is most prominent and can be said to have the primary stress, the second—the *o* which terminates *polio,* unmarked as the word is written above—comes closest to being unstressed but does maintain long /o/ and so can be said to have weak stress, and the first and third can be said to have secondary stress. The ordinary spellings ignore differences in stress. *Simply* and *imply* have very different patterns of stress, and these affect their vowel sounds; but the written forms give no hint of this fact. The noun *entrance* and the verb *entrance* are written alike, so that without the help of context the combination of letters which represents these two words cannot be pronounced.

Used alone, every word can be said to have one primary stress.

451

Inflectional endings are characteristically unstressed; the "inflected" pronoun forms in *self* (*myself, themselves, oneself,* etc.) have primary stress on *self,* however. Simplexes tend to have only one stressed syllable even when they are several syllables in length: this is true, for example, in *cannibal* and *Missouri.* But many simplexes have more than one stress: for example, *antenna, barbecue, hurricane, Massachusetts, moron.* Repetitives such as *hobnob, hocuspocus, hodgepodge, hushhush, rolypoly,* and *willynilly* have two stresses. When words combine to form compounds, ordinarily each retains stress. Even though the first component in compounds is likely to have the relation of modifier to what follows it, it generally has primary stress.

backfire	boathouse	homesick	nowhere
browbeat	houseboat	waterproof	sometime

But in some compounds the primary stress comes later.

outgrow	afternoon	overconfident	whenever
overpay	undergraduate	herein	nevertheless

In letter compounds such as *TV* and *CIO,* the primary stress seems to come at the end. In some compounds the position of primary stress depends on whether or not the compounds have following heads that they modify.

> We still shop at 'downtown stores.
> We still shop down'town.
> He'll give you an 'offhand answer.
> He'll answer off'hand.

In some compounds there is loss of stress on the last component. Often this component is the noun *man.*

chairman	fireman	gentleman	policeman
congressman	foreman	juryman	seaman
draftsman	Frenchman	kinsman	watchman
Englishman	freshman	marksman	workman

But in *businessman* and *mailman* there is usually some stress on *man.* In *forehead, highland, Iceland, necklace, Sunday,* and *yesterday* there is loss of stress on last components other than *man.* In such nouns as *breakfast, Christmas, shepherd,* and *vineyard* the last component has lost stress and the first has had a short vowel sound substituted for a long vowel sound or a diphthong.

Patterns of stress within complexes are quite varied. Complexes can have one stressed syllable, or several. Prefixes and suffixes tend to be unstressed, but some commonly have secondary or weak stress.

antisocial	nonaggression	captivate	customary
coeducation	uneasy	centralize	optimism
extracurricular	unwrap	childhood	solicitude

For a few affixes, primary stress is normal.

absentee	Japanese	kitchenette	sinusitis

Sometimes affixes for which it is not usual have primary stress.

antifreeze	subhead	allocate	infinite
nonsense	superman	correlate	mishap

Some suffixes have stressed variants with characteristic spellings.

cashier	mirage	mountaineer	urbane
personnel	morale	unique	verbose

The *teen* of such complexes as *fourteen* commonly has primary stress when no head follows.

> Carol's four'teen now.
> She's 'fourteen years old now.

The union of words and noninflectional suffixes is often accompanied by redistribution of stress within the components. In such complexes as the following, primary stresses have moved to the first.

> conference, confidence, excellence, residence
> admirable, comparable, preferable, reputable
> competent, confident, excellent, president
> definite, deputy, desperate, maintenance

In such complexes as the following, primary stresses have moved nearer the end.

> abbreviation, accumulation, exhibition, indication
> abnormality, activity, continuity, sterility, minority
> adjectival, colonial, elemental, memorial
> algebraic, artistic, atomic, poetic, Icelandic

courageous, luxurious, ridiculous, synonymous
photographer, telegraphy, triumphant, indicative

Shifts in stress are especially notable before the suffixes *ence, able, ent, ion, ity, al, ic,* and *ous.* Before *ion* and *ity,* in particular, the habit of bringing primary stress to the end of the uniting word, immediately before *ion* and *ity,* results in notably distinct arrangements of stress. *Exhibition* and *continuity* are therefore quite distinct from *exhibit* and *continue* in the spoken language, though the written language gives no suggestion of this. In such complexes as *capability, stability, curiosity,* and *monstrosity* the shifted pattern of stress affects spellings: *ity* is combined with notably distinct variants of the adjectives with which it is uniting. *Apostolic* shows a similar change before *ic,* and *miraculous* shows it before *ous.* There is no shifting in such words as *convergence, respectable, absorbent, epochal, choleric,* and *adventurous.* Shifts in stress do not accompany the addition of suffixes in genuinely native word formation, it should be said. It is a curiosity of stress patterning that in complexes in which the first components are nonaffixal formatives the primary stress often falls not on the central part of either component but on a stem vowel terminating the first formative.

| biology | isochronal | omniscient | philosophy |
| democracy | lithography | omnivorous | psychology |

Related complexes such as *democrat* and *psychological* put the stresses on parts of the components which seem more central.

Within complexes and compounds of two or more syllables, pattern of stress often varies with part of speech. Sometimes the primary stress is on the last syllable of the verb and the first syllable of the noun or adjective.

com'press, 'compress	,over'hang, 'over,hang
con'duct, 'conduct	per'fect, 'perfect
di'gest, 'digest	per'vert, 'pervert
e'scort, 'escort	pre'sent, 'present
ex'tract, 'extract	pro'gress, 'progress
fer'ment, 'ferment	pur'port, 'purport
fre'quent, 'frequent	re'bel, 'rebel
im'port, 'import	re'hash, 'rehash
,inter'change, 'inter,change	sur'vey, 'survey
off'set, 'offset	sub'ject, 'subject
,over'flow, 'over,flow	trans'fer, 'transfer

A few adjectives and nouns are distinguished in the same way.

in'valid, 'invalid   mi'nute, 'minute

In such a verb as *a'ttribute*, which contrasts with the noun *'attri,bute*, the primary stress is on the syllable next to the last rather than on the last. In such pairs as the following—almost all of them terminating in *ate* or *ment*—verbs have final syllables with secondary stress but nouns and adjectives have unstressed final syllables.

a'ppropri,ate, a'ppropriate	'gradu,ate, 'graduate
a'pproxi,mate, a'pproximate	'imple,ment, 'implement
a'ssoci,ate, a'ssociate	i'niti,ate, i'nitiate
'compli,ment, 'compliment	'mode,rate, 'moderate
de'libe,rate, de'liberate	'ori,ent, 'orient
e'labo,rate, e'laborate	'regi,ment, 'regiment
'esti,mate, 'estimate	'sepa,rate, 'separate

But every word must be learned individually. The following complexes and compounds are both verbs and nouns without distinction in patterns of stress.

comfort	detour	exhaust	promise
command	disdain	exhibit	remark
control	exchange	outline	support
delay	exercise	process	surface

Words normally unstressed.—Irregular alternation between stress and absence of stress characterizes sequences of words as well as single multisyllabic words. Unstressed pronunciations are normal for a number of constantly used monosyllables belonging to a variety of grammatical categories.

1. Unstressed pronunciations are normal for *be* and *been* and for most of the verb forms that (1) precede *not* when *not* functions as clause negator and (2) take positions in front of subjects in questions: *are, am, is, were, was; can, could, must, shall, should, will, would;* in auxiliary uses *have, has, had. May, might,* and *ought* usually have at least weak stress even in such sequences as *we may sell the house* and *I ought to warn you. Do, does,* and *did* are strongly stressed in their emotional uses, as in apologetic, enthusiastic, or merely surprised *he does read the local paper;* in their uses as clause markers they are likely to be unstressed.

2. Unstressed pronunciations are normal for the coordinating
adverbs *and, but, or,* and *nor;* for some clause-marker adverbs used in subordinate clauses, notably *when, where,
if, as,* and *than;* and for a number of prepositional adverbs, notably *at, by, for, from, in, of, till, to,* and *with.*
Clause-marker adverbs such as *why, how,* and *though* are
not likely to lose stress, nor are such prepositional adverbs as *down, like, near, off, on, past, up,* and *worth.*
3. Unstressed pronunciations are normal for the articles *the*
and *a;* for monosyllabic forms of the personal pronouns,
excepting possessives used without following heads (as in
that's his) and also excepting the forms *I, our,* and *they;*
for expletive *there;* for substitute *one* (as in *a yellow apple
and three red ones);* and for clause-marker *that.*

The very frequency of occurrence of these words makes it possible for them to be quite inconspicuous and at the same time
recognizable. But all these words except perhaps expletive *there*
are sometimes stressed. When they merge with *not,* as in *we aren't
late* and *he hadn't been told,* the normally unstressed verb forms
have stress and *not* loses it, so that in informal spoken English the
difference in stressing becomes a part of the indication of negation—though *are* and *had* do take stress in emotional *we* are *late*
and *he* had *been told.* In their uses as clause markers, as in *are we
late?* and *had Bill been told?* the normally unstressed verb forms
may or may not be stressed. Some monosyllabic verb forms not
listed above sometimes lose stress before strongly stressed complements: for example, *get* and *come* in *get up!* and *come in!* Except
occasionally as a result of compounding (as in *chairman* and *highland,* where *man* and *land* are unstressed), nouns, adjectives, and
absolutes are very rarely unstressed; but *sir* is sometimes unstressed
in *yes, sir!* and *times* is sometimes unstressed in its use in connection with multiplication, as in *three times four is twelve.* Clause-
marker adverbs and pronouns seem more likely to be unstressed
in subordinate clauses than in main ones: *when,* for example, in
no one answered when I called but not in *when did you call?* Prepositional adverbs that are "normally" unstressed are unstressed
only when they are used as prepositions with objects following
them. When objects come earlier, as in *who's it for?* the same words
are stressed; and they are stressed when they do not have expressed objects, as in *come in! This* and *that* are generally stressed,

in contrast with *the;* but *this* is commonly unstressed in constantly used *this morning. Some* is often a stressed equivalent of unstressed *a,* as in *some salesman has been trying to call you.* When it modifies plurals and quantifiables, *some* is ordinarily unstressed. In *some students are complaining* stress on *some* would suggest an unstated contrasting *but others are not.* Difference in stress can sometimes indicate which of two essentially opposite meanings of *any* is intended. Thus in *Sarah won't invite any boys to her party* light stress on *any* can indicate that the sentence means that no boys will be invited and very strong stress on *any*—especially if *just* is placed before *any*—can indicate that boys will be invited but Sarah is particular and not all the boys that might be invited will be.

When they are unstressed, various monosyllabic words that are quite distinct in their written forms and in their stressed spoken forms become indistinguishable in pronunciation. *Are* and *or* and *her* are alike, for example; so are *and* and *in,* since *and* usually loses /d/. *Of* and *have* become indistinguishable in pronunciation, and the ungrammatical produce written sequences such as *might of known.* Actually *of* and *have* and *a* often fall together, when the /v/ of *of* and *have* is ignored: in a common pronunciation of *a cup of coffee,* for example, *a* and *of* are indistinguishable. When *I* and *they* are unstressed, sequences like *I love her* and *a lover* become identical in pronunciation, and sequences like *they love her* and *the lover.* Context makes real ambiguity infrequent. Where ambiguity would be likely to result, loss of stress is sometimes avoided even in rather rapid informal speech. Thus *on* and *in* are generally kept distinct by maintaining weak stress on *on,* and *our* and *her* by maintaining weak stress on *our. Her* can safely be pronounced like *are* and *or* because it is generally used in clearly different constructions, but *her* and *our,* like *in* and *on,* are used in the same constructions.

Stress in phrasal units.—In phrasal units, phrase stress tends to come on the last word.

enough tíme	a terrific fíght	boys and gírls
time enóugh	a battle róyal	girls and bóys
the return tríp	Roosevelt's déath	around the wórld
the trip báck	the death of Róosevelt	the world aróund

If the last word has more than one syllable, phrase stress normally centers on the syllable where primary stress falls when the word is spoken alone. When the last word is one that is normally unstressed, phrase stress normally moves forward, as in *Géorge and me* (where coordination gives *me* a degree of stress but *George* ordinarily has phrase stress for the multiple unit), and as in *the néw ones* (where *ones* ordinarily remains unstressed).

In phrasal units in which relationships are exceptional in some way, phrase stress often moves forward. The contrasts in the following pairs of nounal units are significant.

a baby síster	a mother cóuntry	a stone hóuse
a báby sitter	a móther complex	a róck garden
a woman láwyer	a toy cúpboard	a candy cáne
a wóman hater	a tóy cupboard	a cándy store

Each of these units contains a modifying noun and a head noun, and the modifying noun precedes its head. When the modifying noun has the essentially descriptive force of an adjective, the head noun normally has phrase stress. In *a baby síster* the sister is a baby, in *a candy cáne* the cane is candy. When the modifying noun has some other relationship to its head, the modifying noun rather than the head normally has phrase stress. Thus in *a báby sitter* the sitter is not a baby but a sitter with babies, and in *a cándy store* the store is not candy but sells candy. When it is used of a cupboard that is itself a toy, *a toy cupboard* has phrase stress on *cupboard;* when it is used of a cupboard which is not itself a toy but is used as a place for toys, the same sequence has phrase stress on *toy*. Adjective modifiers of noun heads tend to have phrase stress when the relationship is exceptional, as in *the síck room* (where the room is not sick), *the légal profession* (as compared with *the legal solútion*), and *a proféssional man* (as compared with *a professional musícian*). When a gerundial adjective or noun modifies a following head noun, the pattern of stress normally indicates the nature of the relationship somewhat similarly. When the gerundial is a gerundial adjective with the force of a modifying clause with progressive-aspect predicator, the head noun normally has phrase stress: when the gerundial is a noun, and often when it is an adjective with the force of a common-aspect predicator, the gerundial has phrase stress.

growing chíldren	visiting fíremen	traveling sálesmen
gró̵wing pains	vísiting hours	vánishing cream
a living sóul	the waiting mó̵ther	wáshing machines
lívin̤g conditions	the wáiting room	wó̵rking people

Here growing chíldren are children that are growing, but gró̵wing pains are the pains of growing. Vánishing cream is cream that vanishes, and wó̵rking people are people that work. Phrase stress sometimes moves to the front of fixed combinations composed of adjective modifiers and noun heads.

the hígh schools   réal estate   yéllow jackets

But *yellow féver* is a fixed combination too. Many phrasal units disregard the usual patterns of stress. Thus in *ghóst writers* and *próblem children* phrase stress is on the modifying nouns, though the writers are ghosts and the children are problems. In *student activities*, on the other hand, phrase stress is on *activities*, though the activities are not students but rather are for students. With identical relationships *apártment house* and *apartment hótel* employ different patterns of stress. Similarly *chocolate cáke* and *chócolate bar* follow different patterns of stress. Running wáter is commonly water that runs when it is turned on, not water that is running; a living wáge is a wage that permits living, not a wage that is living. *Working mó̵thers* has phrase stress on *mothers*, though *wó̵rking people* has it on *working*.

In phrasal proper names phrase stress tends to come at the end.

Samuel Bútler	Wick Ávenue	the Republican
Robert Morss	Swarthmore Cóllege	Párty
Lóvett		St. George's
		Chúrch

In *New York* phrase stress is on *York* and *New* is likely to have weaker stress than that on *new* in *new homes*. But in phrasal proper names such as *West Forty-second Street* and *the General Electric Company* phrase stress precedes such fairly obvious nouns as *street* and *company*.

In phrasal units which require part-of-speech classification as units, phrase stress is variously placed. It is on the first word in such phrasal nouns as *hánd-me-downs*, *hás-beens*, *ín-laws*, and *tó-do*, and in such phrasal adjectives as *unhéard-of* and *uncálled-for*. It is on the last word in such phrasal verbs as *soft-sóap* and *double-párk;* in such phrasal nouns as *about-fáce, at-hóme, commander-in-chíef, B-flát,* and *New Yórker;* and in such phrasal adjectives as *big-héarted* and *matter-of-fáct.*

Stress in sentences.—In sentences, patterns of stress are determined by complex combinations of influences that can only be suggested here. The tendency is toward putting dominant stress at the end. There is a parallel to this tendency in the assignment of time in long-known hymn tunes. Thus the first lines of one of Charles Wesley's hymns are as follows.

> A charge to keep I have,
> A God to glorify.

In the tune to which this hymn is most often sung, "Boylston," the syllables *have* and *fy,* ending their lines, have twice the time any other syllables have. Dominant stress is of course more than extended duration, and normally centers on syllables that would have primary stress or phrase stress if the words or longer units they are parts of were spoken alone: a dominant stress given to *glorify* would normally center on its first syllable rather than its last. But the parallel is significant. When the answer to *what's wrong now?* is *Bill's broken a chair,* dominant stress will usually be on the complement *a chair.* From the point of view of syntactic analysis the head word in the statement is the predicator *has broken,* and from the point of view of meaning it would seem that the trouble centers in the breaking; but dominant stress will be assigned to *broken* only in rather exceptional versions of the sentence. In *I know one thing* dominant stress will usually be on the complement *one thing;* in *one thing I know* it will usually be on the predicator *know.* In *small-town people are very friendly* dominant stress will generally be on the complement *very friendly;* in the double sentence *the smaller the town, the friendlier the people* it will generally be on the subjects *the town* and *the people.* In *what's a linguist?* dominant stress will generally be on the subject *a linguist;* in *who's a linguist?* it will generally be on the complement *a linguist.* Dominant stress is on *her luggage* both in *that's her luggage,* where *her luggage* is the complement, and in *there's her luggage,* where it is the subject. Adverbial second complements, however, are likely not to have dominant stress when they terminate sentences. If the answer to *what was that noise?* is *George put the cat out*, dominant stress will ordinarily be on the first complement, *the cat*, not the second complement *out*. Final adjuncts may or may not have dominant stress. If the answer to *what was that noise?* is *George reads the news emotionally*, dominant stress may or may not be on the adjunct *emotionally*. When prepositional complements are divided as in *what are you looking for?* they are likely to lose dominant stress.

Context is of extreme importance. What is new in the context is likely to be made more prominent than what is not. Thus in a context in which there has been discussion of snow but mention of local conditions is new, dominant stress will probably be on *here* in *it rarely snows here;* but in a context in which there has been discussion of local weather but no mention of snow, dominant stress will probably be on *snows*. The personal pronouns and substitute *one* are normally unstressed because they refer to what is prominent in the immediate context. In *I'll go with George* dominant stress is probably on *George;* but if George has just been mentioned prominently (and the trip to be made has been under discussion), what is said is probably *I'll go with him*, and dominant stress is probably on the preposition *with*. When a gesture accompanies *who's he?* the personal pronoun has dominant stress because "he" has not been mentioned previously. If both George and a piece of information George does not have are prominent in the context, but the idea of telling George is new, then dominant stress will probably be on *tell* in *why not tell George?* But when what is new in a particular context is also fairly obvious, there is normally only light stress or no stress at all. Thus the unstressed *it* of *it rarely snows here* gets its significance from its use with *snows:* nothing can snow snow but "it." In *there aren't many young people in the neighborhood* the modifier *young* takes dominant stress away from its head *people:* the fact that the young creatures of interest are people seems rather obvious. If *women* replaced *people*, it would normally have dominant stress. In *I have things to do* the word *things* makes little real contribution to meaning and has weaker stress than *do*. If *work* is substituted for *things* (with more exact contribution to meaning), it will have dominant stress. In *I know one thing* dominant stress is likely to go to *one* rather than to semantically pale *thing*. In *I knew you when you were a child, and you were pretty then* dominant stress on *then* implies that the young woman spoken to is still pretty. Dominant stress on *pretty* would be almost insulting here. In the written language *then* can be underlined or italicized to guide the reader here, but much of the time the written language simply depends on the reader's alertness, and a careless reader will have to back up and reread.

Often dominant stress simply indicates a centering of attention or emotion. Thus in *it's incredible what that boy can eat* dominant stress is likely to be on *incredible*, and *eat* will have strong stress also. In *she has it in for George* dominant stress will ordinarily be on *in*, where the notion of stored-up antipathy seems to center. In *we're painting at our garage* strong stress on *at* indicates that the job being done is not real painting but simply an effort at painting. Where there is comparison or contrast dominant stresses normally operate to center attention. Thus in *his friends are stranger than his sisters'* strong stresses are normal for *his* and *sisters'*, but in *his friends are stranger than his sisters* strong stresses are normal for *friends* and *sisters*. In *he's hurting himself more than he's hurting you* both *himself* and *you* have stronger stress than they would ordinarily have if there were no contrast. In *is she Chinese or Japanese?* the desire to contrast the first parts of words which are alike in their last components produces an exceptional disregard of the normal patterns of stress of *Chinese* and *Japanese*. Sometimes strong stress serves to focus an important secondary relationship. Thus in *Mary wrote an account of the trip first* strong stress on *Mary* marks Mary as the first in a series of people who wrote accounts of the trip, strong stress on *wrote* marks the writing as the first of a series of actions of Mary's concerned with an account of her trip (about which she may later have made speeches, for example), and strong stress on *trip* makes the trip the first of a series of subjects about which Mary wrote accounts. In *hunger stimulates man too* the situation is very similar. Strong stress on *hunger* treats hunger as an additional stimulus, strong stress on *stimulates* treats stimulation as an additional effect of hunger, strong stress on *man* treats man as an additional creature who responds to the stimulation of hunger. Here again, in the written language it is possible to help the reader get his stresses right by using underlining or italics, but much of the time there is simply reliance on his understanding in the light of context.

When a word represents a larger construction of which it is the only expressed part, it normally has more stress than it would have in fully expressed construction. Thus when *yes, I have* is the response to *have you finished reading the paper?* the stress on *have*, which here represents *have finished reading the paper*, is quite strong. In *Mack's the leader at camp, but Jack is here* the *is* of the second main declarative represents *is the leader* and therefore has stress. *Mack's the leader at camp, but Jack's here*, with this *is* deprived of stress, makes *here* the complement in the clause. In *of all the suggestions that were made, his was the silliest* the possessive *his* represents *his suggestion* and is stressed. When *go* represents itself and a complement (being equivalent, say, to *go to Martinique*) in *which boat did Jack go on?* it has strong stress; when it represents only itself and *on which* is its complement (so that *go on* is semantically equivalent to *board*), *on* has stronger stress than *go* does. Omission of a subordinator pronoun, however, does not result in an increase in stress on a prepositional adverb for which the subordinator pronoun would be object. Thus *to* has light stress both in *that was the conclusion that I came to* and in *that was the conclusion I came to*. But when *to* represents *to consciousness* in *that was the moment that I came to*, and similarly in *that was the moment I came to*, there is much stronger stress on *to*. In *I wanted to tell him, but I was afraid to* the final *to* is lightly stressed because it represents *to tell him*. In *to tell him*, of course, *to* is normally unstressed. When *I have instructions to leave* is equivalent in meaning to *I have instructions that I am to leave this place*, dominant stress is ordinarily on *leave*. When the same sequence is equivalent in meaning to *I have instructions which I am to leave*, dominant stress is ordinarily on *instructions*.

It is clear that patterns of stress sometimes show construction unambiguously in the spoken language where without the help of context it would be ambiguous in the written. Other examples follow.

> I'll come by Tuesday.
> I can't be happy long without drinking water.

In the first of these sentences if *by* is the complement of *come* and *Tuesday* is an adjunct of time equivalent to *on Tuesday*, there will be strong stress on *by* in the spoken language; but if a complement for *come* is implied and *by Tuesday* is a prepositional unit used as an adjunct, *by* will be unstressed or lightly stressed at most. In the second sentence if *drinking water* is a gerundial clause and *without drinking water* is roughly equivalent in meaning to *unless I drink water*, there will be stronger stress on *water* than on *drinking;* but if *drinking* is a gerundial noun modifying *water* and *without drinking water* is equivalent to *without water for drinking*, there will be stronger stress on *drinking* than on *water*. But the use of stress in comparison and contrast, for example, can undermine distinctions such as these. And patterns of stress are not always unambiguous by any means. In *the Steiners have busy lives without visiting relatives* only context can indicate whether *visiting relatives* is equivalent in meaning to *paying visits to relatives* or to *relatives who are visiting them*, and in *I looked up the number* and *I looked up the chimney* only the meanings of *number* and *chimney* make it clear that *up* is syntactically a second complement in the first sentence and a preposition followed by its object in the second.

Syllabification.—Syllables are linguistic units centering in peaks which are usually vocalic but, as has been noted, are consonantal under certain circumstances, and which may or may not be combined with preceding and/or following consonants or combinations of consonants. Syllables are genuine units, but division of words and sentences into them presents great difficulties. Sometimes even the number of syllables is not clear. Doubt on this point is strongest before /l/ and /ɚ/ or /r/. From the point of view of word formation *real* might be expected to have two syllables. Historically *re* is the formative that is employed also in *republic*, and *al* is the common suffix. When *ity* is added, *real* clearly has two syllables. But there is every reason to regard *deal* as a monosyllable, and because of the fact that /l/ commonly has the quality of /əl/ when it follows vowel sounds, *deal* seems to be a perfectly satisfactory rhyme with *real*. Similarly spelling and history suggest regarding *power* as a word of two syllables; yet *power* seems to be a good rhyme for monosyllabic *sour*. We are dealing with borderline cases, and we must expect borderline cases in all attempts at classification of linguistic phenomena.

The problem of deciding where syllables begin and end is a more fundamental one. Often there simply are no clear division points: syllables flow into the syllables that follow them much as the distinctive sounds of which they are composed flow into the sounds which follow them. In comfortable rapid speech the following sequences may become indistinguishable to the ear.

> May could answer.
> Make a dancer.

Division points between syllables are generally clearest before stresses. But even before stresses we must face the fact that such pairs as *a notion* and *an ocean,* and *a name* and *an aim,* have long tended to be indistinguishable, so that the McGuffey Readers of the last century, with a strong interest in "correct" pronunciation, drilled students on making a distinction that they obviously were likely not to make. In earlier times an /n/ moved from the article to the noun in *a nickname,* and the opposite shift occurred in *an orange. At all* is often pronounced like *a tall,* with the aspirated /t/ that begins syllables. *Bring her over* can be very close indeed to *bring Rover,* and *that's tough* to *that stuff.* When the final /s/ of *miss* and the initial /j/ of *you* unite to make *miss you* a reasonably good rhyme for *tissue,* division into precise syllables becomes troublesome.

In compound words in which all major components retain stress, syllable divisions between major components normally seem clear. Thus *pieplant* seems to divide between *pie* and *plant,* and *pipeline* between *pipe* and *line. Teacup* seems to divide between *tea* and *cup,* and *makeup* between *make* and *up.* In complexes, division into syllables is often a very different matter from division into the components with which word formation is concerned. Thus the clearest syllable divisions in the following complexes come at points inside clear formatives, not before or after them.

absen'tee	Chi'nese	pho'tography	ther'mometer
a'dorn	defi'nition	procla'mation	trigo'nometry
car'nivorous	engi'neer	psy'chology	u'nanimous

Proper nouns often divide with equal clarity, whether or not they
are divisible into formatives in English.

Cor'nelius   Fuji'yama   Massa'chusetts   Pa'tricia

Some formatives are generally merged with their neighbors. This
is notably true of *ion:* for example, in *conviction* and *revision.*

The written language does not attempt to indicate syllable divisions as it does vowel and consonant sounds, words, and sentences.
It does have a set of conventions for dividing words at the ends
of lines, but this is another matter. Thus the convention permits
us to divide *suppose, biggish,* and *revision* into *sup-pose, big-gish,*
and either *re-vision* or *revi-sion.* Accurate syllable division here
would give us *su-ppose* and (if we assume that since short stressed
vowel sounds normally cannot end words they normally cannot
end syllables either) *bigg-ish* and *re-vision* or *revisi-on.* Accurate
syllable division is a highly controversial matter, and in the end
has to be uncomfortably arbitrary at important points. For most
purposes it is enough to know how many syllables there are, where
their peaks are, and where stressed syllables begin. The ordinary
spellings will not permit us to mark stresses at the beginnings of
syllables in words like *exact,* where *x* represents one consonant
sound in the first syllable and one in the second: we can bow to
necessity and write *ex'act.*

Intonation and punctuation.—In the spoken language, the
stream of words is interrupted by pauses of varied types; in the written language, by punctuation. The "pauses" of the spoken language
may involve silence, or they may involve simply a slowing down.
Like stress, they also involve characteristic uses of pitch. Where
unstressed words occur, the spoken language does not mark off
words as clearly as the written does. *A lot* and *allot* are generally
indistinguishable in pronunciation, and *lock it* and *locket.* In very
informal speech the merging of words in *what did you take her?*
will make *take her* indistinguishable from *taker* and may make
what did you into a two-syllable sequence rhyming with *rajah.*
But the written language often fails to show syntactic grouping
where the spoken language does. *We need more conscientious
officials* is ambiguous in the written language: it can be equivalent

to *we need officials who are more conscientious* or to *we need a greater number of conscientious officials. Children who have watched this program often show that it has affected their thinking* is ambiguous in the written language: *often* can be taken as an adjunct in the clause whose predicator is *have watched* or as an adjunct in the main statement, whose predicator is *show.* Such sentences as these are not ambiguous in the spoken language, where intonation makes it clear how their components group themselves. Good writing involves avoidance of ambiguities such as these; good conversation is characteristically less demanding.

The spoken language is commonly said to employ three types of terminal pauses, which can be called fading, rising, and sustained. Spoken as a straightforward statement regarded as more or less complete in itself, *Jane's pretty* will normally end with falling pitch and fading away of the sound. Spoken incredulously, or with the force of a question, the same sentence would normally end with rising pitch and without an effect of fading away. Spoken as something which might well be followed by *but* and a comment less favorable to Jane, the sentence might well end with pitch sustained to the end. As a response to *George has bought another ridiculously expensive gadget,* the one-word sentence *what!* with high rising pitch is roughly equivalent to *what are you saying!* With lower fading intonation it is equivalent to *what has he bought?* All three types of "terminal" pauses occur within sentences as well as at the ends of them. The sentences of a minister given to long, elaborately worked out structures and dramatic uses of pitch, stress, and pause will contain many "terminal" pauses. Afterthought, real or pretended, causes them to appear within even very short sentences. Sustained terminals are especially likely to occur within sentences of many kinds. A currently famous bit of phonological analysis places one between subject and predicator in *Long Island is a long island.*

From the point of view of grammatical analysis, the most important function of intonation in the spoken language and punctuation in the written is to show what goes with what. Thus the following responses to the question *what has kept Harriet from marrying?* employ the same sequence of words but are very different grammatical structures.

> You know. Her mother.
> You know her mother.

A variety of intonations is available for each of these responses. The attitude of the speaker is inevitably reflected in the intonation he employs: a great deal of intonation is packaging. This is not to say that it is unimportant. For delicate subject matter intonation can be of tremendous importance. The grammatically significant fact about the two responses given above is that the first response is two sentences, both of them reduced as is often the case in replies to questions, and the second response is a single sentence. Unpunctuated headlines can be misleading, as the following example shows.

GIRLS SAY DOCTORS HAVE MORE BIRTHMARKS THAN BOYS

But neither intonation nor punctuation provides a detailed guide to analysis. The following sentences—the last one reduced, and most likely to occur as the reply to a question—can employ identical intonation and identical punctuation and yet be structurally quite distinct.

> That's her luggage.
> There's her luggage.
> Bring her luggage.
> With her luggage.

The interrogative *where's her luggage?* can employ the same intonation but is marked by special punctuation in the written language.

Punctuation between sentences and main divisions of multiple sentences.—Terminal punctuation and initial capital letters together mark the sentences of the written language. The basic sentence-terminating mark is of course the period. The question mark indicates that a reply is desired. Like the period, it follows clauses and clause equivalents of various types; and it certainly is not confined to association with particular intonation patterns.

> Where's her luggage?
> Did you finish?
> That's her luggage?

But declaratives such as *that's her luggage?* gain question force in the spoken language wholly from rising intonation and perhaps manner. So do isolates with no clausal form at all.

> Ready?   Friend of yours?
> Sugar?   Yes?

Exclamation points, too, can terminate sentences of varied syntactic types: their value is emotional, and they suggest emotional intonations quite imprecisely.

> That's her luggage!
> Is it hot!
> What a mess!
> If only she'd get here!
> Well!

Within multiple sentences the general practice is to use commas to separate the major divisions if these are linked by coordinators (*and, but, or, nor*) and do not themselves contain commas. Where something stated in the first major division is implied in the following one, the divisions are tied together more tightly and the comma can well be omitted.

> Parents were notoriously indulgent of their children and children notoriously disrespectful of their parents.

Where comma punctuation occurs within a major division, and where there is no coordinator, a semicolon normally replaces the comma.

> Nations with large resources, good organization, and a willingness to face economic facts can perhaps hope to remain unaffected by world economic upheavals; but nations which are less fortunate cannot.
> It was very delicate work; consequently errors were inevitably made.
> At that time the electroencephalograph was still a laboratory novelty; today it is standard clinical equipment.

Where the first major division amounts to a preparation for the second, a colon is appropriate.

> He shows more than disregard of ideas: he shows fear of them.
> Matilde is like most girls with backgrounds such as hers: she shows her emotions freely.

Exceptions to the general rule for punctuating between the major divisions of multiple sentences must be noted. When the second main division of a multiple sentence begins (somewhat informally) with a *so* which means *therefore*, a comma is usual as the separating mark.

She went to school in France, so her French is excellent.

A comma is quite possible without a coordinator between short major divisions of multiple sentences, especially when they are parallel in content and structure.

He likes garlic, she hates garlic.
The past has not ceased to exist, it has only ceased to be useful.
What history did the nineteenth-century American know, what stories did he treasure, what heroes and heroines of literature did he cherish, what songs did he sing?

A comma is normal without a coordinator between proportionative-assertive main clauses united in interdependent multiple sentences.

The less building you have, the more light and air you get.

A comma is also normal without a coordinator (1) between a declarative and a confirmational interrogative, (2) between a declarative and an emotional or meditative interrogative, (3) between an imperative and a reiterative interrogative, and (4) between *yes* or *no* and a reiterative declarative, reduced or not reduced.

You live here, don't you?
He's late again, is he?
Take me along, won't you?
No, I haven't.
Yes, I said it.

Split sentences are normally distinguished, in careful punctuation, from multiple sentences.

If the inspector will approve it, this project can be considered finished and a new one can be begun.
Sometimes we invite him but he refuses.

In each of these sentences a single adjunct, *if the inspector will approve it* in the first and *sometimes* in the second, modifies two following nucleuses and punctuation between the nucleuses is therefore not desirable.

Punctuation after clausal adjuncts in pre-subject position.—Within sentences and major divisions of multiple sentences, four principles of punctuation are grammatically significant.

First, clausal adjuncts or complements (including those within which clauses are contained) are best followed by commas when they precede the subjects of the larger clauses which contain them, unless they are short and the construction is quite clear without punctuation.

> If the language policy of the United States in Puerto Rico had been more judicious in those early years, the present position of English on the island would be more satisfactory.
>
> After serving as pastor of a Moravian church on St. Croix for many years, he retired and returned to Winston-Salem in 1948.
>
> How long the communal life of these tribes will continue, only time can tell.

A clausal adjunct or complement which follows an adjunct followed by a comma should often dispense with its own following comma.

> In log-cabin days, when a family moved into a new neighborhood the people of the community would gather and in a matter of hours would construct a house at practically no cost.
>
> If you don't hear from me again before you start, when you reach Columbus be sure to telephone me and let me make arrangements for you to see the Dean immediately.

No comma is used after pre-subject adjunct clauses functioning as clause markers in assertives.

> Not since Wilson nosed out Hughes had the country seen such an upset.
>
> Only when Spain lost control did the island experience freedom of religion.

Punctuation between coordinates.—A second principle of punctuation within sentences and major divisions of multiple sentences is that contained coordinates not linked by one of the coordinators *and, but, or,* and *nor* must ordinarily be separated by punctuation. The basic mark for the purpose is the comma.

It was a cold, wet day.
We visited Nicaragua, Costa Rica, and Panama.

When the contained coordinates have commas within themselves and the multiple unit is either first or last in its sentence, semicolons are likely to be used to separate the coordinates.

At the airport to meet us were the principal of the high school, an energetic and enthusiastic man; the president of the school board, well fed and grayish; and the secretary of the Chamber of Commerce, obviously a professional greeter.

Hyphens are used between coordinates in two-word numerals from *twenty-one* to *ninety-nine,* and in prepositive modifiers such as *Spanish-American* in *the Spanish-American war.* Where numerals are used in highly reduced coordinates without coordinators, they are sometimes set side by side with no punctuation at all.

He's five feet ten.
It's almost twelve thirty.

It is generally best not to punctuate where coordinates linked by coordinators occur within sentences and major divisions of multiple sentences.

It is true that being ordinary is not only the natural way of life for most of us but the surest safeguard against being hurt by our fellows.
Startling theories of geology ruined the comfortable chronology of Bishop Ussher and reduced the history of man to an inconsiderable second of infinite time.
We were disturbed because the man was obviously drunk and his companion was somewhat less than sober.

Punctuation to set off loose adjuncts.—A third principle of punctuation within sentences and major divisions of multiple sentences is that loose adjuncts must ordinarily be set off by punctuation. The basic mark for this purpose is the comma. Loose-adjunct status is normal for adjuncts of interjection, direct address, reason for speaking, and evidence.

Well, why don't you try another store?
Are you reading, Milton?
The water is wonderful today, in case you're interested.
He grew up in Virginia, judging by his speech.

Main clauses used as adjuncts in upside-down construction are treated as loose; so are most gerundial-clause adjuncts with expressed subjects, most combinations of the preposition *for* and a declarative-clause object, and most clauses subordinated by *although*.

> She isn't exactly poor, you know.
> Behind us stood about a dozen young men, most of them workers from the steel mills.
> Mother would enjoy a trip to Juniata very much, for after all she grew up there.
> Automobiles are much more dangerous than planes, although they have less spectacular crashes.

Half modifiers, half appositives, and half coordinates are generally treated as loose adjuncts and set off by commas.

> In institutions of this type professional training begins in the third year, after the student has achieved a solid background in mathematics and the sciences.
> The political capital, Washington, is the capital only in politics.
> The Americans, or "North Americans," knew almost nothing about Juarez.

Year dates attached to names of months or to month-and-day dates, and names of larger containing geographical or organizational units attached to names of smaller units, are usually set off by commas.

> On July 10, 1956, the building was finally opened.
> Parkersburg, West Virginia, has the nearest airport.
> His address is simply Department of English, Earlham College, Richmond, Indiana.

From the point of view of grammatical analysis, loose-adjunct status is assigned somewhat arbitrarily in some of the constructions just noted. The year date in *July 10, 1956*, for example, would seem to be an identifying modifier of what it follows, and therefore deserving of tight-modifier status. When *10 July 1956* is written, as is done increasingly, there is no punctuation, though the older *the tenth of July, 1956*, retains punctuation. Actually the complexity of dates and (even more) of many addresses makes punctuation necessary for clarity, just as in the spoken language pauses are necessary. The written language distinguishes direct address more unfailingly than the spoken. Spoken incredulously, with high pitch and strong stress on *reading*, the following sentences are likely to be indistinguishable in the spoken language.

> Are you *reading*, Milton?
> Are you *reading* Milton?

In any normal context, of course, there is no question whether Milton is the person spoken to or the seventeenth-century poet. The distinction between tight and loose construction affects structure and meaning basically in pairs such as the following.

> In institutions of this type professional training is begun in the third year, after the student has received a solid background in mathematics and the sciences.
>
> In institutions of this type professional training is begun in the third year after the student has received a solid background in mathematics and sciences.

In the first of these sentences, the third year is the third year in the institution; in the second, it is the third year in a sequence beginning after a solid background in mathematics and sciences has been achieved.

Dashes replace commas in setting off adjuncts which are genuinely parenthetical and have the form of main clauses, and in setting off adjuncts which themselves contain commas.

> An officer said that the dead man's family—he was known to have a mother and sister living—would claim the body in a few days.
>
> Of the three great public agencies of transportation—the bus, the train, and the plane—the bus brings the traveler closest to the life of the country he passes through.

Dashes also tend to replace commas for loose adjuncts which begin repetitively, and also for loose adjuncts with half-appositive relationships to the nucleuses to which they attach.

> Hayes was an extraordinarily enlightened man—enlightened both in his attitudes toward the problems of his profession and in his views of the world beyond his profession.
>
> With the dogs barking furiously at him, he renewed his shouts of "Ave Maria"—the proper thing to do when you approached a strange house in that region.

Curves compete with dashes in the uses mentioned here. Curves are usable to inclose quite clearly what occurs where commas would be confusing and dashes a little strong.

Zephir hated to leave King Babar, Queen Celeste, the Old Lady (his teacher), and his beloved Arthur.

Here the curves tie *his teacher* together visibly and relate the unit to its context, somewhat as the hyphens in *modern-language teaching, a single-level house, all-wool suits,* and *the fast-changing customs* relate the units they tie together. Curves can also inclose sentences and series of sentences.

Colons function as introductory marks before loose adjuncts ending their sentences.

In time everyone organized: boys and girls in schools, businessmen and scholars, friends and neighbors, old settlers and newcomers, vegetarians and teetotalers, those who survived a blizzard and those who grew roses.
On this mesa the Indians found the hope of all suffering and tormented creatures: safety.

In particular contexts, adjuncts are sometimes assigned loose status for the sake of clarity of construction or of improved rhythm or of special effect. It is generally wise to set off clausal adjuncts interrupting the nucleuses of the larger clauses within which they are contained.

We all realize, when we face the facts, that local control over schools and teachers can have disastrous effects.

Adjuncts of various other types are often set off to prevent them from being related too closely, in reading, to what follows them.

Jerry had a year of school in Mexico. Ever since, he spends all his vacations there.
After that, school in the States seemed a little dull.

Sometimes what could be the second coordinate in a double unit is set off by commas as a way of showing that something that follows attaches not just to it but to two constructions.

The mother is more nervous, and also a little more exacting, than the father.

Impinging modifiers are sometimes set off for similar reasons.

> The most likable, if not the most dependable, student in the
> group is the boy from Iowa.

The second of what could be two coordinated subordinate clauses
is often set off with commas.

> If you like the house, and if you don't think the rent is too
> high, you'd better go ahead and take it.

Commas often indicate that the closer of two grammatically possible relationships is not the intended one.

> Wrestlers avoid fights with little men who are trying to prove
> something to themselves, by simply allowing the little men
> to have their way.
> I talked to the man that seemed to own the sailboat, and
> learned that it was leaving for St. Kitts in an hour.

Inclosing commas indicate outermost layer of modification in the
following sentence, which would be misread without them.

> We read, most of the time, because reading is one of our bad
> habits.

A comma changes the character of the question in the following
sentence.

> Do you speak Spanish, or Portuguese?

Without a comma this question may be taken as equivalent to *do
you speak either Spanish or Portuguese?* Considerations of rhythm,
and of distance between marks, will determine whether the commas
indicated in the following sentences are used or not.

> She'll marry him one of these days, even though she knows
> he never will have any money.
> He gave an excellent examination, involving thought as well
> as memory.

Desire for special effects of afterthought or, at the other extreme,
exceptional emphasis often lead to setting off items for which
tight construction would seem normal.

> It's quiet here, today.
> Given reasonably favorable conditions, and good will, we can
> hope to get real results.

Punctuation separating the parts of nucleuses.—The fourth principle of punctuation within sentences and major divisions of sentences is that ordinarily the parts of nucleuses—subjects, predicators, and complements—should not be separated or inclosed by punctuation. Thus long subjects are usually not followed by punctuation, or long complements preceded by it, whether or not pauses occur in the spoken language.

> The loneliness of his early life, the constant nagging of his mother, and his long-continued bad health combined to produce in the boy a considerable distortion of personality.
> The group includes a small number of devout churchmen, a few people who see no place for religion in modern life, and the usual majority of people with no very clear opinions in the matter.

But adjuncts set off by commas often interrupt nucleuses, especially in careful and formal styles.

> A few minutes later the people at the next table, who had looked familiar to us from the first, asked us whether we were from Portland.

Main clauses used as complements of *be* are preceded by commas.

> He fulfils the community's ideas of what a good teacher should be; that is, he keeps the liking and respect of his students and enters into the life of the town.

And of course when direct quotations are incorporated in larger clauses punctuation occurs.

> Then she asked me, "Have you visited Houghton before?"

But if the quotation is fragmentary and is woven smoothly into the larger structure, only quotation marks occur.

> Edward is probably right in saying that grammars are "cookbooks the best cooks never consult."

A GLOSSARY OF GRAMMATICAL
TERMINOLOGY

The terms that are listed in quotation marks in what follows are not used in this grammar.

ABSOLUTES. Words that normally function as sentences, or like nucleuses of sentences, not as components within clauses. *Ouch*, *hello*, and *yes* are examples.

"ABSOLUTE PHRASES." This term is sometimes applied to gerundial clauses with expressed subjects—for example, *this being the case*—used as adjuncts within larger clauses.

"ABSTRACT NOUNS." This term is sometimes used of quantifiable nouns such as *goodness* and *ignorance*.

"ACCENT." The term *stress* is employed here. See Vowel Sounds.

"ACCUSATIVE CASE." See Cases.

"ACTIVE VOICE." See Voices.

ADJECTIVES. Words (1) characteristically used as prepositive modifiers of following nouns and as complements after *be* and (2) characteristically modified prepositively by adverbs. The syntactic behavior of *enormous* in the following sentences can illustrate.

> The neighbors have another *enormous* car.
> The neighbors' new car is *enormous*.
> Our own car is rather *enormous* too.

In the nounal unit *an enormous silver buckle* only *enormous* is an adjective.

"ADJECTIVAL CLAUSES." This term is widely used of subordinate-interrogative clauses attaching to nounal heads, as
478

who really know the city does in *we spent the day with friends who really know the city,* and also of clauses of the same type used as loose adjuncts as *who really know the city* is used in *we spent the day with the Robertsons, who really know the city,* where *who* refers to *the Robertsons* though the interrogative clause does not really modify *the Robertsons.* Sometimes clauses of other types are also called "adjectival" because they attach to head nouns: for example, the declarative clause *that Horton would enter the race* in *the announcement that Horton would enter the race was poorly timed.*

ADJUNCTS. Clause components syntactically outside subject-predicator-complement nucleuses, and so (in terms of layers) outer modifiers of the predicators. Thus in *but I've always put hard work off too long, George* there are four adjuncts: *but, always* (which interrupts the nucleus and even the predicator), *too long,* and *George. I* is subject, *have put* is predicator, *hard work* and *off* are complements. Adjuncts can also attach to isolates, as *George* does in *yes, George.*

ADVERBS. Words belonging to the most miscellaneous of the part-of-speech categories, including words characteristically used as adjuncts (as *occasionally* is used in *I get to New York occasionally*), as prepositive modifiers of adjectives and other adverbs (as *quite* is used in *it wasn't quite right* and *too* in *he makes his points too undiplomatically*), and as prepositions (as *through* is used in *the highway goes through Lexington*).

"ADVERBIAL CLAUSES." This term is widely applied to clauses of a variety of patterns used as adjuncts within larger clauses (as *when I left* is used in *Dawson was there when I left*) and as modifiers of adjectives and adverbs (as *than I do* is used in *you argue more convincingly than I do*). Adjuncts composed of prepositions and subordinate-declarative objects are often classified as adverbial clauses also: for example, *until he died* in *Jones taught high-school Latin until he died.*

AFFIXES. See Formatives.

ANOMALOUS SPELLINGS. Spellings of frequent occurrence which nevertheless go against the basic principles of the spelling system: for example, the *ea* of *bread* and the *ou* of *cousin,* which employ two-letter representations for short vowel sounds represented in conformity with the spelling system in *bred* and *buzzing.*

"ANTECEDENTS." This word is often applied to words and multiword units to which pronouns refer.

APPOSITION. See Principals and Appositives.

ASPECTS. Almost all verbs distinguish common and progressive aspects. Progressive-aspect forms employ *be* as auxiliary and follow this auxiliary by gerundials; common-aspect forms lack this construction. Thus the *tries* of *Landon tries to be diplomatic* is a common-aspect form contrasting with the progressive-aspect *is trying* of *Landon is trying to be diplomatic*.

ASSERTIVES. Clauses belonging to a cluster of patterns used, like declaratives, to express fact and opinion but differentiated from declaratives in form. Thus assertive *what a day that was!* is roughly equivalent in meaning to *that was a phenomenal day* but the clause pattern is clearly distinct.

"ATTRIBUTIVE ADJECTIVES." This term is often applied to adjectives that modify following noun heads, as *new* modifies *typewriter* in *I need a new typewriter*.

AUXILIARIES. Within phrasal verb forms the final word indicates the verb to which the whole unit belongs and the preceding words, or reduced words, are auxiliaries. Thus in *I've been looking at the magazines* the phrasal verb form *have been looking* is a form of *look*, used with subject *I* and complement *at the magazines* as *look* itself might be used, and *have* and *been* are auxiliaries of tense and aspect. Auxiliary-verb status is best confined to the *be* of passives, the *be* of progressives, the *have*, *will*, and (in formal use) *shall* of perfect and future tenses, and the *do* of expanded forms. A kind of auxiliaries occurs also in phrasal comparative and superlative adjectives and adverbs in which *more* and *most* and *less* and *least* function much as *er* and *est* function in such forms as *bigger* and *biggest* and *sooner* and *soonest*.

CAREFUL STYLES. See the Introduction.

CASES. Among the nouns and pronouns changes in form are common accompaniments of changes in syntactic function. The personal pronoun *I* has four case forms in three cases: nominative *I*, objective *me*, possessives *my* and *mine*. The nouns have common-case forms that function both where nominative pronoun forms are used and where objective forms are used, and possessive-case forms that are used without change both before heads and elsewhere.

I'm looking for *George*.
George is looking for *me*.
My car is parked in front of *George's*.
George's car is parked behind *mine*.

There is no reason to speak of accusative and dative cases in modern English or to speak of nominative and objective cases in connection with modern-English nouns. *Possessive* seems preferable to *genitive* as a name for the case here represented by *George's*, *my*, and *mine*, though neither term is completely satisfactory.

CLAUSES. Syntactic units in which predicators function as heads. Clauses always include subjects, expressed or implied. Often they include complements and adjuncts also. The main declarative is conveniently regarded as the basic clause pattern. Other main- and subordinate-clause patterns can be regarded as transforms of the main-declarative pattern, among them the pattern of verbid clauses with infinitival and gerundial predicators.

CLAUSE EQUIVALENTS. Words and multiword units that lack clause structure, stated or clearly implied, and yet are given the kind of status clauses are given. Absolutes such as *ouch* and *yes*, the latter sometimes in combination with adjuncts (as in *yes, John*), are commonly treated as main clauses are treated and given sentence status; so are such phrases as *good morning*, which is not felt as a reduction of any clearly formulated clause. Clause equivalents are grammatically quite different from reduced clauses. Thus when *ten twenty* answers the question *what time is it?* it is understood as a reduction of the declarative *it's ten twenty*, not as a true clause equivalent.

CLAUSE MARKERS. This term is here applied to words and longer units which syntactically distinguish clauses of other types from main declaratives, as the use of *who* distinguishes *who said that?* from, for example, *John said that*, and as the use of *are* in front of the subject distinguishes *are the pictures up?* from *the pictures are up*.

COACTUAL SUBJUNCTIVES. Present subjunctives used in main- and subordinate-imperative clauses without rejection, even provisional, of actualization. Thus the *be* of *be diplomatic* and that of *it is important that you be diplomatic* do not imply that the speaker lacks hope of diplomatic action from the person spoken to and can therefore be called coactual.

"COGNATE OBJECTS." This term is sometimes used of such semantically repetitive adjuncts as the one in *he died a painful death*, where *a painful death* is syntactically equivalent to the one-word adjunct *painfully*.

COLLECTIVE NOUNS. Nouns that name groups and have basic forms sometimes felt as singular and sometimes as plural. *Family* and *team* are examples.

"COLLOQUIAL STYLES." This term is often used much as *informal styles* is used here. See the Introduction.

COMMON ASPECT, COMMON CASE, COMMON MODE, COMMON PERSON AND NUMBER, COMMON VOICE. See Aspects, Cases, Modes, Persons and Numbers, and Voices.

COMPARISON OF ADJECTIVES, ADVERBS, AND SOME PRONOUNS. Many adjectives and adverbs, and the pronouns *much, many, little*, and *few*, have comparative forms employed when modifying *than* clauses are used or implied with them, and superlative forms much like the comparatives but unlike them in construction. Thus *big* and *soon* have the comparatives *bigger* and *sooner* and the superlatives *biggest* and *soonest*. *More* and *less* are employed in phrasal comparatives such as *more industrious* and *less industrious*, and *most* and *least* in phrasal superlatives such as *most industrious* and *least industrious*.

COMPLEMENTS. In minimally complete sequences in which they function as predicators, many verbs require not only subjects but also complements, which in the basic declarative order follow them. Thus in *John likes noise* there is no minimal completeness without the complement *noise* or some similarly used word or multiword unit. In *John makes people angry* minimal completeness, with *makes* meaning what it does, requires the two complements *people* and *angry*. In *Harriet is in New York* minimal completeness, with *be* meaning what it does, requires some such complement as *in New York*.

COMPLETERS. Many words require completers. Complements are completers of certain verbs, objects are completers of prepositions. Many contained modifiers are really completing modifiers. For example, in *I'm dubious about the second point* the prepositional unit *about the second point* is a completing modifier of *dubious*, which requires something of the kind, expressed or implied, when it is used with the meaning it has here.

COMPLEXES. Words which contain clear noninflectional formatives, themselves without word status, in combination with words (as *un* is combined with *tie* in *untie*) or with other formatives (as *vitri* is combined with *fy* in *vitrify*).

"COMPLEX SENTENCES." This term is often applied to sentences which include subordinate clauses other than verbids.

COMPOUNDS. Syntactically unified combinations of two words—infrequently more than two words, as in *nevertheless*—which are given the status of single words and written without hyphens or spaces intervening. *Highway* and *afternoon* are examples; *high school*, on the other hand, maintains phrasal status—in spite of the fact that *high* and *school* are not separately modifiable as they are in *high price*, where *a very high retail price* is a normal enough expansion. The normal meaning of the question *is* spark plug *one word or two?* is *is it written solid or not? Spark* is obviously a word, and so is *plug:* the question is whether the combination is given the status of a single word in standard written practice. We cannot ignore standard written practice.

"COMPOUND PREDICATES." See Split Clauses.

"COMPOUND SENTENCES." See Multiple Sentences.

CONDITIONAL SENTENCES. Sentences including adjunct clauses of condition and main nucleuses expressing the conditioned result. Conditional sentences are of two types. Noncommittal conditional sentences characteristically have common-mode predicators, as in *if we take the boat to Guadeloupe next Friday, we'll have five days there*. Rejected conditional sentences characteristically have hypothetical-subjunctive predicators, as in *if we took the boat to Guadeloupe next Friday, we'd have five days there*.

CONFIRMATIONAL INTERROGATIVES. Reduced interrogatives following declaratives for which they request confirmation. Thus in *there are planes to Guadeloupe, aren't there?* the reduced interrogative *aren't there?* asks confirmation for what precedes it in the same double sentence.

"CONJUGATION." This term is often used of the inflection of verbs.

"CONJUNCTIONS." This term is often applied to a syntactically miscellaneous category made up of (1) the four basic coordinators *and, but, or,* and *nor* and the precoordinators *both, not, either,* and *neither* which sometimes accompany them; (2) clause-marker adverbs such as *when, how,* and *if* when they mark subordinate-interrogative clauses; (3) prepositions such as *after* and *because* when they are used with declarative-clause objects (as in *after he died*); and (4) clause-marker *that* when it marks subordinate-declarative, subordinate-imperative, and subordinate-assertive clauses. Sometimes conjunctive adverbs such as *therefore* and *nevertheless* are also included in the category of "conjunctions."

CONJUNCTIVE ADVERBS. Nonprepositional adverbs which relate without explicitly coordinating as the coordinators do and without marking clause types. Thus in *though Mathews came to the University to work in contemporary literature, he has nevertheless taken course after course in English language* the conjunctive adverb *nevertheless* is an adjunct in the main clause and relates the subordinate clause marked by *though* to the main nucleus. *Nevertheless* is much like *but* semantically but it does not coordinate. In *Mathews came to the University to work in contemporary literature, but he has nevertheless taken course after course in English language* the coordinator is *but.* Conjunctive adverbs often reinforce coordinators, and most of them can come later in their clauses than either coordinators or clause markers normally come. They also have considerable use at the first of sentences and of major components in multiple sentences, without other linking words.

CONTAINED SYNTACTIC FUNCTIONS. Subjects, predicators, complements, adjuncts, and isolates are often divisible into components of other types, performing the "contained" syntactic functions. Thus the greeting *good morning* is an isolate composed of a contained modifier and a contained head. The contained functions are contained head and contained modifier, principal and appositive, preposition and object, and coordinate.

COORDINATES. The components making up multiple units are coordinates. Thus in *Nancy speaks Spanish, Portuguese, and*

French the complement is a multiple nounal unit made up of the three coordinates *Spanish, Portuguese,* and *and French.*

COORDINATORS. The function of coordinator is a secondary one performed by words that also perform major or contained syntactic functions. In the multiple sentence *Jorge doesn't like to speak English, but he understands it* the adverb *but* is an adjunct in the second main declarative and a coordinator. In *Nancy speaks Spanish, Portuguese, and French* the adverb *and* is a contained modifier of the noun that follows it and is also a coordinator. The basic coordinators are *and, but, or,* and *nor;* precoordinators often employed with them are *both, not, either,* and *neither.* Conjunctive adverbs often reinforce coordinators, as *too* does in *I was told, and George was too;* but they are also used where there is no syntactic coordination, as *too* is in *if I was told, George certainly was told too.*

COPULATIVE PREPOSITIONS. See Prepositions.

COPULATIVE VERBS. Verbs that take adjectival complements with half-modifier relationships to their subjects. *Be, become,* and *seem* are among the verbs that commonly function in this way. Thus in *the visitors look unhappy* the adjective *unhappy* is the complement of *look* but it also has a relationship to *visitors* much like the relationship it has in *the unhappy visitors.*

"CORRECTNESS." Such terms as *right* and *wrong* and *correct* and *incorrect* are avoided here. *Standard* and *nonstandard* do not suggest feelings of virtue and of vice and therefore seem preferable terms for use in dealing with the same inevitable distinctions.

"CORRELATIVE CONJUNCTIONS." This term is often used for combinations of precoordinators such as *neither* and basic coordinators such as *nor.*

"COUNTABLE NOUNS." See Pluralizer Nouns.

DECLARATIVES. The main declarative is here defined as the clause pattern used in giving the most ordinary main-clause expression to facts and opinions. Subjects are normally stated and precede predicators; if there are complements, these follow predicators. There is more variety in position for adjuncts, though most adjuncts are not movable very freely. The subordinate declarative is identical with the main declarative in pattern except that a clause-marker *that*, corresponding to nothing that would occur if the main-declarative pattern were employed, is added or (except when subordinate declaratives are made objects of certain prepositions) can be added. Thus in *I don't believe the room is big enough* the subordinate declarative *the room is big enough* is syntactically suitable for use as a main declarative without change, and as a subordinate declarative can be begun by an added clause-marker *that*.

"DECLENSION." This term is often used of the inflection of nouns and pronouns.

"DEPENDENT CLAUSES." See Subordinate Clauses.

DETERMINATIVE PRONOUNS. Pronouns which function both as prepositive modifiers of nounal heads (as *these*, *other*, *several*, and *one* function in *these ducks*, *the other ducks*, *several ducks*, and *one duck*) and, except *the*, *a*, and *every*, without stated heads (as the same words function in *whose ducks are these?* in *your ducks are bigger than the others*, in *several have gone up the creek*, and in *I'd like to buy one*). *The*, *a*, and *every* are exceptional among the determinative pronouns in requiring stated heads.

DETERMINERS. Among prepositive modifiers of nounal heads, special notice must be given to the determinative pronouns and to one-word and phrasal possessives used similarly. This is especially true when determinative pronouns and possessives modify basic forms of pluralizers and unite with them to form units freely usable in such nounal functions as that of subject. Thus *this garage, the garage, any garage, no garage, our garage*, and *Mr. Goodman's garage* are all freely usable as subjects as *garage, new garage*, and *brick garage*, lacking determiner modifiers, are not. *This, the, any, no, our*, and *Mr. Goodman's* are all full-determiner modifiers of identification. Partial-determiner modifiers of identification (*other* and *fourth*) occur in *our other garage* and *the fourth garage*. Determiner modifiers of number occur in *three garages* and *several garages*.

DIPHTHONGS. See Vowel Sounds.

"DIRECT OBJECTS." This term is commonly applied to nounal first, or only, complements of verbs other than those which, with closely related meanings, also take adjectival complements that are half modifiers of their subjects. Thus in *such training makes men* the word *men* is described as a direct object, and so is the word *boys* in *such training makes boys into men;* but in *boys become men* the word *men* is not so described.

DIRECTION OF PREDICATION. Particular subject-predicator-complement sequences commonly show semantic relationships of particular types, and these are commonly determined by the predicators. Thus in *children like dogs* in contemporary English the predicator expresses favorable emotion which the subject feels and the complement inspires. In *dogs please children* the subject inspires the emotion and the complement feels it. Passives reverse basic directions of predication: *we were hit by a truck* is opposite in direction of predication from *a truck hit us*. Reversal of direction of predication occurs under other circumstances also, as in *someone opened the door* and *the door opened*. Something very much like it occurs when, for example, the adjective *desperate* means now *feeling despair*, as in *I was becoming desperate*, and now *causing despair*, as in *the situation was becoming desperate*.

DISTRIBUTIVE SINGULARS. *Bend your right knee* has a distributive singular, *your right knee*, when it is spoken to a group of people, such as a class in physical training. *Your right knees* might seem more consistent here, but on the other hand it might seem to suggest a plural number of right knees belonging to each person. Distributive singulars occur with relative infrequency in careful and formal styles.

"ELLIPSIS." See Implied Components.

"EMPHATIC VERB FORMS." See Expanded Verb Forms.

"EXCLAMATORY SENTENCES." See Assertives.

EXPANDED VERB FORMS. Present-tense and past-tense forms employing *do* as auxiliary, used (1) emotionally, as in *I do like that music!* (2) in many clauses negated by *not*, as in *Mary doesn't like it* and in *don't be silly*, and (3) where *do* provides a needed clause marker, as in *did Genevieve get there?* and in *neither did I*.

EXPLETIVES. This term is applied here only to the *there* which takes the subject position in sentences such as *there are many beautiful beaches* and which is the total stated subject in reduced clauses such as *are there?*

EXTREMITIVES. Exceptional syntactic patterning some-times accompanies feelings of extremeness. Thus in *Warren is too small a town* modification by extremitive *too* pulls *small* in front of the determiner *a*.

"FACTITIVE VERBS." This term is sometimes used of verbs of influencing or affecting that take nounal first comple-ments followed by nounal or adjectival second complements of result or effect. Thus *makes* can be called factitive in its use in *it makes me sad*, and *elect* in its use in *they elected Susan secretary*. The construction is of course essentially the same where the second complement is adverbial, as in *such training makes boys into men*.

"FINITE VERB FORMS." This term is sometimes used of verb forms employed in common or subjunctive modes, as op-posed to infinitival, gerundial, and participial verb forms.

FORMAL STYLES. See the Introduction.

FORMATIVES. Recognizable noninflectional components which occur in words but are themselves without word status in contemporary English. Formatives include (1) prefixes, such as the *un* of *unlucky;* (2) suffixes, such as the *y* of *lucky;* and (3) non-affixal formatives, or stems, such as the *aristo* and the *crat* of *aristocratic*.

FUTURE TENSES. See Tenses.

GENDER. Contemporary English does not have true gram-matical gender. But in modern English choice among the third-person-singular pronoun forms *he, she,* and *it* is normally on the basis of personality and sex or the lack of them, and choice be-tween such nouns as *boy* and *waiter* on the one hand and *girl* and *waitress* on the other is ordinarily on the basis of sex. Thus a kind of gender does make itself felt, if not true grammatical gender.

"GENITIVE CASE." See Cases.

GERUNDIALS. The *ing* forms of verbs are here called ge-rundials. Thus *playing* is classified as a gerundial both in *playing the piano is Randolph's greatest pleasure* and in *Randolph is happiest playing the piano*, a distinction between "gerunds" and "present participles" not being attempted. Gerundial verb forms are re-garded as constituting a mode, like subjunctive verb forms. Ge-rundial nouns and adjectives are also recognized here: thus *living* is classified as a gerundial noun in *a living room*, which is equivalent to *a room for living*, and as a gerundial adjective in *a living soul*, which is equivalent to *a soul that is living*.

GLIDES. The consonantal initial sounds of *yet, win,* and *rock* (represented phonemically by /j/, /w/, and /r/) and the closely related vocalic final sounds of *toy, now,* and *car* (represented by /ɪ/, /ʊ/, and /r/) are called glide sounds here, and the letters *y, w,* and *r* are called glide letters.

HALF APPOSITIVES, HALF COORDINATES, HALF MODIFIERS. Many words and multiword units which often are classified as appositives, coordinates, or contained modifiers seem better classified, instead, as adjuncts with secondary functions as what are here called half appositives, half coordinates, and half modifiers. In this use *half* is roughly equivalent to *quasi*. This double classification sometimes seems necessary because the units given it come too late to be true appositives, coordinates, or contained modifiers: their sentences have gone ahead without them.

> I've done such things *myself*.
> Mary was there—*and Sarah*.
> The leftovers were eaten *cold* as a midnight supper.

Here the subjects are *I, Mary,* and *the leftovers;* and *myself, and Sarah,* and *cold* simply come too late in their sentences to be parts of subjects that seem quite complete without them. In the following sentences the subjects include what are primarily adjuncts in the preceding ones.

> *I myself* have done such things.
> *Mary and Sarah* were there.
> *The cold leftovers* were eaten as a midnight supper.

It seems necessary also to assign adjunct status to all words and multiword units which are given inclosing punctuation in the written language. Some of these have secondary relationships of the kinds here described as half apposition, half coordination, and half modification.

> One student, *the best in the class*, questioned the analysis.
> Mary—*and Sarah too, for that matter*—went to entirely too many parties that week.
> Some of the students, *eager to raise their grades*, practically memorized the historical chapters.

HEADS AND MODIFIERS. In the commonest type of syntactic combination, a word-or-multiword unit, a head, combines with another or others, a modifier or modifiers, and determines the syntactic character of the total combination. Thus *new houses* has the syntactic potentialities of *houses*, not those of *new: houses* is head and *new* modifier. *Houses of that kind* has the syntactic potentialities of *houses* also: *houses* is head once again, and *of that kind* is a prepositional unit used as modifier. Reduction is responsible for the theoretical difficulty presented by such a sequence as *several of the houses*. Here *several* is head and *of the houses* is modifier, but *several* is a reduction of *several houses*, which would be undesirably repetitive with *of the houses* following as modifier "of the whole." Upside-down construction offers further complications. *That kind of houses* exists alongside *houses of that kind*, and has *kind* as head and *that* and *of houses* as modifiers. Informal *he's sort of nice* carries upside-down construction a step farther: *sort* is head in the complement and *of nice* is prepositional-unit modifier, and yet the whole unit *sort of nice* has the grammatical potentialities not of *sort* but of the adjective *nice*. Predicators are a special type of heads, modified by subjects and complements within nucleuses and by adjuncts syntactically outside them. Nonclausal transforms make this clear. Thus the clause *that children like dogs* of *never forget that children like dogs* can be replaced by the nonclausal transform *children's liking for dogs*, and in this transform the head word is *liking*, which obviously corresponds to *like* in the clausal equivalent. Subjects and complements trade places in passive reversals, where *a local dentist owns the building* becomes *the building is owned by a local dentist;* predicators hold their ground.

HYPOTHETICAL SUBJUNCTIVES. Verb forms of the four past tenses are employed in the subjunctive mode, with time values different from those of the common mode, to indicate unreality and improbability. The subjunctive past of *I wish I had red hair* (indicating unreality) has the same time value as the common-mode present *have* of *I'm sorry I have brown hair;* and the subjunctive past *left* and past future *would miss* of *if I left next week, I'd miss two examinations* (indicating improbability) have the same time value as the common-mode present *leave* and present future *will miss* of *if I leave next week, I'll miss two examinations.*

"IMMEDIATE CONSTITUENTS." This term is often used of what are here called simply components. Thus in *people with talented children have problems too* the clause components are the subject *people with talented children,* the predicator *have,* the complement *problems,* and the adjunct *too.* Within the subject the components are the head *people* and the modifier *with talented children.* Within the modifier the components are the preposition *with* and the object *talented children.* Within the object the components are the modifier *talented* and the head *children.* The example is a simple one, but it does illustrate the necessity of doing syntactic analysis step by step.

IMPERATIVES. Main imperatives normally give main-clause expression to requests and desires.

> Be quiet.
> Everyone be quiet.
> Heaven help us!

The predicators in such clauses are here said to be in the subjunctive mode. Subordinate imperatives are like main imperatives in force and like them in the mode of their predicators, but are distinguished from them by the use of a marker *that* such as declaratives commonly employ and by the normal occurrence of stated subjects. *That everyone be quiet,* in *it is important that everyone be quiet,* can serve as an example.

IMPINGING CLAUSES. Clauses that are used as the words or multiword units in which they terminate are ordinarily used. Thus in *he'll take us heaven knows where* the clause *heaven knows where,* in patterning a main declarative with a clause-marking adverb used as a grammatically exceptional complement, is used as an uncharacteristic second complement of the main predicator *will take,* much as *where* is used in the incredulous *he'll take us where?* or as *somewhere* is used in the declarative *he'll take us somewhere.*

IMPLIED COMPONENTS. It is necessary to recognize the force of unstated components at many points, though this recognition should not involve actually adding these components. Thus when it serves as answer to *where's the car?* the prepositional unit (and sentence) *behind the Club* is the complement in a main declarative whose subject and predicator are both implied. We cannot be sure of the exact form the implied subject would take if it were stated: probably it would be *it*, but it might well be *the car* if emotion were involved. In *he has a wife to support* the one-word verbid clause *support* has an implied subject suggested by the main subject and an implied complement suggested by the main complement; in *he has a wife to support him* the verbid clause *support him* has an implied subject suggested by the main complement. In *a woman I knew was my friend spoke next* the implied subject of *was* is suggested by *a woman:* a stated subject here might be *that, who,* or (whether we like it or not) even *whom.*

"INDEFINITE PRONOUNS." This term is often applied to a somewhat miscellaneous group of words here called determinative pronouns, sometimes with nounal pronouns such as *someone* thrown in.

"INDEPENDENT CLAUSES." See Main Clauses.

"INDICATIVE MODE." See Modes.

"INDIRECT OBJECTS." This term is commonly used of what are here considered simply nounal second complements preceding first complements in their clauses. Thus *you* is commonly considered an indirect object in *I'll give you an answer tomorrow,* while *to you* in *I'll give an answer to you tomorrow* is likely to be viewed quite differently in spite of the fact that it serves the same syntactic purpose.

INFINITIVES. Infinitives are here regarded not as "verbal nouns" but as modal forms of verbs just as subjunctives are. The *to* which often precedes infinitives is here regarded as a preposition with verbid-clause objects, like the *to* of *June objects to being told the truth about her boy friend,* where the verbid clause has a gerundial predicator. It is of course true that the *to* which precedes infinitives often occurs where prepositions are otherwise not usual.

INFLECTION. The varieties of inflection recognized here are as follows: in verbs, inflection for voice, aspect, mode, tense, expansion (with *do*), and person and number; in nouns and pronouns, inflection for case and number; in adjectives and adverbs, inflection for comparison. Obviously the different varieties of "inflection" listed have very different grammatical values. Thus the singular *man* and the plural *men* perform the same syntactic functions, but the possessives *man's* and *men's* most characteristically perform the basically pronounal function of determiner modifiers of nounal heads, as in *men's goals in life*. The term *inflection* is applied very broadly here. Thus *went* is classified among the inflected forms of *go*, though in origin and in form it belongs rather with *wend*, and such a phrasal form as *will blow* (as in *I'm afraid all our tires will blow out on the trip next week*) is classified among the inflected forms of *blow* exactly like *blew* (as in *two tires blew out last week*).

INFORMAL STYLES. See the Introduction.

"INTERJECTIONS." This term is sometimes applied to relatively emotional words (for example, *ouch*) of the kind here classified as absolutes, and sometimes to emotional isolates in general.

INTERROGATIVES. Main interrogatives are main clauses constructed according to syntactic patterns that are characteristically used to elicit facts or opinions from those addressed. The clause markers employed in main interrogatives are characteristically (1) pronouns or adverbs from a list of seven (sometimes with heads or modifiers) and/or (2) verb forms placed in front of the subjects, these verb forms also being from a restricted list. Subordinate interrogatives employ clause markers of the same types: for example, *when* in *I have no idea when Jane studies* and *had* in *had they taken proper precautions, they would have had no difficulties*. Subordinate interrogatives make much less use of marker verb forms than main interrogatives do, but their list of marker pronouns and adverbs is longer and includes the pronoun *that* when it competes with *who* and *which*, and such adverbs as *if, although, than,* and *as*. What are here called subordinate-interrogative clauses include clauses sometimes called adjectival and adverbial: *when Jane studies*, for example, in *the days when Jane studies are few and far between* and in *we're always surprised when Jane studies*. Many subordinate-interrogative clauses, and some main-interrogative clauses, have no question force. What are often called interrogative pronouns, interrogative adjectives, and interrogative adverbs are here called clause-marker pronouns and adverbs.

"INTRANSITIVE VERBS." This term is sometimes applied to all verbs except transitives: copulatives such as the *be* of *I'm ready*, obliques such as the *insist* of *she insists on paying*, terminants such as the *work* of *Mrs. Phelps works too*.

ISOLATES. Words (such as *yes*, *ouch*, and the *danger* of signs) and multiword units (such as *good morning* and the *no smoking* of signs) which are used as sentences, or total communications, but which have no clearly implied clause structure. Sometimes, as in *yes, John*, isolates are modified by adjuncts much as nucleuses in clausal sentences are.

"KERNELS." This term is applied to stripped-down nucleuses. For example, in *young boys are often exceptionally skillful drivers in spite of an occasional lack of prudence* what is here called the nucleus is *young boys are exceptionally skillful drivers* but what would be called the kernel is *boys are drivers*.

"LEVELS OF USAGE." See the Introduction.

"LINKING VERBS." See Copulative Verbs.

LONG VOWEL SOUNDS. See Vowel Sounds.

LOOSE ADJUNCTS. All sentence components requiring inclosing punctuation in the written language. A wide range of constructions is included, among them such adjuncts of direct address as *Jack* in *that's right, Jack* and such subordinate-interrogative clauses as *who taught me phonemics* in *the third man, who taught me phonemics, was deeply concerned about plus junctures*, which does not mean the same thing as *my third phonemics teacher was deeply concerned about plus junctures*, the "man" being third in some other sequence—and perhaps first or even fifth in the speaker's series of teachers of phonemics.

MAIN CLAUSES. "Independent" clauses, though the independence is commonly no more than grammatical. Clauses whose patterning makes them freely usable as sentences: *why did he resign*, for example, but not *why he resigned* (as in *do you have any idea why he resigned?*).

MAJOR SYNTACTIC FUNCTIONS. The functions performed by subjects, predicators, complements, adjuncts, and isolates.

MARKERS. See Clause Markers.

"MASS NOUNS." This term is often used for what are here called quantifiables, or for some of them. See Quantifiable Nouns.

MODES. Five modes are recognized here: common (or "indicative"), subjunctive, infinitival, gerundial, participial. Participial verb forms are not used as predicators, except with auxiliaries, expressed or implied, in phrasal passive-voice forms and perfect-tense forms—and these phrasal forms belong to other modes. Infinitival and gerundial forms are similarly used with auxiliaries in phrasal forms belonging to other modes, but are also used alone as predicators. The four predicating modes are characteristically used in clauses of various types, as follows:

1. Common mode, in declaratives, interrogatives, and assertives.
2. Subjunctive mode: (1) coactual subjunctives, in imperatives; (2) hypothetical subjunctives, in declaratives, interrogatives, and assertives.
3. Infinitival mode, in verbids.
4. Gerundial mode, in verbids.

"MODAL AUXILIARIES." Such verbs as *can, may,* and *must* are often called modal auxiliaries. No modal auxiliaries are recognized here. In *she must not have understood you,* for example, it seems best to regard *must* as the main predicator and *not have understood you* as its negated complement. This is an analysis comparable to that which would be given for *she seems not to have understood you* or *she gives every indication of not having understood you.*

MODIFIERS. See Heads and Modifiers.

"MORPHEMES." See the Introduction.

"MORPHOLOGY." The internal structure of words, or the analysis of it, in terms of formatives and inflections.

MULTIPLE CONTAINED UNITS. Coordinates combine to form multiple units of varied types within sentences. Thus in *I saw him before and after the meeting* the adjunct *before and after the meeting* has as its first component a multiple preposition, *be-before and after,* in which the first coordinate is *before* and the second is *and after.* In *he's six feet three* the complement *six feet three* is a multiple unit in which the first coordinate is *six feet* and the second is *three*, obviously a reduction of *three inches*.

MULTIPLE SENTENCES. Often two or more main clauses are together given the status of a single sentence, as in *it was raining, and I had a bad cold*. Sometimes clause equivalents function as components in multiple sentences also—as in *yes, I do*, where the clause equivalent *yes* is coordinated with the reduced clause *I do*. The term *compound sentences* is often used for what are here called multiple sentences but does not suggest the relationship of coordination binding the component clauses or clause equivalents.

"NOMINALS." This term is sometimes used of nouns and of other words and multiword units used nounally.

"NOMINATIVE ABSOLUTES." This term is sometimes applied to gerundial clauses with expressed subjects, used as adjuncts within larger clauses.

NOMINATIVE CASE. See Cases.

NONCOMMITTAL CONDITIONAL SENTENCES. See Conditional Sentences.

"NONRESTRICTIVE COMPONENTS." See Loose Adjuncts.

NOUNS. Words (1) characteristically usable as subjects, complements of transitive verbs, and objects of prepositions and (2) characteristically modifiable prepositively by determinative pronouns and by adjectives, except that proper nouns are characteristically used without determiners and have only limited use with adjectival modifiers.

"NOUN CLAUSES." This term is often applied to subordinate clauses, verbids commonly excepted, used in nounal functions.

NOUNAL FUNCTIONS. The functions of subject, complement of a transitive verb, object of a preposition, head in a nounal headed unit, and coordinate in a nounal multiple unit.

NOUNAL PRONOUNS. The pronouns that are strikingly like proper nouns in their syntactic behavior. Thus the nounal pronouns *he* of *he's hopeful* and *everyone* of *everyone's hopeful* are much like the proper noun *John* of *John's hopeful* in the syntactic uses to which they are put. The determinative pronouns are quite different in characteristic behavior. Yet there are frequent parallels in particular situations—as, for example, when *it* and *that* are used almost interchangeably in *I know it* and *I know that.*

NUCLEUSES. Minimal sequences made up of subjects, predicators, and complements, or of such of these as occur. In *sometimes I snore a little* the nucleus is made up of the subject *I* and the predicator *snore.* In *come in!* the nucleus is made up of the predicator *come* and the complement *in.* In *of course small things have always made sensitive people unnecessarily sad* the nucleus is made up of the subject *small things*, the predicator *have made*, the first complement *sensitive people*, and the second complement *unnecessarily sad.* The heads in nucleuses are the predicators: in the last example, *have made*, which in the meaning expressed requires two complements. Nucleuses are minimal in the sense that they contain only minimal sequences of components. The components themselves are often relatively complex. Thus the subject *small things* is more complex than *things*, and the predicator *have made* than *make.*

NUMBER. See Persons and Numbers.

OBJECTS. See Prepositions and Objects.

"OBJECT COMPLEMENTS." See Complements.

OBJECTIVE CASE. See Cases.

OBLIQUE VERBS. Verbs that take adverbial complements, including prepositional-unit complements. The *look* of *look there!* and *look at that!* is an example, the *insist* of *he insists on being told all the details* is another, and the *be* of *she isn't at home* and *she isn't here* is a third.

PARTS OF SPEECH. As described here, the parts of speech are categories of words set up on the basis of different patterns of use in sentences. Noninflectional internal characteristics such as the use of certain affixes do not carry us far enough, and in any case must always be checked against patterns of use. Inflections do not carry us far enough either, and these too must be checked against patterns of use. Almost all verbs do follow distinctive patterns of inflection, but *must* does not inflect at all and yet must be classified as a verb because the verb forms which follow it are clearly not full predicators in the clauses *must* occurs in.

> Horton must *have been* an exceptionally good teacher.
> Horton clearly *was* an exceptionally good teacher.

For many nouns, inflection is rare or nonexistent. This is notably true of such quantifiables as *nonsense, fun,* and *furniture.* Adjectives such as *extinct* do not inflect, nor adverbs such as *here,* nor isolates such as *ouch,* nor pronouns such as *the.* The real basis of part-of-speech classification is characteristic syntactic behavior.

PARTICIPIALS. The term *participle* is here applied only to past forms (or, in the case of irregular verbs such as *cut, spread,* and *run,* to basic forms used where distinct past forms are ordinarily used) employed with auxiliaries expressed or implied, in passive-voice forms and perfect-tense forms.

> We were *stopped* at the door.
> I wouldn't have *come* back.
> I've heard him *criticized* severely.

In the third of these sentences, *criticized* must be described as a reduced passive infinitive with auxiliary not stated: the relation to *I've heard people criticize him severely* is clear. Words of participial origin in other uses seem best classified as participial adjectives.

> He's a *disappointed* man.
> The job simply isn't *finished* yet.

What are often called present participles and present perfect participles are given gerundial classification here.

PASSIVE VOICE. See Voices.

PAST TENSE. See Tenses.

PERSONS AND NUMBERS. Under some circumstances, predicators are affected in form by the person and number of their subjects. Three persons (first, second, and third) and two numbers (singular and plural) are recognized at some points. The verb *be* makes more distinctions than other verbs do, and since *be* is the auxiliary both of the passive and of the progressive the effects of this complexity are far reaching.

> I am   we are
> you are   you are
> he (she, it) is   they are

In the plural the only effect of the person of the subject comes in formal futures employing *shall* as auxiliary in the first person. Much of the time, verb forms are indifferent to person and number. *Played*, for example, is not affected by the person-and-number force of its subject. Common person-and-number forms occur alongside more specialized forms at some points.

I play	we play
you play	you play
he (she, it) plays	they play

Here *play* is common person-and-number and *plays* is third person singular. Pluralizer nouns generally have differences in form distinguishing singulars from plurals, but some of them (such as *sheep* and *Portuguese*) use their basic forms as plurals also, without change. Quantifiable nouns are assigned singular force. Adjectives are not affected by number. Thus *they're Spanish* contrasts with *they're Spaniards* and *they're Canadian* with *they're Canadians*, *Canadian* being both an adjective and a pluralizer noun. Some pronouns are affected by number and some are not. Thus *this street* contrasts with *these streets*, but *any* can replace both *this* and *these* here. At a few points a distinction between two and more than two is made, as when *both of the boys* contrasts with *all of the boys*.

PERSONAL PRONOUNS. The set of pronouns made up of *I, you, he, she, it, we, they*, and their "inflected" forms.

PHONEMES. The vowel and consonant sounds distinguished in the spoken language—or, in this grammar, in the form of it being described. The term is sometimes extended to include matters of pitch, stress, and pause. The analysis of vowel and consonant sounds followed here is that employed in the Kenyon and Knott *A Pronouncing Dictionary of American English*.

PLURALIZER NOUNS. Nouns that have plurals. Quantifiables do not, and proper nouns do not: this basic principle is not affected by the fact that many nouns are both quantifiables and pluralizers, as *noise* is in *too much noise* and *too many noises*, or by the fact that proper nouns in general can be made into pluralizers freely, as *Mary* is in *there are three Marys in the class* and *Johnson* in *the Johnsons are in New York*. Most pluralizers can be described accurately as "countables," but some cannot.

I bought three trousers is hardly standard, for example, or *I've lived in three outskirts of the city.*

POSSESSIVES. See Cases.

"PREDICATES." This term is often used of sequences including what are here called predicators, complements, and adjuncts. Clauses are often thought of as structures generally divisible into two major components, subjects and predicates. Some adjuncts, however, are often called "sentence modifiers" rather than parts of predicates. This is especially likely to be the case with adjuncts which precede the subjects in their clauses and adjuncts which are inclosed in punctuation in the written language. The concept of the predicate is avoided here.

"PREDICATE ADJECTIVES," "PREDICATE COMPLEMENTS." See Complements.

PREDICATORS. In minimal sequences used in expressions of fact and opinion and begun by the pronoun *I*—in contemporary English, one of the most unmistakable of all subjects and therefore an especially satisfactory representative subject—the second component is the predicator.

> I *am* sick.   I *make* Hinton angry.
> I *like* noise.   I *work.*

The predicator is characteristically a verb in part-of-speech classification. Expressed or implied, predicators are heads in all clauses, main and subordinate, and are modified by subjects and complements within nucleuses and adjuncts syntactically outside them.

PREFIXES. See Formatives.

PREPOSITIONS AND OBJECTS. These terms are both used here of syntactic functions, not of part-of-speech classifications. Thus in *I was with him* the complement *with him* is said to be a prepositional unit in which the adverb *with* functions as preposition and the pronoun *him* as object. In prepositional units the prepositions normally determine the syntactic potentialities of the units. *With him* occurs, for example, in *I went to town with him,* in *I argued with him,* in *the boys with him are from the College too,* etc.—where *him* alone would not be usable. But it is easier to think of prepositions as relators, like possessive inflection, than as heads in relation to their objects. The words that function as prepositions are transitive and copulative adverbs from a limited list. Actually, copulative prepositions are few, but *as* is one in *everyone regards him as honest* and *for* in *we took your approval for granted*. Phrasal prepositions must be recognized too: examples are *in spite of* and *because of*. Objects of prepositions are often clausal: for example, in *after thinking it over I decided you were right*, where the object of *after* is a verbid clause, and in *after I thought it over I decided you were right*, where the object of the same preposition is a declarative clause.

PRESENT TENSE. See Tenses.

"PRETERITE TENSE." This term is often used for what is here called simply the past tense.

PRIMARY AND SECONDARY SPELLINGS. When two or more spellings or sets of spellings represent the same phoneme (or, exceptionally, phoneme cluster) in considerable numbers of words, the spelling or set of spellings most in accord with the basic system developed in English is here called primary and the other or others secondary. Thus when *sweet* and *suite* are both pronounced ./swit/ the spelling *ee* is a primary spelling for /i/ and the spelling *i-e* is a secondary spelling.

PRINCIPALS AND APPOSITIVES. Sometimes words and multiword units duplicate the construction of what precedes them. Thus in *our friend Martin is here in Boston* the noun *Martin* repeats the construction of *our friend* within the subject *our friend Martin* and the prepositional unit *in Boston* repeats the construction of *here* within the complement *here in Boston*. *Our friend* and *here* are principals, *Martin* and *in Boston* are appositives. In *it's hard to please Harriet* the subject is the apposed unit *it to please Harriet*, in which *it* is principal and *to please Harriet* is appositive. Postponement of the appositive without loss of appositive status is possible because *it*, without reference to anything already present in the context, is immediately understood here as simply a representative of the real content of the subject, which will be stated later in the sentence. In *I've made that mistake myself* the situation is different. *I* is the subject, and is an entirely adequate subject in most contexts, so that the sentence is taken to proceed with *I* as subject, *have made* as predicator, and *that mistake* as complement— and *myself* can only be an adjunct with half-appositive relation to the subject, not a true appositive within the subject. Words and multiword units which approach repetition of construction but require inclosing punctuation should also be described as half appositives, not true appositives. Thus in *the governor of the territory, Nuño de Guzmán, was distinguished even among the conquerors by his greed and his cruelty* the status of adjunct and half appositive, not of true appositive, should be assigned to *Nuño de Guzmán*.

"PRINCIPAL PARTS OF VERBS." This term is commonly used of sets of three verb forms made up of (1) the basic form, (2) the common-mode and subjunctive past, and (3) the participle. For all regular verbs, and for some irregular verbs, the last two forms are the same. Examples follow, all of them for irregular verbs except the first two.

play, played, played	lead, led, led
rent, rented, rented	shut, shut, shut
keep, kept, kept	speak, spoke, spoken
have, had, had	grow, grew, grown
spend, spent, spent	go, went, gone

Since *s* forms are regular for almost all verbs and gerundial forms are all regular (except for loss of a syllable in the spoken language in such forms as *chuckling*) and phrasal forms are regular without exception, the "principal parts" display all the unpredictable inflectional changes for almost all verbs. But there are advantages in simply listing all the one-word forms in standard use, separating present forms from pasts.

> rent, rents, renting: rented
> have, has, having: had
> grow, grows, growing: grew, grown
> be, are, am, is, being: were, was, been
> shut, shuts, shutting: shut
> come, comes, coming: came, come
> can: could
> must

PROGRESSIVE ASPECT. See Aspects.

PRONOUNS. See Determinative Pronouns and Nounal Pronouns.

"PRONOMINAL ADJECTIVES." See Determinative Pronouns.

PROPER NOUNS AND PROPER NAMES. Proper nouns are nouns that have individual applications without the use of determiners. *Mary* and *Panama* are examples. Proper names include proper nouns but also include multiword units, with and without determiners, that have been given fixed individual applications, often officially. *The United States Steel Corporation* is a proper name within which there are no proper nouns at all. *Iowa State College of Agriculture and Mechanic Arts* is a proper name within which the first word is a proper noun.

QUANTIFIABLE NOUNS. Nouns such as *courage, bacon,* and *scenery* which normally have no plurals and take determinatives of quantity such as *much* and not determinatives of number such as *many* and *one.*

QUESTIONS. Sentences, and main divisions of multiple sentences, intended to elicit expressions of fact or opinion from those addressed. Main interrogatives commonly have question force, but sometimes they do not. Question force is often achieved by nonsyntactic devices of intonation and/or manner, and sometimes circumstances alone produce it. The line between meditative statement and question can be very thin in such a sentence as *you'll be in Lexington tomorrow,* in syntax a main declarative. Such a clause equivalent as *this book* can apparently be given question force by situation alone, or by situation and manner.

RANGES. See Time Ranges and Time Spans.

REDUCTION. See Implied Components.

REJECTED CONDITIONAL SENTENCES. See Conditional Sentences.

"RELATIVE PRONOUNS," "RELATIVE ADVERBS," "RELATIVE CLAUSES." "Relative" pronouns and adverbs are here classified as clause markers in subordinate-interrogative clauses, with references of pronominal type to what precedes them. Thus in *the congress for which Morelos had given his life soon ceased to exist* the interrogative (or "relative") clause *for which Morelos had given his life* includes a clause-marker (or "relative") pronoun *which* that refers to what precedes, *the congress,* as *it* would in the corresponding main declarative *Morelos had given his life for it.*

REPETITIVES. Words such as *poohpooh*, *shillyshally*, and *hubbub*, in which components are repeated with or without variation.

REPRESENTATIVE SINGULARS. Singulars determined by such pronouns as *any* and *the*, in meaning hardly distinguishable from plurals. Thus in *the automobile has changed American life*, obviously *the automobile* is not a particular automobile prominent in the context but a representative, typical automobile, and the meaning of *automobiles have changed American life* is essentially the same.

REPRESENTATIVE WORDS. Words used in reduced construction to represent themselves plus other words or sequences of words. Thus in *my wife's car is in very good condition, but unfortunately mine isn't* the long possessive pronoun form *mine* represents *my car* and the *is* which follows it represents *is in very good condition*.

"RESTRICTIVE MODIFIERS." Punctuated "nonrestrictive" modifiers are classified as adjuncts here. Most of what are here described as contained modifiers are restrictive, though some—for example, the *poor* of *poor George* and *her poor husband*—really are not.

"RETAINED OBJECTS." Nounal complements of passive-verb-form predicators are sometimes called "retained objects." An example is the *time* of *we weren't given time*.

SAMES. The problem of identifying phonemes, words, and clause structures is sometimes difficult, especially if the point of view is that of the hearer or reader. Thus the /t/ of *writer* is commonly quite distinct phonetically from that of *ten*, so that *writer* and *rider* may be indistinguishable to the hearer without help from context. The *rowed* of *we rowed up the river almost to Lowell* cannot be distinguished from *rode*, by the hearer, without the help of context. *You boys drive carefully* can be taken as a declarative or as an imperative unless intonation, manner, and/or situation make clear precisely what is intended. The problem is different when the question is whether *sound* is the same word in *we sounded him out* and *he sounded favorable:* here the answer is a matter of historical fact.

SCHWA. The "obscure" unstressed vowel sound which in

democrat occurs in the second syllable and in *democracy* in the first and third syllables.

SECONDARY SPELLINGS. See Primary and Secondary Spellings.

SECONDARY SYNTACTIC FUNCTIONS. Syntactic functions performed by words or multiword units which also perform major or contained syntactic functions: the functions of half head and half modifier, half principal and half appositive, half coordinate, coordinator, and clause marker. Thus in *the boys went away satisfied* the adjunct *satisfied* performs the secondary function of half modifier of *boys*, and in *who said that?* the subject *who* performs the secondary function of clause marker for the interrogative.

SENTENCES. Main clauses not incorporated in larger clauses, or main-clause equivalents similarly unincorporated, or series of two or more main clauses or main-clause equivalents united in multiple sentences that are given the status of unincorporated single main clauses. The written language marks sentences clearly, beginning them with capital letters and ending them with periods or equivalent marks; the spoken language makes a less unambiguous use of pitch and pauses. In spoken English many sentences are left unfinished and others show nonstandard mixing of patterns.

"SENTENCE MODIFIERS." See Predicates.

SHORT VOWEL SOUNDS. See Vowel Sounds.

"SIGN OF THE INFINITIVE." See Infinitives.

SIMPLEX WORDS. Words which do not contain either other words or clear noninflectional formatives.

SPANS. See Time Ranges and Time Spans.

SPLIT CLAUSES. Clauses with components that function in two nucleuses or even in two clauses. Examples follow:

After twenty years poor Jones is triumphantly emerging from the wilderness of English phonemics and doggedly preparing to enter the jungle of English syntax.

Jones has always been an industrious though unimaginative student of language.

In the first of these sentences there is splitting after *is*, which serves as auxiliary both for *emerging* and for *preparing*. The adjunct *triumphantly* and the complement *the wilderness of English phonemics* continue the clause in one direction; the adjuncts *and* and *doggedly* and the complement *to enter the jungle of English syntax* continue it in another. Like *is*, the initial adjunct *after twenty years* and the subject *poor Jones* belong to both of the continuations that follow the split. In the second sentence the noun *student* serves as head in two complements, one a part of the main nucleus, the other a part of a highly reduced interrogative clause begun and marked by *though*. What are commonly called "compound predicates" are split clauses in which splitting occurs between subjects and predicators, as it would in the first sentence above if *is* were added before *doggedly*.

"SPLIT INFINITIVES." When *to* has verbid-clause objects with infinitival predicators, there is a feeling that the infinitives are undesirably "split" if adjuncts are allowed to separate them from this *to*.

STEMS. This is a convenient term for nonaffixal formatives such as the *fif* of *fifth*, which is obviously a variant of *five*, and the *demo* and *crat* of *democratic*. Complex stems can conveniently be recognized too: for example, the *permiss* of *permissive*.

STRESS. See Vowel Sounds.

STRINGS. This term is here applied chiefly to units made up of two or more clear components whose relationship is not clear: for example, such a name as *Robert Morss Lovett*. All unified sequences of components can be regarded as strings.

"STRONG VERBS." This term is sometimes applied, for historical reasons, to most of the irregular verbs whose pasts are distinguished from their basic forms by differences in vowels rather than by the addition of /d/ (or /ɪd/ or /əd/) or /t/.

STYLES. Formal, careful, and informal styles must be recognized within standard English. See the Introduction.

SUBJECTS. First components in the nucleuses of declaratives. One of the most unmistakable subjects, and therefore a good representative of the category, is the nominative pronoun form *I*. It is not really possible to describe subjects as words or multiword units "about which something is said." In the following exchange, for example, the subject of discourse is "Winston," but the grammatical subjects are quite different.

"What has happened to Winston?"
"An uncle of his died and left him some money."

A tremendous variety of internal forms is to be found among subjects. Thus in *Take It Easy isn't running today* the subject is the proper name *Take It Easy*, which in internal form is felt as a main-imperative clause.

SUBJUNCTIVES. See Modes.

SUBORDINATE CLAUSES. Clauses (1) whose syntactic patterning makes them not freely usable as sentences, at least in standard written practice, and/or (2) whose incorporation within larger clauses is smoother than is ordinary for main clauses. Thus the *when I got home* of *it was almost eight when I got home* is not very satisfactorily usable as a sentence, and the *I can go* of *I'm sure I can go* is incorporated within the larger statement quite smoothly as completing modifier of *sure*.

"SUBORDINATING CONJUNCTIONS." See Conjunctions.

"SUBSTANTIVES." This term is often used of nouns, nounal pronouns, and multiword nounal units.

SUFFIXES. See Formatives.

SYNTAX. The internal structure of sentences, or the analysis of it, in terms of words and combinations of words.

TENSES. Eight tenses are recognized here: a set of four present tenses, including the present itself; and a set of four past tenses, including the past itself. Only two tenses have one-word forms—the present, and the past. Auxiliaries of tense include only *have* in the various perfect tenses and *will* and, in limited formal use, *shall* in the various future tenses.

rent	rented
have rented	had rented
will rent	would rent
will have rented	would have rented

The eight tenses represented here are (1) the present, the present perfect, the present future, and the present future perfect; and

(2) the past, the past perfect, the past future, and the past future perfect. Eight tenses occur only in the common mode; the subjunctive has six, the infinitival two, the gerundial two, the participial one. Time relationships normally determine choice among tenses, but the tenses are differently used in the different modes.

TERMINANT VERBS. Verbs used without complements. *Snore* is a good example. Verbs that are normally transitive, copulative, or oblique often are used terminantly. *Stop* is used terminantly in *the bus stops here*. *Look* is so used in *she refuses to look*, though here it can be said that a complement is implied.

TIGHT ADJUNCTS. Adjuncts not inclosed in punctuation in the written language. In *nowadays Clara always sees movies twice* the adjuncts *nowadays*, *always*, and *twice* are all tight ones.

TIME RANGES AND TIME SPANS. As these terms are used here, time ranges are the divisions of time with which tenses are normally concerned and time spans are the segments of time with which particular verb forms are concerned in particular uses. Thus the progressive present perfect verb form *have been watching* has a time range of indefinite length in the past, extending to the moment of speaking. As the form is used in *I've been watching "The River" on TV this evening*, the time span actually covered is an hour and a half or less—only part of the picture may have been seen—terminating at the moment of speaking or in the last few minutes or perhaps within the last hour or so.

TO WITH INFINITIVES. See Infinitives.

TRANSFORMS. Syntactic patterns that closely resemble other syntactic patterns, from which they are conveniently considered to derive, but that are nevertheless distinct in form and use. Thus the main interrogative *was Jane there?* is conveniently regarded as a transform of the main declarative *Jane was there*. All clause patterns except that of the main declarative are here regarded as transforms of the main declarative, as are some nonclausal patterns—for example, *his dislike for fame*, which obviously parallels *he dislikes fame* closely but has a prepositional completing modifier such as nouns have much more generally than verbs do. Clauses with passive-voice predicators are obviously transforms of clauses with common-voice predicators, though the term *reversals* seems preferable here. *I gave him the book* can profitably be considered a transform of *I gave the book to him,* and *an economics teacher* of *a teacher of economics.* It is possible to regard *the cold roast* as a transform of *the roast is cold,* and even to consider that in *we ate the roast cold* there is transformation of *the roast is cold;* but the value of such analysis is less clear.

TRANSITIVE PREPOSITIONS. See Prepositions and Objects.

TRANSITIVE VERBS. Verbs used with nounal first complements. *Make* is transitive both in *he makes too much trouble* and in *he makes all his colleagues angry.* Even *be* seems best classified as transitive in the uses in which it takes nounal complements regularly, as in *the three girls are sisters.*

UNSTRESSED SYLLABLES AND WORDS. See Vowel Sounds.

UPSIDE-DOWN CONSTRUCTION. See Heads and Modifiers.

VARIANT FORMS. When sets of forms occur where the basic patterning of the language calls for single forms, the forms making up a set can be called variants. Thus among the determinative pronouns the forms *a* and *an* divide determiner-modifier functions performed by more typical *any: any door* and *any entrance,* but *a door* and *an entrance.* Again among the determinatives the forms *no* and *none* divide functions performed by more typical *all: all boys* and *all of the boys,* but *no boys* and *none of the boys.* Among the verb forms *will* is strikingly variable: it is sometimes *'ll,* sometimes *wo,* and sometimes *will.* Among the formatives, in such a complex as *length* it is clear that the stem *leng* is a variant of the word *long.* Spoken-language variation is a great deal more common than written-language practice suggests. Thus, ordinarily, the *the* of *the stove* and that of *the others* are phonemically distinct, and the *can* of *I can drive* is usually distinct phonemically from that of *I can go* as well as from the stressed *can* of *of course I can.* The *long* of *longer* has a /g/ the basic-form adjective lacks. Differences in dialect are of course responsible for a tremendous amount of spoken-language variation that the written language ignores. In a broad sense, all "inflected" forms are variants of their basic forms. *Was* and *will be* can be considered syntactic variants of *be,* the first occurring, for example, with the adjunct *yesterday* in *I was ready yesterday*, and the second occurring with the adjunct *to-morrow*.

VERBS. Words whose characteristic function is that of predicator and whose most distinctive prepositive modifiers are common-case and nominative personal-pronoun forms such as *I*. Almost all verbs inflect in distinctive ways also.

VERBIDS. Subordinate clauses with infinitival and gerundial predicators. Subjects are implied more often than they are stated, and they are objective- and possessive-case forms more often than nominative. Verbid forms with infinitival predicators are often identical in internal syntactic form with main imperatives.

People think you gave up the trombone to *make peace with the neighbors*.
Make peace with the neighbors.

"VOCATIVES." This term is sometimes used of adjuncts of direct address.

VOICES. Most verbs have passive-voice forms employing the auxiliary *be* and participial heads. The use of these indicates that the normal direction of predication is reversed. Thus *the house was built by my grandfather* is a reversal, with passive-voice predicator, of *my grandfather built the house*, in which the predicator *built* is a common-voice verb form. Sometimes common-voice predicators are used with reversed direction of predication also. Thus *the meetings begin at eight* has as subject the complement of *they begin the meetings at eight*. What is here called common voice is often called "active" voice, but the forms so named are often used to predicate events and states of affairs rather than actions, as in *the meetings begin at eight*, where the subject is not an actor and it is not possible to add mention of an actor, *the meetings begin at eight by the chairman* not being standard construction.

VOICED AND VOICELESS CONSONANT SOUNDS. All vowel sounds and most consonant sounds are voiced; that is, they involve vibration of the vocal cords of the type most noticeable, perhaps, in the voiced /z/ of *zoo* as compared with the voiceless /s/ of *sue*. The voiceless consonant sounds of contemporary American English are /h/, /p/, /t/, /k/, /f/, /θ/, /s/, and /ʃ/, the last occurring both separately and in the combination /tʃ/ which is sometimes regarded as a single phoneme.

VOWEL SOUNDS. Any treatment of the vowel sounds of modern English that relates them to the spellings representing them in the written language is facilitated by distinction between the vowel sounds of stressed syllables and those of unstressed syllables. It is necessary to deal with what happens in considerable numbers of pairs (or larger groups) of words such as the following, when stress and the absence of stress are variously distributed.

*a*tom, *a*tomic	dem*o*cracy, dem*o*crat
comp*e*te, comp*e*tition	int*ui*tive, int*ui*tion
conf*i*de, conf*i*dence	lapb*oa*rd, cupb*oa*rd
contin*ui*ty, contin*ua*l	simil*a*rity, simil*a*r
*de*finition, *de*fine	tut*o*rial, tut*o*r

In stressed syllables contemporary American English commonly distinguishes twelve vowel sounds, nine diphthongs, and two triphthongs. Among the twelve vowel sounds of stressed syllables it is convenient to distinguish six "long" sounds, which end words freely and which are commonly given two-letter representations, and six "short" sounds, which rarely end words and after which consonant letters are often doubled. Long vowel sounds occur in *teak, take, talk, stoke, duke,* and *dirk;* short vowel sounds in *tick, deck, tack, dock, took,* and *tuck.* The spellings given the vowel sounds of *talk* and *took* obviously do not follow the system. The diphthongs occur in *buy, bough, boy, beer, bare* with *are* pronounced like the *err* of *ferry, bare* with *are* pronounced like the *arr* of *narrow, bar, bore,* and *boor;* the triphthongs occur in *tire* and *sour.* In unstressed syllables distinctions are much less sharp. Only four unstressed vowel sounds are recognized here: the final vowel sounds of *coffee, virtue, loafer,* and *sofa.* Unstressed words are frequent as well as unstressed syllables: the *can* of *they can damn us* as well as the *con* of *they condemn us.* Degrees of stress are noteworthy.

"WEAK VERBS." This term is sometimes applied, for historical reasons, to all regular verbs and to irregular verbs whose past forms end in added /d/ or /t/ or in unchanged final /d/ or /t/. Irregular verbs commonly described as weak include *make, spend, sell, keep, feed, cut,* and *spread.*

WORDS. Words are minimal units characteristically separable by other words from what precedes and follows, without damage to construction. The written language characteristically distinguishes words by spacing before and after but not inside them. Compound words are combinations of two or even three words written as single words; mergings such as *I'm* and *don't* are grammatically ununified combinations of an exceptional kind; fixed phrasings such as *the College of William and Mary* are not readily interruptible but the words that compose them, like the *to* used with infinitives, are clear in other uses. The distinction between "compounds" such as *highway* and fixed phrasings such as *high school* (and the *high-school* of *high-school students*) is arbitrary.

"ZERO." When grammatical analysis is expressed in formulations of algebraic type, the concept of zero proves quite useful; and indeed the concept can be of value in formulations of traditional types as well. Such a series of paired sentences as the following can illustrate one situation in which the concept can be employed.

The *puppy* is hungry.	The *puppies* are hungry.
The *child* is hungry.	The *children* are hungry.
The *man* is hungry.	The *men* are hungry.
The *goldfish* is hungry.	The *goldfish* are hungry.

In each pair the first sentence has a singular subject—the interest is in a single puppy, etc.—and the second sentence has a plural subject. All the plural subjects except *the goldfish* include explicit indication of their number force. It is reasonable to say that when *the goldfish* has plural force it carries zero representation of plurality. Such a series of sentences as the following can illustrate another situation in which the concept of zero can be employed.

People *eat* very little mutton.
Very little mutton *is eaten*.
People *are eating* very little mutton.
It is important that the average person *eat* mutton.
People *ate* very little mutton.
People *don't eat* very much mutton.
The average person *eats* very little mutton.

Here the *eat* of *people eat very little mutton* contrasts in voice with *is eaten*, in aspect with *are eating*, in mode with the *eat* of *that the average person eat mutton,* in tense with *ate,* in absence of expansion with *do eat,* and in person-and-number with *eats.* It is reasonable to say that in *people eat very little mutton* the predicator *eat* carries zero representation of voice, aspect, mode, tense, nonexpansion, and person-and-number, all of which are clear. Such a set of sentences as the following can illustrate a third situation in which the concept of zero can be made use of.

The hotel *at which we stayed* is high above Port-au-Prince.
The hotel *that we stayed at* is high above Port-au-Prince.
The hotel *we stayed at* is high above Port-au-Prince.

In the last of these sentences the clause *we stayed at* can be said to contain zero representation of a pronoun object of *at*—probably *that,* perhaps *which*—without which it is notably incomplete. Zeros are not employed in the analysis presented in this book, but analyses deserving of the highest respect do make use of them. Grammars are written for different purposes, and for different readers. For the purposes of this grammar, it seems preferable to say that *goldfish* is a noun basic form that is used both as a singular and as a plural; that *eat* is a verb basic form used, in *people eat very little mutton,* in common voice, common aspect, common mode, present tense, and common person-and-number, without expansion; and that *we stayed at,* in *the hotel we stayed at,* is a subordinate clause in which a marker pronoun, *that* or *which,* is implied object of *at.*

A SELECTIVE BIBLIOGRAPHY

STANDARD GRAMMARS

CURME, GEORGE O. *Parts of Speech and Accidence.* Boston: D. C. Heath & Co., 1935.

――――. *Syntax.* Boston: D. C. Heath & Co., 1931.

JESPERSEN, OTTO. *Essentials of English Grammar.* New York: Henry Holt & Co., 1933.

――――. *A Modern English Grammar on Historical Principles.* 7 vols. Copenhagen: Einar Munksgaard, 1909–49.

KRUISINGA, E. *English Accidence and Syntax.* Part II of *A Handbook of Present-Day English.* 5th ed., 3 vols. Groningen: P. Noordhoff, 1931.

PALMER, HAROLD E., and BLANDFORD, F. G. *A Grammar of Spoken English.* 2d ed. Cambridge: W. Heffer and Sons, 1939.

POUTSMA, H. *A Grammar of Late Modern English.* Part I, 2d ed., 2 vols. Part II, 3 vols. Groningen: P. Noordhoff, 1904–29.

SWEET, HENRY. *A New English Grammar.* 2 vols. Oxford: Clarendon Press, 1891, 1898.

ZANDVOORT, R. W. *A Handbook of English Grammar.* 9th ed. Groningen: J. B. Wolters, 1964.

THE GRAMMAR OF THE SCHOOLS

HOOK, J. N., and MATHEWS, E. G. *Modern American Grammar and Usage.* New York: Ronald Press Co., 1956.

HOUSE, HOMER C., and HARMAN, SUSAN EMOLYN. *Descriptive English Grammar.* 2d ed. New York: Prentice-Hall, Inc., 1950.

KITTREDGE, GEORGE LYMAN, and FARLEY, FRANK EDGAR. *An Advanced English Grammar.* Boston: Ginn and Co., 1913.

ROBERTS, PAUL. *Understanding Grammar.* New York: Harper & Bros., 1954.

NEWER APPROACHES TO ANALYSIS

BLOOMFIELD, LEONARD. *Language*. New York: Henry Holt & Co.,
1933.

BOLINGER, DWIGHT L. *Forms of English: Accent, Morpheme, Order*.
Cambridge: Harvard University Press, 1965.

―――. *Interrogative Structures of American English*. ("Publica-
tions of the American Dialect Society," No. 28.) University:
University of Alabama Press, 1957.

CHOMSKY, NOAM. *Syntactic Structures*. 's Gravenhage: Mouton
and Co., 1957.

FODOR, JERRY A., and KATZ, JERROLD J. *The Structure of Language*.
New York: Prentice-Hall, Inc., 1964.

FRANCIS, W. NELSON. *The Structure of American English*. With
chapter on dialects by RAVEN I. MCDAVID, JR. New York:
Ronald Press Co., 1958.

FRIES, CHARLES C. *The Structure of English*. New York: Harcourt,
Brace & Co., 1952.

GLEASON, H. A., JR. *An Introduction to Descriptive Linguistics*.
Rev. ed. New York: Henry Holt & Co., 1961.

HARRIS, ZELLIG S. *Methods in Structural Linguistics*. Chicago: University of Chicago Press, 1951.

HILL, ARCHIBALD A. *Introduction to Linguistic Structures*. New
York: Harcourt, Brace & Co., 1958.

HOCKETT, CHARLES F. *A Course in Modern Linguistics*. New York:
Macmillan Co., 1958.

JOOS, MARTIN (ed.). *Readings in Linguistics*. Washington, D. C.:
American Council of Learned Societies, 1957.

LEES, ROBERT B. *The Grammar of English Nominalizations*.
Bloomington: Research Center in Anthropology, Folklore, and
Linguistics, 1960.

NIDA, EUGENE ALBERT. *A Synopsis of English Syntax*. Norman:
Summer Institute of Linguistics, 1960.

SAPIR, EDWARD. *Language*. New York: Harcourt, Brace & Co.,
1921.

SLEDD, JAMES. *A Short Introduction to English Grammar*. Chicago:
Scott, Foresman & Co., 1959.

TRAGER, GEORGE L., and SMITH, HENRY LEE, JR. *An Outline of
English Structure*. Norman, Okla.: Battenburg Press, 1951.

History and the Problem of a Standard

Atwood, E. Bagby. *A Survey of Verb Forms in the Eastern United States*. Ann Arbor: University of Michigan Press, 1953.

Baugh, Albert C. *A History of the English Language*. 2d ed. New York: Appleton-Century-Crofts, Inc., 1957.

Evans, Bergen and Cornelia. *A Dictionary of Contemporary American Usage*. New York: Random House, Inc., 1957.

Fries, Charles C. *American English Grammar*. New York: Appleton-Century-Crofts, Inc., 1940.

Manual of Style. 11th ed. Chicago: University of Chicago Press, 1949.

Marckwardt, Albert H., and Walcott, Fred G. *Facts About Current English Usage*. Including material reprinted from *Current English Usage* (1932), by Sterling A. Leonard. New York: Appleton-Century-Crofts, Inc., 1938.

Mencken, H. L. *The American Language*. Abridged, with annotations and new material, by Raven I. McDavid, Jr. New York: Alfred A. Knopf, 1963.

Nicholson, Margaret. *A Dictionary of American Usage Based on Fowler's* Modern English Usage. New York: Oxford University Press, 1957.

Style Manual. Rev. ed. Washington, D. C.: United States Government Printing Office, 1959.

Summey, George, Jr. *American Punctuation*. New York: Ronald Press Co., 1949.

Pronunciation

Bronstein, Arthur J. *The Pronunciation of American English*. New York: Appleton-Century-Crofts, Inc., 1960.

Kenyon, John S. *American Pronunciation*. 10th ed. Ann Arbor: George Wahr Publishing Co., 1951.

Pike, Kenneth L. *The Intonation of American English*. Ann Arbor: University of Michigan Press, 1946.

Thomas, Charles K. *An Introduction to the Phonetics of American English*. 2d ed. New York: Ronald Press Co., 1958.

INDEX

Terms in quotation marks are, in general, not used in this grammar.
References to pages numbered between 478 and 513 are to the Glossary.